Qualitative Inquiry in Education

The Continuing Debate

Qualitative Inquiry in Education

The Continuing Debate

Edited by
Elliot W. Eisner
Alan Peshkin

 Teachers College, Columbia University
New York and London

Published by Teachers College Press, 1234 Amsterdam Avenue,
New York, NY 10027

Library of Congress Cataloging-in-Publication Data

Qualitative inquiry in education : the continuing debate/ edited by
    Elliot W. Eisner, Alan Peshkin.
        p.   cm.
    Includes bibliographical references.
    ISBN 0-8077-3017-3 (alk. paper).—ISBN 0-8077-3016-5 (pbk. :
alk. paper)
    1. Education—Research.   1. Eisner, Elliot W.   II. Peshkin, Alan.
LB1028.Q35   1990
370'.7'8—dc20   89-77377
                                                          CIP

ISBN 0-8077-3017-3
ISBN 0-8077-3016-5 (pbk.)

Printed on acid-free paper
Manufactured in the United States of America

96 95 94 93 92 91   8 7 6 5 4 3 2

This book is dedicated to the memory of
Florence and David Friend

Contents

Introduction   1
ELLIOT W. EISNER and ALAN PESHKIN

PART I. SUBJECTIVITY AND OBJECTIVITY   **15**

1. Subjectivity and Objectivity: An Objective Inquiry   19
D. C. PHILLIPS

2. Is Naturalism a Move Away from Positivism?
Materialist and Feminist Approaches to Subjectivity
in Ethnographic Research   38
LESLIE G. ROMAN and MICHAEL W. APPLE

*Commentary on the Papers by Phillips and by Roman
and Apple*
Subjectivity and Objectivity   74
EGON G. GUBA

Response to the Commentary by Guba   92
D. C. PHILLIPS

PART II. VALIDITY   **97**

3. On Daffodils That Come Before the Swallow Dares   101
MADELEINE R. GRUMET

4. On Seeking—and Rejecting—Validity in Qualitative
Research   121
HARRY F. WOLCOTT

Commentary on the Papers by Grumet and by Wolcott
Looking for Trouble: On the Place of the Ordinary
in Educational Studies   153
PHILIP W. JACKSON

Response to the Commentary by Jackson   167
MADELEINE R. GRUMET

PART III. GENERALIZABILITY   **171**

5. Generalizability and the Single-Case Study   175
   ROBERT DONMOYER
6. Increasing the Generalizability of Qualitative Research   201
   JANET WARD SCHOFIELD

   Commentary on the Papers by Donmoyer and by Schofield
   Generalizing from Case Studies   233
   HOWARD S. BECKER

PART IV. ETHICS   **243**

7. The Ethics of Qualitative Research   247
   JONAS F. SOLTIS
8. Ethics in Qualitative Field Research: An Individual
   Perspective   258
   LOUIS M. SMITH

   Commentary on the Papers by Soltis and by Smith
   Toward a Categorical Imperative for Qualitative
   Research   277
   YVONNA S. LINCOLN

   Response to the Commentary by Lincoln   296
   JONAS F. SOLTIS

PART V. USES OF QUALITATIVE INQUIRY   **301**

9. Using the Narrative Text as an Occasion for Conspiracy   305
   THOMAS E. BARONE
10. What You Can Learn from Applesauce: A Case of
    Qualitative Inquiry in Use   327
    CHRISTOPHER M. CLARK

    Commentary on the Papers by Barone and by Clark
    Animadversions and Reflections on the Uses
    of Qualitative Inquiry   339
    MATTHEW B. MILES and A. MICHAEL HUBERMAN

    Response to the Commentary by Miles and
    Huberman   358
    THOMAS E. BARONE

CLOSING COMMENTS ON A CONTINUING DEBATE   **365**
ELLIOT W. EISNER and ALAN PESHKIN

About the Editors and the Contributors   371

Index   377

Qualitative Inquiry in Education

The Continuing Debate

Introduction

ELLIOT W. EISNER and ALAN PESHKIN

Educational researchers have conducted qualitative studies for decades. Their work, however, was not part of an established field of inquiry, with courses and procedures to provide guidance and structure. Indeed, there was about it almost a back-door sense, as if to say that, yes, such work exists, but it truly is a poor and not quite proper relation in the family of scholarship.

Except for the ethnographic tradition in anthropology and the University of Chicago style of case studies in sociology, both of which we would classify as qualitative, there were no accepted models to which educational researchers with a qualitative bent could turn for direction. The psychometric model long dominated educational research, as it has generally dominated the social and behavioral sciences. If professors and their students departed from it, they invited scorn, if not rejection. To conduct experiments and surveys was to be scientific; to do otherwise—and otherwise covered considerable territory—was to be soft-, wrong-, or muddle-headed.

Several characteristics of qualitative researchers of the past stand out: If trained at all, they had concentrated on statistics, measurement, and experimentation; as students, their research was not supervised by mentors who were themselves skilled in qualitative research; and if they labeled their research at all, they did not call it "qualitative." Though that is the general term we use today to subsume the range of types of studies within this tradition, there is no general agreement about the use of this term. It has rivals, such as *naturalistic, case study,* and *ethnographic.* There is, moreover, no general agreement about the conduct of any of the types of qualitative inquiry; perhaps there never will or can be consensus of the sort that is embodied in the standardized procedures of quantitative research, for example in path analysis or single-subject design. In quantitative research, the good may be found in fidelity to design, whereas in qualitative research, relatively lacking in canons and conventions, the good is more elusive because its procedures are more idiosyncratic.

Notwithstanding noteworthy progress in the development and reception of qualitative research, the tradition has denigrators who remain uncomfortable with a nonquantitative approach to research. At best, they are uneasy with what they view as a rival paradigm: They are reacting to the fact of competition. At worst, they dismiss it as unworthy of the name of scholarship: They are reacting to the perception that science is ———. They fill in the blank, and it happens to contain what they do.

In the past, the strong opposition of the denigrators had created a camplike mentality that cast all those they labeled "qualitative" as an antagonist "they" opposed by a protagonist "we." "We" maintained standards, upheld rectitude, and thereby merited the resources available for research and the prerogatives to shape the training of graduate students. The strength of their opposition often created an unequal but opposite reaction from the qualitative "they," who could themselves be shrill and defensive. Clearly outnumbered by their detractors, and clearly outpowered, "they" risked not getting tenure. Their students faced uncertainty in their efforts to get proposals and dissertations approved by faculty who could not conceive that scholarly respectability was attainable without recourse to factor analysis or analysis of variance, and without ever mentioning a null hypothesis. In the encounter between quantitative and qualitative researchers, albeit a lopsided one favoring the former, the politics of method emerged that continues less robust but unabated to the present time. It involved, as politics always does, power, resources, control, policy making, and personnel.

As long as an entrenched majority of the academic community at a particular institution deems quantitative research as the standard, there is virtually no contest and qualitative-oriented students and faculty alike suffer reproach and resistance. For example, doctoral students across the country often face the issue of the lack of correspondence between courses they must take to satisfy degree requirements and the knowledge they need to conduct their research. Recently, a student wrote us of her experience in this regard. Planning to do a qualitative study, she asked her department for permission to take courses in ethnographic methods. For graduation, her department required students to select one course from each of two sets of four. The first set contained only measurement and experimental design courses taught in the department of educational psychology. The second contained an assortment of courses taught by other departments; three of the choices related to history, philosophy, and evaluation, while the fourth was a survey research course. This meant that a student could satisfy requirements by taking two quantitative courses but not a single qualitative methods course. The student's department denied her request: "I explained that my primary interest was in doing nonexperimental research, but was told that I would still have to demonstrate competency in experimental research." Having demonstrated her competency, she could then go on to take whatever courses she wanted. With "core" methodological skills acquired, students then could deviate as they were so inclined.

Fortunately, the judgment that qualitative research is either beyond the pale or substandard no longer generally holds with overwhelming force. Not only is the contemporary interaction between quantitative and qualitative researchers less lopsided, it is increasingly less an encounter and more an interface. The camplike nature of the old quantitative-qualitative debate gradually is giving way to dialogue, so that the politics of method, while it persists throughout our universities, tends to resemble more the academic's ordinary concerns for turf maintenance than the bashing of illegitimate contenders by guardians of the faith.

If much remains to change, much already has changed and the signs are ubiquitous. We see them in the corridors and meeting rooms of the American Educational Research Association (AERA), where the outcomes of qualitative scholarship are regularly heard and where AERA's new Qualitative Research Special Interest Group (SIG) provides a supportive home for those members who for various reasons see opportunity in this SIG that they see in no other. Attendance at the SIG's sessions during the annual national meetings testifies to a degree of interest among AERA members that surpasses the limits of the SIG's official membership.

Of considerable consequence as an indicator of the "legitimation" of qualitative research is the publication of Mary Lee Smith's (1987) invited article in AERA's *American Educational Research Journal (AERJ)*. In her first paragraph, Smith writes that her paper "is meant to signify to the [education] discipline that manuscripts based on qualitative research are being welcomed by AERJ editors" (p. 173). Good news, indeed! Smith's article was one of three solicited by the journal's editor, whose preface to this "special section" states:

> We hope that these steps will encourage those of you who have felt that your manuscripts were inappropriate for *AERJ* to reconsider your judgments and submit them forthwith (Richardson-Koehler, 1987, p. 171).

Although we do not acknowledge the need for legitimation in academic terms, we clearly recognize that legitimation in political terms is another matter. Thus it is a mark of recognition when a journal whose contents have been firmly in the quantitative tradition requests the preparation of a paper (M. L. Smith's) that will set forth the attributes of an "acceptable" paper in the qualitative mode. Less of a break with tradition is the prevalence of articles on qualitative research methodology in AERA's *Educational Researcher*, to the extent that there is now perhaps no better forum for such articles.

The above-mentioned invitation of *AERJ* had been preceded by the thematic issues of other journals devoted to qualitative research. A 1979 issue of *Administrative Science Quarterly* (Van Maanen, 1979) featured qualitative methodology. The October 1984 issue of *Sociology of Education* (Metz, 1984) focused on "Ethnographic Studies of Education," with *ethnographic* used very loosely, such that it is more synonymous with qualitative research than with the anthropologist's strict notion of ethnography. Also in 1984, the *Journal of Thought* (Sherman, Webb, & Andrews, 1984) devoted its summer issue to "Qualitative Research," as it did again in fall 1986 (Sherman & Webb, 1986). Special theme issues are of interest, but less so than journals that regularly publish articles on qualitative research methodology and on the results of studies that use qualitative methods. *Qualitative Sociology* is a prime example, its origins dating back to the late 1920s. The recently renamed *Journal of Contemporary Ethnography* (formerly *Urban Life*), published since 1972, is another. The "ethnography" in its title, as its contents clearly demonstrate, is again broadly conceived, such that "qualitative" would be a more apt term. And the newly introduced *International Journal of Qualitative Studies in Education* is the most recent journal entry in the field.

It is noteworthy that publishers are betting, so to speak, that there is a market not only for qualitative-oriented journals but also for books on qualitative research methodology and for special series. Sage Publications, for example, sponsors the Qualitative Research Methods series, edited by John Van Maanen, that had sixteen books in print as of 1988. The books are meant to provide readers with "the methodological tools and concepts used in qualitative research across the social sciences." Falmer Press's newer Social Analysis Series, edited by Philip Wexler, has a particular ideological focus that also includes the qualitative. Wexler writes that "the study of discourse is central in this new genre of critical social analysis, and there is also a return to careful, original historical work and detailed qualitative research that is theoretically motivated."

Another publication, *Varieties of Qualitative Research* by Van Maanen, Dabbs, and Faulkner (1982), is of interest here for two reasons. First, it was published "in cooperation with Division 14 of the American Psychological Association," a national organization where the psychometric tradition has reigned supreme. Second, the book is part of a series that was funded jointly by the Office of Naval Research and the National Institute of Education. Such funding suggests that federal agencies have been amenable to endorsing research that employs qualitative methods.

It would be reassuring to be able to assert that federal agencies have been consistently amenable to qualitative approaches, but such is not the case. Of course, there have been notable examples of such support. In 1975 the National Science Foundation, under attack from Congress for being out of touch with the state of science education in the nation, issued a request for proposals that stipulated using case studies as one of three major means to explore the status of science education. Also in the 1970s, the National Institute of Education supported case study research on rural schools with grants to Paul Nachtigal and Faith Dunne. These examples, however, do not suffice to establish that federal funding agencies either welcome or are generally responsive to qualitative research.

We began our identification of signs of change with reference to AERA, for it is the prime setting for education researchers in North America. Outside of AERA, further signs of change abound. Taken together they testify to the rooting—no less than this—of qualitative research in American academic life. Tempted to summarize the events that underlie this rooting as a movement, we nonetheless reject this characterization because it implies an ebb and flow: That which is capable of moving in may also move out. On the contrary, qualitative research represents neither a fad nor a trend that in time will fade away or diminish in scope. Indicators of its acceptance and use appear at every turn. The indicators of its acceptance are anchored in the commitment of numerous researchers to what they are fully satisfied is an appropriate alternative or complement to quantitative inquiry.

Where ethnography and education are joined, we find the longest, most secure attachment to qualitative research, for ethnographers have long been comfortable with the efficacy of their nonquantitative means of inquiry. The fruits of their labor are manifest in the approximately twenty-year-old Council on Anthropology and Education and its equally old publication, once a newsletter and now an established periodical, called *Anthropology and Education Quarterly*. The marriage of anthropology and education, among the most robust of the links between education and a social science discipline, is further apparent in the Holt, Rinehart and Winston Case Studies in Education and Culture series that George and Louise Spindler have edited since 1967 and that Wave-land Press has continued to keep in print.

Where history and education are joined, we see a linking of research to methods that are not usually labeled "quantitative" or "qualitative." Notwithstanding an increasing orientation toward the use of quantitative data and analysis, historians still use data-collecting methods—documents of all sorts and interviews—that are qualitative in nature. With their methods labeled "historical" rather than "qualitative," and with the sanction of tradition that placed history outside of science—history is good or bad history, not scientific or unscientific—historians of education basically escaped the opprobrium of being nonquantitative. The research community has considered the methods of the historian as appropriate for doing history; it has not reckoned that the methods have utility for research by nonhistorians whose work would be termed "qualitative."

Conferences represent one of several indicators of academic vitality. One of the earliest conferences, sponsored in 1976 by the Far West Regional Laboratory for Educational Research and Development, resulted in a special issue of *Anthropology and Education Quarterly* (Tikunoff & Ward, 1977). The theme was "Exploring Qualitative and Quantitative Research Methodologies in Education." The most enduring conference is the University of Pennsylvania's Ethnography in Education Research Forum, which held its tenth annual meeting in 1989. Since 1987 the University of Georgia has organized an annual International Invitational Conference on Qualitative Research in Education. We organized the one that is the basis for this book, and Egon Guba, working under the auspices of Phi Delta Kappa, brought together in 1989 several hundred scholars from across the country to explore the theme of "Alternative Paradigms of Inquiry."

What stands out as a general point—extracted from the many cases we have just cited—is that we see qualitative research in places where typically it has not been present and, possibly, not been welcome. The above-mentioned references to AERA and the special theme issues of journals are such examples. There are others that further testify to the expanding presence of the qualitative in the arena of scholarship. Fred Erickson's (1987) article on "Qualitative Methods in Research on Teaching," written for the third edition of the *Handbook of Research on Teaching,* is the first one on qualitative methods that the editors have included in the several handbooks published to date. And the University of Georgia has a cross-disciplinary Qualitative Interest Group of about fifty faculty members, including considerable representation from among professors of education.

A final illustration strikes us as particularly indicative of the qualitative being present where previously it had not. We refer to the "shift" from the quantitative to the qualitative by a host of distinguished American scholars. *Shift* does not accurately characterize the variety of circumstances that describe what may, in fact, represent a conversion by some of them and an embracing of both modes of inquiry by some others. Included in the list of such scholars are Lee Cronbach, Donald Campbell, Robert Stake, Egon Guba, and Philip Jackson, all of whom were trained to be quantitative researchers and gained considerable repute as such. In camp terms, there may be joy among the qualitative brethren to see scholars of the first rank in their midst, but we mean simply to suggest that their shift is one more illustration of the institutionalization of qualitative research.

All that we have noted so far argues for the expanding interest of researchers in qualitative means of inquiry. Of substantial significance, however, are three related developments that suggest the extent to which qualitative research is being institutionalized. These developments augur well for its future. Qualitative methodology courses are now being taught with sufficient regularity and enrollment to encourage major textbook publishers to solicit the writing of books that are appropriate for use in these courses. These two facts are joined to a third: Departments of education have begun to advertise new faculty appointments that specify competence in teaching qualitative research courses as a condition of employment. As a result of these three developments, qualitative research in the near future will more probably be conducted by scholars who have been trained to undertake it, and the training will have been provided by scholars whose own training qualifies them to offer the courses and direct the research of students.

There is a grew-like-Topsy character to the field of qualitative research methodology. The underdog sense of past decades has been replaced by changes that promise students and their mentors that a genuine choice of methodology is available, though future scholars may find that being "bi-methodological" is the true mark of scholarly sophistication.[1] While the Topsylike growth will continue, a new, albeit incipient, phase is evident. We see it most prominently in the intent by Sage Publications to prepare the first handbook on qualitative research methods. Handbooks are intended to be seminal documents; done well,

---

1. We owe the notion of "bi-methodological" to conversations with Professor Judith Goetz of the University of Georgia, who attributes the concept to her colleague Linda Grant.

they can shape a field of study for many years. By their predisposition to define terms, identify issues, and clarify boundaries, handbook writers orient and structure the work of the scholars who follow them.

To be sure, we have not prepared a handbook. Such a monumental undertaking far exceeds our expectations, but it was clearly in that spirit that we organized a two-and-one-half-day meeting at Stanford University in June 1988. In addition to the two of us and fifteen program speakers, fifteen other participants attended the conference, which was cosponsored by Teachers College Press. The conference presentations form the basis for this book. We invited outstanding scholars to address the issues that constitute the five parts of this book: subjectivity and objectivity, validity, generalizability, ethics, and uses of qualitative inquiry. At the conference each issue was explored by two paper presenters and one discussant, and that is the format followed in each part of this book. In addition, for the book, each presenter was invited to write a response to the discussant. About half chose to do so, and those responses are included at the end of the appropriate part.

In inviting conference participants, we knew we wanted papers written by persons who could draw on their personal experience of qualitative research. We did not ask our authors to make explicit the frameworks within which they conduct their research, but when they do so, we get a firmer grip on their particular point of view. The reasons that all do not routinely present their frameworks we can only speculate about. Many, perhaps most, of us evolved as qualitative researchers by taste rather than by socialization. Thus we had not learned to view the conduct of our inquiry within the philosophical context of methodological issues. In a sense, we did what we did without giving a name to it. The result was pragmatic and eclectic, which is not a comment on its quality but on its blurring genres. Our sense is that the pragmatists and eclecticists will continue their work, but, increasingly, we all are becoming usefully aware that frameworks not only exist, they usefully alert us to a logical thread that can run through the various aspects of the research process. This thread varies by framework and it, like the framework itself, has value insofar as it avoids the encrustation of orthodoxy.

Our hope, by no means immodest, is that our book's exploration of these five issues will provoke and promote dialogue of high quality among our colleagues. Far from offering the last word on any of the issues, we intend instead to offer words that promise to extend the dialogue on matters of consequence to those who are committed not only to qualitative research but also to research of quality. We see our conference and this volume as part of a growing disposition to identify and clarify matters that are foundational to the continuing evolution of qualitative research.

So much for context. Although it is reassuring to know that the avenues to research in education have widened, the issues pertaining to legitimate methods still remain. Just what does constitute reliable and valid claims to knowledge about human affairs? What knowledge can we really trust? Must results be replicable? In the end, do we not ultimately seek to discover the regularities of nature and culture, and if so, what can be learned that is generally useful by studying particulars in idiosyncratic ways?

One way in which such questions have been answered is to remind the skeptical or the puzzled that the problem itself should be used to identify the methods appropriate to it. Once the problem has been adequately conceptualized, the question or method can be easily answered.

While such advice is comforting, it is too simple. First, what constitutes a problem is not independent of the methods one knows how to use. Few of us seek problems we have no skill in addressing. What we know how to do is what we usually try to do.

But the problem is still more complex. The methods into which we have been socialized provide powerful filters through which we view the world. If we are predisposed to focus upon the unique features of a person or situation and skilled in their literary description, we are likely to attend to classrooms in ways that emphasize or make salient the idiosyncratic. If we are inclined toward the description of measured relationships or the incidence of events, if what we are inclined to think about is how things co-vary, we see the "same" classroom from a very different angle and with a very different intent. In short, our methodological concepts influence our perception. Thereafter, cognitive maps help us find our way in the territories we wish to explore. Those with different maps tend to take different roads.

Complexities do not stop here. Being socialized into method also means being socialized into a set of norms that define acceptable scholarship. Not a few whose major methodological commitments are in conventional quantitative methods regard qualitative research acceptable for exploratory efforts, believing that the real work of science must be couched in terms more robust. The operative word is often *hard*, as in "hard" data. Hard is good and soft is not.

We mention these matters not to exacerbate tension, increase separation, or deepen antagonism between those whose proclivities lead them in one direction and those who travel in other directions, but because genuine differences, we believe, ought to be acknowledged rather than swept under the rug. There are genuine differences. Ultimately these differences bear upon matters of epistemology. What does it mean to know? Is the term *knowledge* better conceived of as a verb, rather than as a noun? Is it something we do rather than something we have? Is there, at base, a superordinate framework or criterion to which we can appeal to resolve differences in what we think we know? If so, what features does such a framework possess? If there is no such framework, can we resolve differences among those who study the educational world? Will we not wind up with a Tower of Babel if anyone can choose his or her own framework or method? And if there is only one framework, how will we avoid dogmatism? After all, those who believe that there is only one right road, and who also believe they know what it is, are not the easiest people with whom to live.

Consider further the issue of generalization. Do case studies have lessons to teach? Is it possible to talk about "educational implications" of the research when the situation studied is nonrandom and the method unique to the investigator? In conventional research paradigms the logic of random selection, a logic fundamental to inferential statistics, is well developed. Where are the parallels in qualitative research methods? Can there be such parallels? If the answer is negative, what are the grounds—if any—for generalization? And if no generalizations are possible, how can knowledge accumulate? Thus, what does one make of an approach to the study of the educational world that depends upon the unique aptitudes and proclivities of the investigator, that possesses no standardized method, that focuses upon nonrandomly selected situations, and that yields questionable generalizations by conventional research criteria? Indeed, are we justified in referring to the use of such a collection of procedures as "research"?

And yet, how really different are these features from the *real* methods used in conventional studies? By *real* we mean not textbook versions of research, nor the tidy portrayals that find their place in research journals, but the ways in which research actually occurs in practice. How many studies of the conventional kind actually use a randomly selected sample? How much of the significance of such research is a matter of the interpretive dispositions and abilities of the researcher? How much of the planned method is actually employed, and how much of what is employed is a function of the artistry of the researcher? In short, just how much idiosyncrasy is there in conventional research? How much of it is replicable? To what degree is there overlap between approaches to research—qualitative and nonqualitative—considering the real world of research practice, not its textbook version?

What we have, then, are multiple perspectives on the state of research methodology. There are those who regard conventional and qualitative approaches to research as complementary. They argue that each approach is good for a particular class of problems. They cope with methodological pluralism by holding that it is the question that should drive the method, not vice versa. There are others who hold that qualitative research is basically a soft and less trustworthy version of the real stuff, the stuff that good quantitative studies deliver. Their view is that qualitative research might be good for exploratory work, but real knowledge is generated through other, more tough-minded methods. Another group holds that it is conventional methods that are suspect. They argue that such methods, derived from a natural science paradigm, are ill suited for the likes of a human community. After all, they remind us, electrons, unlike children, have neither motives nor aspirations. They do not strategize, they do not think, they are neither devious nor helpful. Methods based upon a deterministic causal model simply do not fit the arenas in which human action takes place. Another group denies that there are any differences between qualitative and conventional research. A good qualitative study, they argue, is subject to and meets the same criteria as the conventional, quantitative one does. Epistemological differences are, in their view, grossly exaggerated.

What is particularly promising from our perspective is that conversations such as these should have such an important place in educational discourse. It suggests to us that consciousness has been raised and that what was once considered settled and sacrosanct is now being reexamined. With this examination, old and secure assumptions are being reconsidered. New ways of thinking about knowing and knowledge are emerging, fresh conceptions of generalization are being offered up for consideration, validity and reliability are being nudged by concepts that are not quite the same. In short, the conversation is getting deeper, more complex, and more problematic.

We function under no illusion that the papers in this book have settled the issues once and for all. Indeed, we would be unhappy if they had. Having arrived at your destination, to where do you now travel? For us, the journey is more than half the fun, and that journey occurs in the dialogue.

The long-term consequences of the dialogue now taking place will, of course, provide much more than the rewards of good conversation. We believe the nature of that dialogue will create a legitimate plurality of methods that will shed greater light on educational matters than any single set of methods can provide. Knowing what it feels like to be a

student in a middle school can be just as important to the educational
well-being of children as knowing the measured effects of a new approach to the teaching of algebra. Qualitative approaches to research
may be better able to make the feel of the place more vivid than a
precise measured description of what students say they experience.
Empathy might be every bit as important for cognition as detachment.

How students are prepared in qualitative research programs, the
courses deemed relevant, the kind of writing considered acceptable,
the aptitudes that are given a place in the sun, are all influenced by the
process and by the products of the growing conversation. The journals
that will continue to emerge, the positions that will become available,
the evidence of scholarship that will be considered on such weighty
matters as promotion and tenure, may be irrevocably altered by a
broader, more catholic conception of inquiry in general and research in
particular.

On projecting the potential consequences of the new conversation,
we do not claim that standards or, better yet, criteria for the assessment of the value of qualitative work are less rigorous than the standards applied to research of a conventional kind. On the contrary,
because there are no algorithms, no statistical significance tests for
qualitative studies, that most exquisite of human capacities must come
into play: judgment. But good judgment is not a mindless activity. It
depends upon attention to detail, sensitivity to coherence, appreciation
of innuendo, and the ability to read subtext as well as text. Essays
written by the left hand need to be read with as much rigor as those
written by the right.

This brings us to our final point. As we see it, the past two decades
have seen the gradual emergence of what we have called the new
conversation. Philip Jackson's *Life in Classrooms* (1968) was a mix of
qualitative work and research in a conventional form. Louis Smith and
William Geoffrey's *Complexities of an Urban Classroom* (1968) was like an
ethnographic account. The former publication had one foot in the
conventional and one in the qualitative. The latter was aligned with
ethnography, a social science discipline. As the varieties of qualitative
work are explored, new forms are emerging that do not fit comfortably
under the anthropological umbrella. Some of this work is a species of
literary criticism, some is phenomenological, others are called portrai-
ture and the like. The point is that the boundaries are being pushed,
and the tidy categories of the conventional disciplines are often ill suited
to encompass them. Where, for example, should we place Lightfoot's
The Good High School (1983), or Connelly and Clandinin's *Teachers as
Curriculum Planners* (1988), or Barone's *Daedalus* piece (1983)?

This exploration has created a new need to find criteria, or at least to develop forms of judgment that suit the new genre of work now being published. The same situation, we might add, has emerged in the field of anthropology. This efflorescence is helping redefine the parameters through which inquiry into educational matters can go forward. These new parameters, we expect, will lead not only to new "answers" to old questions but to new questions. We also expect that the conversations now occurring will widen and that in the decade ahead a new cadre of researchers will occupy positions in universities throughout the world, providing not only good guidance to graduate students but role models for a new generation of students whose instincts lead them their way. Should that occur, this period in which we now work will be remembered as a kind of quiet revolution, one that did not depose the king but converted the monarchy into a coalition government.

Finally, our hopes for the future: We hope that the material presented in each of the papers stimulates deep discussion about the fundamental ideas they address. Each presentation and commentary constitutes a dialogue. Responses, in those cases where they appear, push that dialogue even further. What is left out in this volume is the reader. We hope that dialogue with the authors occurs both in the solitude of a quiet walk and in the privacy of the morning shower. We hope it is stimulated in university lecture halls and in small seminars. We hope that it leads to better questions and to new paths to follow. We hope it opens up some new seas on which to sail. Scholars, particularly experienced ones, often create text that exudes a sense of authority. We can tell you that none of the papers in this volume went unchallenged by those whose experience told them to sail by different stars. We hope that you will join the debate and, eventually, find your own stars with which to guide your ship.

REFERENCES

Barone, T. (1983). Things of use and things of beauty: The story of the Swain County Arts Program. *Daedalus, 112*(3), 1–28.

Connelly, F. M., & Clandinin, D. J. (1988). *Teachers as curriculum planners: Narratives of experience.* New York: Teachers College Press.

Erickson, F. (1987). Qualitative methods in research on teaching. In M. Wittrock (Ed.), *Handbook of research on teaching* (3rd ed., pp. 119–161). New York: Macmillan.

Jackson, P. W. (1968). *Life in classrooms.* New York: Holt, Rinehart and Winston.

Lightfoot, S. L. (1983). *The good high school.* New York: Basic Books.

Metz, M. H. (Ed.). (1984). Ethnographic studies of education [Special issue]. *Sociology of Education, 57*(4).

Richardson-Koehler, V. (1987). Editor's statement. *American Educational Research Journal, 24*(2).

Sherman, R. R., & Webb, R. B. (Eds.) (1986). Qualitative research [Special issue]. *Journal of Thought, 21*(3).

Sherman, R. R., Webb, R. B., & Andrews, S. D. (Eds.). (1984). Qualitative research [Special issue]. *Journal of Thought, 19*(2).

Smith, L., & Geoffrey, W. (1968). *Complexities of an urban classroom.* New York: Holt, Rinehart and Winston.

Smith, M. L. (1987). Publishing qualitative research. *American Educational Research Journal, 24*, 173–184.

Tikunoff, W. J., & Ward, B. A. (Eds.). (1977). Exploring qualitative and quantitative research methodologies in education [Special issue]. *Anthropology and Education Quarterly, 8*(2).

Van Maanen, J. (Ed.). (1979). Qualitative methodology. *Administrative Science Quarterly, 24*(4).

Van Maanen, J., Dabbs, J. M., Jr., & Faulkner, R. R. (1982). *Varieties of qualitative research.* Beverly Hills, CA: Sage.

Part I

SUBJECTIVITY
AND OBJECTIVITY

In the best tradition of scholarship, D. C. Phillips, Leslie Roman, Michael Apple, and Egon Guba, the writers in this section on subjectivity and objectivity, take a firm position, identify its detractors, clarify who stands with them, and submit that while they do not have the last word, they are certainly on the right track. Together they address one of the most fundamental issues in research. We all have been socialized to believe that persons, processes, and products bearing the stamp of "objective" deserve acclaim and acceptance, while persons, processes, and products stamped "subjective" do not. To be sure, the real world of researchers and research is not as simple as these polarized designations suggest, but the effect of goodness, on the one hand, and badness, on the other, is part of our received wisdom. Nowadays, though researchers of any paradigmatic and philosophical stripe may join Gunnar Myrdal in acclaiming that there is no value-free inquiry, they may still part company thereafter, and, as do Roman/Apple and Phillips, disagree vehemently.

Thoughts have consequences: how we think about subjectivity and objectivity affects research procedure because these issues typically are embedded in the broader framework, albeit most often implicitly, that directs the conduct of our inquiry. Roman and Apple, in keeping with our general lack of specificity about how to approach the topic we invited them to address, focus on subjectivity and its inevitable and appropriate presence in social inquiry; they rarely mention objectivity, and, by their lights, they need not. We readily infer where they stand on objectivity—the province of a paradigm they reject—when they articulate where they stand on subjectivity. Their discussion is grounded extensively in Roman's recent study of Punk young women. Of course, they do much more than explore subjectivity because their position encompasses a worldview—"feminist materialist ethnography"—in which subjectivity occupies a certain place. Accordingly, to understand their conception of subjectivity, their worldview must be grasped.

Guba rightly observes that Phillips, as a postpositivist philosopher, stands a world apart from Roman and Apple; Phillips, however, is comfortable there. As regards an attribute of the general contexts of their arguments, we learn that Roman and Apple are moved by an abiding concern for justice, whereas Phillips is moved, no less abidingly, for a concern to get things straight. They do not, of course, confront each other's concerns, except inferentially. We, the readers, are left to do that as we scan their persuasive arguments.

In contrast to Roman and Apple, Phillips addresses, indeed insists on, the feasibility of objectivity, albeit in a reconstructed form that he feels holds up to the critiques that an earlier conception received. On the way to stating and making his case, he takes issue with those who presume they have seen objectivity's demise, only to find that Egon Guba, the session's discussant, must be included among those who have created the obituary.

Guba recapitulates each paper's central points and then concludes with a "commentary" section that positions their arguments in the philosopher's basic notions of ontology, epistemology, and methodology. Never a fence sitter, Guba casts doubt on both arguments but concludes by finding Roman and Apple's conception of "feminist materialist ethnography" quite close to his and colleague Yvonna Lincoln's "constructivist" paradigm. Indeed, he suggests a reconsideration of Roman and Apple's stance that would bring them closer to his preferred position and, therefore, to what he sees as a welcome consensus.

Roman and Apple do not offer a rejoinder to Guba's discussion. Phillips, whose position rests on divergent philosophical grounds that offer Guba no comparable prospect of consensus, does write a response. In the best scholarly tradition, he claims, quite directly, that Guba got him wrong: There is, he argues, genuine light to be derived from "critical scrutiny" conducted in a nonrelativistic world, and objectivity, rightly construed, is no chimera.

In this assemblage of internal and external point and counterpoint, we have strong claims rendered in strong language. Dialogic? We think so. With matters settled? That depends. Some methodologists speak and write as if the light within which they conceptualize is clear and true. Their language, carrying the authority of resolution, suggests that they have matters settled. Their premises intact, they confidently take issue with those that diverge. And when they do so, they engender intellectual interactions that are the stuff of the dialogue we cherish. For methodological codification is premature now, and probably always will be. Thus, while as educational researchers we trust that something of value for the world of learners and learning will result from our studies, as qualitative researchers we subject the nature of our processes to continuing scrutiny, as if to say, "Here's some good stuff, but as we get wiser and better at what we do, our stuff will improve."

1 Subjectivity and Objectivity: An Objective Inquiry

D. C. PHILLIPS

A person does not have to read very widely in the contemporary methodological or theoretical literature pertaining to research in the social sciences and related applied areas, such as education, in order to discover that objectivity is dead. When the term happens to be used, it is likely to be set in scare-marks—"objectivity"—to bring out the point that a dodolike entity is being discussed. Or "there is no such thing," authors confidently state, unmindful of the fact that if they are right, then the reader does not have to break into a sweat—because if there is no such thing as objectivity, then the view that there is no such thing is itself not objective. But, then, if this view is the subjective judgment of a particular author, readers are entitled to prefer their own subjective viewpoint—which, of course, might be that objectivity is *not* dead!

A couple of illustrations should suffice to set the stage. The first is from Gunnar Myrdal (1969):

> The ethos of social science is the search for "objective" truth. The faith of the student is his conviction that truth is wholesome and that illusions are damaging, especially opportunistic ones. He seeks "realism," a term which in one of its meanings denotes an "objective" view of reality. . . . How can a biased view be avoided? (p. 3)

After an interesting discussion of the deep-seated sources of bias and opportunism in belief, Myrdal suggests that some techniques exist to help achieve at least a degree of objectivity.

A second example comes from Elliot Eisner; unlike Myrdal, he does not try to soften the blow but boldly sets out to face a future in which the demise of objectivity is not mourned:

19

> What I have even more quarrel with is the view that a scientifically acceptable research method is "objective" or value-free, that it harbors no particular point of view. All methods and all forms of representation are partial. (1986, p. 15)

Or, from a different work, "What is meant by objective? Does objective mean that one has discovered reality in its raw, unadulterated form? If so, this conception of objectivity is naive" (1979, p. 214).

It is not intended that the present chapter will develop into a paradoxical discussion of the self-referential puzzles generated by such remarks. But it is the intent, at the outset of the inquiry, to point out the oddity of trying to write an essay for a learned symposium—a paradigm case of an exercise in the marshaling of objective considerations—if, indeed, there is no escape from subjectivity. It would be too quixotic; and it would be better to take the bull by the horns and proceed by using rhetoric (much as is being done now), or special pleading, or appeals to the readers' baser motives.

Believing the task *not* to be quixotic, the present author is inspired to inquire why objectivity has sunk into such disrepute and to investigate whether it deserves the fate that has befallen it. Because the issues concerning objectivity and subjectivity transcend disciplinary and methodological boundaries, the discussion will have to be far-ranging, but it will keep returning to the specific issues raised by qualitative research.

The issues, then, are these: Why is it doubted that qualitative research—or, indeed, any research—can be objective, and are these doubts reasonable? What notion of objectivity is involved here? Is Eisner correct in suggesting that the traditional notion of objectivity is naive? If all views are subjective, are they all on a par, or are some more subjective than others? (And does the notion of degrees of subjectivity make sense?)

One further point remains to be made in this prelude. It is clear that in normal parlance the term *objective* is commendatory, while *subjective* carries negative connotations. After all, it is not a good thing for a judge, a physicist, an anthropologist, or a professor to be subjective. It is even worse to be biased—this latter term being sometimes used to mark the contrast with objectivity.[1] (Such negative evaluations are likely to change, of course, if it turns out the objectivity is dead, and that there is no option but to be subjective.) In what follows, the discussion will attempt to avoid using the terms in a judgmental way—at least until it has been established, objectively, that either term can justifiably be so used.

THE INTELLECTUAL ROOTS
OF THE ATTACK ON OBJECTIVITY

The fields of philosophy of science and epistemology have undergone something of a revolution in recent decades. The traditional foundationalist or justificationist approach to epistemology has largely been abandoned in favor of a nonfoundationalist approach; in philosophy of science, the work of Popper, closely followed by that of Kuhn, Hanson, Feyerabend, and Lakatos, has been the center of much debate. Acting under these influences, some individuals have moved in the direction of relativism (although this is not what had been intended by most of the individuals just mentioned). But the very same forces—supplemented by one or two others—have also given rise to the strong attack on objectivity. It will be as well to discuss the major influences in turn.

Nonfoundationalist Epistemology

Traditional epistemologies, whether of rationalist or empiricist persuasion, were foundationalist or justificationist in the sense that they regarded knowledge as being built upon (or justified in terms of) some solid and unchallengeable foundation. It was the presence of this solid foundation that served as the justification for the knowledge claims that were made. Where the traditional schools of epistemology fell out with each other was over the issue of what, precisely, constituted this foundation. Empiricists (such as Locke, Berkeley, and Hume) saw the foundation as being human experience—sense impressions or some such item. Rationalists (like Descartes) claimed it was human reason; the starting place for the construction of knowledge was to be those beliefs that appeared indubitable after scrutiny in the light of reason.

In the twentieth century there has been a steady erosion of foundationalism of both varieties. It is now recognized that there is no absolutely secure starting point for knowledge; nothing is known with such certainty that all possibility of future revision is removed. All knowledge is tentative. Karl Popper (1968) is probably the best-known advocate of this newer perspective, but he is not, by far, a solitary figure. In his words:

> The question about the sources of our knowledge . . . has always been asked in the spirit of: "What are the best sources of our knowledge—the most reliable ones, those which will not lead us into error, and those to which we can and must turn, in case of doubt, as the last court of appeal?"

I propose to assume, instead, that no such ideal sources exist—no more than ideal rulers—and that *all* "sources" are liable to lead us into error at times. And I propose to replace, therefore, the question of the sources of our knowledge by the entirely different question: *"How can we hope to detect and eliminate error?"* (p. 25; emphasis in original)

It is important to note that abandonment of the notion that knowledge is built on an unshakable foundation does not mean that the traditional notion of truth has been abandoned. Popper constantly reminds his readers that truth is an essential regulative ideal. He offers this nice image:

The status of truth in the objective sense, as correspondence to the facts, and its role as a regulative principle, may be compared to that of a mountain peak which is permanently, or almost permanently, wrapped in clouds. The climber may not merely have difficulties in getting there—he may not know when he gets there, because he may be unable to distinguish, in the clouds, between the main summit and some subsidiary peak. Yet this does not affect the objective existence of the summit. . . . The very idea of error, or of doubt . . . implies the idea of an objective truth which we may fail to reach. (p. 226)

It makes little sense to search for a summit if you do not believe that a summit exists; and it makes little sense to try to understand some situation if you believe that *any* story about that situation is as good as any other. In this latter case, to inquire is to waste one's energy—one might as well have just invented any old story. But if some stories are regarded as being better than others, then this belief, upon unpacking, will be found to presuppose the notion of truth as a regulative ideal.

The crucial point for the present discussion is that it does not follow from any of the recent developments in epistemology outlined above that the notion of objectivity has been undermined. This would only follow were objectivity equated with certainty. This is to say that the following argument is a *non sequitur*, at least until some further premise is added to link the antecedent to the consequent: If no knowledge is certain, then there is no possibility for any viewpoint to be objective. It might be objected here that Popper himself referred to the real existence of his cloud-covered mountain top and that he said it might never be possible to know one had reached it—showing that attainment of "objective truth" might not be possible. But it is crucial to note that here he was not discussing objectivity, he was discussing truth. When we abandon foundationalism, we abandon the assurance that we can know when we have reached the truth; but, as Popper's story also illustrates, we do not have to abandon the *notion* of truth, and we do not have to abandon the view that some types of inquiries are better than others.

Leaving the notion of truth, and returning to the issue of the objectivity of inquiries, there is good reason to hold that certainty and objectivity should not be linked. For if they were, all human knowledge would thereby become subjective (for no knowledge is certain), and this would have the effect of washing out a vital distinction. Consider two observers of a classroom in which a science teacher has been conducting a lesson on a difficult topic. One observer claims to have noticed that the students did not understand the material, but the only evidence she gives is that "I did not understand the material myself"; the other observer also claims that the students did not learn, but offers by way of evidence the test scores of the students, a videotape of the classroom showing the puzzled demeanor of the students, and interview protocols where a random sample of the students seemed rather confused about the topic. The new epistemology would have us recognize that neither of these two views is absolutely certain, but it is not the consequence of the new epistemology that we would have to judge both views as being equally subjective. For it is evident that one of the observers was greatly influenced by her own personal reactions to the lesson, and this unduly affected how she perceived the classroom; whereas the other observer had taken pains to marshal relevant evidence (even if that evidence was not absolutely incorrigible). In a straightforward and nontroublesome sense, the second observer's opinion would be regarded by all normal language users as being more objective (even if the opinion later turned out to be wrong).

This example suggests the following hypothesis: "Objective" seems to be a label that we apply to inquiries that meet certain procedural standards, but objectivity does not *guarantee* that the results of inquiries have any certainty. (It implies that the inquiries so labeled are free of gross defects, and this should be of some comfort—just as a consumer prefers to buy an item that has met rigorous inspection standards, although this does not absolutely insure that it will not break down.) The other side of the coin is that a biased, bigoted person who jumps to some subjective conclusion about, say, a political candidate who happens to be of different ethnicity may not always be wrong. His or her biased judgment may turn out to be true. Thus the narrow-minded black Democrat who had no time for Richard Nixon, and who claimed he would be a dishonest president, nevertheless turned out to be right. (Just as a consumer who purchases a shoddy piece of merchandise occasionally "lucks out" and never has any trouble with it.) Or, to use a less loaded example but one that is historically accurate, in its heyday Newtonian physics was supported by a wealth of objective evidence, that is, evidence that was free from personal contamination and that was, in large part, accepted by an international community whose members had subjected it to critical scrutiny and cross-check. Nevertheless, in our day evidence has accumulated that makes it hard to believe that the Newtonian framework is anything but a reasonably good approximation of the truth (but not as good, for example, as the Einsteinian framework, which itself is probably not absolutely true). Thus those scientists of earlier times who rejected Newton for their own personal (subjective) reasons turned out to have been right in doing so (although, of course, whatever positive views they did hold may well have been defective also).

To put the point pithily, neither subjectivity nor objectivity has an exclusive stranglehold on truth. But why, then, should objectivity be preferred if it is not guaranteed to lead to the truth? The answer is implied in the discussion above: At any one time, the viewpoint that is the most objective is the one that currently is the most warranted or rational—to deny this is to deny that there is any significant difference between the warrants for the views of the two classroom observers in the earlier example. If we give this up, if we hold that a biased or personally loaded viewpoint is as good as a viewpoint supported by carefully gathered evidence, we are undermining the very point of human inquiry. If a shoddy inquiry is to be trusted as much as a careful one, then it is pointless to inquire carefully. The philosopher Ernest Nagel (1979) put it well:

> Those attacks on the notion that scientific inquiry can be objective are tantamount to an endorsement of the view that the grounds on which conclusions in the sciences are accepted are at bottom no better than are the grounds on which superstitious beliefs are adopted. Those attacks may therefore . . . justify almost any doctrine, no matter how unwarranted it may be. (p. 85)

In light of these remarks, it would seem that Elliot Eisner (1979) was both right and wrong when he stated that "to hold that our conceptions of reality are true or objective to the extent that they are isomorphic with reality is to embrace a hopeless correspondence theory of truth" (p. 214). He was right to criticize the identification of objectivity as "isomorphic with reality"; however, he was wrong to treat "objective" and "true" as synonyms, and he was wrong to suggest that nonfoundationalism leads to the rejection of the correspondence theory of truth. It is worth commenting here, to forestall a philosophical misunderstanding, that the correspondence theory of truth is firmly entrenched in contemporary philosophy, and it is supported by weighty—but not by absolutely conclusive—considerations. Eisner runs together two issues that philosophers keep separate, for good reasons: The first is the issue of what account best clarifies the *meaning* of the term "truth," and it is here that the correspondence theory is alive and well, as Popper's story of the cloudy mountain illustrates. The second is the issue of what *test* or *criterion* we can rely upon in order to judge if a theory actually *is* isomorphic with reality. On this second matter, nonfoundationalists would answer that there is no such test or criterion, as once again Popper's allegory illustrates. Eisner has reasoned back, invalidly, from the negative response to the second, to a negative judgment about the first.[2]

Hansonism

It is now widely accepted that observation is always theory-laden. Due largely to the work of N. R. Hanson (although Wittgenstein and Popper could claim priority), researchers are aware that when they make observations they cannot argue that these are objective in the sense of being "pure," free from the influence of background theories or hypotheses or personal hopes and desires.[3] Qualitative researcher John Ratcliffe (1983) was reflecting this view when he wrote that "most research methodologists are now aware that *all* data are theory-, method-, and measurement-dependent" (p. 148; emphasis in original). And he continued on to turn this point into a thinly veiled attack on objectivity: "That is, 'facts' are determined by the theories and methods that generate their collection; indeed, theories and methods *create* the facts" (p. 148; emphasis in original). If the observer's prior theoretical commitments do, indeed, determine what he or she sees as being the facts of a situation, then subjectivity would seem to reign supreme.

It is here that the distinction between low-level and high-level observation becomes relevant. The distinction is similar to the one that research psychologists have in mind when they speak of "high-inference" and "low-inference" variables. While observation is never theory-free, it does not follow that many (or most) observations are such that people from a wide variety of quite different theoretical frames will be in total disagreement about the facts of the case. There are many situations where all frameworks are likely to lead to the same results—they overlap, as it were. This is particularly so in cases of low-level observations, such as "there is a patch of red," or "the object on the left is heavier." Even people who do not share the same language can agree on such matters, for the only problem they face is the relatively trivial one of translation. (Thus my Korean students might not understand when I speak of "a patch of red," but with the help of a bilingual dictionary they can quickly come to comprehend—and to agree with me!) To put it in a nutshell, relatively speaking, low-level observation is high in objectivity, in the sense that the reports of my observations transcend the merely personal or subjective. My observations are open for cross-check, testing, and criticism by other inquirers, and there is nothing in Hanson to suggest that people with beliefs that differ from my own are *bound* to disagree with me about such observations. Contrary to what some radical Hansonists claim, there is no evidence that people with markedly different theoretical frames—for example, Freudians and behaviorists—actually see different things at the basic or low-inference level being discussed here. They might notice—or fail to notice—different things, but when these are brought to their attention they agree about what they have seen. Of course, they might still disagree about the significance of what they have observed, but this is not a point under contention in the present context.

Even Hanson's (1965) famous claim that the astronomers Tycho Brahe and Johannes Kepler would see different things while watching the dawn is a claim that can be recast to support the point being made here.[4] Both scientists would agree that the sun was moving higher in the sky relative to the horizon—a point Hanson acknowledges; but of course Brahe would interpret this as the sun's moving, while Kepler would regard it as a case of the earth's rotating away from the sun. Their disagreement is spectacular, and Hansonists get good mileage from it, but what gets obscured is the agreement of the two men at the "low-inference" level. Ernest Nagel (1979) has made a similar point, using a different example:

> It is simply not true that every theory has its own observation terms, none of which is also an observation term belonging to any other theory. For example, at least some of the terms employed in recording the observations that may be made to test Newton's corpuscular theory of light (such terms as "prism," "color," and "shadow"), underwent no recognizable changes in meaning when they came to be used to describe observations made in testing Fresnel's wave theory of light. But if this is so, the observation statements used to test a theory are not necessarily biased antecedently in favor of or against a theory; and in consequence, a decision between two competing theories need not express only our "subjective wishes," but may be made in the light of the available evidence. (p. 93)

If, however, the results of observation are couched in abstract theoretical terms—in "high-inference" terms—then there might well be disagreement or misunderstanding. Consider the following example: Most people, whether Freudians or behaviorists, Republicans or Democrats, Americans or Australians or Koreans, deists or atheists, astrologers or astronomers, would agree upon a visit to a classroom that they saw a teacher working with a particular number of pupils. They also probably would agree with the low-inference observation that at a certain stage in the lesson the teacher asked one pupil a series of questions. They might not all agree, however, with the high-inference observation that at this point the teacher was forcing the pupil to do some high-order cognitive task involving Piagetian abstract reasoning. For all the observers to agree with *this* observation and, more to the point, to be able to discuss, to criticize, and to evaluate warrants, they would all have to share the same theoretical framework as well as speak the same language (and this is what Hanson seemed to have in mind when he wrote of "theory-laden perception"). And it is worth noting, in passing, that even if they all did have the same framework, it is not certain that they would necessarily agree—for some might judge that the Piagetian categorization of the pupil's task was erroneous. Similarity of framework is, at best, a guarantee of communication, but not of much else.

The moral of the example is this: Just because, on some accounts, the more abstract description is "less objective" in the sense that it is less "pure" and more "contaminated" by theory, it does not follow that there is no hope for observers to enter into mutual and fruitful discussion, criticism, and evaluation. At a lower level of abstraction there might well be full overlap of categories and terminology (and thus the possibility of a higher degree of objectivity), and this more objective, low-inference observation would serve both as a constraint on the nature of the abstract accounts that could be put forward and as a springboard for critical evaluation.

Israel Scheffler (1967) seems to have had something like this in mind when he stated that the fact that none of the statements we assert

> can be *guaranteed* to be an absolutely reliable link to reality does not mean that we are free to assert any statements at will, provided only that they cohere. That the statement "There's a horse" cannot be rendered theoretically certain does not permit me to call anything a horse. (p. 119; emphasis in original)

Scheffler points out that language offers constraints on what is to count as a horse (just as, in the earlier examples, it provided constraints on what is to count as a patch of red and what is to count as a pupil answering a question), and "such constraints generate credibility claims which enter my reckoning critically as I survey my system of beliefs" (p. 119). In short, then, Hanson has pointed to a problem that ought to be in the forefront of the minds of observers; but in pointing out the theory-laden nature of high-inference observations he has not offered grounds for abandoning the notion of objectivity.

There is a further consideration that strengthens this optimistic conclusion. In the earlier discussion the point was made that the term *objective* is used more or less as a seal of approval, marking the fact that an inquiry or conclusion meets certain quality standards. There are poor inquiries, infected with personal biases, and there are more worthy inquiries, where the warrants that are offered are pertinent and have been subjected to critical scrutiny. The same situation exists with respect to observations. There are certain well-documented factors that influence observers and that can make their work less credible. (In social science terminology, they can be spoken of as "threats to the validity" of observational or qualitative work.) For example, it is known that observers are prone to misjudge frequencies of occurrence of events they are watching, unless they use some quantitative scoring; and they are prone to be overinfluenced by positive instances and underinfluenced by negative instances. (For a discussion of the significance of these factors, see Phillips, 1987b.) Thus the conclusions reached by a shoddy observer who has not controlled these factors would be properly judged by the research community as being less objective than the conclusions reached by a more careful person. Once again, objectivity is seen to be a vital notion, and its abandonment would be fatal for the integrity of the research endeavor.

The Myth of "The More the Merrier"

In an influential essay, Michael Scriven (1972) points out that sometimes objectivity is thought about in terms of the number of inquirers or observers—data that only one person has been able to collect are regarded as subjective and dubious, but there is usually a more favorable judgment when a number of people have been involved.[5] Scriven argues, however, that quality and number of investigators do not always go together. Thus he distinguishes between qualitative objectivity, where the data are of high quality (no matter how many observers or inquirers were involved), and quantitative objectivity, where more than one person has replicated the findings (which does not guarantee veracity). Scriven writes of the two types of objectivity:

> Now it would certainly be delightful if these two senses coincided, so that all reports of personal experience, for example, were less reliable than all reports of events witnessed by a large number of people. But as one thinks of the reliability of reports about felt pain or perceived size, on the one hand, and reports about the achievements of stage magicians and mentalists on the other, one would not find this coincidence impressive. (pp. 95–96)

Scriven's points are crucial; he has shown that it is untenable to give an account of objectivity solely in terms of group consensus— qualitative objectivity is not reducible to quantitative. Thus the audience consensus that a magician has made a woman levitate freely in the air and the group consensus that the world is flat are objective views in the quantitative sense only, that is, those things are what the groups concerned are agreed upon. But the consensus is *only* that; and the agreement does not mean that the views concerned are correct, or warranted, or that they have been reached in a way that has avoided sources of bias and distortion. And yet the number of observers remains a crucial factor in many influential accounts of objectivity. Fred Kerlinger (1973), for example, in his widely used textbook on behavioral research, refers to an "objective procedure" as "one in which agreement among observers is at a maximum" (p. 491). Kerlinger neglected to point out that what is crucial is *how* the agreement was brought about!

Something more is needed to account for the qualitative sense of "objectivity"—some account has to be given of what makes a viewpoint objective in the sense of having a respectable warrant and being free from bias. Alternatively, one could follow Elliot Eisner's lead; in effect he denies that there is any such thing as qualitative objectivity, and thus there is *only* group consensus or quantitative objectivity. The problem here—apart from the issue of whether he is right about the null status of qualitative objectivity—is that quantitative objectivity is not worth very much. Indeed, it is not worthy of the label "objectivity" at all; a more appropriate term is simply "consensus." And the problem, of course, is that consensus about an incorrect or untrustworthy or substandard position is hardly worth writing home about. Eisner's (1979) view has the same defect as Kerlinger's: "What so-called objectivity means is that we believe in what we believe and that others share our beliefs as well. This process is called consensual validation" (p. 214).

It is important to realize, along with Scriven, that "consensual" and "validation" are uncomfortable bedfellows. Scriven makes it clear that "validity" is a term that belongs with "qualitative objectivity," not with "quantitative" or "consensus." Nevertheless, Eisner's and Kerlinger's concern with the role of the community of believers is not entirely misplaced, as will soon be seen.

The missing ingredient, the element that is required to produce objectivity in the qualitative sense, is nothing mysterious—but it has nothing to do with consensus. Gunnar Myrdal, Karl Popper, and Israel Scheffler have put their fingers on it: It is acceptance of the *critical tradition*. A view that is objective is one that has been opened up to scrutiny, to vigorous examination, to challenge. It is a view that has been teased out, analyzed, criticized, debated—in general, it is a view that has been forced to face the demands of reason and of evidence. When this has happened, we have some assurance (though never absolute assurance) that the view does not reflect the whim or bias of some individual or group; it is a view that has respectable warrant. Myrdal (1969) states:

> The method of detecting biases is simple although somewhat laborious. When the unstated value premises of research are kept hidden and for the most part vague, the results presented contain logical flaws. When inferences are confronted with premises, there is found to be a *non sequitur* concealed, leaving the reasoning open to invasion by uncontrolled influences. . . . This element of inconclusiveness can be established by critical analysis. (pp. 53–54)

Popper (1976) expresses a similar point in a manner that makes even clearer that a community of inquirers can only hope to be qualitatively objective when conditions allow them to subscribe to—and actually apply in practice—the critical spirit:

> What may be described as scientific objectivity is based solely upon a critical tradition which, despite resistance, often makes it possible to criticize a dominant dogma. To put it another way, the objectivity of science is not a matter of the individual scientists but rather the social result of their mutual criticism, of the friendly-hostile division of labour among scientists, of their co-operation and also of their competition. For this reason, it depends, in part, upon a number of social and political circumstances which make criticism possible. (p. 95)

Thus Eisner and Kerlinger need to do two things to strengthen their accounts. In the first place, they have to stress that the community of inquirers must be a critical community, where dissent and reasoned disputation (and sustained efforts to overthrow even the most favored of viewpoints) are welcomed as being central to the process of inquiry. Second, they must abandon their references to agreement or consensus. A critical community might never reach agreement over, say, two viable alternative views, but if both of these views have been subjected to critical scrutiny, then both would have to be regarded as objective. (Once again, the term *objective* does not mean true.) And even if agreement is reached, it can still happen that the objective view reached within such a community will turn out to be wrong—this is the cross that all of us living in the new nonfoundationalist age have to learn to bear!

Kuhnism

Thomas S. Kuhn popularized the notion that inquirers always work within the context of a paradigm—a framework that determines the concepts that are used and that also contains exemplars, or model inquiries, which direct attention toward some problems as being key and away from other problems or issues regarded (from that perspective) as somewhat trivial. Many scholars have interpreted Kuhn as supporting a relativistic position whereby it does not make sense to ask which one of various competing paradigms is the correct one; since such judgments can only be made from within a paradigm, inquirers are not able to step outside to examine their paradigms etically. In a sense, then, all inquirers are trapped within their own paradigms; they will judge certain things as being true (for them) that other inquirers in other paradigms will judge as being false (for them). To those who have taken such relativism seriously, there has seemed to be little place in the Kuhnian universe for objectivity.

Thus, sometimes when the possibility of achieving objectivity is being questioned, the focus of attention is the framework within which inquiry is being pursued. For example, Freudians use a particular theoretical frame—they are guided by distinctive concepts and hypotheses—and, of course, for a dedicated worker in this psychoanalytic tradition, the possibility of using some quite different framework does not arise as a practicable alternative. The same situation exists, it has been argued, even if the inquirer does not subscribe to some well-known paradigm; for even here, the inquirer must be working with *some* concepts and hypotheses that serve as bedrock for the endeavor. Thus, to repeat Ratcliffe (1983):

> Most research methodologists are now aware that *all* data are theory-, method-, and measurement-dependent. That is, "facts" are determined by

the theories and methods that generate their collection; indeed, theories and methods *create* the facts. And theories, in turn, are grounded in and derived from the basic philosophical assumptions their formulators hold regarding the nature of and functional relationship between the individual, society, and science. (p. 148; emphasis in original)

Gunnar Myrdal, Elliot Eisner, and the "anarchist" philosopher of science Paul Feyerabend (1978) are among those making similar points.

It is a somewhat controversial point whether choice of a framework or paradigm can be made objectively; but it is clear that the tide of philosophical debate has been running steadily against Kuhn (and relativism) and hence in favor of the view that it *is* possible to judge as better or worse the considerations that are advanced in support of any particular paradigm. (For a summary of the relevant arguments, see Newton-Smith, 1981; Siegel, 1987.) More to the point, the following is also very clear: *Within* any particular framework inquirers can go about their work with more or less facility. Not all Freudians are equally adept; some are bunglers, some are misogynists or suffer from homophobia, and some may even be anti-Republican or anti-Democrat in orientation, and their work as Freudians might be indelibly stamped by these predilections. So sometimes when objectivity is being discussed, the focus of interest is whether it is possible to escape from bias while working or making judgments inside one's framework. Myrdal (1969) seems to have had this focus when he wrote:

Biases are thus not confined to the practical and political conclusions drawn from research. They are much more deeply seated than that. They are the unfortunate results of concealed valuations that insinuate themselves into research at all stages, from its planning to its final presentation. As a result of their concealment, they are not properly sorted out and thus can be kept undefined and vague. (p. 52)

The point, of course, is that the two foci—choice between paradigms, and choices and work within a particular paradigm—must not be confused. An argument that establishes that at one of these levels objectivity is impossible to achieve (accepting, for the moment, that such an argument could be mounted) does not address the issue of whether the other type of objectivity lies out of reach. There are, however, grounds for believing that this confusion does exist. Eisner, for example, argues strongly that it is naive to believe in framework objectivity, but his published advice on the methodology of qualitative research does not stress the dangers of bias in judgment within frameworks, and he does not discuss in any detail the steps that can be taken to avoid it. As was seen earlier, with one broad stroke he does away with objectivity in all its senses, replacing it with consensual validation. (For a further discussion of these issues, see Phillips, 1987b.)

Can objectivity of judgment within a framework or paradigm be achieved? It seems clear that the answer is in the affirmative. Consider a group of qualitative researchers who are working on similar problems, using the same intellectual framework to shape their approaches. What property must their judgments have in order to be regarded as objective? As was shown earlier, it will not suffice for these inquirers merely to *agree* in their judgments. Instead, they would have to show that their own personal biases and valuations had been exposed to critical examination, and the role that these predilections played in their investigations would need to have been rigorously examined. Furthermore, as already mentioned, qualitative research (no less than quantitative research) is subject to a variety of threats to its validity—qualitative researchers are liable to misjudge the frequency rate of certain behaviors that are of interest, they are likely to be unduly influenced by positive instances and not so sensitive to the significance of negative instances, they are likely to be unduly influenced or "anchored" by experiences undergone early in the research, and so on (Sadler, 1982). To achieve objectivity within a paradigm, then, the researcher has to ensure that his or her work is free from these problems, and again the presence of a critical tradition is the best safeguard. When work is sent to blind peer review, when researchers are forced to answer their critics, when researchers are supposed to be acquainted with the methodological and substantive literature (and when others can point out when they are not), and when researchers try honestly to refute their own dearly held beliefs, then bias and the other obvious shortcomings are likely to be eliminated, and the judgment (or judgments) reached by the community of scholars should be objective in the relevant sense.

The Conflation of the Contexts
of Discovery and Justification

The philosopher of science Hans Reichenbach (1953) drew what is now a well-known distinction between the context of discovery in science and the context of justification. In recent years some have argued that the distinction between these is blurry at best, and a few seminal writers seem to have ignored the distinction altogether—though with arguably disastrous results.[6] Nevertheless, for heuristic purposes Reichenbach's distinction turns out to be a very fruitful one.

The relevant point in the present context is this: processes involved in, and even central to, the *making* of discoveries during the pursuit of a research program may not be involved—and might be counterproductive if allowed to intrude—when the discoveries are *checked* and *tested* and *critically evaluated*. Both Israel Scheffler (1967) and Karl Popper (1976) see this distinction as crucial for understanding objectivity in research. Thus Popper, having in mind the context of discovery, writes that

> We cannot rob the scientist of his partisanship without also robbing him of his humanity, and we cannot suppress or destroy his value judgments without destroying him as a human being *and as a scientist*. Our motives and even our purely scientific ideals . . . are deeply anchored in extra-scientific and, in part, in religious valuations. Thus the "objective" or the "value-free" scientist is hardly the ideal scientist. (p. 97; emphasis in original)

Objectivity in research is not, for Popper, a property of the individual researcher: "It is a mistake to assume that the objectivity of a science depends upon the objectivity of the scientist" (p. 96). Objectivity, in this view, is a property of the context of justification; as we have seen in the earlier discussion it is in a sense a social matter, for it depends upon communal acceptance of the critical spirit.

CONCLUSION

Before bringing this discussion to a close, a penultimate point must be made. It may have been noted that, throughout, nothing has been made of the distinction between quantitative and qualitative inquiry. For many authors, of course, the distinction is crucial, and qualitative inquiry can only be objective insofar as it approximates to quantitative inquiry. Fred Kerlinger (1973) seems to be representative of this stance:

> Objective methods of observation are those in which anyone following the prescribed rules will assign the same numerals to objects and sets of objects as anyone else. An objective procedure is one in which agreement among observers is at a maximum. In variance terms, observer variance is at a minimum. This means that judgmental variance, the variance due to differences in judges' assignment of numerals to objects, is zero. (p. 491)

He acknowledges that all methods of observation are inferential but sees procedures that assign numbers as "more objective."

From the point of view of the new nonfoundationalist epistemology, there is little difference between qualitative and quantitative inquiry. Bad work of either kind is equally to be deplored; and good work of either kind is still—at best—only tentative. But the good work in both cases will be objective, in the sense that it has been opened up to criticism, and the reasons and evidence offered in both cases will have withstood serious scrutiny. The works will have faced potential refutation, and insofar as they have survived, they will be regarded as worthy of further investigation.

Another way of putting this is that in all types of inquiry, insofar as the goal is to reach credible conclusions, there is an underlying epistemological similarity. Even in hermeneutics—a mode of qualitative inquiry that at first sight seems far from the "objective" science of physics—there is appeal to evidence, there is testing and criticism of hypotheses (Follesdal, 1979).

It turns out, then, that what is crucial for the objectivity of any inquiry—whether it is qualitative or quantitative—is the critical spirit in which it has been carried out. And, of course, this suggests that there can be *degrees*; for the pursuit of criticism and refutation obviously can be carried out more or less seriously. "Objectivity" is the label—the "stamp of approval"—that is used for inquiries that are at one end of the continuum; they are inquiries that are prized because of the great care and responsiveness to criticism with which they have been carried out. Inquiries at the other end of the continuum are stamped as "subjective" in that they have not been sufficiently opened to the light of reason and criticism. Most human inquiries are probably located somewhere near the middle, but the aim should be to move in the direction that will earn a full stamp of approval!

Acknowledgments

I wish to thank the members of the California Association for Philosophy of Education, and especially Harvey Siegel, for the comments and criticisms that have helped to make this paper more objective.

NOTES

1. Myrdal seems to use "bias" in this way throughout his book.
2. A similar confusion bedeviled critics of William James's work; see Phillips (1984).

3. Hanson's work and its general impact—and the ways in which it has been misinterpreted—is discussed in Phillips (1987a).
4. See particularly the concession Hanson (1965) makes at the bottom of p. 23.
5. Ernest House (1980) discusses Scriven's essay admiringly and in some depth.
6. See, for example, the mischief this causes in some of Piaget's work, as discussed by Phillips (1982).

REFERENCES

Eisner, E. (1979). *The educational imagination*. New York: Macmillan.
Eisner, E. (1986, September). *The primacy of experience and the politics of method*. Lecture delivered at the University of Oslo, Norway.
Feyerabend, P. (1978). *Against method*. London: Verso.
Follesdal, D. (1979). Hermeneutics and the hypothetico-deductive method. *Dialectica, 33*(3–4), 319–336.
Hanson, N. R. (1965). *Patterns of discovery*. Cambridge: Cambridge University Press.
House, E. (1980). *Evaluating with validity*. Beverly Hills, CA: Sage.
Kerlinger, F. (1973). *Foundations of behavioral research* (2nd ed.). New York: Holt, Rinehart & Winston.
Myrdal, G. (1969). *Objectivity in social research*. New York: Pantheon.
Nagel, E. (1979). *Teleology revisited*. New York: Columbia University Press.
Newton-Smith, W. (1981). *The rationality of science*. London: Routledge.
Phillips, D. C. (1982). Perspectives on Piaget as philosopher. In S. & C. Modgil (Eds.), *Jean Piaget: Consensus and controversy* (pp. 13–29). London: Holt.
Phillips, D. C. (1984). Was William James telling the truth after all? *The Monist, 67*(3), 419–434.
Phillips, D. C. (1987a). *Philosophy, science, and social inquiry*. Oxford, UK: Pergamon.
Phillips, D. C. (1987b). Validity in qualitative research. *Education and Urban Society, 20*(1), 9–24.
Popper, K. (1968). *Conjectures and refutations*. New York: Harper.
Popper, K. (1976). The logic of the social sciences. In T. Ardono et al. (Eds.), *The positivist dispute in German sociology* (pp. 87–104). New York: Harper.
Ratcliffe, J. (1983). Notions of validity in qualitative research methodology. *Knowledge Creation, Diffusion, Utilization, 5*(2), 147–167.
Reichenbach, H. (1953). *The rise of scientific philosophy*. Berkeley & Los Angeles: University of California Press.
Sadler, D. (1982). Intuitive data processing as a potential source of bias in naturalistic evaluations. In E. House et al. (Eds.), *Evaluation Studies Review Annual* (Vol. 7, pp. 199–205). Beverly Hills, CA: Sage.

Scheffler, I. (1967). *Science and subjectivity*. Indianapolis: Bobbs-Merrill.
Scriven, M. (1972). Objectivity and subjectivity in educational research. In
  L. Thomas (Ed.), *Philosophical redirection of educational research* (71st Yearbook of
  the NSSE; pp. 94–142). Chicago: National Society for the Study of Educa-
  tion.
Siegel, H. (1987). *Relativism refuted*. Dordrecht, The Netherlands: Reidel.

2 Is Naturalism a Move Away from Positivism?
Materialist and Feminist Approaches to Subjectivity in Ethnographic Research

LESLIE G. ROMAN and MICHAEL W. APPLE

POWER, SUBJECTIVITY, AND METHOD

There are certain concepts that seem so simple at first glance that one is often surprised by the complexity lurking beneath their surfaces. "Subjectivity" is such a concept. It is often used to signify a form of pollution in social and scientific inquiry. To be "subjective" is to be "biased," allowing one's values to enter into and prejudice the outcome of one's research. Here, the ideal is the disinterested inquirer, the scientific equivalent of Mannheim's (1936) "unattached intelligentsia" who stand above the structure of social conflicts and can see what is truly real and what is ideological or false. In various guises, this position has found its proponents on the right and left sides of the political and research spectrum.

For others, subjectivity is not something to be purged from the research community. It is, rather, something to be acknowledged, understood, and learned from in the process of constructing the relations and representations of cultural selves and others. Its significance lies in the recognition of the joint construction of meaning in all social and scientific inquiry. *Verstehen* acts in such a way as to close the hermeneutic circle.

There are those for whom the distinction between subjectivity and objectivity (when treated as a binary opposition in which the absence of one implies the presence of the other) is not a simple one, but is the result of constantly shifting relation. Rather, according to this conceptualization, subjectivity is a signpost that distinguishes human consciousness of the social and material world. Its interaction with objectivity is a point of contention in which different but related power struggles take place between and among subordinate and dominant groups over what counts as "true" knowledge. Within this view, subjectivity is not merely an individual's psychological state of mind. While encompassing human consciousness, this conceptualization also allows for the recognition of consciousness as asymmetric, that is, as invariably defined by the multiple power relations and conflicting interests of class, race, gender, age, and sexual orientation. To put it more simply, when we act in the world, we act simultaneously within and against our contradictory interests by gender, class, race, age, and sexual orientation. These power relations set perceptible and imperceptible limits upon the range of choices and actions in which we may engage to further one or more of our interests and, in turn, variously affect our subjectivities. In the construction of our arguments, we will acknowledge the reciprocal determinacy that "subjectivity" and "objectivity"—the conflicting sets of historically specific power relations and material interests—have upon one another. This acknowledgment thus makes previous dualistic and binary oppositional treatments of subjectivity and objectivity inadequate. They are inadequate to the tasks of both raising and answering certain questions that we believe are essential in the democratization of knowledge in educational research, and, more particularly, in a form of qualitative inquiry known as naturalistic ethnography.

We will argue that such democratization is part of a broader project of recognizing that questions confronting researchers about their methods and design, as well as the validity of their conclusions, are not only procedural and technical matters but political ones as well. They place all researchers (whether they acknowledge it or not) squarely within the conflicting power relations and subjectivities that comprise human consciousness of the social and material world.

Examining the Subject-Object Dualism

Working for theoretical and practical alternatives to the subject-object dualism entails self-consciously confronting several questions. We intend to raise those questions that we believe to constitute critical interventions into the construction of a politically transformative epistemology for qualitative inquiry, in general, and ethnography, in particular. First, for whom is research or inquiry conducted? This issue concerns the role of social research in empowering certain social actors and silencing or disempowering others. Second, who decides what the "problems" of a research agenda are? Both questions require us to examine the macro- and microrelations of power that construct the local setting in which one makes an inquiry, as well as the differential power relations between the researcher and the researched. Third, we ask whether the rigid binary opposition between subjectivity and objectivity is one consequence of adhering to a masculinist and positivistic logic in which the more one distances oneself from the "object of study," the better one is as a researcher. Fourth, and conversely, is naturalistic ethnography—a method involving a great degree of intimacy and apparent mutuality in the potential for self-exposing subjectivity between the researcher and the researched—in more danger of exploiting subordinate groups than allegedly more positivistic, quantitative, and masculinist research methods? Fifth, what ethical principles and epistemological traditions can be evoked to guide ethnographers facing the contradictions invariably entailed in the often unacknowledged power relations of conducting fieldwork and writing ethnographies?

The previous questions lead to another. *Whose subjectivity are we talking about?* In our minds, it is crucial to discuss the concept of subjectivity in relation to consciousness of and power relations surrounding both researchers and researched. All too often, we focus on the subjectivity of one group or the other, thereby missing their interaction and the power differentials constructed in their social relations with each other. Thus, as many feminist researchers have argued, and as we shall claim, meaning is jointly constructed between researchers and research subjects in the context of interests that are formed out of contradictory power relations. The recognition of such a process, we shall argue, allows genuine progress to be made in understanding the power of research to make an emancipatory difference in people's lives.

Finally, while our arguments call for a critical reexamination of the rigid binary opposition between subjectivity and objectivity, we also intend to ask what social function is performed inside and outside of the research community by quests for a positivistic conception of objectivity, or what feminist philosopher of science Sandra Harding (1987a) calls "objectivism." By objectivism, Harding means the stance often taken by researchers in the attempt to remove, minimize, or make invisible their own cultural beliefs and practices, while simultaneously directing attention to the subjectivities, beliefs, and practices of research subjects as the sole objects of scrutiny. If qualitative researchers, following Harding's lead, reject objectivism and its claim to disinterested research that separates the context of discovery from the justification for research, must they necessarily resort to subjectivism and relativism? Must they discard the concept of objectivity altogether? How might the nature of objectivity be reconceived as an alternative to the pitfalls of objectivism? In short, how are the beliefs and practices of the researcher constitutive of the empirical evidence for or against the ethnographic descriptions and analyses the researcher draws or advances?

We ask these questions from our different positions as gendered social subjects, both of us continuing to be politically active inside and outside of the academy, but one of us having experienced subordination as a woman. The questions we ask and the implications they pose structure our arguments. They act as a backdrop against which we judge not only the adequacy of the procedures used by many qualitative researchers in education but also their claims regarding the justification for research and the context of discovery.

Educational Research as an Ethical and Political Act

As argued at the outset, our overarching concern in reexamining the epistemological questions surrounding naturalistic ethnography is to link research to the project of democratizing the institutions of our unequal society. Because forms of oppression by gender, class, race, sexual orientation, and age are structured into the very warp and woof of our society, to study schooling is not simply to inquire into an assemblage of neutral institutions whose role is to pass on "the common culture." It is to see schools as places that were and are formed out of cultural, political, and economic conflicts and compromises (Apple, 1979, 1982).

For example, to study elementary school teaching is also to study the paid labor of millions of *women*. The control of teaching and curricula was strongly influenced by a set of gender dynamics between women and men that continue to this day (Apple, 1986). The same holds true for the dynamics leading to the outcomes of student examinations. As many ethnographers have demonstrated, while the relationship between, say, school achievement, attitudes, and the relations of class, race, gender, sexual orientation, and age in the society as a whole is complicated, one would have to be nearly blind to miss the importance of these interrelationships in structuring the lives, hopes, and futures of students inside and outside the school. It is unwise to think of the curriculum itself as neutral. Out of the vast universe of possible knowledge, it is clear that only certain groups' knowledge tends to become legitimate in schools. For these reasons, the educational system is implicated in processes that are connected to the patterns and social relations of unequal power that permeate this society (Apple, 1982).

The conduct and uses of social research are not immune from these power relations. Therefore we see educational inquiry as an ethical and political act that is strongly connected to conflicts over knowledge, resources, and power outside as well as inside of education, even when its practitioners wish otherwise. Therefore we shall argue that one of our tasks is to participate in emancipatory and democratizing social transformation, not simply the "neutral" collection, analysis, and reportage of data.

The criticisms we offer of positivistic tendencies within qualitative research emanate from our dissatisfaction with naturalistic ethnography as well as our dissatisfaction with the determinism of structuralist neo-Marxism in educational scholarship. Within structuralist neo-Marxism, culture and the individual and collective experiences of people often have been treated merely as reflections of economic interests and class-based power relations (Bernstein, 1977; Bowles & Gintis, 1976). Thus, while we shall be critical of the ways the discourse of naturalistic ethnography affirms the purging of the researcher's subjectivity in the various stages of research, we do believe that qualitative inquiry (and ethnography in particular) has offered an important step beyond many of the deterministic positions taken by other critically oriented forms of scholarship in education.

By making these criticisms, we will acknowledge some affinities with what is known as the "culturalist" position in critical educational studies. Work within this tradition emphasizes nonreductive treatments of social subjects' active sense-making processes. It does not, however, eschew an awareness of the structural forces and social relations of capitalism, patriarchy, and racial domination that impinge upon and determine the range of choices available to social subjects. Recently, such analyses have argued and shown how race and gender are as important as class in understanding the practices and social relations of institutions and culture in this society (Apple, 1982; Apple, 1986; McCarthy & Apple, 1988).

Our positions also have been strongly influenced by the traditions of critical ethnography, feminist sociology, and feminist materialist analyses of the methodologies, epistemologies, and praxis of research. Until recently (Roman, 1987, 1989; Stacey, 1988) there has been little cross-fertilization among these traditions. Yet we believe that they, and especially the feminist materialists' explicitly committed stance of democratizing qualitative research, offer crucial points of departure for the articulation of practices that are grounded in both an ethical and a socially transformative political vision of the rationale for and the uses of ethnography (Harding, 1986; Lather, 1986; Oakley, 1981; Roman, 1987, 1989; Rosaldo, 1983; Scott, 1984, 1985; Stacey, 1988). It is important to state, however, that the arguments we shall present, while generally shared by both of us, emerge in their empirical and theoretical specificity from Roman's (1987) ethnography. This work examines how middle- and working-class Punk young women formed their gender and class identities and relations within the extramural curriculum of their subculture, while they also traversed their families and schools.

The Dialectics of Theory and Practice

At the outset of this examination, I (Roman)[1] would like to clarify two points to try to avoid the development of misunderstandings in the reading of my arguments because I present them as theory largely in the absence of the practical social relations that helped give rise to them. In fact, the arguments advanced in this paper emerged from a specific set of social relations—a middle-class, white, academic researcher studying middle- and working-class Punk young women in the context of their interactions with Punk young men. Elsewhere (Roman, 1987, 1989) I describe in detail the dialectical interaction between my fieldwork practice and emergent theory.

Here I would first like to point out that the issues of practice and ethics surrounding my ethnographic research did not emerge out of nor were they derived from my rigid adherence to feminist materialist theory. Rather, it is more accurate to say that my ethnographic practice and ethics in the field emerged and transformed as I attempted to square the conflicts and contradictions they presented with my training as a naturalistic ethnographer and my prior conscious political beliefs as a feminist materialist. The interaction of practice with my deeply held political beliefs and theoretical commitments was dialectical; that is, as practical ethical dilemmas shaped and transformed my feminist materialism, the resultant emergent theory in turn caused me to rethink my ethical stances toward the young women I researched.

A second and related potential misconception I would like to dispel is the idea that ethnographic decisions are a matter of choosing between the priorities of politically and ethically motivated methods and ones that are scientific and epistemologically founded. The reality discovered in my fieldwork relationships with the Punk young women and men reveals the epistemological reasons why it is both wrong and impossible to escape political and ethical decisions in methodological choices. To crystallize these arguments, I am not advancing a "feminist materialist method or procedure" for the conduct of ethnographic research. Rather, I am advancing those theoretical and methodological features of my research that may indicate possible applications of a general structure of social scientific theory to the conduct of research on women and gender.[2] These features are epistemological because they entail the production of theories of knowledge that offer an alternative to masculinist ones and because they challenge the class essentialism often assumed in neo-Marxist ethnographies.[3]

NATURALISM AS DISCOURSE AND IDEOLOGY

The Appeal of Naturalistic Ethnography

Initially, I selected the naturalistic approach to ethnography as the primary method for my study (1987) for two compelling reasons. First, ethnography insists upon rendering "thick" contextual descriptions of social subjects as they actively and creatively make sense of their social worlds (Geertz, 1973). As Woods (1985) states:

> Ethnography by definition is descriptive. In anthropology it means, literally "a picture of the way of life of some interacting group. . . ." Faithfulness to a culture as it is found is one of the guiding principles of ethnography, and immersion in the culture under study is the general strategy towards this end. (p. 52)

The idea of thoroughly immersing oneself as a participant-observer in a setting in order to render a picture of people's common-sense knowledge, cultural practices, and agency within their subcultures, families, and schools had a particular appeal for me. Such a method seemed consistent with the culturalists' political critique of the determinism embedded in structuralist theories of social reproduction.

Like some other critically oriented researchers, such as Willis (1981), I shared those elements of such a critique that were opposed to reducing human agency and social subjectivity to the mere passive effects of social structure. Ethnography, I reasoned, with its focus on microlevel patterns of social interaction among people, would provide a useful antidote to the tendency of structuralist reproduction theories to grossly abstract and overtheorize about what goes on in the daily life of cultural institutions or informal settings, whether they are schools, families, or youth subcultures.

Second, I was drawn to naturalistic ethnography because for the most part structuralist theories of social reproduction relied upon methods that were either opaque or overly formalistic and totalizing in their account of social subjects' collective self-making processes. I wondered whether Willis's (1977) lads or the young women in McRobbie's (1978) influential study of the role of the school in reproducing class and gender relations would have recognized themselves in the resultant theoretical accounts had their subcultural practices and subjectivities been interpreted strictly through Bernstein's (1977) structural and linguistic schema of classification and framing or through Bourdieu and Passeron's (1977) typology of linguistic and cultural competence. Could such structural approaches account for the richness and complexity that occurs in daily life?

In contrast, ethnographic accounts, as they had been used by culturalists such as Willis (1977), McRobbie (1978), and others, seemed at first glance to be explicit in their methods and rationales for participant-observation. Willis (1977) even went so far as to include a methodological appendix that attempted to provide a reflexive account of his field research, as well as the lads' responses to his theoretical interpretations of their subcultural practices and subjectivities. Unlike the overbearing formalism and inaccessibility of structuralist theories of social reproduction and their attendant methodologies, ethnographies seemed immediately accessible to a wide range of readers. They appeared to invite the readership into dialogues with the research subjects themselves. Moreover, the texts of these culturalist ethnographers appeared to function as written proxies for the agency of working-class people and the "oppositional" or "resistant" aspects of working-class culture. As such, interview data, descriptive accounts, and extracts from fieldwork with working-class groups, much like narrative realist texts, seemed to clarify powerfully—as if told in their own voices—the underlying structural mechanisms and material conditions that enabled society's cultural and social reproduction.

Given such a compelling (and, I might add, politically correct) rationale for "doing" ethnography, I worked toward my adoption of the conventional role and subject position of the naturalistic ethnographer. According to the discourse of naturalistic ethnography, I would enter the Punks' subculture as an anthropological stranger, explore them in the context of their own natural settings, and yet remain careful not to disturb the ecology of their social world by introducing my own subjectivity, beliefs, or interests as a white, middle-class, academic researcher.[4]

As an ethnographer of a Punk subculture, I would participate covertly or overtly in people's lives for an extended period of time, watching what happens, listening to what is said, asking questions; in fact, collecting whatever data are available to throw light on the issues with which he or she is concerned. (Hammersley & Atkinson, 1983, p. 2)

And I would enter the field research heeding the words of Schatzman and Strauss (1973):

The naturalistic researcher will not in advance presuppose more than the barest rudiments of social order and value. What he [sic] will do is maximize the possibilities of discovering these as they are developed within the situation. (p. 14)

Thus a key element of naturalistic ethnography is the attempt by the researcher to hold in abeyance any of her or his prior political assumptions and theoretical commitments about what is happening in the world under study. According to the naturalistic view of ethnographic research, I would arrive in the Punk subculture only to discover that much of what I took for granted as knowledge about how the social world works would be disconfirmed or proven false in the context of a new environment. As an ethnographer, my tasks would then be to gain an insider's knowledge of what is going on and to gradually and inductively generate theory to explain what is seen. As Schutz (1964) argues, entering the field in such a manner would allow me to acquire a certain objectivity not available to the Punks themselves, whose underlying assumptions regarding their own practices would remain fundamentally and unconsciously obscure to them.

According to Schutz (1964), I as researcher might expect to find some overlap in assumptions, beliefs, and worldviews between myself and the researched, given that we live in the same society. However, this would not minimize the value of the ethnographic account as a social science method. Ethnography could still render a description of the cultural patterns and practices that vary across and within society, especially those that shed light upon the social meanings and contexts that constitute such variations. By seeking to ascertain the Punks' everyday ways of perceiving the world, the naturalistic ethnographer could glimpse the ongoing constitution of social reality. I would conceive of social reality mainly as the situations and meanings widely available among the people being studied in order to construct and reconstruct the social world of their own culture (Reynolds, 1980; Sharp & Green, 1975).

Writing the ethnography would entail my documenting and pre-serving an accurate description of how the Punk young women saw things in the context of interactions with other Punks, their fellow students, teachers, parents, and so forth. My analysis would emerge out of the Punks' accounts as members of a particular "taken-for-granted" reality. I would therefore be describing the commonsense rules—whether tacit or explicit—that organized the various practices and subjective meanings constituting social reality in the subculture, families, and schools. The analysis then would emerge inductively out of the field research alone (Edwards & Furlong, 1985; Schatzman & Strauss, 1973).

According to such a view of naturalistic accounts anything more would constitute an *imposition* of my own "arbitrary and simplistic cate-gories on a complex reality" (Hammersley & Atkinson, 1983).[5] If I followed the main tenets of naturalistic ethnography as Hammersley and Atkinson have summarized and ambivalently critiqued them, I would be reassured by the claims of numerous ethnographers repre-senting a variety of disciplines and political traditions (including neo-Marxist sociologists of education) that naturalistic ethnography dia-metrically opposes and provides a methodological alternative to the allegedly intrinsic positivism of the natural sciences, quantitative sociol-ogy, and experimental research. In the process, I would feel comforted by the idea that the methodological criteria of naturalism would "solve" the "problem" of subjectivity as it is represented and reified in the subject-object dualism.

According to this view of the naturalistic ethnographer, I would not place the Punks in a laboratory setting, introduce them to standard-ized questionnaires written in neutral-sounding observational lan-guage, or subject them to artificial simulations (the plans for which some educational psychologist may have already conceived). I therefore could take heart that both the field research and the written account of the ethnography would be free of such unnatural and intrusive mea-sures. Having alternated in the researcher's role between acting as a fully immersed participant-observer, who surrenders herself to the "native" experience and account of their subculture, and participating as an unobtrusive "fly on the wall," who gleans privileged knowledge and insight into the participants' culture, I could proceed unproblemati-cally to write the ethnography. Because the ethnography itself would not rely upon the deductive mode of explanation or universal covering laws that would attempt to posit, predict, or generalize from the obser-vations of the subjects' interactions, I could rest assured that I had not succumbed to positivism[6] (Giddens, 1979; Hammersley & Atkinson, 1983; Keaṭ & Urry, 1975).

Naturalistic Ethnography's Affinities with Positivism

It cannot be denied that a research method that closely attends to the ways social subjects form their commonsense knowledge in their everyday contexts and situations makes some important modifications to the assumptions traditionally associated with a positivistic conception of scientific method. For example, while positivistic science usually asserts the experimental mentality, with its emphasis upon the discovery of universal laws and deductive explanations that rely on value neutrality and quantifiable precision, naturalistic ethnography forsakes generalizations in favor of the image of contextually and inductively built qualitative description and theory. Now certainly one of the values of naturalistic ethnography is its potential to generate theory that may challenge unwarranted preconceptions or conclusions on the parts of researchers. It is also important to recognize, however, that beneath such distinctions, *naturalistic ethnography often constitutes an extension of rather than a break from positivism.*

First, whereas positivism usually employs the discourse of hypothesis testing and controlled experiments to speak of the research process, naturalistic ethnography uses the discourse of the discovery and exploration of the culture of "others." Both discourses take for granted the assumption that the researcher is a detached observer who "minimizes" the research subjects' "reactivity" to the researcher (Aggleton, 1984; Hammersley & Atkinson, 1983; Hargreaves, Hester, & Mellor, 1975; Lofland, 1971). Just as positivistic science and, more particularly, quantitative sociology have been accused by naturalistic and qualitative researchers of standardizing the research process in order to minimize the effects of the researchers upon the data or the research subjects, naturalistic ethnographers have been equally obsessed with the effects of their presence in creating "distorted" or "unnatural" interactions among those they research.

Aggleton (1984) provides one typical example of an ethnographer who works to erase his presence in the fieldwork and in the written account of it. Aggleton set out to study a group of what he termed "new middle class," subcultural youth, whom he identified as "underachievers," attending an English college of further education. Since he had been a teacher at the same college in which he hoped to conduct the research, Aggleton went to elaborate lengths to disguise the nature of his research with former faculty colleagues and the students who were the prospective research subjects for the study.[7] Inside the school and with his former teaching colleagues, Aggleton represented himself in "vague" terms as taking a leave of absence from his teaching, allowing them to draw their own conclusions that he was either conducting research on "something to do with youth culture" or "taking the time off dossing at the University" (p. 110). Outside school, however, he represented himself to the students as just another person who, like themselves, had become "disillusioned" with school, was "pissed off with teaching," and was having "difficulty" with his "work."

Of course, the very idea that the ethnographer works to "increase naturalism" or gain rapport by reconstructing accounts of her or his self-presentation and purposes with different groups of research subjects exposes the discourse's own contradictory ideology. It is analogous to women being sold cosmetics to use in creating a natural appearance. The researcher uses nonreciprocal and nondialogical means of entry and communication to gain access into sets of social relations (e.g., subcultures and school faculties) that are themselves structured by their interactive and dialogical features among and between groups. Aggleton's attempts to build rapport in this manner, which I (1987) have called "going native," shares with positivism the assumption that one can simply refrain from making the and/or revealing ethical considerations that motivate and are embedded in the practice of field research. Maintaining these different and less-than-open accounts with the students and faculty appears to pose no major ethical problems for Aggleton in terms of examining how he obtained his data or the conditions under which people opened up to him. Instead, like most ethnographers who work within the discourse of naturalism, Aggleton—though very sensitive in other ways—tends to construct himself as a "neutral" and "unobtrusive observer" whose main interest in establishing rapport or "building commonality" (1984, p. 111) with the research subjects is the quest for better data.

It is this similarity in the underlying logic and methods of positivism and those of naturalistic methods such as participant-observation and ethnography that prompts Willis (1981)—in one of the rare discussions of the limitations of naturalistic ethnography by a neo-Marxist—to warn against creating a false distinction between quantitative research as intrinsically positivistic and qualitative research as free of positivism:

> The duality and mutual exclusivity of the overly neatly opposed categories, "qualitative methods" and "quantitative methods," suggests already that the "object" is viewed in the same unitary and distanced way even if the

mode is changed—now you measure it, now you feel it. (p. 88; emphasis in original)

In either "mode" of research, Willis argues, the researcher assumes that knowledge of the social world can be constructed by drawing inferences from immediate sensory experiences of the "object" under study. These inferences are then made distant from the researcher's own subjectivity, interests, and values.

Like the positivistic concern to create the aura of neutrality on the part of the researcher, naturalistic ethnographers generally offer a similar rationale for minimizing the reactivity of their research subjects to themselves. They do so by adopting various field roles, such as "going native" to become a fully immersed participant or becoming the unobtrusive "acceptable incompetent" (Lofland, 1971). They stress their concern not to contaminate the natural relations and interactions among research subjects with the "biases" of the researcher (Popkewitz, 1981; Schatzman & Strauss, 1973). Such preconceptions on the part of the reseacher are seen as ultimately distorting or falsifying the results of the study. According to this view, data retrieved under conditions that acknowledge the researcher's presence and her or his possible effects upon what the research subjects said in interviews or how they interacted among themselves pose a threat to the ecological validity of the analysis.

Instead of treating the inevitable reactions to and interactions with the researcher by the research subjects as valid data occurring within a specific set of social relations, a good deal of naturalistic ethnography legitimates a number of misconceived distinctions premised upon the positivistic logic that neutrality in research and on the part of the researcher's established field role is both attainable *and* desirable. The apparent prevalence of such a premise in naturalistic ethnographies inspired Johnson (personal communication, March 1982) to coin the phrase "the phenomenon of the missing researcher." Johnson uses this phrase to describe how researchers adopt authorial voices in their written accounts in which they absent themselves from acknowledging that they held prior theoretical assumptions or nascent hypotheses when they entered and conducted the field research.

One fundamental problem with such a logic is its affirmation of the false distinction between "natural," or ecologically valid, and distorted, or "artificial" or "imposed," modes of doing ethnographic field research. Such a distinction holds in common with positivism the assumption that the social reality and social relations associated with field research can be treated as entirely distinct from the social relations of the wider society, which are structured in part by the inequitable power relations and divisions of gender, class, race, age, and sexual orientation. One could imagine different practices, behaviors, and social meanings arising in the field when a researcher is physically present among the research subjects and when she or he is physically absent. How a group responds to and understands the presence of the researcher is as informative as how it makes sense of the researcher's absence; both are sets of meaningful social relations.

It is difficult, however, to argue that the context in which the researcher is present can be seen as less meaningful or socially constructed than one in which the researcher is absent because in both cases there are underlying power relations structuring social life that affect whatever understandings and accounts of reality the given groups generate to articulate "what is or is not going on" for them. To ignore an account of such power relations as they underlie the field research is to assert an argument that reinforces naive realism and empiricism. It presumes that social reality is atomistic (Jaggar, 1983) and can therefore be reduced to descriptions of "the ways things are," that is, the appearances of social life as they are observed by the research subjects (Jones, 1986, p. 34). Just as critically, in sanctifying the absolute primacy of how subject members see their social reality, naturalistic ethnography fails to account for any of the structural mechanisms and material conditions that might contribute to the determination of how members see things or articulate what they understand.

Taking such a view also asserts the erroneous notion that inductive reasoning, or what Glaser and Strauss (1967) call "grounded theory" (p. 55) and the cultural description it renders in ethnographic accounts, can be separated from the researcher's *prior* assumptions, theory development, testing, and explanation. In response to such a view, Hammersley and Atkinson (1983) find themselves most critical of naturalistic ethnography's affinities with positivism. They first make the rather obvious argument that all research methods, whether they are more quantitatively or qualitatively structured, involve processes of selection and interpretation in which the researcher describes and explains a limited or partial construction of the social totality under study. In their view, no researcher is privy to the structural totality of the culture under study since "even in a small-scale setting we [ethnographers] could not begin to describe everything, and any description we [ethnographers] produce is inevitably based on inferences" (p. 13).

However, they later advance a more sophisticated argument, implying that all description is theory-laden. Hence they critique the assumption within naturalistic ethnography that limits the project of ethnographers to cultural description:

> While there may be nothing wrong with such cultural description, the kind of empiricist methodology enshrined in naturalism renders the [researcher's] theory implicit and thus systematically discourages its development and testing. (p. 13)

In pursuit of this argument, Hammersley and Atkinson come close to a critical break with naturalistic ethnography. This nearly critical break occurs when they challenge the restriction placed upon ethnographers merely to describe the social world under study rather than to theorize systematically and explicitly one's transforming relationship to it. By refusing to accept naturalistic ethnography's distinction between description (seen as value-neutral) and theory (seen as value-laden or as the consequences of the researcher's imposition of her or his prior assumptions), they implicitly reserve a role for the ethnographer's reflexive[8] theory development and testing as a form of "critical praxis," that is, as a way of transforming the differential power relations that exist between the researched and researcher and within the social setting itself. However, the boundaries and principles of that role remain unclear as their discussion ultimately seems to vacillate between casting the ethnographer in either a relativistic or an objectivistic position. They do little more than recognize that ethnographers are part of the social worlds they study. Beyond equating such a recognition with reflexivity, Hammersley and Atkinson's critique of naturalism gives us little purchase on the relation of ethnographers and ethnographic research practice to understanding and transforming (however modestly) the structural power relations underlying the field research.

WORKING FOR A FEMINIST MATERIALIST ETHNOGRAPHY

Although specific critiques of naturalistic ethnography by materialists and feminist materialists, particularly within cultural studies, remain nascent and rare, far-reaching criticisms of naturalism's affinities with positivism and the ways it deals with the issue of subjectivity can be found in the elaboration of materialist, feminist, and feminist materialist theories outside debates on naturalistic ethnography per se. I draw upon both sets of debates in order to extend my own critique of naturalistic ethnography from a feminist materialist perspective. The purpose of the critique is not merely to say what feminist materialist ethnography is by way of negation, that is, by way of saying what it is *not* in its opposition to positivism. I also aim to elaborate the principles and practices that might inform feminist materialist ethnography in a way that both acknowledges how the subjective and objective positions of all participants—researcher and researched—enter into the research process and deals with the reality of differential power.[9]

As I have just shown, the discourse of naturalistic ethnography gives primacy to the subjective or intersubjective states of social members' accounts. Since this discourse still too often leans toward a positivistic notion of objectivity and an atomistic view of knowledge, it renders the researcher a purportedly distant and neutral observer who merely describes the "appearances of social life." Yet as political philosopher Jaggar (1983) so persuasively argues, every method entails at least an implicit commitment to a certain theoretical understanding of the social world and to particular criteria for empirical and theoretical adequacy. And it is at this level of analysis that it becomes clear that all too often naturalistic ethnography affirms a social world that is meant to be *gazed upon but not challenged or transformed*.

The Implications of Materialism for Ethnography

In her superb analysis of social reproduction in a New Zealand secondary school, Jones (1986) cogently summarizes a representative materialist critique of naturalistic ethnography. She quotes Rachel Sharp (1982), who maintains that

> Ethnography reinforces ontological and epistemological social atomism: the atoms of social life are individuals; their beliefs, intentions, assumptions and actions form both the starting point of, and dictate the explanatory procedures for grasping social reality. (Sharp, 1982, p. 49; quoted in Jones, 1986, p. 35)

Jones draws upon Sharp's theoretical critique of naturalistic ethnography to explain the theoretical and epistemological basis of her own materialist ethnography. She draws the implication from Sharp's language that ethnographers cannot afford to ignore the fact that social subjects are born into and socially constituted by "a world already made," and that "structured patterns of social relations pre-exist the individual and generate specific forms of social consciousness, . . . linguistic and, hence, cognitive possibilities that socially structure available life chances" (Sharp, 1982, p. 50). Furthermore, in order to get beyond the phenomenal level of analysis, ethnographers need to explain the underlying social relations that set objective limits on the "appearances" of people's practices and their accounts of the social world.

According to Jones, such an analysis would make explicit use of the crucial materialist distinction between the appearances of social life and the material conditions and social relations structuring them. This call for a method that works dialectically on the relation between the phenomenal appearances of social life and the objective nature of the social relations that structure them is a dramatic departure from naturalistic ethnography, but it is also one that enables researchers to generate and test theories in the process of doing the research. Jones concurs with the statement of sociologist E. O. Wright (1978) about the value of examining such a distinction:

> The point of the distinction between appearances and underlying reality is not to dismiss appearances, but rather to provide a basis for their explanation. The central claim [in Marxist theory] is that the vast array of empirical phenomena immediately observable in social life can only be explained if we analyze the social reality hidden behind those appearances. If we remain entirely at the level of appearances we might be able to describe social phenomena, but we cannot explain them. (Wright, 1978, p. 12)

Thus a materialist conception of ethnography provides an explanatory theory that situates the understandings of the research subjects and the researcher within the underlying social reality (i.e., the modes and forces of material production and their relations of domination and subordination; Sharp, 1982).

In contrast to naturalistic ethnography's assertion of value-neutrality as a criterion for theoretical and empirical adequacy, materialism makes an explicit commitment to understand and transform the various forms of subordination that exist in society (Jaggar, 1983). Rather than seeing knowledge as the construct of either the social members under study *or* the researcher as the detached observer, materialism views knowledge as arising through practical social struggle to change the social world, a struggle that in turn changes the human subjects themselves. Speaking very generally, since all human productive activity grows out of specific material conditions and social relations of society (we can call them here capitalism, patriarchy, and racial domination), social knowledge constitutes definite historical forms.

Given such a premise, it follows that doing ethnographic research entails asking several related questions that are grounded in the issues raised at the outset of this paper:

- What are the social locations and backgrounds of the researcher and the research subjects?
- Whose knowledge gets articulated in the field as well as in the written account?
- Who benefits from the research?
- Is it possible within the confines of naturalistic ethnography to capture the active agency of people without ignoring or minimizing the structural determinants that set limits on people's practices and subjectivities?

It is clear that these questions raise a particular set of epistemological issues concerned with attempts to ground accounts of the social world in a basis that is less partial and distorting than dominant atomistic and traditional modes of social and scientific inquiry. In this aim, materialist and feminist perspectives are in agreement. However, materialist and feminist strategies for responding to these questions and extending the issues they raise into areas of ethnographic research practice differ in at least one way that is germane to our discussion. Broadly speaking, materialist epistemology (as reflected in the work of neo-Marxist ethnographers and sociologists of education) tends to maintain the subject-object dualism without question,[10] while feminists of various orientations have attempted to challenge the androcentric rigidity of the categorical bounds of this dualism. As Harding (1987b) argues in her edited volume, *Feminism and Methodology*, if women's perspectives and knowledge claims were already legitimate within both traditional and Marxist approaches to social and scientific inquiry, then the development of specifically feminist approaches would no longer be necessary.

Therefore, the focus in this essay hereafter will be on the implications of different feminist epistemologies for ethnographic research. Yet I believe strongly that the issues raised by feminist epistemologies pertain to all forms of qualitative research and inquiry in which the primary goal is the development of a self-critical stance toward the ethics and politics of the power relations between the researcher(s) and the researched in the constitution of social subjectivity.

The Implications of Forms of Feminism for Ethnography

Feminists of various orientations (particularly radical and materialist) have worked to revise Marxism's gender-blind epistemology and appropriate its conceptual arguments in order to understand and transform women's gender-specific experiences of subordination (Barrett,

1982; Coward, 1980; Jaggar, 1983; Lather, 1986; McRobbie, 1982; Oakley, 1981; Scott, 1985; Smith, 1974; Spender, 1980). They disagree, however, as to what constitutes a feminist understanding of women's subordination. Feminists widely debate such questions as:

- Is a research method and theory feminist simply because it is developed by a woman or consists of women as research subjects?
- Are research methods and theories feminist because they raise the question of women's subordination in the context of focusing exclusively on women's experiences of it?
- Can it be assumed that there are enough commonalities in women's experiences across and within groupings by class, race, age, and sexual orientation to speak of a shared experience of subordination?

One position taken by some feminists implies uncritically that feminist research, methods, theories, and practice constitute any research done by women about women or with women as research subjects (Bernard, 1973; Scott, 1984; Spender, 1980). Such a position assumes that there is an understanding, whether it is tacit or explicit, among women about what feminism is or what gender interests may unite them. Insofar as it applies to interactive or qualitative research methods, it holds in common with radical feminism the assumption that women researchers and research subjects form a natural bond based on their identification with each other as women.

Although the specifics of their argument vary, researchers working within this paradigm frequently view academic research—its traditional interviewing techniques, including those within naturalistic ethnography; its positivistic canons for establishing rigor, validity, and truth; and its gatekeeping for publishing—as inherently masculinist and therefore objectifying of female research subjects (McRobbie, 1982; Oakley, 1981; Spender, 1980). In contrast, for example, they characterize the practice of challenging such a paradigm through dialogical interview strategies in which female respondents "talk back" and pose questions to a female researcher as an instance of woman-to-woman identification based on their common experiences of motherhood, childbirth, using a "female language," and so forth. They then argue that the rapport established among female researchers and their research subjects is a special and *natural one*, representing their common understanding of women's experiences. This view of what makes research feminist, whether one speaks of method, theory, or practice, tends to romanticize the biological nature of the origins of rapport between women researchers and research subjects, establishing a gender-essentialist argument as its basis for both doing and challenging naturalistic or qualitative research.[11]

As an overreaction to the gender essentialism of the first position, some feminists articulate an admittedly minority view among feminists by asserting quite the opposite. They hold that feminist research can be separated from the issue of whether it is conducted by women, about women, and/or with women. Such a position rejects the assumption that a shared interest or unity around women's experiences can be said to unite women researchers and research subjects and, hence, be presumed to constitute feminism. As feminist post-structuralist Rosalind Coward (1980) argues:

> Feminism can never be the product of the identity of women's experiences and interests—there is no such unity. Feminism must always be the alignment of women in a political movement with particular political aims and objectives. It is a grouping unified by its political interests, not by its common experiences. (p. 63)

Yet, as Barrett (1982) contends from a feminist materialist position, whatever problems may be generated by premising feminism (and for our purposes, feminist research, methods, theories, and practices) on the effort to understand and transform what is shared in women's experiences of subordination, far greater problems emerge in the attempt to separate feminism (as a political effort) from women's experiences. Divorcing feminism from women's experiences could lead to the position that women researchers and their women research subjects experience nothing in common with regard to shared experiences of gender oppression in the process of the field research or in the attempt to construct a feminist alternative to such experiences, for example.

As an alternative to the first two positions, feminist materialists argue along the lines of Jaggar (1983) that while there is no unified experience of feminine subordination, "a primary condition for the adequacy of a feminist theory . . . is that it should represent the world from the standpoint of women" (p. 370). By "women's standpoint," Jaggar means uncovering the ways in which

> Women's perceptions of reality are distorted by male-dominant ideology and by the male-dominated structure of everyday life. The standpoint of women, therefore, is not something that can be discovered through a

survey of women's existing beliefs and attitudes. . . . Instead, the standpoint of women is discovered through a collective process of political and
scientific struggle. The distinctive social experience of women generates
insights that are incompatible with men's interpretations of reality and
these insights provide clues to how reality might be interpreted from the
standpoint of women. The validity of these insights, however, must be
tested in political struggle and developed into a systematic representation
of reality that is not distorted in ways that promote the interests of men
above those of women. (p. 371)

These remarks by Jaggar imply a tendency to universalize women's
experiences of subordination. The major import of her argument, however, with which I agree, refines the concept of "women's standpoint"
in such a way as to consider the epistemological and political consequences for feminist theory and practice when the differences as well
as commonalities in women's lives are taken into account. For Jaggar as
well as for Smith (1974), Hintikka and Harding (1983), Harding (1986,
1987a, 1987b), and Barrett (1982), the criterion that distinguishes
whether a research method and theory is feminist is not its claim that
women's experiences are homogeneous or unified in a common viewpoint of subordination. Rather, research is feminist when its methods,
theory, and practice draw on the differences among groups of women
to theorize about what is common or different in their experiences of
various forms of oppression and privilege.

Jaggar (1983) identifies both the research goals and the political
praxis underlying genuinely feminist materialist methods. In fact, quite
unlike the assumption of naturalistic ethnography, feminist materialist
epistemology renders theory, method, and praxis inseparable from one
another, especially in their aim to transform women's subordinate
positions within and across dominant power relations of our cultural
institutions. She argues that in order to develop a systematic theoretical alternative to the prevailing modes of interpreting the world,

A way must be found in which all groups of women can participate in
building theory. Historically, working-class women and women of color
have been excluded from intellectual work. This exclusion must be challenged. *Working class women, women of color, and other historically silenced women
must be able to participate as subjects as well as objects in feminist theorizing.* . . . Within
a class divided and racist society, different groups of women inevitably
have unequal opportunities to speak and be heard. *For this reason, the goal that
women should begin to theorize together is itself a political goal and to succeed in collective
theorizing a political achievement.* Women who theorize together can work
together politically; indeed, in theorizing they are already doing one kind
of political work. (pp. 386–387; emphasis added)

For Jaggar as well as for most feminist materialists the test of adequacy for any research method, theory, and practice is its usefulness in developing a "scientific reconstruction of the world" from their own standpoint(s). The integration of feminism as both theory and practice comes when the "representation of reality" is tested "constantly by its usefulness in helping women transform that reality" (p. 387).

In contradistinction to naturalistic ethnography's naive realism, which does not question the constitution of existing power relations (particularly those that manifest themselves in procedural norms for observation and interviewing), the realism to which feminist materialism aspires democratizes the production of theory and the research process itself. The aim is action on the everyday world by women as subjects and objects of their own experiences. The test for adequacy is measured not in absolutist or atomistic terms, in which all competing knowledge claims can be reduced to an essential "women's standpoint." Instead, the test constitutes the successfulness of actual struggles in transforming for women "what constitutes fully human activity" (p. 387), a test that has societal ramifications that go well beyond the confines of any one ethnography.

Furthermore, according to Jaggar, most feminist materialists are open to the possibility that the development of theories, methods, and practice from the standpoints of women is accessible to men. In fact, the vision of social change entailed in feminist materialism encourages women to build alliances with men in the context of discovering how not to become dominated by them. This said, however, feminist materialists do predict that men would have less incentive for comprehending such gendered perspectives than women. They also predict that the threat to the male privilege posed by women acting collectively in their own behalf would militate against such perspectives' being widely accepted by or worked for among men (Jaggar, 1983).

Ethnography as Socially Transformative Praxis

If we take feminist materialist epistemology seriously, then the implications for ethnographic research practice are significant. First, within such a position positivism in principle finds no quarter either in establishing the relationship of theory to data or the relationship of the researcher to the research subjects. Second, positivism also finds no quarter in establishing the relationship between tests for theoretical adequacy and the political usefulness of research praxis in making social change. A clear statement against ethnographers' depicting themselves or their research as denying their subjective experiences, or as being disinterested and neutral, can be drawn as a main implication from feminist materialist epistemology.[12]

Third, a genuinely feminist materialist ethnographer would attempt to show how the specific social relations and material conditions underlying the field research set limits upon the access and rapport she or he could establish with particular groupings of research subjects. The ethnographer would take into account her or his own class background, race, gender, age, and sexual orientation, as well as those of the research subjects, in any account of the field research. Clearly then, a crucial task for the ethnographer is the *elaboration of the structural power relations* that formed the basis for conducting the field research and the study and not just a simple recounting of method as a set of techniques to gain rapport with people so as to have access to better data.

It is important here to give readers a sense of the practical dilemmas and contradictions I faced during the course of the fieldwork and writing of the ethnography in the attempt to integrate practice with my feminist materialist theory in a dialectical manner. Although the examples are not detailed in this paper, they touch upon the specificity of the social relations out of which the resultant theorizing of my ethnographic research practice grew. Further, they provide a context for understanding why global or universalizing language would not locate the researcher within specific social relations at a particular historic juncture.

For example, in the academic written account (1987), I explained why it was easier for me as a middle-class university researcher initially to gain access to and establish rapport with the middle-class Punks and their families than with the working-class Punks and their families, who more often rightly viewed me as an intruder. I also described how the young women came to see me as a "big sister," "friend," or an "adult intruder," while the young men treated me as a potential "groupie" to their bands, "Dear Abby" confidante, or threat to their relationships with their girlfriends. By taking such interests and social relations into account, I began to analyze critically the social functions of my attempts to establish rapport with the Punks. I had to question whether the alliances I had made (intentionally or unintentionally) reproduced or transformed forms of class exploitation and gender oppression that existed between myself and the Punks and among the Punks themselves.

This kind of reflexivity engages the researcher in confrontations over the tendencies within naturalistic ethnography to affirm the idea that ethnographers ought to present themselves to research subjects and later to their readers as having become either the fully immersed, "gone native" participant or the "fly on the wall" fieldworker. Similarly, many ethical dilemmas posed by the fieldwork's social relations caused me to question as well as to provide an alternative to the ethnographers' convention of presenting themselves in the written account as the absent presence, or what historian and cultural analyst Richard Johnson calls "the missing researcher" (Personal Communication, March 1982). I argued through the use of painful examples from the fieldwork that by not challenging these dominant positivistic tendencies within naturalistic ethnography—tendencies that limit the subject positions and authorial voices of ethnographers—researchers are likely to find themselves maintaining residual or creating emergent forms of domination and exploitation of the research subjects, which I called voyeurism and intellectual tourism.[13]

Fourth, given the centrality of feminist materialism's fundamental theoretical commitment to understand and transform women's (and in other contexts, other people's) subordination, "emancipatory praxis" would play an integral role in conducting the ethnographic fieldwork and in generating and testing theory. In this regard, Lather (1986) argues, "emancipatory theory-building" (p. 262) sharply contrasts with inductive or grounded theory building. The researcher's aim is to use feminist materialist theory in an explicit, open-ended, dialogical, and reciprocal manner with research subjects while struggling against any tendency to impose her or his theory where it is unwarranted.

Of course, there are enormous tensions here concerning what counts as "theoretical imposition" on the part of the researcher. Does any explanation offered by the researcher that disagrees with those of the research subjects constitute imposition? Clearly, as I have argued earlier, the importance of a feminist materialist analysis is its attempt to understand the structural conditions that underlie social subjects' everyday actions without resorting to a phenomenological explanation. As Lather (1986) puts it:

> How does one avoid reducing explanation to the intentions of social actors, by taking into account the deep structures—both psychological and social, conscious and unconscious—without committing the sin of theoretical imposition? (p. 262)

This tension is further connected with the underlying realization, as argued earlier, that social subjects (including the researcher) have different stakes and contradictory interests in maintaining or challenging their own or others' oppression. Any analysis that attempts to get beyond the appearances of social life in order to examine the historically specific and objective forms oppression and power relations take "therefore must be premised on a deep respect for the intellectual and political capacities of the dispossessed" (Lather, 1986, p. 262), which does not equate contradictory subjectivity with false or inferior consciousness.[14] This poses a rigorous demand upon the researcher to honor the subjectivities of and possible criticisms to be made by those women research subjects from a different class, race, culture, sexual orientation, gender, or age than that of the researcher.

Consistent with such a precondition is the commitment on the part of the researcher to allow her or his prior theoretic and political commitments to be *informed* and *transformed* by the lived experiences of the group she or he researches. An ethnography whose theory is produced democratically, that is, as a collective effort among the researcher and the research subjects, is less likely to generate propositions that are imposed by the researcher and more likely to be responsive to the logic of evidence that does not fit the researcher's preconceptions. Unlike the process of naturalistic ethnography, an ethnography that is dialogical and aims to build theory democratically encourages the research subjects' empowerment through systematic reflection upon their own situations and roles in reproducing or transforming existing power relations. Introducing this subjective element and its jointly constructed interaction into the research, in fact, increases the potential for historically specific forms of objectivity rather than objectivism, which does not disclose this evidence or the dialogue that produced it. It also decreases the possibility that theoretic imposition on the part of the researcher will occur as a form of unexamined subjectivism.

For example, in keeping with the logic of emancipatory praxis in my study (1987), I showed how I attempted to work collectively with the young women Punks, holding small-group interviews and discussions, which eventually operated in a fashion similar to women's consciousness-raising groups in the building and testing of theory. I described how I encouraged the young women to give me feedback that would check my emerging hypotheses and descriptions of particular subcultural practices and rituals for unwarranted interpretations and conclusions. I provided examples in the written account where the young women's interpretations of the subculture's gender and class relations differed from or concurred with mine. Full collaboration at every stage of the research was not attempted or achieved—far from it. Yet even though successful moments of genuine democratic and collective dialogue as well as theoretic reciprocity were modest and few, I found them worthy of mention because they represented times when the young women and I knew that some of the inequalities imposed by class and by virtue of being a researcher or research subject were not as great as our efforts to struggle against them.

Theoretical and Political Adequacy

The tests for theoretical and political adequacy that ought to be applied to the ethnography can be framed in the following questions. I have sought to preserve the reference to the Punk young women as a reminder of their centrality in the process of formulating these questions, which is to say one could imagine other or additional questions emerging in the context of racially mixed groups or groups of researchers and research subjects from different backgrounds than those participating in this study. The parenthetical remarks within the questions serve to broaden the issues raised regarding the implications of feminist materialist ethnography for ethnographic research in education more generally. Readers may use the parenthetical remarks to envisage how these questions would apply or could be transformed in order to be relevant to their own experiences of research with different groups.

- Does the ethnography (as a research process and as an interpretive account) resonate with the Punk young women's (the research subjects') actual lived experiences?
- Is the ethnography useful to the young women (research subjects) in terms of enabling them to comprehend systematically their experiences of feminine subordination, some of which varied by class (and with other groups could vary by race, age, or sexual orientation)?
- Did the process of meeting in groups (or whatever strategy that developed mutually between the research subjects and the researcher to foster dialogue and democratic theory building) lessen the structural divide between my own intellectual work (or that of other mostly middle-class researchers) and the research subjects' commonsense ways of articulating their identities and relations of gender, class, race, age, and sexual orientation?
- Are my (the researcher's) theoretical understandings and concepts accessible, that is, written in language that is neither pretentious nor condescending?
- Do the young women (research subjects) find that the written account demystifies or clarifies the underlying structural power relations that shaped their everyday experiences?

- How have their theoretical experiences and interpretations modified my (the researcher's) theoretical understandings of what it
  meant to become Punk (or in other contexts to belong as a
  member of a specific social or subcultural group)?
- Have I (the initial inquirer) taken seriously these issues, which
  are simultaneously methodological, ethical, and political, or
  have I sought refuge in the subject positions of the "intellectual
  tourist" and "voyeur" who watches and takes from the community of research subjects and gives little back that is of value to
  them?

CONCLUSION

This essay has sought to do a number of things. We have acknowledged
the real gains that qualitative research has made in helping us to reflect
on the subjectivity of the researcher and the researched and in assisting
those critical researchers who wish to go beyond the static models that
dominated many of the earlier studies of the role of education in social
reproduction. Yet we set out to criticize some of the remaining weak-
nesses and silences within one tradition of qualitative research, naturalistic ethnography. We have questioned whether most forms of naturalistic ethnography have constituted as genuine a break as they
might have from positivistic epistemologies for social and scientific
inquiry. Tacit theoretical and political assumptions underlie all research
methods regarding the role of research to affirm or challenge and
transform the inequalities of the society researchers and research subjects inhabit. By showing its affinities with positivism, Roman's analysis
has enabled us to be critical of those assumptions within naturalistic
ethnography that affirm atomistic accounts of complex social realities
and the intellectual tourism and voyeurism of researchers.

In clarifying these issues, we have turned to a position that recog-
nizes the gains made by naturalistic forms of inquiry, especially the
aspirations of qualitative researchers to inquire into the real material
conditions and social relations of daily life in different cultural contexts.
We have, however, argued a position that does break with naturalism
by providing an alternative to its reified notions of subjectivity, which
we have shown are unmediated by analyses of the relationships of
researchers and research subjects to the unequal power relations and
material conditions often structuring daily life. This position of feminist materialist ethnography attempts to democratize the research pro-

cess and enable the social and intellectual positions and meanings of the researcher and researched to be transformed and transformative. By confronting ethical and political dilemmas presented in the course of conducting her ethnography, and by drawing upon the growing literature of feminist materialist inquiry, Roman has provided a set of questions that are essential, but not exhaustive, as guides for an emancipatory difference to be made by ethnographic research.

Because we do not believe it possible as researchers to escape from our prior theoretical, ethical, and political commitments, we have attempted to integrate them into the theoretical arguments presented here. In so doing, we have interrogated important aspects of critical ethnographic theory and practice in education and feminist analyses of methodologies, epistemologies, and praxis in the social sciences. We have asked whether the work of these scholars is adequate to the educational and political tasks we take as important.

The essence of our reflection depends on an understanding of the dual nature of the very roots of a feminist materialist concept of subjectivity as embodied in the idea of the *subject* itself. Our common-sense intuitions already recognize the contradictory roots out of which this idea arises. First, persons can be the subjects of a ruler, that is, they can be "subjected" (thus being ruled, legislated, and even studied). Second, they can be the subjects of history—not simply objects of study who are moved by external forces, but active subjects, agents of change, of social forces that they in part create (Therborn, 1980).

We have attempted to examine in serious depth the second of these two meanings and its implications for educational ethnographic research. We realize that the position we have advocated raises many theoretically, politically, and methodologically contentious questions that will require more examples of researchers and research subjects articulating the links between practice and theory in the democratization of qualitative research. Our task has been to hold two ends of a rope together: One emphasizes the reality of inequality and the structured patterns of differential power relations; the other brings to bear upon research a feminist materialist politics of praxis involving self-criticism and a commitment to historicize and explain the conditions under which caring, connectedness, and intimacy may or may not develop in the context of inquiries into the existing daily realities of social and material inequalities. By beginning this process of criticism and renewal (however modestly), we can alter the way the two ends of the rope are woven together and, thus, help change that reality.

Acknowledgments

A debt of intellectual gratitude is owed to James Anthony Whitson and Fazal Rizvi for their critical comments on various revisions of this chapter. John Guillory and Monica Kirchweger's thoughtful help in the preparation of this essay is also appreciated.

NOTES

1. I (Roman) retain the first-person pronoun to refer to myself as ethnographer, woman, author, and subject in the text so as to prevent distancing myself from the social relations of the research I conducted or incorporating myself into the stance of an undifferentiated "we." Undifferentiated ethnographic writing, as Stacey (1988) argues, may unintentionally privilege the masculine attribution, which usually accompanies the use of the "official" or "royal we." My attempt to differentiate voices within the text is also in keeping with recent efforts by other critical ethnographers working within deconstructive and postmodern anthropology to provide a more dialogical construction of narrative voices than has previously existed in those ethnographic narratives written in the conventional voices of neutral or detached observation. While these efforts have largely been applied to ethnographic accounts, the same problems exist with the writing of narratives about specific ethnographic research projects. See Stacey (1988) for a feminist analysis of the advantages and limitations of these postmodern developments in ethnographic anthropological work, particularly in the work of Clifford and Marcus (1986).

2. The concept of gender here is not meant as synonymous for women as research subjects or as researchers. Rather, it is meant to describe the relational categories of and meanings for masculinity and femininity. These meanings may differ within and across classes, races, and cultures, as well as between conceptual systems, as ways of naming the social world; that is, the way social actors know "what" they know. Thus, to study gender in a feminist relational manner is to include the possibility that men as well as women can be the subjects of a feminist study and that male researchers can meet the requirements for producing less distorted masculinist or androcentric descriptions, explanations, and understandings of the social world. The issue of whether women and men have experiences that can serve as equally reliable guides in the production of undistorted social research is taken up later in the discussion of the feminist standpoint position.

3. For example, see the works of Willis (1977) and Everhart (1983), which have been widely criticized for their unselfconscious over-identification with the male research subjects, the privileging of class over gender issues, and the emphasis on the waged work experiences of their research subjects over the formation of their identities within their families and intimate relationships,

particularly with females. Roman and Christian-Smith (1988) provide an examination of the history of the masculinist research agendas within cultural studies, as well as of the attempts made by feminists to transform the terms of such debates. See Roman (1988) for an example of an alternative to productivist, masculinist, and class essentialist accounts of subcultural formation.

4. For an accessible and typical account of the ethnographer as "professional stranger," see Agar's (1980) ambivalently proscriptive discussion of the ways ethnographers attempt to handle the "strain" of negotiating across the roles of "detached involvement" from and through immersion into groups or cultures under study, or what he calls "going native" (pp. 50–51). Elsewhere, I (Roman, 1987, 1989) argue that to the extent that naturalism coheres as discourse and as ideology, it does so chiefly through researchers' having to negotiate ambivalently across the conflicting stances of objectivism and subjectivism—what I call respectively "being a fly on the wall" and "going native"—instead of having to develop alternatives to them that have democratizing ethical and political consequences for research praxis.

5. While Hammersley and Atkinson (1983) are liberal critics of some of naturalism's affinities with positivism, they nonetheless fail to challenge the subject-object dualism within naturalism, a dualism that can also be found in the epistemology and discourse of positivism.

6. Although *positivism* has become a term of abuse, its use for my purposes refers to what some philosophers of science have called the "received model" of natural science. This model has been influenced strongly by logical empiricist conceptions of knowledge and hypothetico-deductive method. Such conceptions of knowledge aspire to formulate deductively related covering laws in which observations and events can be separated from their context and subsumed under such laws. Giddens's (1979) and Hollands's (1984) discussions provide illuminating histories and critiques of positivistic logic.

7. I do not mean to suggest that all naturalistic ethnographers work to disguise their identities to research subjects or their purposes for conducting their research. Nor am I suggesting that naturalistic ethnographers never have confessional moments of subjectivity when they acknowledge in a more reflexive manner the frequency of the emotional crises and anxieties generated by their attempts to manage the ethical and political consequences of adhering to the stances of subjectivism and objectivism that are part of the discourse of naturalism. For examples of the tensions for researchers generated by their attempts to achieve objectivist or subjectivist stances simultaneously, see Dentan (1970, pp. 104–107) and Keiser (1970, pp. 234–235); see Rabinow (1977) for a more critical example of a reflexive account of fieldwork by a naturalistic ethnographer. My point is, however, that such examples fail to challenge the subject-object dualism, which permits ethnographers to treat their "subjectivities" as incidental moments rather than as historically contextualized and interested within specific social and power relations.

8. Ruby's (1980) provocative conceptualization of reflexivity is defined as the action of anthropologists (or researchers more generally) revealing their

methodology and themselves as the "instruments of data generation." However, Ruby neglects how the plurality of voices and perspectives, particularly on the parts of research subjects, shape the generation of ethnographic data and narrative (whether self-consciously disclosed by ethnographers or not). The issue then becomes whether the concept should be used when researchers do not take a genuinely dialogical approach to the disclosure of such pluralities, even though they themselves may have been thoughtfully personal and autobiographic in their ethnographies.

9. See Roman (1987, 1989) for an elaboration of the practical ethical dilemmas that shaped and transformed the theory presented here.

10. The differences between feminist and materialist theories and epistemologies on the utility and adequacy of the subject-object dualism is worthy of a paper in and of itself. In this limited space, however, it is worth noting that this dualism in neo-Marxist ethnographic research takes several forms under the guise of other binary oppositions, most notably, the opposition between description and analysis, which is exemplified in the bifurcation of Willis's (1977) narrative voice. The first part of the book, called "Ethnography," is arranged thematically and contains verbatim interview data and dialogue from the lads. Willis is self-consciously present only as an interlocutor who sometimes brings into their dialogue the structural and material world in which the lads' practices are situated. By marginalizing his own gender and class relation to and affinity and identification with the lads, Willis speaks through the first part as methodologist, clearly distinguishing the first part as narrative, realistic "description." Willis re-presents the authenticity of the lads' voices both on the basis of using verbatim extracts from interviews and by constructing these interviews as unmediated and uninterrupted by the lads' social relations with him.

The second part, labeled "Analysis," rhetorically and theoretically analyzes and expounds upon the first. In this part, Willis's narrative voice sounds much more authoritative, summative, and "objective" than in the first part. While the second part refers back to the first part, it relies heavily upon theorized abstractions and academic language to elaborate Willis's analysis of the lads' resistances to their schooling and capitalist social relations. The second part gains its authorial validity by referring back to and relying upon the verbatim data—the data that methodologically symbolize naturalness, authorial nonselection, neutrality, and authenticity. The bifurcation in Willis's narrative voice between description and theory/analysis serves a particular function. It masks the degree to which he participates in the lads' subculture and hence can claim to know and understand the very sense-making process he describes exclusively as "theirs." It is then another form of the subject-object dualism as represented through the ethnographer's bifurcated narrative voice.

11. I do not mean to suggest, however, that only research that theorizes about women's direct experiences of subordination is feminist. There is a danger in ignoring the social relations and constitution of male power when feminists claim that only researching the powerlessness of women can help

transform women's oppression. We also need to know how men experience their positions of power across varying class and racial formations. The incentive for men to conduct such research, however, is less self-vested than the interests of women in understanding their own subordination. Scott (1985) makes this point well.

12. As will become clear, this does not mean that the obverse of positivism is naive subjectivism. In my study (1987), I attempt a synthesis between culturlist and structuralist interpretive approaches, using semiotics to discover the discursive codes at work in the young women's verbal and nonverbal practices. The strategy used avoids the subject-object dualism, since it takes biography and historical moments into account, attempting to locate those moments within the structurally determined limits of the discourses available to produce them.

13. Although these are exaggerated "ideal types," I use the terms to refer to the dominant conventions proscribing roles and narrative authorial voices for ethnographers. By the concept of "voyeur," I refer to the discursive codes and cultural practices to which an ethnographer consents when she or he accepts a privileged vantage point from which she or he discloses minimally the *prior* theory she or he uses to describe, view, interpret, and frame questions in the process of representing the knowledge and meanings of the research subjects. A subject position of ethnographic voyeurism is secured both when the use-value of the research subjects' knowledge is transformed within exchange relations into the commodified pleasure (sexual or economic) of the researcher and when the group under study feels intruded upon by the researcher. The voyeur's rapport is short-lived, having been premised upon the idea that the ethnographer's role is to extract the research subjects' common-sense knowledge and withdraw from the intimacy established when the research is completed.

The concept of "intellectual tourist" refers to the discursive codes and cultural practices to which an ethnographer consents when she or he conducts research as a brief excursion, foray, or sightseeing tour into "other" people's lives. Unlike the voyeur, the ethnographer as intellectual tourist may, for brief periods of time, become deeply involved in the daily lives of the research subjects so as to achieve "cultural immersion" or the status of a participant-observer. Even though the intellectual tourist has worked quite arduously to establish rapport with the research subjects, she or he strains to write an account in which she or he appears as distant and disengaged. She or he recalls copious fieldnotes as "snapshot" descriptions taken on the scene of the research subjects' cultural practices. Yet in the final account, the researcher draws upon dense theoretical language recognizable to those in her or his field, but possibly obscure to those studied. Such language often has the effect of mystifying to the research subjects the very conditions of their lives about which the researcher theoretically aims to develop critical understanding. In either case (voyeurism or intellectual tourism), the research subjects may find the ethnographer's account of little use in grasping or transforming various inequalities they experience in their daily lives.

14. A Gramscian understanding of commonsense knowledge and consciousness as "contradictory" avoids the empiricist trap of seeing social subjects'
practices as mere reflections of material conditions in the "real world" in which
they take practical action. It makes a distinction between those intellectuals
who have the material resources and time to develop a more systematically
theoretic view of their activities and those whose material positions of subordination do not permit such reflections. Yet the distinction is not premised upon
the idea that subordinate classes or social groups necessarily are limited to less
systematic understandings of the social world. As Gramsci (1971) writes, referring erroneously only to men:

> The active man-in-the-mass has a practical activity, but no clear theoretical
> consciousness of his practical activity. One might say he has two theoretical
> consciousnesses (or one contradictory consciousness): one which is implicit in
> his activity and which in reality unites him and all his fellow workers in the
> practical transformation of the real world; and one which superficially explicit
> or verbal, he has inherited from the past and uncritically absorbed. (p. 333).

REFERENCES

Agar, M. H. (1980). *The professional stranger*. New York: Academic Press.

Aggleton, P. J. (1984). *Reproductive "resistance": A study of the origins and effects of youth
  subcultural style amongst a group of new middle class students in a college of further
  education*. Unpublished doctoral dissertation, University of London-King's
  College, London.

Apple, M. W. (1979). *Ideology and curriculum*. Boston: Routledge and Kegan Paul.

Apple, M. W. (1982). *Education and power*. Boston: Routledge and Kegan Paul.

Apple, M. W. (1986). *Teachers and texts: A political economy of class and gender relations in
  education*. New York: Routledge and Kegan Paul.

Barrett, M. (1982). Feminism and the definition of cultural politics. In R. Brunt
  & C. Rowan (Eds.), *Feminism, culture and politics* (pp. 37–58). London: Law-
  rence & Wishart.

Bernard, J. (1973). My four revolutions: An autobiographical history of the
  ASA. *American Journal of Sociology, 78*, 773–791.

Bernstein, B. (1977). *Class, codes and control: Towards a theory of educational transmissions*
  (Vol. 3, rev. ed). London: Routledge and Kegan Paul.

Bourdieu, P., & Passeron, J. (1977). *Reproduction in education, society, and culture*
  (R. Nice, Trans.). London: Sage.

Bowles, S., & Gintis, H. (1976). *Schooling in capitalist America*. New York: Basic
  Books.

Clifford, J., & Marcus, G. E. (Eds.). (1986). *Writing culture: The poetics and politics of
  ethnography*. Berkeley: University of California Press.

Coward, R. (1980). This novel changes lives: Are women's novels feminist
  novels? A response to Rebecca O'Rourke's "Summer Reading." *Feminist
  Review*, No. 5, pp. 53–64.

Dentan, R. (1970). Living and working with the Semai. In G. D. Spindler (Ed.), *Being an anthropologist: Fieldwork in eleven cultures* (pp. 85–112). New York: Holt, Rinehart and Winston.

Edwards, A. D., & Furlong, V. J. (1985). Reflections on the language of teaching. In R. C. Burgess (Ed.), *Field methods in the study of education* (pp. 21–36). Lewes, UK: Falmer Press.

Everhart, R. (1983). *Reading, writing and resistance: Adolescence and the labor process in a junior high school*. London: Routledge and Kegan Paul.

Geertz, C. (1973). Thick description: Toward an interpretative theory of culture. In C. Geertz (Ed.), *The interpretation of cultures: Selected essays by Clifford Geertz* (pp. 3–32). New York: Basic Books.

Giddens, A. (1979). *Central problems in social theory: Action, structure and contradiction in social analysis*. London: Macmillan.

Glaser, B., & Strauss, A. (1967). *The discovery of grounded theory*. New York: Aldine.

Gramsci, A. (1971). *Selections from the prison notebooks*. (Q. Hoare & G. N. Smith, Trans.). New York: International Publishers.

Hammersley, M., & Atkinson, P. (1983). *Ethnography: Principles in practice*. London: Tavistock.

Harding, S. (1986). *The science question in feminism*. Ithaca, NY: Cornell University Press.

Harding, S. (1987a). Introduction: Is there a feminist method? In S. Harding (Ed.), *Feminism and methodology* (pp. 1–14). Bloomington & Indianapolis: Indiana University Press.

Harding, S. (1987b). Conclusion: Epistemological questions. In S. Harding (Ed.), *Feminism and methodology* (pp. 181–190). Bloomington & Indianapolis: Indiana University Press.

Hargreaves, D. H., Hester, S., & Mellor, R. (1975). *Deviance in classrooms*. London: Routledge and Kegan Paul.

Hintikka, M., & Harding, S. (Eds.). (1983). *Discovering reality: Feminist perspectives on epistemology, methodology and the philosophy of science*. Dordrecht, The Netherlands: Reidel.

Hollands, R. G. (1984). *Working for the best ethnography*. Unpublished paper. Birmingham, UK: University of Birmingham, Centre for Contemporary Cultural Studies.

Jaggar, A. (1983). *Feminist politics and human nature*. Totowa, NJ: Rowman and Allenheld.

Jones, A. (1986). *At school I've got a chance . . . Social reproduction in a New Zealand secondary school*. Unpublished doctoral dissertation, University of Auckland, New Zealand.

Keat, R., & Urry, J. (1975). *Social theory as science*. London: Routledge and Kegan Paul.

Keiser, R. L. (1970). Fieldwork among the Vice Lords of Chicago. In G. D. Spindler (Ed.), *Being an anthropologist: Fieldwork in eleven cultures* (pp. 220–237). New York: Holt, Rinehart and Winston.

Lather, P. (1986). Research as praxis. *Harvard Educational Review, 56*, 257–277.

Lofland, J. (1971). *Analyzing social settings*. London: Wadsworth.

Mannheim, K. (1936). *Ideology and utopia*. New York: Harcourt, Brace and World.

McCarthy, C., & Apple, M. W. (1988). Class, race and gender in American educational research. In L. Weis (Ed.), *Class, race and gender in American education* (pp. 9–39). Albany: State University of New York Press.

McRobbie, A. (1978). Working class girls and the culture of femininity. In Women's Studies Group (Ed.), *Women take issue: Aspects of women's subordination* (pp. 96–108). London: Hutchinson of London.

McRobbie, A. (1982). The politics of feminist research: Between text, talk and action. *Feminist Review*, No. 12, pp. 46–57.

Oakley, A. (1981). Interviewing women: A contradiction in terms. In H. Roberts (Ed.), *Doing feminist research* (pp. 30–61). London: Routledge and Kegan Paul.

Popkewitz, T. S. (1981). The study of schooling: Paradigms and field-based educational research and evaluation. In T. Popkewitz & B. Tabachnick (Eds.), *The study of schooling: Field-based methodologies in educational research and evaluation* (pp. 1–26). New York: Praeger.

Rabinow, P. (1977). *Reflections on fieldwork in Morocco*. Berkeley: University of California Press.

Reynolds, D. (1980). The naturalistic method of educational social research—a Marxist critique. *Interchange*, 4, 77–89.

Roman, L. G. (1987). *Punk femininity: The formation of young women's gender identities and class relations within the extramural curriculum of a contemporary subculture*. Unpublished doctoral dissertation, University of Wisconsin–Madison.

Roman, L. G. (1988). Intimacy, labor, and class: Ideologies of feminine sexuality in the Punk Slam Dance. In L. G. Roman & L. C. Christian-Smith with E. Ellsworth (Eds.), *Becoming feminine: The politics of popular culture* (pp. 143–184). Lewes, UK: Falmer Press.

Roman, L. G. (1989). *Double exposure: The politics of feminist materialist ethnography*. Manuscript submitted for publication.

Roman, L. G., & Christian-Smith, L. C. (1988). Introduction. In L. G. Roman & L. C. Christian-Smith with E. Ellsworth (Eds.), *Becoming feminine: The politics of popular culture* (pp. 1–34). Lewes, UK: Falmer Press.

Rosaldo, Michelle Z. (1983). Moral/analytic dilemmas posed by the intersection of feminism and social science. In N. Haan, P. Rabinow, & W. M. Sullivan (Eds.), *Social science as moral inquiry* (pp. 76–95). New York: Columbia University Press.

Ruby, J. (1980). Exposing yourself: Reflexivity, anthropology, and film. *Semiotica*, 30, 153–179.

Schatzman, L., & Strauss, A. L. (1973). *Field research: Strategies for a natural sociology*. Englewood Cliffs, NJ: Prentice-Hall.

Schutz, A. (1964). The stranger: An essay in social psychology. In A. Schutz (Ed.), *Collected papers* (Vol. 2) (pp. 91–105). The Hague, The Netherlands: Martinus Nijhoff.

Scott, S. (1984). The personable and the powerful: Gender and status in socio-logical research. In C. Bell & H. Roberts (Eds.), *Social researching: Politics, problems and practice* (pp. 165–178). London: Routledge and Kegan Paul.

Scott, S. (1985). Feminist research and qualitative methods: A discussion of some of the issues. In R. Burgess (Ed.), *Issues in educational research* (pp. 27–46). Lewes, UK: Falmer Press.

Sharp, R. (1982). Self-contained ethnography or a science of phenomenal forms and inner relations. *Journal of Education, 164,* 48–63.

Sharp, R., & Green, A. (1975). *Education and social control: A study in progressive primary education.* London: Routledge and Kegan Paul.

Smith, D. (1974). Women's perspective as a radical critique of sociology. *Sociological Inquiry, 44,* 7–13.

Spender, D. (1980). *Man-made language.* London: Routledge and Kegan Paul.

Stacey, J. (1988). Can there be a feminist ethnography? *Women's Studies International Forum, 11*(1), 21–27.

Therborn, G. (1980). *The power of ideology and the ideology of power.* London: New Left Books.

Willis, P. (1977). *Learning to labor: How working class kids get working class jobs.* Westmead, UK: Saxon House.

Willis, P. (1981). Notes on method. In S. Hall, D. Hobson, A. Lowe, & P. Willis (Eds.), *Culture, media, language* (pp. 88–95). London: Hutchinson.

Woods, P. (1985). Ethnography and theory construction in educational research. In R. C. Burgess (Ed.), *Field methods in the study of education* (pp. 51–78). Lewes, UK: Falmer Press.

Wright, E. O. (1978). *Class, crisis and the state.* London: New Left Books.

Subjectivity and Objectivity

EGON G. GUBA

When Elliot Eisner and Alan Peshkin invited me to be a discussant of two papers on the topic of subjectivity and objectivity, I very nearly demurred, despite the awesome reputations of the individuals to whose ideas I was expected to react. I believed that the issue of objectivity/subjectivity had been debated to death and that to engage in further polemics on the topic would simply beat a dead horse. I am therefore especially pleased to report that the authors have lived up to their reputations, furnishing a plethora of ideas with which to conjure. I can only hope that they will find my response as engaging as I found their stimuli. I will begin with some comments on the paper by Denis Phillips.

PRESENTATION BY D. C. PHILLIPS

I hope Denis Phillips will forgive me if I cite a quotation that he himself selected as the frontispiece for his recent book, *Philosophy, Science, and Social Inquiry* (1987): "Whoso loveth correction loveth knowledge, but he that hateth reproof is brutish" (Proverbs 12:1). While the terms *correction* and *reproof* may be a bit strong for what I have in mind to do, they capture the essence that I intend to convey.

It seems reasonable to expect that a philosopher would begin a discourse on a term like *objectivity* with some sort of definition of it (we will see later how Roman and Apple manage to avoid the same dilemma). As a matter of fact, I intended to get a head start on reading Phillips's paper by seeing what he had to say about objectivity in the book from which I have just cited the frontispiece. It contains an extended index as well as an unusual and exceptionally good glossary, so I confess that I was taken aback when I failed to find the term *objective* in either place. Nor would a reading of the book (done quickly by me, I admit) suggest that any exceptional weight is placed on this concept.

My curiosity was piqued. I turned to the paper with heightened expectations.

What I found was a variety of statements from which it is possible to tease a variety of possible intended meanings, but nothing that really nailed things down. As close as one comes to a formal definition is found where Phillips suggests a "hypothesis":

> "Objective" seems to be a label that we apply to inquiries that meet certain procedural standards, but objectivity does not *guarantee* that the results of inquiries have any certainty. (It implies that the inquiries so labeled are free of gross defects, and this should be of some comfort—just as a consumer prefers to buy an item that has met rigorous inspection standards, although this does not absolutely insure that it will not break down.) (Emphasis in original)

To be sure, as Phillips reassures us, objectivity and certainty can not be equated, nor can objectivity and truth. But while I may take some small comfort in knowing that the Underwriters' Laboratory has put its seal of methodological approval on an inquiry by labeling it "objective," I am nevertheless anxious to know just what standards they applied in reaching that judgment.

So I was not helped much by this hypothesis. I looked further. First, I noted that there were some disclaimers about what objectivity was *not*:

- It is not truth and not to be equated with truth.
- It is not correspondence (isomorphism) with facts.
- It is not certainty.
- It is not consensual validation (indeed, Phillips avers that the terms *consensual* and *validation* are themselves "uneasy bedfellows" and implies that their conjunction usually signals some error in logic).

Second, I found some ways to tell whether an inquiry is objective:

- It rests on relevant and weighty evidence; it is based on warranted and rational evidence; it is based on carefully gathered evidence; and/or it has been forced to meet the demands of reason and evidence. In these statements we cannot fail to notice the implied but unspecified standards, for example, What is relevant?
- It is free from personal contaminations, and/or personal biases

and values have been exposed to critical examination. Again, we note the undefined terms.

• It fits within a "critical tradition": it has been subjected to critical examination and cross-checking by an international community; it is able to be evaluated critically; it has been opened up to scrutiny, vigorous examination, and challenge; and/or it has been tested out, analyzed, criticized, and debated. The means for carrying out these tasks are unspecified.

• It demonstrates how threats to validity have been handled. But this requirement seems to contradict the earlier assertion that objectivity and truth are not to be equated; apparently objectivity *is* a function of validity, at least.

• It is carried out with great care and responsiveness to criticism. This requirement does seem to make objectivity at least a second cousin of politics.

Labeling an inquiry *objective*, Phillips tells us, certifies the inquiry and not the inquirer; the label means that the inquiry is worthy of trust. Objective inquiries are to be preferred to subjective ones because while there are no guarantees that truth is actually exposed, it is the case that the objective viewpoint is the one that is "currently . . . most warranted or rational." I could not help but wonder whether that is a case of consensual validation.

Whatever *objective* may mean, Phillips suggests that for many people the issue is moot because objectivity is dead. Among the pallbearers hastening the concept to its final resting place, he tells us, are these:

• The nonfoundationalist philosophers, who have argued, apparently convincingly, that all knowledge is tentative. Now Phillips counterposes the argument that this consideration is irrelevant to the concept of objectivity because, as he was careful to point out earlier, objectivity has nothing to do with either truth or certainty. Phillips faced a choice here: *either* to believe that objectivity has *something* to do with certainty, in which case, given the tentative nature of knowledge, all knowledge would have to be taken as subjective, *or* to believe that objectivity is unrelated to certainty, in which case he can say, "No problem!" Apparently he preferred the latter option. The values on which he resolved the dilemma that way are unclear.

• The Hansonists, who point out that facts are theory-laden. Phillips agrees that if theoretical commitments tend to determine facts, subjectivity gets a big boost. But he has an out: Distinguish *levels* of observation, note that low-level observations can be easily agreed upon even by those whose theoretical positions may differ widely, and be prepared to negotiate the rest, entering into fruitful discussion, criticism, and evaluation. His conclusion: The theory-laden nature of high-inference observations does not offer grounds for abandoning the notion of objectivity. Of course, this position begs the question whether it is possible for theorists with high-level differences to come to terms on *what* to discuss; even less does it offer hope that there may be agreement on some emergent position. And if they did agree, would that agreement represent consensual validation?

• The "more the merrier" pixies, who, by holding the untenable position that objectivity is a matter of intersubjective agreement (hence the more the merrier), give objectivity a bad name and hasten its demise. Holding to that definition, Phillips suggests, implies unwarranted consensus and suggests the possibility of bias. The way out of that dilemma, Phillips proposes, is to have warranted consensus, which is reached via a critical community. Indeed, it may not be possible to reach consensus exactly, because there may exist equally viable views. But whether consensus be distributed normally or bi-, tri-, or multi-modally, consensus still retains a subjective flavor, a form of consensual validation.

• The Kuhnists, who, having misinterpreted what Thomas Kuhn intended, insist that knowledge is relative after all, thereby excluding the possibility of objectivity (so much for the assumption that truth and objectivity are unrelated). Well, Phillips responds, it may be the case that choices between or among paradigms cannot be made objectively (although he asserts his belief in that possibility), but it is surely the case that it is possible to be objective *within* a paradigm once one has selected it. The possibility that the defining assumptions of a paradigm may militate against objectivity (a key point in the case of the Roman and Apple paper, as we shall see) has apparently not been considered.

• The conflaters of the contexts of discovery and of justification, who fail to understand the critical importance of keeping these two contexts separate. Phillips avers that "the *making* of discoveries during the pursuit of a research program may not be involved—and might be counterproductive if allowed to intrude—when the discoveries are *checked* and *tested* and *critically evaluated*" (emphasis in original). But, says Phillips, it is only an ideal that we should keep these contexts separate; we cannot, after all, "rob the scientist of his partisanship without also robbing him of his humanity" (quoting Popper, 1976, p. 97). The solution, Phillips suggests, is to quit thinking of objectivity as a property of the individual scientist and instead regard it as a property of the context of justification itself. He says, "It is in a sense a social matter, for it depends upon the communal acceptance of the critical spirit." Another example of consensual validation?

It seems clear that Phillips not only declines to be a pallbearer at objectivity's funeral but also believes that the concept is reasonably healthy, or can be fixed up to be. Indeed, a number of ways to approach objectivity exist; following are some that appear directly or by implication in Phillips's paper (I have added one myself).

A. *By Focusing on the Inquirer*
  1. *Reflexivity and openness on the part of the inquirer.* I have heard this approach described elsewhere as "coming clean." One should make an effort to unload one's personal baggage and report on one's own biases. "Coming clean means a creation of awareness, and not the divestiture of self" (Locke, Spirduso, & Silverman, 1987, p. 93). But it is hard to see how an inquirer can do a good job of "coming clean" simply by dint of the resolution to do so. Moreover, this mode of approaching objectivity is at best weak, in view of Phillips's own insistence that objectivity should be thought of as a characteristic of the inquiry rather than of the inquirer.

B. *By Focusing on the Inquiry and Its Context.* There are three varieties.
  2. *Method.* Methodological processes and safeguards represent the traditional ways to deal with objectivity. The proper use of method can accomplish four things to protect objectivity.
       a. It interpolates procedures and instrumentation between the inquirer and the inquired-into, for example, the "objective" test or the "double-blind" experiment.
       b. It separates the contexts of discovery and justification—ideas are tested in an arena different from the one in which they were spawned. It often distances the discoverer (a theoretical physicist, say) from the tester (an experimental physicist, say).
       c. It separates design from implementation. Design must be pre-specified and cannot be altered once the study is under way so as to prevent the exploitation of serendipities in the data—especially those that delight the investigator.
       d. It provides safeguards against the intrusion of unwanted (and confounding) variables, especially values and political influences.

  3. *Critical tradition* (or critical history). Time affords the opportunity to critique, evaluate, and dispute—processes that expose error and that

may ultimately lead to consensus! Despite subjectivity, we eventually come to an ultimate grasp of truth at some given time or in some given study. The development of a critical tradition is in turn dependent on the existence of a critical community.

4. *Critical community.* This is the community of scholars in which we all claim membership by virtue of a joint (even if unspoken) commitment to subject ourselves to critical disputation. We agree to peer review and the discipline of the marketplace of ideas. The critical community includes, perhaps first and foremost, the formal gatekeepers we appoint to monitor our channels of communication (professional conference programs, journals, and the like). Their joint judgment of a given inquiry is a strong guarantee of its objectivity. As a somewhat marginal man in the community of scholars for which Denis Phillips is clearly a leading spokesperson, I cannot resist inserting a perfectly irrelevant quotation from James Gleich's recent book *Chaos* (1987), in which the author describes this emergent theory:

> Those who recognized chaos in the early days agonized over how to shape their thoughts and findings into publishable form. Work fell between disciplines—for example, too abstract for physicists and yet too experimental for mathematicians. To some the difficulty of communicating new ideas and the ferocious resistance from traditional quarters showed how revolutionary the new science was. Shallow ideas can be assimilated; ideas that require people to reorganize their picture of the world provoke hostility. A physicist at the Georgia Institute of Technology, Joseph Ford, started quoting Tolstoy: "I know that most men, including those at ease with problems of the greatest complexity, can seldom accept even the simplest and most obvious truth if it be such as would oblige them to admit the falsity of conclusions which they have delighted in explaining to their colleagues, which they have proudly taught to others, and which they have woven, thread by thread, into the fabric of their lives." (pp. 37–38).

Perhaps conventionalism is as much buttressed by the critical community as objectivity is claimed to be!

C. *By Focusing on Groups of Inquiries*
5. *Meta-analysis.* I have taken the liberty of introducing this means of (among other things) achieving objectivity even though it is not included among those suggested by Phillips. Meta-analysis is a technique that has been widely applied and that seems well designed to deal with problems of irregularities and errors in extant research. The technique depends upon the availability of literature in some area or

discipline, or related to some research topic of interest. While any given study may have problematic objectivity, that study, when combined with others like it in method and intent, contributes to a more stable objectivity than would otherwise be possible. If studies (rather than subjects) are taken as analytic units, statistical power is increased and the nonobjectivity and/or invalidity of the single study "wash out." Meta-analysis is powerful because it does not matter, in the end, whether (some) individual studies would be judged not to be objective because of the "coming clean" of the inquirer, or because method, critical tradition, or critical community would suggest that they are not. Bad studies wash out. Of course, it helps if the studies are high on objectivity when you decide to include them in the analysis, but the process is highly forgiving of an error in judgment; successive refinements will take care of things.

Where does all this leave us with respect to the thesis advanced by Phillips? He does admit that some of the arguments brought to bear by critics of objectivity have a certain validity. There is no question that we need to be aware of them and to do what we can to offset the difficulties that are thereby posed, I am sure he would say. But I am reminded of two comedic sequences. One is brought to mind by the line from the song, "When I'm not near the girl I love, I love the girl I'm near." Since Phillips cannot be near the objectivity he loves, he will settle for the objectivity he can get. He devises new definitions that make the concepts more tolerable. It is a lover's desperate effort to deny the flaws of his lady love, conspicuous though they may be to everyone else, and to patch things up cosmetically. Thus the old girl can be made reasonably presentable, even if she does look a bit like Phyllis Diller.

Or consider the following exchange between a rejected suitor and the object of his affection:

Suitor: Why don't you love me? Give me one good reason!
Object: Well, for starters, because you're ugly, stupid, selfish, and malevolent.
Suitor: Yes, but aside from that . . . !

Which translates metaphorically:

Positivist: Why can't I be objective? Give me one good reason!
Critic: Well, for starters, because you can't stand outside your humanness; because you inevitably interact with the phenomenon, human or otherwise, that you happen to be studying;

because the data you get are literally created by the questions you ask and the order in which you ask them; and because all "factual" data are subject to the interpretations that you bring to them, whether theoretical, prejudicial, or serendipitous. And besides, your name is Hanson.

Positivist: Yes, but aside from that . . . !

There are those who, with Phillips, believe that objectivity is not only not dead, but so little battered that a bit of first-aid and sprucing up will make that concept serviceable again. Others believe that it is badly flawed. Clearly I must number myself as one of the latter (a kind of "coming clean"?). I think you will agree that Roman and Apple must be counted in that number also.

PRESENTATION BY LESLIE ROMAN AND MICHAEL APPLE

One need not read very far into the Roman/Apple (hereafter R&A) paper to discover that they are not interested in conventional objectivity; they cite a good many reasons why, in their view, objectivity is neither especially prized nor assiduously pursued. But they *celebrate* subjectivity, a term they define very differently from Phillips, as we shall see.

What could lead to this stunning reversal of conventional values? Nothing less than a completely different philosophic base from which to project the nature and meaning of inquiry. In the first few pages of the paper we are informed of the basic assumptions that undergird this different approach:

- That this is an unequal society whose relations of domination (e.g., social and economic class, race, and gender) are deeply patterned
- That schools are places formed out of cultural, political, and economic conflicts and compromises; the curriculum is not neutral since only certain groups' knowledge is legitimate to incorporate
- That social research and its conduct and use are not immune from these patterns
- Thus, that educational inquiry is an ethical and political act
- Finally, that the educational inquirer is obligated (!) to participate in social transformation

By these statements, R&A make it very evident that conventional conceptions of what inquiry is and how it should be done do not apply. They spend most of the paper recounting their own search for a method that accomplishes what they wish to do—clearly ideological inquiry. However, they are not unmindful that they may at any time be called to account for the quality of the inquiry that they do under this banner, and, as we shall see, they do finally offer up certain criteria for judging goodness. Objectivity, we can easily surmise, is not one of these criteria. But we are getting ahead of our story.

In their search for a viable methodology, R&A tell us, they fastened first on ethnography (sometimes they call it "naturalistic ethnography" or even "critically oriented ethnography"). Ethnography seemed to offer many advantages: providing a useful antidote to the gross abstraction and overtheorizing of structuralism, avoiding formalism, tending toward holism, providing a product accessible to a wide range of readers, inviting "the readership into dialogues with the research subjects themselves," serving as proxy for the agency of subordinated groups, and telling it all in the subjects' own voices. But curiously, they came to reject ethnography because (among other reasons) it was *too* objective in orientation: Ethnographers are expected to work as anthropological strangers; to minimize reactivity even if to do so requires deception; to eschew reciprocity; to strive to prevent their own biases from entering into the final depiction, which nevertheless represented facts about the subjects, whose "own practices . . . remain . . . fundamentally and unconsciously obscure to them"; to adopt an authorial voice in writing "in which they avoid acknowledging that they held any prior . . . assumptions or nascent [!] hypotheses"; and finally, to presume that social reality is atomistic, independent of power relationships between researcher and subjects.

Obviously none of the above postures and practices, typical of conventional objectivity, serve the assumptions with which R&A started; indeed, it is immediately apparent that their assumptions are entirely abrogated by them. Conventional (naturalistic, critical) ethnography has, as the authors note, a pervasive and remarkable affinity to positivism. It affirms that the "social world . . . is meant to be *gazed upon but not challenged or transformed*" (emphasis in original).

The realization, R&A assert, sent them looking in other directions for help. They turned first to materialist ethnography, which had several important insights to contribute:

• "Ethnographers cannot afford to ignore the fact that social subjects are born into and socially constituted by 'a world already made,' and that 'structured patterns of social relations pre-exist the individ-ual and generate specific forms of social consciousness, . . . linguistic, and hence, cognitive possibilities that socially structure available life chances.'" (quoting Sharp, 1982, p. 50)

• "Such an analysis would make explicit use of the crucial material-istic distinction between the appearances of social life and the material conditions and social relations structuring them. This call for a method that works dialectically on the relation between the phenomenal ap-pearances of social life and the objective [*sic*] nature of the social rela-tions that structure them is a dramatic departure from naturalistic ethnography, but it is also one that enables researchers to generate and test theories in the process of doing research." If I didn't know better, I'd think the last quotation came from Denis Phillips, after he'd had a mild conversion to neo-Marxism!

• Research is aimed not only at understanding but also at trans-forming "various forms of subordination"; knowledge is neither the construction of "social members under study" nor the researcher as "detached observer," but arises "through practical social struggle to change the social world, a struggle that in turn changes the human subjects themselves."

• Emphasis is on the relative "social locations and backgrounds" of researcher and researched, dealing with such questions as "*whose* knowl-edge gets articulated" and "*who* benefits" (emphasis added).

• The "agency of people" is captured "without ignoring or mini-mizing the structural determinants [!] that set limits."

But materialism did not offer everything that was needed—it is gender blind (the authors' failure to mention that it is also ethnicity blind is interesting). Hence R&A explored feminist critique, which, while embracing a variety of formulations about the nature of "wom-en's experience," nevertheless seems to be intent on somehow discover-ing what R&A call "women's standpoint." The effort to discover this standpoint involves "a collective process of political and scientific strug-gle" (quoting Jaggar, 1983, p. 371). Research, they aver, "is feminist when its methods, theory, and practice draw on the differences among groups of women to theorize about what is common or different in their experiences of various forms of oppression and privilege." The-ory, method, and praxis thereby become inseparable, they assert.

The lessons of materialist ethnography and feminist critique are complementary and mutually supportive; indeed, R&A combine them into a single approach to which they apply the label "materialist femi-nist ethnography." Inquirers in this mode cannot depict "themselves or their research as denying their subjective experiences, or as being disinterested and neutral." Instead, "a crucial test for the ethnographer is the *elaboration of the structural power relations* that formed the basis for conducting the field research" (emphasis in original). She or he cannot avoid the ethical and political questions involved in the presentation of self.

"The researcher's aim is to use feminist materialistic theory in an explicit, open-ended, dialogical, and reciprocal manner . . . while struggling against any tendency to impose her or his theory where it is unwarranted." (Does that imply that warrant does exist under some circumstances?) The problem that arises is how "to understand the *structural conditions* that underlie social subjects' everyday actions without resorting to a phenomenological explanation" (emphasis added). Subjects' and researchers' different stakes and contradictory interests add to the tension. But there must be a "deep respect for the intellectual and political capacities of the dispossessed" (quoting Lather, 1986, p. 262). At the same time, the researcher must be committed to allowing "her or his prior theoretic and political commitments to be *informed* and *transformed* by the lived experiences" of the subjects (emphasis in original). Theory must be "produced democratically" as a collaborative effort.

R&A recognize that if this new methodology is to be pursued, nonconventional criteria for judging the goodness of inquiries must be devised; the old positivist ones do not apply—most particularly, not objectivity. What are these new criteria?

- The report must resonate with the subjects' actual lived experiences.
- The report must enable the subjects to comprehend their experiences of subordination.
- The report must lessen the "structural divide" between academics and actors.
- The report must not be pretentious or condescending—interpretations and concepts must be generally accessible.
- Subjects must find the report demystifying and clarifying.
- The researcher's prior theoretical understandings must also be modified.
- The inquirer must take ethical and political issues seriously—no intellectual tourism is allowed.

From all of this we conclude that the concept of objectivity is neither relevant nor useful to the materialist feminist ethnographer. Subjectivity is—but what is subjectivity?

R&A are hardly more careful in defining this crucial term than is Phillips. Their paper begins with commentary on the nature of subjectivity, noting that subjectivity may be viewed, on the one hand, as an unmitigated evil (when the ideal is the disinterested inquirer, what could one say in praise of its opposite?), or, on the other hand, as an unalloyed good (if knowledge depends on the joint construction of all meaning, insistence on objectivity can result only in a one-sided view). But R&A indicate that there is an intermediate position:

> There are those for whom the distinction between subjectivity and objectivity (when treated as a binary opposition in which the absence of one implies the presence of the other) is not a simple one, but is the result of constantly shifting relation. Rather, according to this conceptualization, subjectivity is a signpost that distinguishes human consciousness of the social and material world. Its interaction with objectivity is a point of contention in which different but related power struggles take place between and among subordinate and dominant groups over what counts as "true" knowledge.

Thus, R&A avoid the difficulties of defining either objectivity or subjectivity precisely, preferring to leave the issue unsettled, perhaps to be engaged via the self-same "struggle" that, in their paradigm, characterizes all efforts to arrive at understandings. Subjectivity is a moving target, defined differently as constructions of it change and as they are informed through continuing participation in the "struggle."

The R&A paper may then be understood as an attempt to lay out the arguments that they might advance as participants in such a struggle. They conclude their paper by saying:

> The essence of our reflections depends on an understanding of the dual nature of the very roots of a feminist materialist concept of subjectivity as embodied in the idea of the *subject* itself. Our commonsense intuitions already recognize the contradictory roots out of which this idea arises. First, persons can be the subjects of a ruler, that is, they can be "subjected" (thus being ruled, legislated, and even studied). Second, they can be the subjects of history—not simply objects of study who are moved by external forces, but active subjects, agents of change, of social forces that they in part create. (Emphasis in original)

We may presume that the researcher is also a creative social force that absolutely requires subjectivity as a precondition for its operation. Lack of subjectivity leads at best to sterile research that may be descrip-

tive, perhaps even enabling prediction and control, but cannot be transformative.

COMMENTARY

It is clear that the Phillips and R&A papers are worlds apart; objectivity
is crucial for one and irrelevant to the other. How can one account for
this difference? And is there no possibility of bringing these points of
view into harmony? Obviously Phillips believes that an accommodation
is not only possible but mandatory; R&A seem unconcerned. What's it
all about?[1]

It seems to me that the issues raised here turn on the different
basic belief systems that these authors espouse. I suggest that these
belief systems can best be described in terms of the responses they
would give to the fundamental questions that have intrigued philosophers, and specifically, philosophers of science, for millennia; to wit:

- What is there that can be known—what is knowable? This question has conventionally been called the *ontological* question; essentially it deals with the assumptions one is willing to make about
  the *nature* of reality.
- What is the relationship of the knower to the known? This
  question has conventionally been called the *epistemological* question; obviously the assumptions one makes about this *process*
  aspect depend heavily on what one is willing to assume ontologi-
  cally.
- How can one go about finding out things? This question is
  conventionally called the *methodological* question; how one answers
  depends heavily on what one has decided earlier at the ontological *and* the epistemological levels.

Phillips deals with the ontological question in the conventional
postpositivist way. He eschews *naive* realism; inquiry will never be able
to converge on reality; all knowledge is tentative and cannot be justified
on some solid and unchallengeable foundation. But reality is still there;
simply because (to pursue the Popper metaphor) we cannot tell

---

1. I am happy to acknowledge the contributions made by my colleague, Yvonna S.
Lincoln, to the propositions and assertions of this section of the paper. I absolve her of
any blame that may stem from a misapplication of our joint ideas in this specific instance,
however.

whether the peak we are climbing is the highest summit does not negate the fact that we are looking for the summit and that the summit *is there*. The image of truth is not that of some ultimate, permanent reality, but of some regulatory ideal, which exists whether we can see it or not. Phillips might well be numbered among the so-called *critical* realists, a point of view described by Cook and Campbell (1979) as stressing that

> Many causal perceptions constitute assertions about the nature of the world which go beyond the immediate experience of perceivers and so have objective contents which can be right or wrong (albeit not always testable). The perspective is realist because it assumes that causal relationships exist outside of the human mind, and it is critical realist because these valid causal relationships cannot be perceived with total accuracy by our imperfect sensory and intellective capacities. (p. 29)

And indeed, knowledge must be certain, in principle, at least, for as Phillips himself asserts, "If no knowledge is certain, then there is no possibility for any viewpoint to be objective."

And that is precisely my point, except that I wish to champion its reverse. For objectivity to make any sense as a criterion, knowledge must (in principle) be certain. For it is only through the adoption of a realist ontology that one can gain warrant for posing objectivity as a criterion. The term *objectivity* is not a descriptor for the reality that an inquiry (partially) discovers, but for the *process* whereby the putative discovery takes place. Remove the realist ontology and the possibility of an objective epistemology disappears. *The need for objectivity is gone.*

I will assert that postpositivism is a coherent philosophic system. It begins with a realist ontology (although admitting, in good postpositivist fashion, that true knowledge cannot be certain; it remains an ideal). It is the realist ontology that drives the demand for objectivity. The methodology of the paradigm likewise follows: If there *is* a reality (even if it is not ultimately accessible), the purpose of science must be to describe it and to ferret out its dynamics. The latter task is accomplished by hypothesizing *why* the descriptive data appear as they do (that is, by theorizing) and then verifying (or more properly, falsifying) those hypotheses. The aim is always to find out how things really are. Further, when one believes that things really do exist in some prefigured constellation and operate in accordance with natural laws, it is entirely appropriate to demand an objective stance, for otherwise we will achieve only a distorted and unreal characterization. We must be able to put questions directly to nature and arrange for nature to answer back directly, as Donald Campbell put it in his 1977 William James Lecture (Brewer & Collins, 1981). The call by Phillips for objectivity is thus entirely appropriate; indeed, he would be inconsistent with the fundamental belief system of postpositivism were he to do otherwise.

The issue for us today is whether this justification for an objective process extends to the materialist feminist ethnography that R&A advance and defend. That approach clearly calls for subjectivism. It requires the investigator to become intimately involved—she or he cannot be the anthropological stranger, minimizing reactivity, eschewing reciprocity, writing with an authorial voice, or otherwise displaying the characteristics that R&A find embedded in conventional ethnography. Instead, the "structural divide" between investigator and investigated must be minimized; the researcher's own theories must be open to modification; the researched must be able to comprehend better their own experiences of subordination; both researcher and researched must have input into the inquiry process; and both must be open to being "informed and transformed" as a result of the inquiry. There is no objectivity here, certainly not in the positivist sense.

But there is a problem. Despite their apparent sensitivity to the "affinities" that conventional ethnography has for positivism, R&A do not seem to recognize their own affinities for positivism's basic ontological beliefs. They, too, are realist. To cite a few examples:

- It is essential that a feminist materialist ethnography deal with the "crucial materialist distinction between the appearances of social life and the material conditions and social relations structuring them."
- A proper conception "provides an explanatory theory that situates the understandings of the research subjects and the researcher within the underlying social reality."
- "The importance of a feminist materialist analysis is its attempt to understand the structural conditions that underlie social subjects' everyday actions without resorting to a phenomenological explanation."

Now it seems appropriate at this point for Phillips to say, "If you accept a realist ontology, you cannot at the same time eschew objectivity. If there is some real state of affairs out there, you are obligated to describe it and to deal with it *as it is*, not as you might wish it to be under conditions more acceptable to you on ideological grounds." And I would have to agree with him; materialist, feminist ethnography is hoist on its own petard just as soon as its advocates elect to follow (in principle) a realist ontology.

But of course the election of a realist ontology is not the only option open to adherents of materialist feminist ethnography. There seems to be little doubt expressed either in the papers before us or in any other sources I have seen that the phenomena we are talking about studying are *social* in nature. There is no need to posit a natural state of affairs and a natural set of laws for phenomena that are socially invented—I shall say socially constructed—in people's minds. I suggest that materialist feminist ethnography should be based on an ontology that is relativist in nature. It begins with the premise that all social realities are constructed and shared through well-understood socialization processes. It is this socialized sharing that gives these constructions their apparent reality, for if everyone agrees on something, how can one argue that it does not exist? Thus the ideas that realities are negotiable, that they can be informed and transformed, that they can be democratically arrived at, and that the processes whereby this can be done are dialogic in nature make very good sense indeed. It is under this ontological assumption that the epistemological assumption of subjectivity not only becomes desirable but is seen as the only alternative logically available.

I cannot help noting the similarity of this reconstructed version of materialist feminist ethnography to the naturalist paradigm that Yvonna Lincoln and I have been espousing, as shown in the accompanying table. (We have come to use the term *constructivist* to label our own paradigm for reasons I will not take time to describe. I will simply use that label without justifying it as meaningful.) Now R&A began by

Ontological, Epistemological, and Methodological Positions of Three Alternative Paradigms of Inquiry

	Alternative paradigms		
Domain	*Postpositivism*	*Materialist feminist ethnography*	*Constructivism*
Ontology	Realist	Realist	Relativist, consensual
Epistemology	Dualist, objective	Interactive, subjective	Interactive, subjective
Methodology	Descriptive, verificatory	Dialogic, transformative	Hermeneutic/ dialectic, reconstructive

Note: This table is the mutual work of Yvonna S. Lincoln and Egon G. Guba.

asking whether it would be possible to conduct meaningful but unabashedly ideological research that would replace the objective positivism they found repugnant for all the reasons they cite. Lincoln and Guba, and others like us, began at a very different point, asking whether it would be possible to devise a new paradigm that would replace positivism, which we found repugnant for other reasons—including those that Phillips cites as the basis for his claim that positivism is dead. I think it not unreasonable to assert that if advocates of materialist feminist ethnography (a term I abhor if for no other reason than because it is so awkward to say and to write!) were to alter their ontological stance, not only would they become impervious to charges of nonobjectivity (could one think of them then as practicing a teflon-coated paradigm?) but they would also have a great deal in common with constructivists, among whom I number myself. I, for one, would welcome the consensus that might emerge.

There are some other points of difference, of course, that need to be considered. The methodological position of materialist feminist ethnography is *dialogic*, a term that I think does not carry quite the implication of negotiation that we attempt to portray by our term *hermeneutic/dialectic*. Our intent is not to "transform" so much as it is to "reconstruct," to make it possible for all concerned to develop more informed and sophisticated constructions than anyone, *including* the investigators, held prior to the inquiry. And, I note in passing, our criterion might well be "consensual validation" of emergent constructions. Indeed, if inquirers in this paradigm have a *moral imperative*, it is not only to be open to information and levels of sophistication that challenge one's existing constructions but also to seek out such *with deliberate intent*.

It must be apparent, even without further confession on my part, that I reject Phillips's position and accept Roman and Apple's, albeit not without some qualifications. I do feel a closer affinity to the latter than to the former. I cannot justify to myself the proposition that some changes and adjustments in positivist methodology will be sufficient to overcome what I see as that paradigm's fatal flaws—many of which are cited by Phillips himself. At the risk of joining the ranks of those who misunderstand Kuhn, let me assert that it is time for a paradigm shift in the social sciences.

REFERENCES

Brewer, M. B., & Collins, B. E. (Eds.). (1981). *Scientific inquiry and the social sciences* (a volume in honor of Donald T. Campbell). San Francisco: Jossey-Bass.

Cook, T. D., & Campbell, D. T. (1979). *Quasi-experimentation: Design and analysis issues for field studies.* Chicago: Rand McNally.

Gleich, J. (1987). *Chaos.* New York: Viking Press.

Jaggar, A. (1983). *Feminist politics and human nature.* Totowa, NJ: Rowman & Allenheld.

Lather, P. A. (1986). Research as praxis. *Harvard Educational Review, 56,* 257-277.

Locke, L. F., Spirduso, W. W., & Silverman, S. J. (1987). *Proposals that work.* Newbury Park, CA: Sage.

Phillips, D. C. (1987). *Philosophy, science, and social inquiry.* Oxford, UK: Pergamon.

Popper, K. (1976). The logic of the social sciences. In T. Adorno et al. (Eds.), *The positivist dispute in German sociology.* New York: Harper.

Sharp, R. (1982). Self-contained ethnography or a science of phenomenal forms and inner relations. *Journal of Education, 164,* 48-63.

Response to the Commentary by Guba

D. C. PHILLIPS

It is obvious from his response to my paper that Egon Guba belongs to the group I was criticizing—he does, indeed, think that objectivity is dodolike. No more evidence is needed than *his* paper to support my charge that there are reputable people who are misreading a number of recent intellectual developments and are drawing the *mis*inference that there is no room in the late twentieth century for a notion of objectivity. He offers a number of criticisms of my arguments; I will start by commenting upon three matters that I find annoying but not particularly central, by way of preface to a more vital issue.

First, Guba opens his onslaught by pointing out that I did not define the term *objectivity*, and it is obvious that he considers this to be a serious failing. "It seems reasonable to expect that a philosopher would begin . . . with some sort of definition," he writes in his opening page. However, it was not incompetence that led to my shattering his expectations here; the point is that offering a definition, at the outset of the discussion, would have been worse than irrelevant.

Popper once said that he denigrated the giving of definitions, for it was a serious mistake to suppose that the dictionary definition of a word was at issue in philosophical discussions. No one at the present conference on qualitative inquiry in education, no matter what his or her personal epistemological position may be, is ignorant of the dictionary definition of *objectivity* or *objective*. It is noteworthy that, after offering this criticism of me, Guba himself does not bother to offer a dictionary definition. (It is noteworthy, too, that Myrdal, Eisner, and others I cited in my paper also do not start out by offering definitions.) The real issue (and it is a nontrivial one) is how in this day and age one can continue to hold—or not hold—beliefs such as the following: that things exist independently of the mind, or that they are real, or that viewpoints can be unbiased. And these issues, of course, are just the ones I did grapple with in my paper. I adopted the honorable philosophical strategy of showing that the factors that have led some people to abandon objectivity as a useful concept do not, when properly understood, lead in this direction at all. And I can argue in this way without having recourse to a dictionary.

Regarding the second matter, in several places Guba confronts my point that achieving objectivity depends upon the presence of a community that espouses the critical spirit; he hints that I have been inconsistent, for he claims that this comes close to my embracing the consensual validation that I claim to have rejected. Here he simply has not read my paper carefully enough; following Scriven, I *do* specifically reject the view that objectivity is related to consensus. I made it abundantly clear that there may never be consensus about several rival and objectively held positions; but even if there were, what is important is not the consensus itself but *the manner* in which the consensus was reached.

Guba correctly points out that I do not say much about the criteria that will be used within a critical community. Let me acknowledge that, being a mere mortal, I am unable to describe them with a great deal of precision—for the fact is that the critical endeavor is, and must be, open-ended. It cannot be governed by a closed set of rules, and so the criteria *cannot* be completely codified. Guba's tone throughout suggests that he thinks there are no criteria at all—a view that I regard as patently silly, and on which I will offer a further comment shortly.

As to the third matter, Guba opens his paper with a lengthy but rather idiosyncratic summary of my paper, in which he not only ignores the spirit or general thrust of my arguments but also gets some of these arguments *wrong*. As a consequence my paper appears as worse than mistaken—in his recounting it comes out as well-nigh incoherent. I am, as an advocate of critical rationality, open to the first possibility, but I reject the second!

I offer two samples by way of evidence; the first comes from early in the paper where he summarizes me thus:

> Phillips suggests that for many people the issue is moot because objectivity is dead. Among the pallbearers hastening the concept to its final resting place, he tells us, are these:
>
> The nonfoundationalist philosophers, who have argued, apparently convincingly, that all knowledge is tentative. Now Phillips counterposes the argument that this consideration is irrelevant to the concept of objectivity because, as he was so careful to point out earlier, objectivity has nothing to do with either truth or certainty. Phillips faced a choice here: *either* to believe that objectivity has *something* to do with certainty, in which case, given the tentative nature of knowledge, all knowledge would have to be taken as subjective, *or* to believe that objectivity is unrelated to certainty, in which case he can say, "No problem!"

This seems to me to be neither a fair summary of the point I was making nor a valid analysis of it—it makes my train of reasoning tortuous in the extreme. In fact, I did *not* suggest that nonfoundationalist philosophers are pallbearers who regard objectivity as being dead (Popper, for example, is clearly nonfoundationalist, and he believes in objectivity). My point was that *some* readers—among whom I now must number Egon Guba—misunderstand recent developments such as nonfoundationalism and erroneously suppose that if one abandons foundationalism one must also give up the notion of objectivity.

My second example is shorter; near the end of his paper, in the course of an argument that is difficult to follow, Guba states the following: "And indeed, knowledge must be certain, in principle, at least, for as Phillips himself asserts, 'If no knowledge is certain, then there is no possibility for any viewpoint to be objective.'" The point is that I did *not* assert this at all; what I said was almost the opposite. I claimed that this argument (I will label it as statement X for future reference)—"if no knowledge is certain, then there is no possibility for any viewpoint to be objective"—is, as it stands, a *non sequitur!*

So much for my three introductory points. To turn to a deeper matter: Why has Egon Guba done all this? I do not consider him to be an intemperate man, nor a bad scholar. What has happened in his response to me is a fine example of the sort of thing that he himself consciously advocates: All knowledge is a human construction, and motives and interests and points of view are so involved in its production that there is no room for objectivity. His very way of dealing with my paper is, as it were, his philosophy writ large! He has seen what I have written through his own theoretical lens. As he says in the comic dialogue in the middle of his paper, you cannot be objective

> because you can't stand outside your humanness; because you inevitably interact with the phenomenon, human or otherwise, that you happen to be studying; because the data you get are literally created by the questions you ask and the order in which you ask them; and because all "factual" data are subject to the interpretations that you bring to them, whether theoretical, prejudicial, or serendipitous.

Guba's summary of my paper, then, is itself apparently a validation of his *Weltanschauung.*

Please note that I said "apparently." Consider the following: Because I am human, the arguments that I construct are human constructions; and because Egon Guba is human, his arguments also are human constructions. But it does not follow from these truisms that objectivity is impossible. In his paper, Guba claimed that I said certain things, for example, that I asserted statement X; anyone literate in the English language may check back and see if he is right! His views are his constructions, but they have been expressed publicly, and so they are open to criticism and check. Guba's mistake lies in supposing that if knowledge is a human construction, it is thereby private and immune from criticism and testing.

Consider another (in this instance, hypothetical) example: It may be the case that data I collected when engaged upon an inquiry were *made* by the questions I asked during the course of my investigation; but having been made, these data then become open to public scrutiny—the fact that the data were made by a human is no hindrance to their being objective data. So, I might be studying a tribe of headhunters, and I might ask them some questions about their own beliefs and rituals that they had never thought of before; in a sense my questions have made the data, but nevertheless the data—their answers to my questions— are then on public record, and it is possible for my account of these things to be objective! (Furthermore, the answers are *real*; even Guba, an avowed nonrealist, would have to concede that!)

In sum, Egon Guba has been led, by his misinterpretation of modern developments in philosophy of science and epistemology, to live in a shadowy and inhospitable nonrealist and relativistic world. There is no reason—no good reason that can withstand critical scrutiny—for us to cohabit with him. And that is my objective opinion.

Part II

VALIDITY

One of the fundamental beliefs of researchers is that efforts to describe the world become increasingly valid as descriptions correspond to the world described. Validity, in a basic sense, pertains to the congruence of the researcher's claims to the reality his or her claims seek to represent. Valid interpretations and conclusions function as surrogates through which readers of research reports can know a situation they have not experienced directly. Thus a valid description or interpretation of a state of affairs is closely aligned to matters of truth. Truth, in turn, is related to matters of correspondence. Correspondence, in turn, is related to a distinction between a subjective self and an objective world. What we want, in traditional terms, is an account that tells the truth about some objectively described state of affairs. Such an account would be a valid one.

Although this line of argument seems to most unassailable, it is not one shared by either Madeleine Grumet or Harry Wolcott. For Grumet, the search for detached objectivity and pristine validity is a hopeless quest. We cannot, she says, detach ourselves from the world we study in order to meet a scientific standard of validity. We are a part of what we study. Wolcott's view of validity proceeds through initial skepticism about the appropriateness of the term in the first place, to an effort to enumerate the tactics he employs as an ethnographer to increase the validity of his ethnographic accounts. Finally, he offers a more fundamental critique and ultimately rejects the concept as an appropriate one for qualitative research. For Wolcott, to ask about validity in qualitative research is to ask the wrong question.

The reasons for his iconoclastic position are related to the context within which the concept of validity initially emerged and its fitness—or lack thereof—for the aims of ethnography, the form of research he employs. *Validity*, he tells the reader, is a term that functions within a psychometric tradition. Its context is tests and measurement. Its epistemology is rooted in something called knowledge, and *knowledge* is a term that regards science as an effort to frame the world as it really is. Knowledge is something you can kick; it is discoverable, collectible, and cumulative.

Wolcott's view of the function of ethnography is a more dynamic one. Ethnography is less concerned with knowledge and more concerned with understanding. *Understanding* is more a verb than a noun. Understanding is a personal achievement, something that one frames for oneself within a community of discourse and a human culture. Furthermore, validity conveys the sense of focusing and verifying with precision something about the course of future events: for example, does a set of test scores predict performance on the job? If it does, the test can be said to have predictive validity. Wolcott's point is that the deepest and most important aspects of social situations are not quite that focused and are far more complex and subtle. The problem is not validity, but understanding, or some new term as yet to be invented that will capture the significance of the drama the qualitative researcher wishes to share with readers. What comes through in Wolcott's personal narrative is an account of such authenticity, coherence, and cogency that we do not doubt the reality of the situation that Wolcott describes, or his feelings about it. His account exemplifies the deeper issue he has attempted to address under the concept of "validity."

The major point of Wolcott, Grumet, and others who aim at describing the deep, intimate moments of life is the need to elude the traditional concepts and norms that blinker sight. What they are getting at is the need to find a new lexicon that will do justice to even those aspects of life that are, at base, ineffable. For Grumet, the mode that comes closest is art—a literary art. For Wolcott, it is something else not yet named, but it is not the tidiness of the concepts and criteria normally found in an experimental paradigm. What both Wolcott and Grumet allude to are the spaces between the lines, the subtexts as well as the text itself, the *form* of the narrative as well as its explicit content. It should be noted that in emphasizing the complexity of understanding and the intimacy of knowing, Wolcott remains meticulous about the ways in which he secures information, uses it in preparing text, and revises the text he has prepared. Great care is apparent in the several criteria he puts forward as relevant.

Given the views expressed in these chapters, can we now dismiss the concept of validity in qualitative research? Is it an inappropriate notion? We think not. We think that while we cannot dismiss the concept, we need not treat it in the way in which it has been used in conventional research efforts. We need not be constrained by standards that we developed for another game during another era. Both Grumet and Wolcott adumbrate some of the features of the newer enterprise. The conceptual work that will lead to the generation of better and more appropriate notions remains to be done.

Philip Jackson takes us on another tack. While the drama Wolcott and Grumet portray makes interesting reading, the real life of the school, Jackson reminds us, lives in the ordinary. It is that most difficult-to-see ordinary educational world that we must learn to look *at*. What interferes is our penchant for looking *for*. Our hunt to find, paradoxically, limits our sight. It creates a form of instrumentalism that obliterates from our sight what does not fit our intentions. Ultimately, to appreciate the ordinary, we must develop a different attitude, a different way of being in the world, at least in the classroom or school. This new attitude is not a passive one, nor is it one that is focused on the achievement of aims or goals. It is one that allows the scene to speak to us: Our attitude needs to be one that is receptive. Furthermore, disclosures, Jackson claims, ought not to persuade, but to reveal. Those with a mission are less likely to see and are more likely to obscure what they try to describe. Thus Jackson's pitch is, ironically, to persuade us that persuasion, rhetoric, and intention ought to be replaced with an openness to tell it like it is. Validity—if that is the right term—is located in the way we address the world. In that sense, Wolcott, Grumet, and Jackson share a common agenda.

3 On Daffodils That Come Before the Swallow Dares

MADELEINE R. GRUMET

For some time many of us have been arguing that qualitative inquiry is an art rather than a science. Having made that assertion, we quickly crawl into it for comfort. No longer radically disassociated from the object of our inquiry and subjugated to the epistemological loneliness that plagues the scientist, we bring together that which science has separated and declare our connectedness, our continuity with our world. The problem of validity—ascertaining a concept's adequacy to the phenomenon to which it corresponds—is relegated, we think, to the skepticism of the Cartesians who must struggle to assert connections they have denied.

The artist, on the other hand, admits the relation to the object that the scientist represses. That is the message of Henry James's artist in "The Real Thing" (1893/1979). After struggling in vain to illustrate a text on the aristocracy by working with authentic models, the artist finally has his servants pose, and it is their perception of class difference that strikes the gestures he draws. His canvas depicts a relationship to the phenomenon rather than a display of the thing itself. Ah, but then what am I to do when Virginia, herself, disagrees? "Art is being rid of all preaching: things in themselves: the sentence in itself beautiful: multitudinous seas; daffodils that come before the swallow dares" (Woolf, 1953, p. 183). Immediately I am convinced. Good-bye. I will go to Half Moon Bay, where I will walk on rocks and watch for whales.

"Daffodils that come before the swallow dares." I write these lines in Rochester in March. Seven days past the vernal equinox and still it shows.

"Daffodils that come before the swallow dares." This semblance dissembles. It hides in what it reveals. It hides her surprise and her

101

relief. It hides her despair of the long grey months, her doubt, her loss, her dread. But I forgive her sleight of hand that makes her self disappear before our eyes. It is a clever trick. In her absence, I lean on her windowsill, I walk her path. I inhabit her very body, the tilt of her head, her glance (first down, then out above.) I abandon my scrawny snowy crocus for her daffodils. I purchase them at the price of me.

Neither science that denies connection, nor art that displays connection, can design the relation to the world that I struggle to achieve. For I am neither an artist nor a scientist. I am a teacher. Here is the difference. Teaching simultaneously performs the connection of art and practices the so-called abstention of science. To adopt the stance of the artist is to perform one's relation to the world for one's students. That is what the charismatic teachers we are, and have all admired, do. They lean on our windowsills, they long for our daffodils. It is the process of learning that we call mimesis. It is that teacher's passion for a beautiful line, for multitudinous seas that sends us to Half Moon Bay or to the stacks.

"I begin to understand a philosophy by feeling my way into its existential manner, by reproducing the tone and accent of the philosopher," Merleau-Ponty tells us (1962, p. 179). Moved by the eros that makes identity fluid, so that we abandon our own ground to stand in another's place, we love this teacher who gives us another world. That is how I first received Merleau-Ponty, leisurely, swaying through the ironic southern drawl of Harmon Holcomb, the professor who taught me existential philosophy. He was a fisherman, and most of the examples he offered us of phenomenological concepts were drawn from reveries in drifting rowboats or battles with sharks in shallow waters where I will never wade. In the seminar room it was perfectly foggy, and with Holcomb I would cast my line and reel Merleau-Ponty in. But as I walked to the parking lot, wondering whether I had defrosted something for dinner, in the 5:00 P.M. (premicrowave) twilight, I could feel phenomenology wriggle off the hook to make its way back to the Mississippi.

This is the way, after all, we found the world in the first place, as we mimicked our mother's song, followed her glance, and then the sweep and destination of her gesture. The very word *mimesis*, Atwell (1988) points out, has roots in the words *mim* and *mum*, which refer to an echoic pursing of the lips as well as the imitative but silent acts of mimes or mimics. The lip pursing that makes sucking possible does not in this case bring that which is other and sustaining in, as in the case of the nursing infant, but reverses direction and sends air out, summoning the object of its own desires and making the sound that names both the one who gives us the world and our own silence, "mum."

So the world is constituted, within the relationships within which it and we come to form. But her world is not ours, we come to learn. If we are male and mother-raised, we also come to learn that we are not she and repress our original experiences of connection to both her and the world. Connection is denied and becomes the thing to be proved; ergo, the null hypothesis. If we are female and can sustain in gender identity our original sense of being both like our mothers and connected to their worlds, we are ambivalent about that continuity. We still sustain her in our own identities but resist the identification in order to experience that clarity and distinct organization of our own egos.[1] "Daffodils that come before the swallow dares." Male gender, achieved by identifying with what has been distant and abstract, valorizes those attributes, thinking that what is important, what really matters, must be out there. Spring comes to such a man from afar, on the wings of the migrating swallow. Female gender, maintaining its identity with its first love, its first world, finds spring, with some ambivalence, perhaps, on home ground.

For all of us, the process of development has required this mimetic tracing of the other's relation to the world and then the negotiation, once we have arrived, of a new itinerary that will bring us back to ourselves. Male or female, wistful, yearning, repudiating, or celebrating, we repeat the histories of our own identifications and differentiation throughout our lives. The classroom, the class period, provide the stage for transference of the relations within which we came to form; teachers and students, the cast of characters with whom we endlessly repeat, or perhaps transform, those relations. For the world is never an outright gift, no strings attached. And when we, in Merleau-Ponty's (1962) words, "slacken the intentional threads which attach us to the world and thus bring them to our notice" (p. xiii), we risk losing both the world and each other. That is the paradox and fascination of teaching, its ceaseless alternations of presence and absence, mimesis and transformation.

In *The Practice of Teaching*, Philip Jackson (1986) names mimesis and transformation as the two major traditions that organize our understanding and practice of teaching. He says that he will discuss mimesis before transformation just because it is easier to describe. He claims to be describing neither a history of an individual's experiences of merging and differentiation in the process of ego development nor the historical antecedence of the sophistic to the Socratic method. Nevertheless,

mimesis does maintain a position of priority in relation to transformation, and it is the necessary priority of intentionality to reflexivity. It is
mimesis that has given us a world to think about. Mimesis of the sophist's
rhetoric was not merely a copy of his speech but was, indeed, a reproduction of his relation to a mundane and metaphysical system, to the polis,
the world, the universe (Silverman, 1973). Participation in the Socratic
dialogue implied a willingness to see those relations questioned and
transformed. It is tempting to assert that just as ontogeny recapitulates
phylogeny, ego development recapitulates this capitulation of mimesis to
transformation. But I hesitate to follow the trajectory of repudiation that
this analogy represents, for it takes us further and further from our
beginnings. The hole in the ozone layer reminds us that we forget our
gills, our webbed feet, and our wings at our peril, and illiteracy and the
dropout rate remind us that deconstruction is hardly urban renewal.

Daily experience continually moves through the phases of mimesis
and transformation as we move between intentional and reflexive
thought. Nevertheless, as Jackson has pointed out, teaching too often
clings to one approach or another, dichotomizing what is continuous
and related in human experience. My response is mimetic, filled with
the words, the rhythms, and the relations of Paulo Freire.[2] It is impossible
to think about teaching without thinking about a relation to the object
to be known. It is impossible to think about the object to be known
outside the human relationships that designate it as meaningful in our
world. And it is impossible to think about teaching without making all
these relations as well as their objects the matter of our study.

Now it may be argued that this portrayal of teaching begs the
question, that it presupposes the character of the phenomenon that we
would investigate. But at the outset I identified myself as a teacher
rather than an artist or a scientist. Neither my purpose nor my method
will admit their exemptions. In one way or another both the artist and
the scientist deny or disguise their relation to the object.

The scientist's alienation from the object is accompanied by the
consolation of epistemology. Unwilling to assert a vivid, situated, and
compelling relation to the object, the scientist takes comfort by closing
ranks with others in a club of rational discourse, where, Rorty (1979)
tells us, "everybody agrees on how to evaluate everything everybody
else says" (p. 320):

> The dominating notion of epistemology is that to be rational, to be fully
> human, to do what we ought, we need to be able to find agreement with
> other human beings. To construct an epistemology is to find the maximum
> amount of common ground with others. (p. 316)

In contrast, the artist's connections to the object, as Woolf has maintained, ignores consensus. It is grounded in the world of seas and daffodils and repudiates the analysis that would drive a wedge between what the Greeks called *hyle*, or quality, and matter. The artist will not discriminate the connection from the object, the way she knows, what she knows, is it. "Daffodils that come before the swallow dares." But the artist finds another loneliness. Her rush to the object is a solitary sprint. She hardly has time for the interaction that hermeneutics, Rorty's (1979) alternative to epistemology, requires:

> For epistemology, conversation is implicit inquiry. For hermeneutics, inquiry is routine conversation. Epistemology views the participants as united in what Oakshot calls a *universitas*—a group united by mutual interests in achieving a common end. Hermeneutics views them as united in what he calls a *societas*—persons whose paths in life have fallen together, united by civility rather than by a common goal, much less by a common ground (p. 318; emphasis in original).

In the civil conversations of hermeneutics, Rorty (1979) tells us, the speaker refrains from trying to measure meaning against a common set of terms but instead is "willing to pick up the jargon of the interlocutor rather than translating it into one's own" (p. 318). Here mimesis, so often portrayed as a slavish replication, is presented as less controlling and authoritarian than Rorty's depiction of transformation: "the Platonic philosopher-king who knows what everybody else is really doing whether they know it or not, because he knows about the ultimate context (the Forms, the Mind, Language) within which they are doing it" (pp. 318–319). Here mimesis, situated, specific, and material, provides specificity and presence, and transformation, always pointing elsewhere, undermines the moment and the integrity of the persons whose lives it holds.

If it is as a teacher that I engage in inquiry into teaching, then I do not deny or disguise my relation to the object of that inquiry but make that relation the object of the inquiry itself. If teaching requires that we bring to consciousness our relation to the object both so that the relation may be extended to the student through mimesis and so that the relationship of both student and teacher to the object may be reconsidered and perhaps transformed, then research into teaching demands the most rigorous attention to these relations.

Because both teaching and inquiry about teaching contain the possibilities of control and liberation, qualitative research cannot rest on phenomenology's celebration of the simultaneity of matter and meaning. Nor can it rely on the critique of ideology that strands speakers in language, in discourse, sans sentences, sans seas, sans daffodils.

Teaching is about connection to the world and to the other people with whom we share that world. Science and art, each in its own way, interrupt the natural attitude where things and thoughts, language and material, ideology and reality, mingle. The transformations of epistemology surrender specificity and immediacy. The mimesis of hermeneutics surrenders purpose. But we who are responsible for bringing children to the world and the world to children cannot make such excluding choices. Nevertheless, research offers us exemptions all the time. On one hand, for example, it offers us the transformations of post-structuralism, in which the identity and responsibility of the subject are dissolved into fragmentary and contradictory discourses (Henriques, Holloway, Urwin, Venn, & Walkerdine, 1984). Identity often disappears as well in the categories of the research on "teacher thinking" that describes "teacher planning" (incremental or comprehensive) and strives to conceptualize this complex and marvelous human enterprise such that it can be appropriated as professional knowledge. For example, Clark (1988), reviewing studies of the interactive decision making of effective teachers, reports that it is characterized "by rapid judgment, 'chunking' of many events and cues into a few categories, differentiation of cues and events as to their importance, and a willingness to change the course of classroom interaction when necessary" (p. 10). Teacher decision making is illuminated for us by this wisdom: "Conflicting goals, combined with endemic uncertainty about how to achieve desired outcomes, can lead to knots in teachers' thinking" (Clark, 1988, p. 10, citing Wagner, 1984).

Knots. *Knots* share the same German root as *knitting*, the wool winding of women. Intentionality turned back upon itself. The reflexive recursiveness that goes back to go forward, that loops back and under and then out again. "Daffodils that come before the swallow dares." Knots are material obstacles to the logic of the line they interrupt. They stop the line that slides between our fingers; they anchor the thread to the cloth, the boat to the pier, and thought to the world. Reflexivity means that after being startled by daffodils, the intentional objects of my thought, I recover and reflect on my surprise, my anticipation that spring would come from far away on the wings of the swallow rather than first appearing here, near. But unlike Descartes I do not relinquish these daffodils forever to my thoughts about them.[3] "Language," argues A. D. Nuttal in *A New Mimesis* (1983), "grows when certain schemes prove operable in relation to the real. Literature . . .

lives in language, and the meanings with which it *plays* must first have *worked*, or they would not be meanings" (pp. 192–193; emphasis in original). Reflexivity does not intimidate Merleau-Ponty (1962) either; "there is no inner man," he tells us, "man is in the world, and only in the world does he know himself" (p. xi).

If teaching is about our relations to the world, then we must let the world into our method. If the world we have comes to us though our relations to other people, then those relations as they appear in the transferences, ideologies, and systems of thought that shape our culture must be there too. Narrative is a form for inquiry that can contain both the world and the relations within which it becomes the focus for our attention, a locus of concern, a system of meanings, in short, our world. The narrative encodes time and space. Like our bodies, it literally takes place. Its story line takes up time, as do we, from beginning to end. The language that suits the eye first pleased the ear, Diane Wakoski (1987) reminds us. Its starts and stops, plunges and pauses, have all been poised on a pedestal of breath. The poet Robert Bly (1987) confirms the presence of the body in the text when he seeks to return tension to poetry[4]:

> Why should tension in art always be considered bad? The dislike of tension has something to do with the entire mind set of the New Age, which favors vegetables, which as we all know have no muscles at all, and bland rice, Wyndham Hill music, simple cheerfulness, and books that urge us to get rid of anger and fear.
> Will we ever develop a music that increases the tension in a body? While I enjoy relaxation, I'd be interested in that one. My metaphor then is this: honoring a line with its limits and occasionally knotted shape is a way of increasing the tension in a poem. (p. 55)

"Daffodils that come before the swallow dares." The alliteration of the beginning and end of that line brings the sweep of the swallow to the daffodil's debut. Displaced, but replaced, we find at our feet what we had scanned the horizon to discover. In *Poetry and the Body* John Vernon (1979) tries to reconcile these centrifugal and the centripetal forces of language:

> When our bodies participate in language, they participate in an organization that transcends our individual bodies or the individual things around us, an organization with its own rules and patterns and its own history previous to ours. (p. 14)

Echoes of science and epistemology. But he continues:

> At the same time, the gravity and thingness of the body and earth prevent language from flying off and becoming a self-enclosed or self-referring structure, a pure form. This gravity exists *in* language, at its very heart, in our bodily gestures (p. 14; emphasis in original)

Shadows of art and hermeneutics.

Hear the tension and reconciliation that the contradictory practice we call teaching contains and requires in the discourse, method, and politics that constitute its study. I have asked teachers to write autobiographical accounts of educational experience. These accounts necessarily encompass both mimesis and transformation. The author tries to tell the story as it happened. I ask for all the detail she can recall. Was it raining? Did she see oil rainbows in the puddles? Did she pump the brakes to see if they would hold? Does wet charcoal still make your fingers black? But, of course, a perfect copy is not the point, and the very process of selection of what to tell and its transformation as she writes it—writes it to me—is inevitable. She writes as an artist, rid of all preaching. I read as a scientist looking for the meanings both common and uncommon. My reading of her text must enter its world. I join her in a hermeneutic stroll, meeting the relatives, the neighbors, locating the object, educational experience within her horizons, her body, her language. She joins me on an epistemological perch, from which we survey the territory that she has traveled.

The inquiry that I present here is a conversation between teachers. Kathy Farrar is a teacher and was a graduate student at the University of Rochester, where I was her teacher. I am not a scientist, sitting in the back of the room, waiting for the phenomenon to emerge as the kids file in, take their seats and the class begins. I am not an artist, sketching their energy and their resistance with a gesture that captures my empathy or repugnance. I am a teacher. I ask my student Kathy Farrar to situate the experience of education among the relations within which it has come to form in her own world. At my request, Kathy Farrar writes three narratives of educational experience. After years of working with autobiography I have learned to ask for multiple accounts in order to diminish coherence and the ideologies that accompany stories that attempt to bind together the varied moments of our lives into a logic of development, purpose, or necessity.[5] The first is a story about reading:

> I was probably five years old when I first learned to read and write a word. I didn't experience this first educational step

at school, or even at home. My reading lesson took place in an old farm house which stood empty except for a desk and file cabinet which allowed it to fulfill its role as office for the man who owned it and the homes and pastures nearby.

My parents didn't read to me very often, but they made a practice of reading the Sunday comic strips to me. I have a very vivid memory of standing in the living room on a sunny Sunday morning while my parents remained hidden behind newspaper sheets for what seemed like hours. My memory is of losing patience with them for making me wait so long for my treat. I finally punched in the sheet of newspaper which my father was holding and received a spanking (one of a very few which I clearly recall) for my action. I didn't often "backtalk" my parents, but I remember crying and telling them that I would just learn to read so that I could read the "funnies" myself. I was as dead serious as a small child could be, and I buttonholed everyone I knew to try to get someone to teach me to read.

As a five-year old growing up in St. Louis County in 1954, I was not sent to kindergarten. The local community had not planned for the post war "baby boom" which hit its schools, causing kindergarten classrooms to be needed for upper grades. There was even some dispute about which school I could attend because we lived in a distant corner of the county at a junction called "Shoveltown" and the nearest school was a lengthy busride away from my home. These circumstances hampered my progress in my campaign to learn to read.

The day when I first learned to read a word was, I imagine, in the autumn. I remember a cool, grey day, around suppertime. Everything about that late afternoon seemed softened. House, barn, sheds and cows in the distance were filtered through fading afternoon sunlight. My flannel-lined bluejeans had been laundered many times, giving them a softness which only old, familiar clothing can have. My father and I walked hand-in-hand down the oil-soaked gravel drive for about a quarter of a mile to where "Uncle Gus" kept his office.

Gus's office was in the front room of the one story, white frame farmhouse. The entire front side of the house was faced with a low-slung roof which overhung a grey wooden porch floor. The back of the house opened onto a small hillside and faced the open pastures.

My father had stopped by to pass the time of day and was pleased to see another neighbor was visiting also. I can't remember why, but the two visiting men went outside to check on something, leaving me alone with "Uncle Gus."

Now Uncle Gus was not really my uncle, but some sort of distant relative, as were many of the neighbors nearby. It was just the custom where we lived to call men and women friends uncle and aunt instead of Mr. or Mrs. So-and-So. Gus always seemed old to me and always unchanged in manner and appearance. He was of German descent and spoke with the lilt and cadence of speech common to farmers in our area. If Gus is still alive he probably still looks today as he did over 30 years ago. Sweat-rimmed, soft grey hat (indoors or out), dark grey cotton work shirt (rolled to the elbows in summer) and denim overalls (worn as they were originally intended; for work, not style) comprised his wardrobe.

He must have been a little uncomfortable with just a small girl to talk to. He was more accustomed to speaking with his friends about their broken combines, the price of feed or weather conditions as they related to harvests. Gus managed to ask me the usual kinds of adult-to-child questions which no doubt rewarded him with monosyllabic answers. Finally he hit a responsive chord. "Do you know your ABCs?" he ventured. I replied that indeed I did and then shyly muttered something about wishing I could read.

A twinkle came into his eye as he leaned back in his creaky old oak chair and asked me if I thought I'd like to learn to read a very important word. I sidled up close to his chair and watched intently as he opened his center desk drawer and pulled out a hand-sharpened, soft lead, carpenter's pencil and a thick pad of blue-lined paper. I watched as he carefully drew the letters M-A, and he told me that it spelled Ma. He wrote the letters M-A again right next to the first pair and asked me if I could guess what that word was. I was delighted to be able to read the word Mama, and to feel that I had accomplished at least part of the task by thinking it out for myself.

I must have demonstrated my new skill for my father when he returned for me, and for my mother when we got home, but I don't remember that part of the day. However, I'll always remember my own thrill at being able to read my first word.

In Kathy's account the text is a barrier separating her from contact with her parents and with the world. On a sunny Sunday, reading suspends both activity and presence. Her parents are hidden behind the sheets of the newspaper. She makes contact, punching and being spanked. The spanking is "received" and in this scene it may indeed be a gift—of contact, visceral, engaged, at once humiliating and triumphant. Communication with her parents is a struggle against the text; her mother remains sequestered behind the papers. "Backtalk," which may well be the developmental prerequisite of reflexivity, is forbidden.

The absolute boundaries that the text presents in the first scene, violated only by the contact of bodies, are blurred in the second scene. The public school is closed to her. She walks to Gus's place with her father, holding hands. I note the reconciliation. It closes off the violence of the first narrative and resolves it in familial romance. My response is mimetic. I accept the closure and follow her transference to Gus, who is neither the absent mother nor the spanking, hand-holding father. It is Gus who offers to mediate between the child and the adults in her world. Gus is given the title of "uncle"; he stands between stranger and family. Gus crosses all the boundaries. His space is both private and public, home and office. His clothing, "soft grey hat, (indoors or out)," transcends the division of nature and culture. With his carpenter's pencil he teaches her the word MAMA. He is the one who shows her how to encode the relation that is strangely absent from this narrative of childhood.

The second narrative is a recollection of the first day of school.

My first day of school was one of the most miserable days of my school experience. I can't recall the events of the day exactly, but I can compose a picture based on recollections of several events early in my career as a first grade student.

The first hurdle of the day arrived with the school bus which seemed to be enormous and extremely loud. My short legs could barely make the stretch from step to step to climb aboard. The bus travelled over miles and miles of rural roads and passed farms which I had never seen before. We were on the road for such a long time that I could not imagine how we would ever be able to return home the same day.

I sat between Becky and Ross, children from a farm down the road from my house, with whom I had only slight acquaintance. Becky was my age, but outspoken and self-confident. Ross was a year ahead of us and he seemed very sophisticated and wise. We listened enthralled as he told us what he considered to be mandatory information about which teachers were mean and how often children were sent to the principal's office for doing "nothing at all." Near the end of our ride, Ross wrapped up his story with vivid details about the principal's paddle and how many swats to expect for any given offense. Of course I arrived at school frightened to the point of being unable to utter a word.

Somehow we got from the bus to our classroom. When I discovered where our class was located, I felt truly sick at heart. We didn't have a quiet, pretty classroom down a brightly decorated hall waiting for us. We were stuck in a classroom-size square in the corner of the school gymnasium. There were 6 or 8 classes in the gym, divided only by heavy curtains which afforded neither quiet nor privacy.

After the warnings from Ross and the discovery of my miserable classroom, I was certainly not eager to meet my teacher. Mrs. Larimore eventually became one of the most beautiful people in the world to me, but I was not receptive to her at the time. When she asked me my name I started to cry for my mother and my home.

Somehow we got through the morning and time came for lunch. Our lunchroom was in the basement of the school. I remember only that the room was crowded, poorly lit and very chaotic. After our teacher herded us to a table I discovered that I could not open the paper tab on top of my 8 ounce, glass bottle of milk. Some other child ended up opening it for me, and lunch period ended before I was close to being finished.

The afternoon became unbearably hot in our classroom. It was hard to keep my eyes open, and I just wanted to put my head on my desk and sleep. Our teacher took us to the playground for recess before any of us actually fell asleep. The playground was built on a foundation of hard, packed dirt. Some areas of the playground were for larger children and others were set aside for those of us in the lower grades. A chain-link fence delineated the playground boundaries. I stood by the fence and tried not to cry as I wondered if any child would ask me to play.

At the end of the day a "big girl" came to the classroom to take a group of us to our bus. As we walked along the sidewalk between the buff brick building and the long line of yellow buses, I felt that I was lost in a tunnel or maze. I felt that the older girl must be very smart to find her way, and I was convinced that I would never be able to find my way alone.

On the way home, the older children were loud and happy. I merely struggled to stay awake and to keep from bouncing out of the seat. At the last stop on the bus route, I cautiously crept down the enormous steps and ran across the yard to my family.

Happy just to be home, my spirits soon plummeted when my mother started talking to me about how much easier everything was going to be "tomorrow."

Again, the threat of violence accompanies her contact with the text. Her father's spanking is generalized here to the threat of the principal's paddle. Is the threat of contact, however sadistic, a consolation to a child who fears that she may never find home again as the bus makes its way past farms she has never seen before? Time, space, and sustenance close around her in this place. The chain-link fence encodes the contradiction, the passage to the world that schooling has promised is an illusion, and she is stranded in this space that is neither the world nor her home. And home itself fails to be a refuge when her mother's talk of tomorrow interrupts her relief.

Sequestered behind the papers in the first story, mother is missing in this one too. She is felt as an absence, desired; eventually the comfort that only she provides and withholds will be provided by Mrs. Larimore. But Mrs. Larimore, her teacher, remains abstract here: "Mrs. Larimore eventually became one of the most beautiful people in the world to me, but I was not receptive to her at the time."

The third narrative brings us to the city of Chicago, where the exile of the student has become the exile of the teacher.

The listing in my address book reads, "Antoine and Ruby Mills, 7020 S. Morelle, Chicago, Illinois." Antoine was seven years old when I met him over thirteen years ago. We met at the neighborhood center where I worked as a volunteer tutor. Antoine was all eyes, bony legs, and fidgets as he came through the door that Saturday morning in the firm grip of his mother's hand. Ruby left after admonishing Antoine to be good and assuring me that if he gave me any trouble I could hit him "up alongside his head." My instincts told me that I was in for problems.

Antoine didn't have school work with him, so I scrounged for battered copies of Dr. Suess books in the daycare section of our building. Armed with books, paper and crayons, I settled Antoine into a quiet corner to work. His idea about what we were going to do was very different from mine. He was too busy looking around for left behind daycare center toys to pay any attention to the questions I was trying to ask him. Sometimes he would seem to listen to my question, then respond with a comment that had nothing to do with the subject which we were supposed to be discussing. He also had real difficulty with sitting and looking at books while I read to him.

Ruby returned for her son at the correct time. She was tall, large-boned and slender, and wore her hair pulled back in a turban style hat. She asked first if Antoine had been good, then asked if I thought that I could help him. With some misgivings I agreed to try to tutor Antoine. I told her that I needed information from his teacher about specific areas in which help was needed, and that Antoine should bring his schoolwork to the next tutoring session.

I walked to my Hyde Park apartment building as I pondered the events of the morning. As a newcomer to urban living I was eagerly drawing conclusions about my experience. The child behaved in a hyperactive manner. "Maybe he had donuts and soda for breakfast," I thought. I felt that a mother who would urge me to use corporal punishment on her son was probably a poor, single mother, living in the ghetto with no outlet for her anger. Antoine's teacher had sent me no information about his needs. Was he learning disabled? Was he being treated for a medical problem? What was being done for him at school? By the time I reached home, I had convinced myself that Antoine was the perfect example of a little child who had become lost in the middle of an uncaring, overwhelmingly incompetent, urban public school setting.

The next Saturday Antoine arrived with math and reading workbooks, but without a note from his teacher. That week he still was unable to sit and carry on a discussion about the lessons. However, I did find that he was able to respond directly when we discussed which foods he liked. The discussion turned to what we had eaten for breakfast, and I discovered that my fears that he was eating unbalanced meals were completely unfounded. However, by the time his mother came to take him home, I had some new ideas for the next week's lesson.

I reported to Ruby on the small amount of work which we had accomplished, and I remarked that Antoine had behaved well and that I was enjoying my work with him. Her face opened into a lovely smile and she offered me a ride home. I was amazed at the offer since I never would have guessed that she owned a car. I was even more surprised to find that she drove a Volkswagen van just like many of my graduate student neighbors.

On the way home I asked Ruby more questions about Antoine's school and his teacher. I discovered immediately how wrong my initial assessment of the situation had been. Antoine's school was a private parochial school near his home in an area called South Shore. His neighborhood was hardly the ghetto existence I had imagined. It turned out that the Sister who was Antoine's teacher had not recommended him for tutoring. Ruby had found the notice about tutoring and was eager to find help for Antoine on her own. She was very anxious for her son to be a successful student, and a little impatient with his progress in school.

The following Saturday, and for several subsequent sessions, I tailored Antoine's lessons around the subject of food. We counted cookies (then ate some), cut, pasted and labeled food collages, and even read stories about food. Eventually Antoine relaxed with me and we began to be able to spend more time on his lessons.

One Saturday in the Spring, Ruby invited me to her home for barbecued ribs. I was surprised when she told me that Antoine's father would be picking me up, because it was the first time that she even mentioned his existence. My single-parent theory was also incorrect.

My visit to their home made all of my early notions about their ghetto life seem even more ridiculous. The Mills lived in a lovely apartment building with a house-sized apartment. Ruby even kept a room in the apartment for a small upholstery and furniture refinishing business.

By the end of the school year, Antoine and I had made a little progress on his education and a lot of progress on mine. His attention span improved enough to allow him to follow a storybook or complete a brief math or reading lesson. I learned how misleading first impressions can be.

Once again violence introduces pedagogy. But now it is no longer associated with father or principal but with Kathy herself, as Ruby offers her this access to Antoine's body and soul: "Hit him 'up alongside his head." Antoine is the pure possibility of action, "all eyes, bony legs, and fidgets." I remember the five-year-old on the summer Sunday. Antoine comes to her as she came to Gus, delivered from a parent's hand. But she does not turn to the place from which he has come. She turns instead to Dr. Seuss, a place where none of us lives.

Kathy transfers all of her own feelings of being out of control and abandoned to Antoine, but class and race intervene to protect her from the identification. The diagnostic objectifications of the professional pedagogue are deployed to resolve her anxiety about how to work with him, and then the attributions of inadequacy are shifted onto the deficiencies of school and family. Kathy cannot discover Antoine until she can discover Ruby, his mother. The narrative becomes the story of that reconciliation. For it is Ruby who is bringing Antoine into the world. And it is not through default that it is Ruby who takes him by the hand rather than his father. As Ruby's home and Ruby's business and Ruby's energy to make a world for Antoine become visible, so does the relation within which text can live evolve in this pedagogy. Kathy finds Gus's solution as domestic culture is encoded in the cookie collages that she makes with Antoine. "Daffodils that come before the swallow dares."

My comments and questions are written to Kathy. They encode a mimetic as well as a transformative response. The object relations theory of Winnicott (1971) provides the transitional space and the mediating language for Kathy's reflections on these narratives. Winnicott's theories of space, play, and transitional objects provide concepts that symbolize the role of culture in the processes of identification and differentiation that constitute both ego and knowledge. The move is epistemological as it shifts our discourse from the specificity of narrative to the generality of theory. Qualitative inquiry requires both languages. They are present in Freire's (1973) dialogical method as he moves from the encodings of specific lived situations, to their analysis as "limit situations" (p. 94), to the identification of the "generative themes" (p. 86) that tie them to history and the ideologies of power. Both languages are present in what Geertz has called "experience-near" and "experience-distant" concepts:

> An experience-near concept is roughly one which an individual—a patient, a subject, in our case an informant—might feel himself naturally and effortlessly use to define what he or his fellows see, feel, think, imagine and so on, and which he would readily understand similarly applied by others. An experience-distant concept is one which various types of specialists—an analyst, an experimenter, an ethnographer, even a priest or an ideologist—employ to forward their scientific, philosophical, or practical aims. (quoted in Bernstein, 1983, p. 90)

Richard Bernstein comments:

> We need to employ both concepts in a subtle dialectical interplay if we are to come to an understanding of the incommensurable phenomena that we are studying. We need to realize that experience-distant concepts are not

merely blind prejudices that get in the way of understanding but enabling concepts that allow us to understand. (p. 90)

This shift in language does change the context. It is a language in the middle that can mediate the conversations of Kathy and Gus, of Kathy and Antoine, and of Kathy and me. It is continuous with, but not identical to, her own history. It permits her to recollect it without obligating her to repeat it.

The tensions between the mimetic and the transformative, between art and science, between hermeneutics and epistemology, are negotiated in this pedagogical discourse. I say less than I mean, mean more than I say. I offer various texts—Winnicott, Chodorow, Sartre, Plato, and Dewey—and invite Kathy to write again about these educational experiences in a language that is both mimetic and transformative. Kathy will use what she finds useful. In *Critical Hermeneutics* John B. Thompson (1981) argues that the crucial "non-empirical criterion for the selection of theoretical reconstructions is provided by a principle of self-reflection" (p. 208):

> The interpretations derived from a reconstruction of institutions and social structure may be initially disavowed by the actors who may not recognize themselves under the descriptions thereby produced. Nevertheless the decisive condition for the acceptance of the interpretation, and hence for the defence of the reconstruction from which it is derived, is the ultimate appropriation of the interpretation by the subjects concerned. The principle of self-reflection thus asserts that the redemption of the truth claim expressed by theoretical reconstructions is dependent, in the last analysis, upon the ability of such reconstructions to generate interpretations which clarify conditions of action for the actors themselves, and which thereby provide the actors with the means to free themselves from the circumstances within which they are enmeshed. (p. 208)

Kathy makes her choices. I ask her to write another essay that intertwines the languages of transformation and mimesis. It is a meditation that takes the relations encoded in the three narratives as the objects of reflection. Object relations theory provides the epistemological perch.

> I believe that there is a relationship between how people "know themselves" and how people come to "know" other kinds of knowledge. . . . In intentional thought the subject comes to know the object by directing attention to it. In object relations

theory this knowing is a process of negation and mediation through intentional objects. In reflexive thought we examine the whole process of how we come to knowledge.

In my first narrative account I engage in the intentional process of learning in order to know how to read. It was a totally voluntary process and I had the freedom to choose not only the object, but the mediating objects in the experience as well. At the time of the experience I doubt that I engaged in any reflective thought concerning the experience. In the "first day of school" narrative, the objects which might have mediated the experience for me were not effective because my will had no say in their selection.

The narrative involving Antoine illustrates the reflexive process in a more meaningful way. In this experience I needed to select a series of transitional objects for myself in order to know Antoine and his lifestyle before I could work with him. I also needed to remove myself from the situation so that I could examine our interactions in a reflexive manner. In this instance it was necessary for me to identify my "self" before I am able to teach Antoine. The role of the teacher is not to form little "selves" by filling children with information in the classroom. However, an increased awareness of the world around them may enable children to better engage in the creation of "self" through reflexive thought.

In our autobiographies we attempt to move our private experiences into a public domain. By sharing my private experience in the autobiographical narratives in conjunction with studying object relations theory and reviewing the autobiographical accounts, I have reached what may be an ironic conclusion. I believe that there is merit in moving our educational experiences from very public to more private or familiar spaces. In our own class we have used our personal narratives from the very beginning, interweaving them with the autobiographical accounts and philosophical ideologies which we studied. As a new student in an unfamiliar situation I appreciated the use of personal, familiar materials to mediate the learning experience.

Well, it appears that to some degree Thompson's (1981) criteria have been satisfied by Kathy's appropriation. But his altruism excludes me and excuses me from responsibility for my own participation and my own learning. In mimesis I have joined Kathy. In transformation I also work to understand the relations within which I have learned, within which I teach. Kathy's acknowledgment is not perfunctory in my reading. For I work to make present the relations to that absent mother, to make the reconciliation with Ruby possible, and to bring the history and process of connection, the history and possibility of our love and our desire into the language and politics of knowing. Around the time that I worked with Kathy's text, I was also writing an essay on women and teaching. The processes of identification and differentiation that constitute the ego development of women have been muted in psychological and political theory. The absence of the mother too often encodes her overwhelming presence in the life of the child. The absence of the mother in our understandings of education exacerbates the alienation of teachers from parents and of teachers from each other. Now, like Kathy, at the end of her text, I am preaching. Sorry, Virginia. Kathy and I work not only to know the world, not only to show the world, but also to change the world. But this is not the guilty confession of an incompetent artist or an errant scientist. This work that I have done with Kathy is motivated by my interest as well as hers. It has been a conversation, not an interview or a portrait.

Teaching, which has, in our time, come to be the work of women with children, has lacked the status of art or science and has borrowed their stances and methods to know itself. But teaching, as I have tried to show, is both art and science. And we must study teaching as teachers. For us, teaching *is* research and research *is* teaching and daffodils often come before the swallow dares.

NOTES

1. This brief description of male and female processes of merging and differentiation in the development of gender identity is drawn from the object relations theory presented by Nancy Chodorow (1978).

2. Conversations with Paulo Freire, April 1988, at Hobart and William Smith colleges.

3. Jo Anne Pagano (1988) describes the image of Descartes sitting before the fireplace wearing his dressing gown as "one of the most chilling images in western literature. . . . Perhaps all of western philosophy is a footnote to Plato, but Descartes certainly achieved the total split between life and thought that Plato did not. Every thinker since Descartes has had to cross an abyss, to escape the yawning jaws of metaphysical oblivion." (p. 516).

4. I am indebted to James McCorkle for suggesting the Bly and Wakoski essays.

5. The theoretical rationale for multiple accounts is more fully presented in Grumet (1987).

REFERENCES

Atwell, W. (1988). *The application of reader response theory to the personal reading experiences of three secondary English teachers and their literary curricula.* Unpublished doctoral dissertation, University of Maryland, College Park.

Bernstein, R. (1983). *Beyond objectivism and relativism.* Philadelphia: University of Pennsylvania Press.

Bly, R. (1987). Free verse and muscle tension. *The Ohio Review, 38,* 53–57.

Chodorow, N. (1978). *The reproduction of mothering.* Berkeley: University of California Press.

Clark, C. (1988). Asking the right questions about teacher preparation: Contributions of research on teacher thinking. *Educational Researcher, 17,* 5–12.

Freire, P. (1973). *Pedagogy of the oppressed* (M. B. Ramos, Trans.). New York: Seabury Press.

Grumet, M. (1987). The politics of personal knowledge. *Curriculum Inquiry, 17,* 319–329.

Henriques, J., Holloway, W., Urwin, C., Venn C., & Walkerdine V. (1984). *Changing the subject.* New York: Methuen.

Jackson, P. (1986). *The practice of teaching.* New York: Teachers College Press.

James, H. (1979). The real thing. In R. Gottesman (Ed.), *The Norton anthology of American literature* (Vol. 2) (pp. 388–409). New York: W. W. Norton. (Original work published 1893)

Merleau-Ponty, M. (1962). *The phenomenology of perception* (C. Wilson, Trans.). New York: Humanities Press.

Nuttal, A. D. (1983). *A new mimesis.* New York: Methuen.

Pagano, J. (1988). The claim of Philia. In W. Pinar (Ed.), *Contemporary curriculum discourses* (pp. 514–530). Scottsdale, AZ: Gorsuch, Scarisbrick.

Rorty, R. (1979). *Philosophy and the mirror of nature.* Princeton, NJ: Princeton University Press.

Silverman, J. (1973). A critical analysis of the philosophical foundations of secondary school humanities programs. (University Microfilms No. 73-19448).

Thompson, J. B. (1981). *Critical hermeneutics.* Cambridge: Cambridge University Press.

Vernon, J. (1979). *Poetry and the body.* Urbana: University of Illinois Press.

Wagner, A. (1984). Conflicts in consciousness: Imperative cognitions can lead to knots in thinking. In R. Halkes & J. Olson (Eds.), *Teacher thinking: A new perspective on persisting problems in education* (pp. 163–175). Lisse, The Netherlands: Swets & Zeitlinger.

Wakoski, D. (1987). Eye and ear: A manifesto. *The Ohio Review, 38,* 14–19.

Winnicott, D. (1971). *Playing and reality.* London: Tavistock.

Woolf, V. (1953). *A writer's diary.* New York: Harcourt Brace Jovanovich.

4 On Seeking—and Rejecting—Validity in Qualitative Research

HARRY F. WOLCOTT

The topic of this paper is validity in qualitative research in education. The topic was assigned. I would not have thought of myself as one to address this question, while certain other names came immediately to mind (e.g., Dobbert, 1982; Goetz & LeCompte, 1984). "Of all people, why me?" I asked. "I'll have to look up the term just to make sure I don't have it confused with reliability!"

No sooner had I voiced my concern, however, than it became part of the rationale for inviting me. "No, don't do that," Alan Peshkin quickly reassured. "We don't want a literature review. We are inviting you as someone who has done research and who deals with the issue *implicitly* in your work. How do you deal with validity if you are *not* self-conscious about it?"

Had he said "oblivious to it," I would have kept my guard up. But Alan is a gentle man, and, contrary to the old saying, flattery will get you everywhere. Assured that I was the right person for the assignment and (tacitly, at least) that whatever validity is, I apparently "have" or "get" or "satisfy" or "demonstrate" or "establish" it, I accepted the challenge.

Like other ethnographers—and qualitative researchers in general—there are strategies I follow to "strengthen the validity" (which, according to word roots, is something of a redundancy) of my work. I offer them here for consideration by anyone contemplating fieldwork, as well as to subject them to review by others. As a result of these reflections, I am no longer quite so un-self-conscious about validity. On the other hand, I am even less concerned with it than previously.

I have responded to the assignment in the manner suggested by my title, first by inventorying some procedures for achieving validity and then by raising the central issue of whether validity serves us well as a criterion measure or objective for qualitative research.

VALIDITY: EARLY ENCOUNTERS

Although it is not recorded in the annals of science, I first confronted the issue underlying validity by an act of independent discovery almost half a century ago. For about two years after I was given a Swiftset Printing Press one Christmas, the kids in our neighborhood published a usually weekly "newspaper." (To help you locate this in time, the only edition we ever printed early—but, alas, never delivered as the surprise Extra we planned—carried the headlines, "Willkie Wins! Roosevelt Out, So Is Eleanor and the New Deal!") Our source of paper was a huge roll that could be cut into long strips so the tiny rotary press would actually "roll" at press time. When one of the "little kids" in the neighborhood received a gift of toy electric scissors, we decided to award her the position of paper cutter on the newspaper staff. However, we felt she should demonstrate her qualifications for the job. We designed a convoluted test pattern and watched with approval as she swiftly and adroitly cut along our meandering line.

Our measurement error was classic. She cut the paper for the printing press the same way she cut the test pattern, with jagged and curvy margins of such uneven widths that about half the time the paper jammed between the edges of the press and the rest of the time was in strips too narrow to reach both drive wheels. In our penchant for rigorous testing, we had overlooked the only critical skill involved: precision in cutting along an extended straight line.

More than a cautionary tale about the excesses of testing (as well as an interesting reflection on how as children we had acquired a sense of the cultural ethos surrounding it), my story also serves two other purposes. First, it points to the essence of validity, which asks whether one is measuring whatever it is that is supposed to be measured. Obviously, we were not.

Second, it points to the arena in which the concept has acquired its formidable status: tests and measurement. It is my distinct recollection that in the 1950s (and actually much earlier) the terms *validity* and *reliability* were associated almost exclusively with testing. Validity has not been totally ignored as an issue in field research, however. Through the years there have been discussions on questions of validity in its general sense of obtaining accurate data (e.g., Becker, 1958), on assessing the validity of data already collected (e.g., Vidich & Bensman, 1954), on drawing valid meaning from data (e.g., Miles & Huberman, 1984), and on validating theoretical ideas (e.g., McEwen, 1963).

Virtually everyone who has ever addressed the issue, quantitatively and qualitatively oriented researcher alike, seems to have written on its behalf. Every source I consulted takes a position contrary to my validity-rejecting one, whether claiming that everybody is doing it ("Most anthropologists rank informants for validity and reliability, at least in their own minds," Dobbert, 1982, p. 263); we already have it (our "major strength," Goetz & LeCompte, 1984, p. 221); we desperately need it (external validity identified as the single greatest weakness in case studies, Campbell, 1975); we are nowhere without it ("In order to be believed . . . it is absolutely necessary to have the property of being true or false," Phillips, 1987, p. 10); or that all roads lead to it—if you can follow the directions:

> What I join him [Habermas] in rejecting is the currently fashionable hermeneutic nihilism, in which validity of interpretation is rejected as a goal. Like the nihilists, I applaud the achievement of radical interpretations, but only because I see these as the inevitably wasteful route to a potential future consensus on a more valid interpretation. (Campbell, 1986, p. 109)

My effort to catalogue various "types" of validity and clarify the relationships among them—on the assumption that to be forgiven the assignment of a literature review did not give me license to ignore the literature itself—has revealed a proliferation of qualifying adjectives that may enhance validity for those who set store by it but often confuses those who do not. Validity is variously presented as a twosome: external and internal; as a threesome: instrumental (pragmatic, criterion; also predictive, concurrent), theoretical (construct), and apparent (face); and as a foursome: content (face, apparent; also sampling), predictive, concurrent, and construct (or theoretical). If I have correctly situated these major terms, there are still others not easily placed—conclusion validity, ontological validity, overall validity, and practical validity. One also finds references to consensual validation (Phillips, 1987, p. 19), cross-validation, final validation, self-validation (Geertz, 1973, p. 24), validity coefficient, and even "validity-seeking hermeneutics," as Campbell (1986, p. 109) characterizes the position of Habermas.

Two recent sources that attempt conceptual clarification about validity and thus help differentiate among critical nuances are Brinberg and McGrath (1982) and Weber (1985). Educational psychologist Lee Cronbach's 1971 article "Test Validation" stands as a definitive statement. His opening sentence provides an intentionally narrow definition of validation: "The process of examining the accuracy of a specific prediction or inference made from a test score" (p. 443). A footnote addendum on the same page suggests that Cronbach might have preferred to see validity applied in a broader context, although his own efforts produced the opposite result. Limiting his discussion to tests, Cronbach nonetheless noted that validation refers to the "soundness of *all* the interpretations of a test—descriptive and explanatory interpretations as well as situation-bound predictions":

> For simplicity, I refer to tests and test scores throughout the chapter. The statements, however, apply to all procedures for collecting data, including observations, questionnaires, ratings of artistic products, etc. Most statements apply to protocols and qualitative summaries as well as to numerical scores. For some writers, *to validate* means to demonstrate the worth of, but I intend to stress the openness of the process—i.e., *to validate* is *to investigate*. (p. 443n; emphasis in original)

Perhaps it is ironic that the "enshrinement" of construct validation—as Cronbach himself describes it (1986, p. 86)—occurred with publication of his own co-authored article "Construct Validity in Psychological Tests" (Cronbach & Meehl, 1955). At that time, as Sandy Charters has observed (personal communication, April 21, 1988), validity became "irretrievably ensconced in the positivistic tradition and the hypothetico-deductive mode of explanation." If the word *test* did not appear at every mention of validity, it was nonetheless implied. Consider, for example, this explanation from Roger Brown's *Social Psychology* (1965), an authoritative source in its day:

> The problem of validity is the problem of what the data *indicate*. Have we measured what we have undertaken to measure? In one very limited sphere the notion of test validity has a precise meaning. If a psychologist has devised a test for the purpose of selecting men who will be able to do well on some job or task then the validity of the test is the correlation between test scores and the quality of job performance. The job is the *criterion* for the test and the test's validity is measured against its criterion. (p. 438; emphasis in original)

Somewhere between then and now—and I refer specifically to three decades when I thought I had been paying attention to such things—the word *test* seems to have been eased out. In an age of growing self-consciousness and sophistication about scientific measurement, the evolution of validity as a desirable but ambiguously defined criterion for *all* research may have been something like this:

Test validity
Validity of test data
Validity of test and measurement data
Validity of research data on tests and measurements
Validity of research data
Validity of research

Today one finds enthusiastic endorsements for validity easily at hand. This one is from anthropologists Pertti and Gretel Pelto (1978):

"Validity" refers to the degree to which scientific observations actually measure or record what they purport to measure. . . . In their field research anthropologists have invested much effort to achieve validity, for we generally assume that a long-term stay in a community facilitates the differentiation of what is valid from what is not, and the assembling of contextual supporting information to buttress claims to validity. (p. 33)

An adaptation of this definition for educational research appears in Goetz and LeCompte (1984):

Validity is concerned with the accuracy of scientific findings. Establishing validity requires (1) determining the extent to which conclusions effectively represent empirical reality and (2) assessing whether constructs devised by researchers represent or measure the categories of human experience that occur. (p. 210)

Who would have dreamed that educational researchers in any number might someday pay heed to so-called qualitative approaches or comprise a ready audience for books with titles such as *Doing the Ethnography of Schooling* (Spindler, 1982) or *Ethnography and Qualitative Design in Educational Research* (Goetz & LeCompte, 1984)? Even twenty-five years ago, who would have believed that quantities-oriented educational researchers would make room for and eventually begin a dialogue with qualities-oriented ones? We should hardly be surprised or offended by the assumption that the vocabulary of *their* perceived world would constitute the language of the dialogue. Questions they addressed to us were the ones they pondered among themselves, for example, "How do you deal with the issue of validity?"

And instead of replying, "That's your problem," we too hastily replied, "We've got it." From whatever moment concern for formal validity was first expressed, qualitative researchers in education appear to have been defending and, for the most part, successfully demonstrating claims about validity. Perhaps we wanted to divert attention from uneasy anticipation about a parallel question concerning reliability, the extent to which studies can be replicated, which, as Goetz and LeCompte (1984) note, poses a "herculean problem for researchers concerned with naturalistic behavior or unique phenomena" (p. 211). Given the choice, we've steered the conversation toward validity: "Reliability poses serious threats to the credibility of much ethnographic work. However, validity may be its major strength" (p. 221).

The reason I tend to confuse the two terms is that for me their esoteric meanings among researchers are the very opposite of their everyday ones. The synonyms and "related words" given for *validity* in my thesaurus include *cogency* (appealing, convincing), *efficacy* (power to produce an effect), *force, punch, persuasiveness,* and *potency.* For me, these terms conjure up a "might makes right" approach. Among the qualities I seek in research, I would rather my work be regarded as *provocative* than as *persuasive.* On the other hand, I feel honored when someone describes me (as observer) or one of my accounts as *reliable.*

I suspect that claims about validity reveal a similar kind of confusion—the consequence of taking a term overspecified in one domain and reassigning it a more satisfying, intuitive, and global definition in another. Validity has a technical set of microdefinitions relating to correspondence (Brinberg & McGrath, 1982). It can point to critically focused macrodefinitions as well, relating at one extreme to truth value and, at the other, to external validity as implied in such terms as *dependability, generalizability,* or "robustness" (p. 12). But my sense is that except for those hypothetico-deductive types mentioned earlier, validity serves most often as a gloss for *scientific accuracy* among those who identify closely with science and for *correctness* or *credibility* among those who do not.

What is it about ethnographic and other qualitative approaches to research that leads us to boast that validity may well be our "major strength"? Let me address that issue before turning to the broader one: whether validity is well suited as a criterion, guideline, or objective for qualitative approaches to research.

SEEKING VALIDITY, OR
ON NOT GETTING IT ALL WRONG

I have quoted the following words from Clifford Geertz's (1973) essay "Thick Description" so often that I am coming to think of them as my own:

Cultural analysis is intrinsically incomplete. And, worse than that, the more deeply it goes the less complete it is. It is a strange science whose most telling assertions are its most tremulously based, in which to get somewhere with the matter at hand is to intensify the suspicion, both your own and that of others, that you are not quite getting it right. (p. 29)

I assume that by "cultural analysis" Geertz refers both to what one is attempting to describe and how one interprets it. Thus we can say of field studies in general that "to get somewhere with the matter at hand is to intensify the suspicion . . . that you are not quite getting it right."

But I also go to considerable pains not to get it all wrong. At least in its broad sense of scientific accuracy or correctness, validity haunts qualitative researchers as a specter, even if it may not be precisely the quality we seek. Others have offered arguments to show why validity can be claimed, either in their work or on behalf of qualitative researchers in general (e.g., Goetz & LeCompte, 1984, p. 221), and I take this opportunity to do the same.

In nine points that follow, I have described what I do, try to do, or think I do to satisfy the implicit challenge of validity. I hasten to add that I probably do some of these things to keep the question from being raised at all, since it can be one of those accusations not lightly dismissed even if subsequently refuted. There is no particular order to the points as presented, although I more or less follow a progression from early stages of fieldwork, devoted primarily to getting information, through later stages given more fully to analysis and writing.

Talk Little, Listen a Lot

Like any fieldworker, I have some personal qualities that I believe serve me well in research. A seemingly unlikely one (about which others may disagree) is that I regard myself as neither particularly talkative nor particularly gregarious. I am basically a loner in thought and work; I do not like to be lonely, but I enjoy and need solitude when pursuing my academic tasks. It requires great patience under any circumstances for me to "sit and visit." A rather inevitable consequence of being inquisitive without being a talker is that my conversational queries usually prompt others to do the talking. During fieldwork, I make a conscious effort to be sociable, thus providing opportunities for people to talk to me. My work ethic takes over to help me become not only more social but more attentive and responsive, and out pour the informants' stories and explanations so essential to good fieldwork.

(Parenthetically, I note my suspicion that many fieldworkers talk too much and hear too little. They become their own worst enemy by becoming their own best informant. (This is especially serious in school research, where we often presume to "know" what is supposed to be happening and consequently may never ask the kinds of questions we would ordinarily ask in any other research setting. I have suggested elsewhere [Wolcott, 1984] that educational researchers need to be wary of this "ethnography minus one" approach.)

Since no one ever can say everything about anything, in virtually any conversation, and especially during fieldwork, I find myself pondering what part of the whole story is being told and what part of that I am actually understanding. Like most of us, I *think* I sense when I am getting a straight story, when I am getting a story straight, and when I am on a detour of my own or another's making. If the latter, I usually try to swing by that way another time. I never confront informants with contradictions, blatant disbelief, or shock, but I do not mind presenting myself as a bit dense, someone who does not catch on too quickly and has to have things repeated or explained—what Kirk and Miller (1986) describe as "willing to look a fool for the sake of science" (p. 49).

Record Accurately

Whenever I engage in fieldwork I try to record as accurately as possible, and in precisely their words, what I judge to be important of what people do and say. I note that this occurs during formal fieldwork because, unlike some ethnographers, I am not a regular diary keeper. Rather, like most of them, I detest notetaking, in part because I tend to be so meticulous about it. I record field notes only when my work ethic demands. When I do take notes, I endeavor to make them as soon as possible after an event, if not at that moment. I prefer to make notes *during* observations or interviews—including written notes to supplement mechanically recorded ones. (It is not a bad idea to remind people of one's research presence and purposes.) By recording as soon as possible, to capture words and events as observed, I try to minimize the potential influence of some line of interpretation or analysis that might have me remembering and recording too selectively or reinterpreting behavior prior to recording it.

Begin Writing Early

Since I do not work quickly anyway, I make something of a fetish of taking my time at fieldwork. In seeming contrast, however—because I have come to regard writing as an integral part of fieldwork rather than as a separate stage initiated after fieldwork is completed—I often begin preparing a rough draft soon after fieldwork begins. Most recently I have suggested that qualitative researchers consider writing a preliminary draft of a descriptively oriented study before even venturing into the field (Wolcott, 1990). The intent is twofold: to make a record of what one already knows or suspects and to identify obvious gaps where more information will be needed.

In every study in which I have begun writing early, I have been able to share a draft (but not that first one, by any means) with others knowledgeable about the setting. Thus I obtain valuable feedback for myself and sometimes provide welcome feedback for others who may have expressed curiosity or concern about what I was observing and what kind of story I would tell.

To borrow a phrase from linguistics, my accounts move forward by "successive approximations." It would be nice if that meant they became successively more accurate; I suspect they only become successively better contextualized (i.e., more complex). But I try to "stick around" long enough, and keep in touch long afterward, so that events observed can be reviewed from the perspective of time—for observer and observed alike. Twenty-seven years after beginning fieldwork, I am still in contact with Kwakiutl families I met in 1962 (Wolcott, 1989). Twenty years after initiating a study of the principalship in 1966, I sat down with "Ed Bell" to record his reflections on that study and his now-completed career as an educational administrator. And in neither of those studies—nor in any of my others—does it seem that I have ever quite gotten it right.

In spite of extending one's fieldwork and one's subsequent reflections over time, I begin making detailed notes immediately upon initiating fieldwork, as I pointed out before. Right or wrong as first impressions may be, I feel they should be carefully recorded as a baseline from which the work proceeds. First impressions also serve as a useful resource in subsequent writing. Through them, researchers can introduce readers to settings the way they themselves first encountered them, rather than in the presumably more discerning way they have come to see them through extended time for observation and reflection.

Let Readers "See" for Themselves

I make a conscious effort to include primary data in my final accounts, not only to give readers an idea of what my data are like but to give access to the data themselves. In striking the delicate balance between providing too much detail and too little, I would rather err on the side of too much; conversely, between overanalyzing and underanalyzing data, I would rather say too little. Accordingly, my accounts are often lengthy; informants are given a forum for presenting their own case to whatever extent possible and reasonable. This poses a dilemma: In reading the descriptive accounts of others, I confess that I often skip over the quoted material in my haste to "get right at it" and see what the researcher made of it all; yet I knowingly risk boring my readers with potentially tedious detail.[1]

More subtly, my growing bias toward letting informants speak for themselves is exactly that—a bias in favor of trying to capture the expressed thoughts of others rather than relying too singularly on what I have observed and interpreted. The extent to which participant-observation and interviewing are a natural complement or get at quite different aspects of thought and action has always vexed experienced fieldworkers (see, for example, Bernard, Killworth, Kronenfeld, & Sailer, 1984; Dean & Whyte, 1958; Freeman & Romney, 1988). Terms like *triangulation* and *multi-instrument approach* may strike neophytes as ample safeguard against error in qualitative research, but anyone who has done fieldwork knows that if you address a question of any consequence to more than one informant, you may as well prepare for more than one answer. I try to report what I observe and to offer an informed interpretation of those observations, my own or someone else's. But only the most central of issues in one's research warrant the thorough probing implied by triangulation. We are better off reminding readers that our data sources are limited, and that our informants have not necessarily gotten things right either, than implying that we would never dream of reporting an unchecked fact or unverified claim.

Report Fully

I am not disconcerted by data that do not fit the developing account or my interpretation of it. That does not mean I report every discrepant detail, but I do keep such bits and pieces in front of me (often, quite literally, on 5" × 8" cards) as a way of testing my efforts at making sense of things. Sometimes a comment or observation can be introduced via brackets or footnote to flag an issue that is not as well resolved as the prose implies or not developed more fully because my data are "thin" or certain events never occurred during the period of fieldwork.

When I can do so without seeming too obtuse, I also include comments and observations that I do not understand or for which I feel I have no better basis for discerning meanings than might the reader. To illustrate: A Kwakiutl parent commented during a discussion about the kind of teacher best suited to a village assignment, "I think what we need here is a teacher who isn't *too* smart" (Wolcott, 1967, p. 85). I did not know exactly what he meant, and I still do not (although I have a hunch). I included it without comment—and today it continues to provoke *possible* interpretations every bit as plausible as my own.

Be Candid

I opt for subjectivity as a strength of qualitative approaches rather than attempt to establish a detached objectivity that I am not sure I want or need. As I am doing here, I have always put myself squarely into the settings or situations being described to whatever extent seemed warranted for the purpose at hand. With some fear and trepidation, I introduced that strategy in my doctoral dissertation, and committee members raised no concern except for the question of excess. I decided that if I could get away with it there, I certainly could be as forthright in the future when writing to satisfy myself.

To the extent that my feelings and personal reactions seem relevant to a case, I try to reveal them: The greater their possible influence, the more attention they receive and the earlier they appear in the account. In writing *Teachers Versus Technocrats* (1977), I was distressed both by the nature of a project designed to impose greater accountability on public education and by the heavy-handed manner by which it was being implemented. As a result, I began the monograph with a chapter titled "Caution—Bias at Work" to bare my feelings and objections.

How far to go with personal revelation? I see no easy resolution. The issue has become of more immediate concern than I could have imagined, as will become apparent in the course of this essay. Qualitative research has brought researchers self-consciously back into the research setting. That has been healthy for all, including those quantitative types who wanted everyone to believe that they were not part of their own investigations. Yet when someone remarks, often charitably, "I learned as much about you in your study as I did about the people you were studying," I feel dismay at the likelihood of having taken more light than I have shed.

I try to draw a distinction between revealing my feelings and imposing my judgments, however. If circumstances call for me to draw implications or suggest possible remedies, I try to "change hats" conspicuously. There is simply no way one can get from a descriptive account of what is to a prescriptive account of what should be done about it. Those are value judgments. Granted, such judgments are critical to the work of practicing educators. It is appropriate for them to seek whatever help they can, and for us to be prepared to offer help, but we need to clearly mark the boundaries where research stops and reform begins. A different set of principles must be employed to validate our personal or professional authority to offer pronouncements about what needs improving and how to go about it.

The big value judgments are easy to spot because words like *should* and *ought* abound in sentences containing them. There are opportunities for eliminating little judgments as well, simply by careful use of the editing pencil. Little words of judgment creep into all kinds of sentences but can be rounded up and marched right off the page again. Consider the difference between reporting, "Only one villager had ever graduated from high school" versus "One villager had graduated from high school," or "Few pupils were at task" versus "Five pupils appeared to be engaged in the assignment."

Seek Feedback

I share my developing manuscripts with informed readers as part of the process of analyzing and writing. Rather than a mass distribution of a manuscript in next-to-last draft, what I have in mind is a continuous process of asking one or more individuals to read the current version. Academic colleagues are usually good for one careful reading at most; there is little point in pressing busy people for more, but no excuse for not asking at all.

Accuracy of reported information is one critical dimension, and readers close to the setting provide yeoman service by checking for correctness and completeness. Further, their reactions sometimes help me recognize where the reporting or the interpretation (or both) seems overblown or underdeveloped. Readers not so closely involved can also be helpful in assessing the suitability of my analytical concepts, my sensitivity to the people involved, or the adequacy and appropriateness of interpretations made and lessons drawn. Readers who disavow their expertise or their familiarity with protocol in qualitative research may offer valuable suggestions about style and sequence, may question inadequate explanations or definitions, or may express straightforward but intuitive reactions conveyed in such statements as, "I just don't see what you are getting at here." I also like to circulate working drafts among my graduate students. In terms of providing feedback, they are not necessarily one's severest critics, but even when they are not, they keep me mindful of my audience. In addition, it is valuable for them to have a glimpse of manuscripts in process rather than to have access only to polished final accounts.

Am I straying from validity? I believe not. I am describing a constellation of activities intended not only to help *me* get things right (or keep me from getting them all wrong) but to convey ideas in such a way that the *reader*, who is also not quite getting it right, is not getting it all wrong, either. I am willing to admit that some of this activity is image building, intended to create the *impression* that my accounts are credible. To the extent that is true, I can only add that having gone to great lengths to make such an impression, there is no particular reason not to work to live up to it.

Try to Achieve Balance

At some particular point or points in the writing/revision process, I take time either to return to the field setting or, second best, to read entirely through my field notes one more time (why do I find that so onerous a chore?). Then I reread my current draft to assess the extent to which the account I have created squares with the setting and individuals on which it is based. Objectivity is not my criterion as much as what might be termed *rigorous subjectivity* (or "disciplined subjectivity," following Erickson, 1973, p. 15). It is I who must be satisfied now, with elusive criteria like balance, fairness, completeness, sensitivity.

Ed Bell raised the question of balance in reacting to my study of him in his role as principal (Wolcott, 1973), but the issue exists in every study I have conducted. He found my reporting sufficiently accurate but nonetheless expressed dismay that the recounting of his problems (e.g., teacher evaluation, parent complaints, disagreements with the central office about his "leadership style") received a disproportionate amount of attention. Ed literally worked day and night to smooth out problems and to create a positive, constructive atmosphere. I meticulously uncovered and examined every little malfunction to show what a principal must contend with.

Had I conveyed the minute-by-minute routine of Taft School during those two years, I think I would have fallen asleep writing about it long before anyone could have fallen asleep reading about it. Somehow I had to communicate the customary "hum" of a smoothly functioning elementary school while also assuring readers that the account would probe beneath the surface. Now, years later, Ed insists that my study helped him because it enabled him to see things that "needed improving." Even he has forgotten what he once expressed as "real disappointment" at the perceived lack of balance in my account.

Write Accurately

As a parallel activity to the field check just described, at one or more points during the rewriting process I read through a manuscript with an eye for what might be called technical accuracy. This stage usually comes rather late, prompted by feelings that the content and interpretation are pretty well in place but that I still need to make an almost word-by-word assessment of the manuscript. One such check is for coherence or internal consistency. Much as coherence may appear to be a concession to the strictures of validity, I think of it more as an element of style. I accept as a compliment that something I have written appears to have "internal validity," but frankly I regard consistency (which I think is implied) as much an author's trick as it is revealing of research acumen. That our studies are so free of inner contradiction ought really to set us wondering how they can be describing human behavior. As long as we employ consistency as a criterion, however, we will continue to find it in full measure.

There is another kind of internal review that seems more critical. I have no better term for it than a "word check." I mean a literal sentence-by-sentence examination to check that the verbs are appropriate, the generalizations have real referents in what I have seen or heard, and the points of conjecture are marked with appropriate tentativeness. Admittedly, some part of this task is also a kind of window-dressing. At a minimum I strive to make every sentence technically correct. I confess to having written sentences that virtually defy editing because they cannot be changed and still retain their truth element. (I give my own special meaning to "technical writing"—sentences that are correct as written but actually reveal how little, rather than how much, I know.) Still, in attempting to satisfy canons of technical accuracy, I try as well to be forthright (or sometimes just more modest, if that is what the circumstances warrant). The fact that a sentence needs fine honing serves notice that maybe it should not remain in the manuscript.

If such intentional wordsmithing seems unbecoming in scholarly work, it seems better dealt with head-on than by wishing it away from so human an undertaking as the human reporting of human social life. Qualitatively oriented studies of what goes on in laboratory life, the bastion of true science, do more than hint that comparable efforts at the social construction of facts are not unknown among so-called hard scientists as well (see, for example, Gould, 1981; LaTour & Woolgar, 1986).

Wordsmithing also has its complementary and lighter side in sometimes allowing researchers to convey more, rather than less, information or to keep confidences. Let me illustrate with two sentences from *A Kwakiutl Village and School* (1967) describing tensions that arose over thefts of teachers' personal property in outlying villages:

> During the year five teachers in local day schools suffered losses by theft either of personal property taken from the teacherages or of skiffs and kickers [small outboard motors]. Two thefts were privately resolved between teachers and villagers, two were reported to the RCMP, and no action was taken on the fifth. (p. 87)

Over the Christmas holiday, someone literally had "taken the fifth," a bottle of liquor hidden among the belongings of an older female teacher concerned as to whether she was breaking the law by bringing liquor onto the reserve in the first place. She dared not report the loss. She also felt some personal awkwardness, recognizing that the theft implicated a particular villager. Those of us who knew about her missing liquor had our chuckle and felt vindicated because all the thefts—with their demoralizing impact on everyone involved—had been reported accurately without exacerbating hard feelings.

Having reviewed some of the procedures I follow that provide the basis on which I would claim validity—were I pressed to claim it—I have come to the end of this part of my paper. These activities are my "answer" to validity, but reviewing them has only confirmed my feeling that the more important issue before us is to examine whether validity is the right question.

WHEN IT REALLY MATTERS, DOES VALIDITY REALLY MATTER?

The points developed in the preceding discussion of validity-enhancing procedures were extracted from my own experience and my completed studies. Four monographs constitute the major evidence I can present on behalf of validity or any other criterion on which qualitative research may be judged: *A Kwakiutl Village and School* (1967), *The Man in the Principal's Office: An Ethnography* (1973), *The African Beer Gardens of Bulawayo: Integrated Drinking in a Segregated Society* (1974), and *Teachers Versus Techno-*

crats: An Educational Innovation in Anthropological Perspective (1977). Two modest field-based studies have been reported in shorter articles, one describing efforts at community development (1983b), another dealing with the introduction of a program for instructional television (1984). Although I would be loathe to dissect the studies of others in a critical essay on validity, neither would I ordinarily have put my own works forward on its behalf. As already noted, validity neither guides nor informs my work. What I seek is not unrelated to validity, but "validity" does not capture its essence and is not the right term. I am hard pressed to identify the expression that is.

To support my position, let me turn from cases concluded and published to some personal experience coupled with ongoing research that currently occupies some of my time and much of my thought—a study begun but not completed. In this current preoccupation, I am not the least preoccupied with validity. By describing these circumstances, I hope to raise valid questions about validity for you as reader. Be forewarned: The account may also raise some question for you about me.

The case has its origins in three rather independent events. (There are similar "event chains" in all our work.) One was an effort I made at "fine-tuning" my professional career. Coinciding with my fiftieth birthday, I made a self-conscious decision to focus my teaching and research more on how culture is acquired—a social process in which humans engage individually—and less on schools and what is done in their efforts to transmit it. Originally I referred to this as "the anthropology of learning" (Wolcott, 1982a), although "culture acquisition," the phrase I use today, points more accurately to my particular interest. I raised the idea of an "anthropology of learning" in conversation with colleagues and asked what they felt it should embrace and how we might approach it. Frederick Erickson's personal counsel was direct and to the point, "First of all, get yourself a learner." I was on the lookout for a learner.

The second event was an invitation from the director of a federally funded project at the U.S. Department of Education to prepare an essay on educational adequacy. The intent of the project, as I understood it, was to explore ways of assessing whether each state was providing "adequate" education and to suggest how state efforts might be subsidized with federal funds, were they to become available. It sounded like a task for economists, and apparently a number of them had been commissioned to write papers. The project now sought broader perspectives, I was told, "such as you might provide as a sociologist." Wrong discipline, I realized, but the project officer seemed undaunted when I asked whether I could prepare an anthropologically oriented case study of one individual rather than take on so ambitious a topic as an equitable way to allocate federal dollars. I was assured that I was free to approach the topic as I wished, provided that I addressed the issue of educational adequacy. I sensed an opportunity to dramatize the useful but often overlooked distinction between schooling and education by presenting a case contrasting adequate schools and inadequate education.

The third element of this story had its beginning about a year earlier, in the kind of circumstance ethnographers often refer to as serendipity, although in retrospect I am not sure that is the right term. In a remote part of the hilly and densely wooded twenty-acre tract on which I live, a young man, then aged nineteen, had been constructing a crude but sturdy cabin and was also attempting to construct an independent survival-style life on his own. He had freed himself from most of the trappings of the workaday world, eking out a living on food stamps, reducing cash expenses to the minimum, scrounging what he could, and taking whatever else he felt he needed. Although he had roamed this countryside as a youth, he did not know on whose property he had built his cabin, perhaps hoping he had chosen public land adjacent to mine. His first question when I discovered him and his cabin after several weeks was, "Can I stay?" Belligerence seemed just beneath the surface, but I could not see how I could claim to be any kind of humanitarian and throw him off the property. I allowed him to remain.

I seldom saw him in the next few months, although I did stop by from time to time to see how he was getting on and occasionally hired him to work for me. The following winter he asked if I would let him dig a 700-foot trench for a new water line to the house rather than contract the work out as I had planned. Together we installed the line, a major undertaking. In the course of a year of casual contact, then working together on an ambitious project, he became more talkative and revealing about himself. We found ourselves becoming more intimately involved, psychologically at first, and, in time, physically. After that there seemed no topic that we could not discuss, no aspects of his (or my) life about which we did not talk freely.

On the basis of the long-term and now candid nature of our relationship, I began thinking about doing a life history with him, recognizing that he seemed willing, even eager, to discuss his "experiences," his outlook, and his deliberate effort to put his life together. He presented an unusual opportunity to learn about a life dramatically different from my own or those of the people I ordinarily meet as a university professor. About this time I received the invitation from Washington, D.C., giving me both impetus and focus to proceed more systematically on a project that until then was only a gradual realization that I had found my "learner"—literally in my own backyard.

He agreed to the study, estimating that it would take him about six hours to narrate his life story into a taperecorder. To start, we planned to record in sessions of up to an hour. On the day we began, he spoke quickly and uninterruptedly for about twelve minutes, concluding with, "So here I am up at the cabin." Then he announced, "That's it!" His account was finished.

From that moment, getting his life story in more detail and putting it together into a cohesive narrative was up to me. He was paid for his interview time, the dollars providing adequate motivation once initial enthusiasm waned. He also was paid to review the manuscript, and at his request I deleted minor portions that sounded "dumb" to him. "If only to please me," I noted in a subsequent footnote, "he even commented that he hoped his story might 'help people understand.'"

I felt that his story did reveal a different lifestyle, presented in an integrated fashion, in contrast to the bits and pieces of most newspaper articles or educator and sociological accounts of dropouts, drifters, or the young alienated-and-unemployed. I received encouragement to make the case more widely available. I retained the title but changed the subtitle of the original report (Wolcott, 1982b) when it appeared in slightly revised and elaborated form in the *Anthropology and Education Quarterly* as "Adequate Schools and Inadequate Education: The Life History of a Sneaky Kid" (Wolcott, 1983a). "Sneaky Kid" was a reference he once made to himself; I assigned him the pseudonym Brad.

By that pseudonym, Brad is on his way to becoming fairly well known in educator circles, particularly among qualitative researchers. In spite of the intrigue and events subsequent to publication of "Sneaky Kid," methodologically I think the piece offers a good model for life history in educational research, and I unabashedly point to it as such. Subsequently, when I was asked to identify an illustrative example to accompany my chapter, "Ethnographic Research in Education" (Wolcott, 1988), for an edited volume describing several "alternative" approaches to research in education, the Sneaky Kid article was my choice, for several reasons. It is journal length. It is told largely in the (edited) words of a key informant. It is well focused. And it attempts to offer some insight at the same time that it raises a host of provocative questions.

(Needless to say, eyebrows have been raised about becoming intimately involved with an informant, even for those who recognize that the ways humans become involved with each other—physically and emotionally—far exceed the prescriptions our various societies endeavor so diligently to impose. I note emphatically that our mutual involve-ment *preceded* the life history project and in a sense opened the way for another dimension in our relationship and dialogue. It was during our long conversations—or, more accurately, innumerable short conversa-tions over what was becoming an extended period of time—that I realized how, with a host of personal concerns now an open topic between us, Brad talked fairly easily about everything that comprised his "world." Here, at last, was one time I would finally get it right.)

A few days after celebrating a twenty-first birthday that marked his second full year at the cabin, Brad abruptly announced that he had decided to leave. The previous weeks had been a time of terrible mental turmoil for him, coupled with strange behavior and increasingly longer periods when he appeared depressed and disoriented. As he tearfully announced his decision, he consoled me with, "I'm sorry; I know you liked me." By this time, with the exception of occasional and almost rib-crushing hugs, our physical relationship had ended, but the dialogue had not. He insisted that he had to "hit the road," although he seemed to have no corresponding idea about where he would go or what he would do. I urged him to take a few days to review his options, which he agreed to do. He became more distraught with each passing day. I was able to get him to talk to counselors at the county mental health office, but they offered no dramatic action and he was impatient for some-thing—anything, really—to happen. By the end of the week, he was gone.

Several weeks later I received an unexpected telephone call from Brad's mother in southern California. Contrary to his stated inten-tions, Brad had returned to the community (but not the home—he was not welcome in the home of either of his estranged parents) where his mother had relocated after divorce and where he himself had briefly attended high school before dropping out. She succeeded in getting him under psychiatric review and county outpatient care. Brad made one telephone call to me shortly after arriving in southern California, during a brief period when he voluntarily committed himself to a mental institution. After that, I did not hear from him again. He did not respond to my letters.

I had scant information about his current status. In reflecting about his final days at the cabin, however, I realized that I had gained considerable insight into a whole new set of alternatives facing young people like Brad—options quite different from any that would ever occur to me. Without any particular audience in mind, I began drafting a sequel to the Sneaky Kid article focused on events precipitated during that final week. (Geertz, 1973, p. 19, asks rhetorically, "What does the ethnographer do? He writes.") I hoped that the process of writing would help me sort out complex and conflicting feelings of personal loss and social responsibility and provide a genuine test for the power of cultural explanation.

The writing did not come easily, and I felt that for the most part I was writing to and for myself. When eventually completed, however, the account seemed to fit with a collection of qualitative studies being planned and edited by George Noblit and William Pink as *Schooling in Social Context*. My paper "Life's Not Working: Cultural Alternatives to Career Alternatives" (Wolcott, 1987) was accepted for that volume.

In the body of the chapter, I reported that after his departure, I never saw Brad again. But in that always-interminable delay between rushing off a contributed chapter and waiting to see the final copy-edited version of it, Brad did come back, unexpectedly and unannounced. With him came tragedy. At that point all I could do was add a long footnote recording events recently past and presaging others yet to come:

> In the interim between completion of the manuscript and publication of the book, Brad did return, just as several readers of early drafts predicted. Within hours of his arrival he provided sufficient evidence of "craziness" to be incarcerated. Long beyond the moment for timely help, the state's resources for dealing with him punitively seemed limitless.
>
> I do not yet understand those events or their meaning in terms of Brad's life or my own well enough to relate them; I am not sure I ever will. Bizarre as they are, the ensuing events do not change what I have written. In retrospect, my comments seem almost prophetic. But Brad had been equally prophetic years earlier when he reflected on what had been and what was yet to be: "I always seem to screw things up at the end." (Wolcott, 1987, p. 317n)

Initially, Brad was charged with attempted murder. I was the principal victim. The district attorney's office decided not to press that charge ("Too hard to prove," they explained), opting for assault and battery instead. But the major crime for which he was charged was arson. Hours before my return home from the campus one evening in November 1984, Brad had broken into the house, siphoned 500 gallons of stove oil onto the floors from a storage tank on the hillside above, taken my chainsaw to cut holes in the ceilings and roof, and trashed the house, so that the instant he poured on gasoline and ignited it, the place would become an inferno. Then he waited until I walked into his deadly ambush.

My long-time companion, Norman, returned home during the course of Brad's maniacal attack and interrupted what had to that moment seemed my quick and inevitable demise. Norman's arrival lent an element of distraction that provided opportunity for me to escape only seconds before Brad "torched" the house. The arson inspector described it as the hottest fire he had ever investigated. The destruction was total.

While still in the emergency room being stitched back together, I realized that my worldly possessions now numbered three: an old Chevrolet and two Bic pens. Even the clothing I had worn—blood and oil soaked—was confiscated for evidence. Neither did anything of Norman's survive, except the clothes he was wearing. Our losses included my entire professional library—a devastating loss to me—as well as field notes from my studies, all my lecture and reading notes, and, for each of us, a lifetime accumulation of family memorabilia and household goods, as well as slide photography, recorded music, art and artifacts from all over the world. (Except in latest revision, however, working manuscripts were spared—from my first days in the field, I have always kept backup copies of manuscripts at my campus office.)

Brad was quickly apprehended. By morning he had confessed to the arson and assault, basing his rationale on damage I had caused to his delusional "Hollywood career" and insisting that everything about our relationship had been anathema to him. He left unexplained the haunting phrase he repeated while battering and attempting to subdue me, "You hate me. You hate me." He voluntarily gave an oral confession to police, but when formally charged he changed his plea to the frequently heard "guilty but insane."

That plea tripped a whole new host of events. Each side, prosecution and defense, got the psychiatric opinion they sought (or bought?), and the case headed into court for a jury vote as to Brad's sanity. Technically the verdict turned on whether he was assumed able to "conform" his actions while planning and carrying out the arson and assault. The consulting psychiatrists were in agreement with each other (and with written reports forwarded from people working with Brad during the previous two and a half years) that his symptoms exhibited what is known as a paranoid schizophrenic disorder.

The trial proved a professional as well as a personal nightmare. Although I was "allegedly" (to use court terminology) the victim, for the first four days of the trial I became the defendant while a carping public defender built a case to suggest I had gotten what I deserved. The Sneaky Kid article was introduced and leveled against us both, destroying intended confidentiality and revealing Brad to have been often at odds with school and society, dating back long before his days at reform school. At the same time, the article was turned against me to show both how gullible and how ruthless I was. Under oath, Brad's mother insisted he had made up most of it—this, the story I felt I had finally gotten right—simply to impress me. A further implication was that I had extracted the story in order to enhance my career and thus had exploited Brad not only sexually but professionally as well.

Eventually the drawn-out trial turned to the issue of Brad's sanity, each psychiatrist having a literal "day in court" as expert witness. (The courtroom approach to validity is a different game entirely. The essence seems not to attempt to validate one's own position but to discredit [impugn] all others.) Three weeks after the jury was convened, they returned the guilty verdict, rejecting the insanity plea. The presentence investigation recommended that Brad be sentenced to a *minimum* of ten years. The judge commented on the severity of the crime, ritually imposed a "severe" twenty-year sentence, and urged that Brad be considered for psychiatric assessment and assistance in prison. However, he imposed no minimum sentence: The bets were that Brad would be released in thirty months. (My next social "cause" may be for truth-in-sentencing!)

Brad's tentative parole date was set for the three-year anniversary of the crime. When he did not do well on a prerelease psychological assessment, his tentative release date was postponed for twelve months.

New victims' rights laws in effect since the trial allow limited access to parole information at the time of such hearings (and would have allowed me to be present during the trial, from which I was then excluded except when testifying). Other than at formal hearings, however, the prison walls effectively barred me from all information about Brad except whether he was actually in custody. For most of the time he was assigned to a special voluntary program for emotionally and mentally disturbed inmates.

Long before this chapter appears in print, Brad will have been released. Unless the risk to society could be shown to be clear and substantial, detaining him longer had to be weighed against the negative effects of the prison environment and, more critically, chronic overcrowding in the state's institutions.

I cannot predict how all this will end: Prediction is not the long suit in social science. The probabilities would be difficult enough to estimate even with all available information at hand, and I have been able to glean virtually no information at all. My own sense is that when he has the opportunity, Brad is likely to return to do more harm. It does not seem unthinkable that he might attempt to kill me or to destroy what Norman and I have attempted to rebuild of our lives.

I make that statement somewhat dispassionately. My last encounter with Brad pretty well eliminated any thoughts I had about immortality. Had Norman not returned at the moment he did, my chances for surviving that evening would not have been good. As I see it, my fate at Brad's hands turns on whether he still nurtures the hatred and convoluted ideas that rationalized his violence in the first place. A psychiatrist whom I consulted—who also expressed surprise at my lack of awareness that April and October are particularly stressful months for mental patients and that the attack had occurred during a period of full moon—suggested that the critical unknown is what triggered Brad's violent response and under what circumstances a similar reaction might be precipitated again. That, in turn, will depend on his present mental health and—more unknowns—the extent and consequences of any current medication or new interpersonal involvement. I assume Brad has been well coached as to appropriate responses in this regard, for he stated in my presence at his earlier parole hearing, "I don't even think about Harry Wolcott any more." How comforting it would be were I able to assess the validity of his claim.

THE ABSURDITY OF VALIDITY

Let me return summarily to my academic purpose. Although there are aspects of all this about which valued colleagues may not be well informed, I am not trying to engage in "confessional" anthropology. Furthermore, should this account suddenly seem to have taken a confessional turn, it is the earlier how-I-really-go-about-fieldwork section to which that label properly applies, at least according to the typology suggested by John Van Maanen (1988) distinguishing among realist, confessional, and impressionist styles for writing ethnography. To the extent I can lay claim to be acting as ethnographer in a case in which I have become so centrally involved, I exemplify Van Maanen's "impressionist" mode. The ethnographer's intention in the impressionist mode, he explains, "is not to tell readers what to think of an experience but to show them the experience from beginning to end and thus draw them immediately into the story to work out its problems and puzzles as they unfold" (p. 103).

I might note here a critical but instructive reaction of my students to an earlier and even more highly personal version of this account.

"Had you been given one of the other conference topics, would this still be the paper you would have written?" they asked. My answer had to be "Probably yes," at least to the extent of seeing the opportunity to clarify certain matters and to write about problems of genuine—and in this case personal and pressing—concern rather than of only "professional" interest. I hasten to add, however, that I *always* try to present issues in terms of concrete and complex illustrations, guided by Geertz's maxim that there is no ascent to truth without a corresponding descent to cases. I also think it instructive and provocative to examine cases that are open, confounding, and of immediate consequence, rather than to retreat always to cases where known outcomes make us appear so much wiser in our ability to explain them. (See Kaplan's [1964] distinction between reconstructed logic and logic-in-use.) My long-held suspicion that validity does not serve well as a criterion or goal for qualitative research seems to me to find firm ground in examining how I am trying to understand the circumstances I have described.

My mind swirls constantly with questions and concerns about the events and circumstances I have related, not only as a personal matter but in terms of a multiplicity of social issues on which they touch. Mental health, justice, social responsibility, morality, mortality, ethics— they are all here. As qualitatively oriented researchers portraying and reflecting upon them, what can we bring to or take from this case? What is the nature of the contribution we can make? And what criteria are most helpful in guiding our efforts or evaluating our results?

For my personal health, safety, and sanity, this time more than ever I need to get things as "right" as possible, and I feel a certain urgency about it. I do not compartmentalize my personal and professional lives: I personalize the world I research and intellectualize the world of my experience. I have presented this case—and, to the extent possible, given its immediacy and my deep involvement, suggested what I can by way of interpretation—in substantially the same manner that I outlined for my previous studies.

I can state unequivocally that I find no counsel or direction in questions prompted by a concern for validity. There is no exact set of circumstances here, no single and "correct" interpretation, nothing scientific to measure that tells us anything important. (The arson inspector could estimate with a high degree of scientific accuracy the relatively inconsequential fact of the heat of the fire; on the pivotal issue of sanity, a lay jury had to decide because the psychiatrists could not.) For every actor in these events there are multiple meanings. In spite of seemingly direct access, I have never been able to sort out even my own thoughts and feelings, for Brad is a person about whom I cared and whom I believed I had not only reached but also "helped." Which are the errors of judgment? Does validity help with that? Will anyone, even Brad, ever know whether I am really antagonist or fall guy?

To the extent that Brad did undergo a dramatic mental breakdown, I was both the caring human and the detached observer closest to him during the time when it became manifest. Yet I did not have access to his mind, and I am certain he himself could not always find reason in it. When, subsequently, he was formally diagnosed, I was astounded to learn that problems related to getting and holding a job were accepted as major symptoms and social indicators in the mental health field. I had no idea of the ambiguity (flexibility?) of mental health diagnoses or their narrow prescriptions for "proper" cultural behavior.[2]

Also, despite whatever physiological basis there was—and Brad as a young male in his early twenties was statistically right on schedule as a candidate for a diagnosis of paranoid schizophrenia—I was aware of his own volition in embracing the social role offered him to be "crazy." I will never know the extent to which his words revealed a reluctant acquiescence or a bold new strategy when he announced after his first visit to the local mental health office, "Crazy Brad! OK, if that's what they want me to be, that's what I'll be." But I could and did share his frustration at systems of schooling that forever tested someone they could not teach and systems of welfare that eventually denied the assistance of less than $100 a month in food stamps (enough to sustain him when he had the freedom of life at the cabin yet could not face more employment refusals) but spent thousands upon thousands of dollars a year to confine and treat (?) him in what I trust was the most restrictive, and assume to be the worst possible, environment for regaining personal equilibrium.

At the same time, I will never, never be convinced that Brad can be depended on to maintain self-control. I am entitled to personal opinion: In fieldwork, I am guided by the maxim that you do not have to be neutral to try to be objective. Although I did not wish him sent to prison in the first place, neither do I relish the idea of his ever being without immediate supervision. I felt "safe" only so long as Brad remained institutionalized. My freedom was placed in jeopardy the moment he regained his.

Has Brad now forgotten about me, as he has learned (correctly) to insist? Can anyone ever discern the true genesis of his hate? Why did it get transformed into his insistence that *I* hated *him* in the final intimacy of the life-and-death struggle between us? What part did I really play in wreaking all this destruction, what part is Brad's (and of his, how much is real, how much delusional?), what part properly should be attributed to family and peers? How many more ways are there to tell the story than the one Brad originally volunteered, the one I have related here, and what was extracted or extrapolated in three weeks of courthouse antics? Is one of these accounts the "valid" one?

A concern for validity in the story of Brad's life and its intersection with mine seems not only an unfortunate choice of objectives but a dangerous distraction. What I seek is something else, a quality that points more to identifying critical elements and wringing plausible interpretations from them, something one can pursue without becoming obsessed with finding the right or ultimate answer, the correct version, the Truth.

Perhaps someone will find or coin qualitative research's appropriate equivalent for "validity"; we have no esoteric term now.[3] For the present, *understanding* seems to encapsulate the idea as well as any other everyday term. Among the definitions offered in *Webster's New Collegiate Dictionary* is the following, in addition to others like "harmony in opinion or feeling" or "kindly tolerance," neither of which I seek at present:

> *understanding*: the power to make experience intelligible by applying concepts and categories

I do not for a minute believe that validity points the way to saving my life or my soul or suggests how to come to grips intellectually with a case study that really matters. Perhaps *understanding* can do little more. But as a human who happens also to be a qualitative researcher, I feel that it sets a more heuristic course than does validity.

Let me hasten to add, as should be evident from the case I have used in illustration, that I do not restrict myself to the phenomenologist's sense of understanding social phenomena from the actor's perspective or, especially, from *an* actor's perspective. That was the goal in my original and focused effort to understand something of Brad. My present concern grows out of events closely linked with individual perspectives that now include my own (and it seems strange to acknowledge that I am not sorting out my "meanings" with much more success than I had with Brad's), but it is system qualities I seek to describe and understand. To attempt to understand a social system is not to claim to understand or be able to predict the actions of particular individuals in it, oneself included.

In a thoughtful essay titled "Understanding People," philosopher Zeno Vendler (1984) contrasts *knowing* and *understanding*, the latter a more ambitious activity requiring one to be able to interpret and explain (e.g., distinctions implied between claiming to know, and claiming to understand, a poem or person). "To understand," he posits, "it may not be enough to know" (p. 204).

Perhaps that is the critical point of departure between quantities- and qualities-oriented research. We cannot "know" with the former's satisfying levels of certainty; our efforts at understanding are neither underwritten with, nor guaranteed by, the accumulation of some predetermined level of verified facts. For us, again quoting Vendler, "There is no 'ready-made world,' a realm of virginal noumena, immaculately perceived and untainted by the perceptual patterns and conceptual network imposed upon it by the human observer" (p. 202.)

I do not go about trying to discover a ready-made world; rather, I seek to understand a social world we are continuously in the process of constructing. (For a "constructionist" perspective on culture, see Peacock, 1986.) Validity stands to lure me from my purpose by inviting me to attend to facts capable of verification, ignoring the fact that for the most part the facts are already in. My present reality includes a case study in which any understanding I may achieve will occur largely in answer to questions that are *not* matters of fact.

Encouraged by Geertz's (1973) reminder that "it is not necessary to know everything in order to understand something" (p. 20), I struggle to understand complex facets of my own everyday, American, middle-class social life that seem almost to defy understanding: ambiguities of mental health definitions and treatments; the social "boundary-maintaining" function of the courts (and the seeming absence of judicial wisdom in them); social welfare systems that do too little until too late; schools that test their problem students with the same zeal they exhibit toward their promising ones—but have little idea and even less authority about what to do with the information they collect; prison systems that lock away information but release inmates; and, always and ultimately, nagging questions about what might be done to check the human waste of young people like Brad in those brief interludes when they signal for help. What interventions might be effective, in what situations? How might we allocate help, recognizing there will never be enough to go around?

I also struggle with questions of the role of research in all this, particularly qualitative research. What contribution can we make to complement what other researchers already do and what (little?) we already understand? If cases like this are "powerful," to what extent is that because they touch a note of reality we ordinarily avoid in setting our research problems? What criteria are relevant to guide and judge our work so that its unique contribution can be retained and nurtured rather than reformed and assessed according to standards developed within and appropriate to other approaches?

Paradoxically, I think that a slippery old chestnut like "understanding" also reminds us that we sometimes learn from poorly reported studies and poorly analyzed ones, while seemingly truthful, or correct, or neatly analyzed accounts may have no impact or provoke no further thought. A preoccupation with validity may be as much a distraction to our collective efforts at qualitative research as it most certainly would be for me individually were I to set my course by it. That is not to dismiss validity but to attempt to put it into some broader perspective. What a surprise to discover that Cronbach concluded his carefully analytical and now-classic discussion of test validation in 1971 with the same words I might have chosen here: "Everything said in this chapter has returned to a concern with understanding" (p. 503).

LAST WORDS

What I have attempted here is to inventory some of the things I (and other fieldworkers) do to achieve and even "enhance" validity and at the same time raise the question of whether validity itself points to a quality about which we should concern ourselves. In an often-cited article written more than thirty years ago and addressed to researchers interested in participant-observation, Howard Becker (1958) wrote, "The researcher faces the problem of how . . . to present his conclusions so as to convince other scientists of their validity" (p. 653).[4] The invitation to write this paper is testimony that "the problem" has not gone away, but I am not convinced it must be addressed in such singular fashion. I do not have conclusions to present. I try to understand, rather than to convince. I do not write to an audience of "other scientists." And I do not accept validity as a valid criterion for guiding or judging my work. I think we have labored too long under the burden of this concept (are there others as well?) that might have been better left where it began, a not-quite-so-singular-or-precise criterion as I once believed it to be for matters related essentially to tests and measurement.[5] I suggest we look elsewhere in our continuing search for and dialogue about criteria appropriate to qualitative researchers' approaches and purposes.

If I have succeeded in making a case for cutting the concept of validity down to size, let me note with fine irony that even in restricting it to its original locus, the concept offers cold comfort. Brad's parole originally was delayed twelve months on the basis of a brief interview and his performance on three tests (Rorschach Psychodiagnostic Technique with Palo Alto Destructiveness Scales, Bender Visual-Motor Gestalt Test, and Draw-a-Person) administered by a consulting psychologist. Once his paper-and-pencil test scores demonstrated a "positive" psychological evaluation, he was reevaluated and, on the basis of his "potential for improvement," was recommended for parole to harried board members eager for that message. I do not envy professional careers built on that kind of validity. I wish even more that I did not feel that henceforth my own life may be hanging in the balance. Under such circumstances, how valid is "valid enough"?

Acknowledgments

I appreciate the invitation extended by Alan Peshkin and Elliot Eisner to prepare this account and the challenge it might have posed for Philip W. Jackson, who was assigned responsibility to react to it. My own earlier critics included, at various stages in the writing, W. W. Charters, Jr., C. H. Edson, and Sakre Edson, all of whom also helped me live through and think through the "Brad" years, as well as Robert Everhart, David Flinders, David C. Potter, Philip D. Young, and editors Susan Liddicoat and Karen Osborne at Teachers College Press. I am particularly grateful to Sandy Charters for his caution that although it was clear that I was not using the term *validity* in the technical manner indicative of its origins, he was not clear about the sense(s) in which I *was* using it. I hope that is now more apparent as the point of the paper: It is not that clear to me how any of us uses the term. Or why.

NOTES

1. Anthropologist Philip Young reminds me that by training and inclination he does just the opposite, that is, he carefully goes through informants' accounts to see what *he* can make of it all. Our difference, I think, lies not in personal styles but in what we read. In anthropologically oriented accounts, one expects to come to know one or a few informants rather well. The quoted material one finds in much of the descriptive research in education, on the other hand, often reads more like conversational snippets than informant accounts.
2. Anthropologist Stephen Tyler (1986) refers to *DSM III*, the *Diagnostic and Statistical Manual* (third edition) that serves as sourcebook for mental health diagnosis, as "that terrorist bludgeon of the psychiatrist" (p. 139).
3. Egon Guba (1981) is among those who have pioneered the effort to identify criteria for judging adequacy within naturalistic research paradigms

that parallel rather than replicate those of the rationalistic tradition. I am not much taken with his early choice of *trustworthiness* as a global term. However, the four "aspects" of trustworthiness that he identifies seem to hold promise. Perhaps the parallels he draws with their quantitative ("scientific") counterparts do not need to be as tight as those he has proposed, in which internal validity is equated with credibility; external validity/generalizability with transferability; reliability with dependability; and objectivity with confirmability.

4. I admit to some initial disappointment at discovering Becker's seeming endorsement of validity in this early statement. I had opportunity to discuss it with him when these papers were presented. As he intended the sentence, he explained, the emphasis was on "convince" rather than on "validity." "And that," he noted, "is still the problem."

5. Substituting *valid measure* might help foster this distinction, consistent with Bernard's (1988) observation, "Valid measurement makes valid data, but validity itself depends on the collective opinion of researchers" (p. 54).

REFERENCES

Becker, H. S. (1958). Problems of inference and proof in participant observation. *American Sociological Review, 23,* 652–660.

Bernard, H. R. (1988). *Research methods in cultural anthropology.* Beverly Hills, CA: Sage.

Bernard, H. R., Killworth, P. D., Kronenfeld, D., & Sailer, L. (1984). The problem of informant accuracy: The validity of retrospective data. *Annual Review of Anthropology, 13,* 495–517.

Brinberg, D., & McGrath, J. E. (1982). A network of validity concepts within the research process. In D. Brinberg & L. H. Kidder (Eds.), *Forms of validity in research* (pp. 5–21). San Francisco: Jossey-Bass.

Brown, R. (1965). *Social psychology.* New York: Free Press.

Campbell, D. T. (1975). "Degrees of freedom" and the case study. *Comparative Political Studies, 8*(2), 178–193.

Campbell, D. T. (1986). Science's social system of validity-enhancing collective belief change and the problems of the social sciences. In D. W. Fiske & R. A. Shweder (Eds.), *Social science: Pluralisms and subjectivities* (pp. 108–135). Chicago: University of Chicago Press.

Cronbach, L. J. (1971). Test validation. In R. L. Thorndike (Ed.), *Educational measurement* (2nd ed., pp. 443–507). Washington, DC: American Council on Education.

Cronbach, L. J. (1986). Social inquiry by and for earthlings. In D. W. Fiske & R. A. Shweder (Eds.), *Metatheory in social science: Pluralisms and subjectivities* (pp. 83–107). Chicago: University of Chicago Press.

Cronbach, L. J., & Meehl, P. E. (1955). Construct validity in psychological tests. *Psychological Bulletin, 52,* 281–302.

Dean, J., & Whyte, W. F. (1958). How do you know if the informant is telling the truth? *Human Organization, 17*(2), 34–38.

Dobbert, M. L. (1982). *Ethnographic research: Theory and applications for modern schools and societies.* New York: Praeger.

Erickson, F. (1973). What makes school ethnography 'ethnographic'? *Council on Anthropology and Education Newsletter, 4*(2), 10–19. [Revised and reprinted in *Anthropology and Education Quarterly, 15*(1984), 51–66.]

Freeman, L. C., & Romney, A. K. (1988). Words, deeds and social structure: A preliminary study of the reliability of informants. *Human Organization, 46*(4), 330–334.

Geertz, C. (1973). Thick description. In C. Geertz (Ed.), *The interpretation of cultures* (pp. 3–30). New York: Basic Books.

Goetz, J. P., & LeCompte, M. D. (1984). *Ethnography and qualitative design in educational research.* Orlando, FL: Academic Press.

Gould, S. J. (1981). *The mismeasure of man.* New York: W. W. Norton.

Guba, E. (1981). Criteria for assessing the trustworthiness of naturalistic inquiries. *Educational Communication and Technology Journal, 29*(2), 75–91.

Kaplan, A. (1964). *The conduct of inquiry.* San Francisco: Chandler.

Kirk, J., & Miller, M. L. (1986). *Reliability and validity in qualitative research* (Sage University Paper Series on Qualitative Research Methods, Vol. 1). Beverly Hills, CA: Sage.

LaTour, B., & Woolgar, S. (1986). *Laboratory life: The construction of scientific facts.* Princeton, NJ: Princeton University Press.

McEwen, W. J. (1963). Forms and problems of validation in social anthropology. *Current Anthropology, 4*, 155–183.

Miles, M. B., & Huberman, A. M. (1984). Drawing valid meaning from qualitative data: Toward a shared craft. *Educational Researcher, 13*(5), 20–30.

Peacock, J. L. (1986). *The anthropological lens: Harsh light, soft focus.* New York: Cambridge University Press.

Pelto, P. J., & Pelto, G. H. (1978). *Anthropological research: The structure of inquiry* (2nd ed.). New York: Cambridge University Press.

Phillips, D. C. (1987). Validity in qualitative research. *Education and Urban Society, 20*(1), 9–24.

Spindler, G. (Ed.). (1982). *Doing the ethnography of schooling.* New York: Holt, Rinehart and Winston. (Revised edition, Prospect Heights, IL: Waveland Press, 1987)

Tyler, S. A. (1986). Post-modern ethnography: From document of the occult to occult document. In J. Clifford & G. E. Marcus (Eds.), *Writing culture: The poetics and politics of ethnography* (pp. 122–140). Berkeley: University of California Press.

Van Maanen, J. (1988). *Tales of the field: On writing ethnography.* Chicago: University of Chicago Press.

Vendler, Z. (1984). Understanding people. In R. A. Shweder & R. A. LeVine (Eds.), *Culture theory: Essays on mind, self, and emotion* (pp. 200–213). New York: Cambridge University Press.

Vidich, A. J., & Bensman, J. (1954). The validity of field data. *Human Organization, 13*(1), 20–27.

Weber, R. P. (1985). *Basic content analysis* (Sage University Paper Series on Quantitative Applications in the Social Sciences). Beverly Hills, CA: Sage.

Wolcott, H. F. (1967). *A Kwakiutl village and school*. New York: Holt, Rinehart and Winston. (Reissued, Prospect Heights, IL: Waveland Press, 1984, 1989)

Wolcott, H. F. (1973). *The man in the principal's office: An ethnography*. New York: Holt, Rinehart and Winston. (Reissued, Prospect Heights, IL: Waveland Press, 1984)

Wolcott, H. F. (1974). *The African beer gardens of Bulawayo: Integrated drinking in a segregated society*. New Brunswick, NJ: Rutgers Center of Alcohol Studies.

Wolcott, H. F. (1977). *Teachers versus technocrats: An educational innovation in anthropological perspective*. Eugene, OR: Center for Educational Policy and Management, University of Oregon.

Wolcott, H. F. (1982a). The anthropology of learning. *Anthropology and Education Quarterly, 13*(2), 83–108.

Wolcott, H. F. (1982b). *Adequate schools and inadequate education: An anthropological perspective*. (Commissioned paper prepared for the School Finance Project, Contract NIE-P-81-0271). Washington, DC: U.S. Department of Education.

Wolcott, H. F. (1983a). Adequate schools and inadequate education: The life history of a sneaky kid. *Anthropology and Education Quarterly, 4*(1), 3–32.

Wolcott, H. F. (1983b). A Malay village that progress chose: Sungai Lui and the Institute of Cultural Affairs. *Human Organization, 42*(1), 72–81.

Wolcott, H. F. (1984). Ethnographers sans ethnography: The evaluation compromise. In D. Fetterman (Ed.), *Ethnography in educational evaluation* (pp. 177–210). Beverly Hills, CA: Sage.

Wolcott, H. F. (1987). Life's not working: Cultural alternatives to career alternatives. In G. W. Noblit & W. T. Pink (Eds.), *Schooling in social context: Qualitative studies* (pp. 303–325). Norwood, NJ: Ablex Publishing.

Wolcott, H. F. (1988). Ethnographic research in education. In R. M. Jaeger (Ed.), *Complementary methods for research in education* (pp. 187–249). Washington, DC: American Educational Research Association.

Wolcott, H. F. (1989). A Kwakiutl village and school—25 years later. Afterword to the second printing of *A Kwakiutl village and school*. Prospect Heights, IL: Waveland Press.

Wolcott, H. F. (1990). *Writing up qualitative research* (Sage University Paper Series on Qualitative Research). Beverly Hills, CA: Sage.

Looking for Trouble:
On the Place of the Ordinary
in Educational Studies

PHILIP W. JACKSON

As I understand my task, it is neither to criticize nor to praise the two preceding papers so much as it is to respond to them with thoughts of my own that have been stimulated or at least altered in some way by the contents of each essay. This task is made both easy and difficult by the richness of both presentations. On the one hand I find I have no shortage of things to say, which makes my job easy. But on the other hand I cannot possibly report on everything that came to mind as I read the two papers, which makes my job difficult, though pleasantly so. To remedy the situation, I have chosen to narrow my focus to a single topic that draws upon ideas from the two papers yet calls for a far more extended treatment than I can give it here. In broadest terms what I wish to discuss is the place of the ordinary in educational studies. This covers the question of where we go to look for things to study and to write about as educational researchers. It also requires us to think about what we hope to accomplish by our work.

Before turning to these matters, however, I would like to comment briefly on what I especially liked about each paper, even though, as already said, that is not the principal reason for my commentary. However, since some of the things I shall later say might be interpreted as being critical, I thought it best to begin on a clearly positive note, if only for the sake of balance.

I start with Harry Wolcott's paper simply because I received it first and it was his thoughts that got my own going. He managed to capture my attention at once by giving short shrift to his assigned topic. Like a backwoodsman in full stride, Wolcott brushes aside the concept of validity as though it were no more than a frail vine or a small cloud of gnats impeding his progress. His chief objection—that validity is essentially a testmaker's concept and is therefore best left to those who pursue that line of work—seems right to me. Ethnographers and others of us who engage in what is increasingly referred to these days as qualitative research usually have more pressing things to worry about than the standard questions that revolve around the idea of validity and that loom so large in textbooks on research methods. Wolcott goes on to remind us of what some of those alternative worries typically turn out to be. The criteria he applies to his own work comprise as good a list as any I have come across. We should all try, he tells us, to be as credible, balanced, fair, complete, sensitive, rigorously subjective, coherent, internally consistent, appropriate, plausible, and helpful as possible. Quite a mouthful, I would say. In fact, it sounds suspiciously like the litany of virtues we used to rattle off as Boy Scouts. But its length alone suffices to remind us that there remains a whole raft of things to think about once we have moved beyond the ancient bugaboos of reliability and validity. All aspiring ethnographers and qualitative researchers of every stripe would do well to paste a summary of Wolcott's advice into the bands of their hats before they themselves go stomping off into the bush.

In a rather more serious vein, I also admired the courage it must have taken Wolcott to tell the story of his relationship with Brad. That kind of openness is rare in academia. It is also a risky business, as Wolcott surely knows. I am grateful to him for taking that risk not only because in doing so he models a degree of candor that others of us might seek to emulate (though the recent spate of "kiss-and-tell" bestsellers may turn many of us the other way) but also because his report raises a host of tantalizing questions about the relationship between the researcher's public and private selves. A couple of those questions lie at the center of the topic I plan to discuss.

Turning next to Madeleine Grumet's paper, I first must express my usual pleasure over the way her writing draws upon literary and philosophical sources. Past experience has taught me that though I do not always fully agree with what Grumet has to say about the topic at hand, I can usually count on being edified, not to say educated, by her scholarship. This time was no exception. I finished my reading of her essay with a list of other items to read, an outcome that often turns out to be a very good indicator of how much I have enjoyed myself in the process. Discovering something new to read has long been one of my greatest pleasures.

What I liked most about Grumet's paper, however, was not its erudite references to folks like Merleau-Ponty and Virginia Woolf.

What pleased me even more was the essay's underlying assumption, more a conscious affirmation in spots, that there is much more to teaching, and, by extension, to everything else that goes on in schools and classrooms, than meets the eye. By itself this observation is not very exciting. In fact, it is downright banal. But if we take it seriously, as Grumet tries to do through her use of autobiographical reports, we wind up having to declare what it *is* about teaching or about schooling in general that remains undisclosed by casual observation. There are multiple answers to that question, as we well might imagine. Grumet has explored some of them in her essay. I shall be exploring others in what follows.

Having said enough, I hope, to establish my basic sympathy with each author's project, I turn now to the central set of questions that emerged from my reading of the papers, those having to do with where we go to look for things to study and to write about as educational researchers and what we hope to accomplish by doing so.

What actually triggered this line of thought was Wolcott's comments about his book *The Man in the Principal's Office* (1973). In describing how he goes about getting his informants to check the accuracy of his written reports, he spoke of taking a draft of the report of that study to the principal of the Taft School, who reacted with "real disappointment." In the principal's eyes the account gave "a disproportionate amount of attention" to his problems as an administrator. In responding to this complaint, Wolcott readily acknowledges that he had "meticulously uncovered and examined every little malfunction to show what a principal must contend with." But he then goes on to defend what he had done. "Had I conveyed the minute-by-minute routine of Taft School during those two years," he explains, "I think I would have fallen asleep writing about it long before anyone could have fallen asleep reading about it." His task as a researcher, at least as he saw it, was to convey the "customary 'hum' of a smoothly run school while also assuring readers that the account would probe beneath the surface."

Wolcott's explanation for why he chose to uncover and examine "every little malfunction" at the Taft School makes perfectly good sense, of course, given his avowed goal of trying to find out what principals do or, more accurately, what *a* principal *did* to make a school run smoothly. We all can easily understand why he chose to "get beneath the surface" of things. Yet when I read the account I could not help but sympathize, at least a tiny bit, with the disappointed principal.

What stirred my sympathy, strangely enough, were lingering thoughts about the concept of validity. "Did Wolcott offer the principal a *valid* picture of the school's operation?" I asked myself, meaning now not what the testmaker's have in mind when they use that term but what ordinary people commonly mean by it. The answer I gave back was both yes and no. Wolcott's report was certainly valid in the sense of being true, that is, not a fabrication, or so we may presume. But it was just as certainly not valid as a picture of the Taft School that one might obtain from a casual inspection of the place, the kind of picture a parent of one of Taft's students might easily recognize, let's say, or even one that might draw a nod of assent from the president of the school board. I realize that neither was what Wolcott was trying to produce, but something like an easily recognizable picture seems to have been what the principal was looking for, and that explains why he was disappointed with what Wolcott presented him. Is the latter account any more valid than the one the principal was looking for? I think not, at least no more than an X-ray of a person's face might be said to reveal a truer, "in-depth" depiction than does a Polaroid snapshot. The two pictures are different certainly, but one is not more true or more valid than the other. They are simply taken for different purposes. They serve different ends.

The idea of there being many different pictures one might take of the Taft School brings me back to what Wolcott has to say about ordinary classroom events, about how they threaten to put him to sleep. That observation raises the interesting question of whether a faithful portrayal of such events is humanly possible. Imagine a painter who was using as objects for a still life a collection of bottles and fruit that was so impossibly boring to look at that she began to doze off each time she gazed in its direction. Is not her project doomed from the start? It would seem so to me. Wolcott obviously does not go so far as to contend that every well-functioning classroom will have the same soporific effect on all observers as the Taft School had on him, but his remarks are unsettling all the same. Moreover, Wolcott is not alone in making them.

N. L. Gage once confided to me that he often felt bored when sitting in the back of a classroom. I nodded with understanding at the time, for I had often felt the same way myself under similar circumstances. Indeed, I suspect that if we inquired around we would soon discover the experience to be common among educational researchers, so much so perhaps that the situation almost calls for trotting out a reworked version of W. C. Field's old joke about winning a vacation trip to Philadelphia, only this time the first prize would be *one* luxurious week of observation in a smoothly running classroom and the second prize, *two* luxurious weeks of sitting in the back of the same room.

Many practicing educators and even some researchers perhaps

would probably object to my use of humor in this way, and understandably so, I suppose. After all, schools and classrooms are important places, as everyone knows. What goes on within them is properly the subject of serious talk and systematic investigation. Treating classrooms facetiously, making their observed dullness the butt of jokes, may seem grossly unfair. At the same time, that an astute observer like Wolcott can barely keep his eyes open when he turns them to the run-of-the-mill happenings of school life and, additionally, that he is not alone in feeling as he does are serious matters, even when treated lightly.

In truth, however, when I first read Wolcott's paper I did not have much time to chortle over the image of him falling asleep inside the Taft School, only to be found there late at night by a surprised janitor, before I was swept up by his story of Brad, which quickly took my mind off schools and classrooms completely and forced me to think of nothing else but the tale itself. And what a tale it turned out to be! The exact opposite, I would say, of what goes on in classrooms. Here was everything most schools lack: drama, passion, madness, crime, you name it. The note of suspense on which it ended brought to mind Professor Moriarty's famous disappearance over the Reichenbach Falls. Will Brad return, or has Wolcott seen the last of him? We reach the end of an episode but not the tale's conclusion. A professional writer of pulp fiction, one whose readers bite their nails to the quick waiting for the next installment to hit the newsstand, could hardly have done better.

"Meanwhile, back in the classroom . . ." my work-oriented conscience urged as I finished the part about Brad's impending parole, but, try as I might, my heart and my imagination refused to budge. They kept me sitting stock still for quite some time, mutely pondering the charred remains of Wolcott's house, together with the yet-to-be-settled aftermath of the horror that took place there. What did manage to coax my thoughts back to more mundane matters was the memory of a conversation I once had with Renato Paggioli, who was then a professor of comparative literature at Harvard.

The topic was academic novels, of which I had read a few and was looking for more. I asked Professor Paggioli if he would recommend a few great ones for me to read. He laughed and said that there was no such thing as a *great* academic novel. Nor would there ever be one. The reason, he explained, was that academic life did not contain enough drama to sustain a great novel. With respectful temerity I protested and quickly nominated a couple of my own favorites, which he promptly dismissed as being "good, but certainly not great." He then went on to name a few works that met his own standard of greatness. *The Brothers*

Karamazov and *Don Quixote* were among them. Our conversation ended with my being convinced by Paggioli's argument but thoroughly disappointed with its conclusion. I continued to read academic novels after that, and still do today, but no longer with my old enthusiasm.

Paggioli's claim, Brad's story, and everything that has been said to this point about drowsy classroom observers all speak to the limits of schools as settings for the kind of drama that makes a good story, not to say a great one. Any number of compelling tales *have* been set there, of course (witness the recent film *Stand and Deliver* as an instance), but typically the school or classroom being depicted is very unusual in some way, or else it is simply a backdrop for a story that has little to do with the day-to-day business of teaching and learning. The latter, it seems, is not sufficiently interesting to hold our attention, at least not when we are out to be entertained. The question is: What, if anything, does the alleged dullness of ordinary classrooms have to do with their status as settings for sustained academic study? I suspect the two have a lot to do with each other for the simple reason that researchers no more relish the prospect of falling asleep at their posts than do novelists or movie-makers and their audiences. Wolcott's testimony bears that out. The natural temptation, therefore, even for serious scholars, is to seek out the dramatic, the troublesome, the unexpected, leaving behind the mundane, the ordinary, the run-of-the-mill.

This inclination is as evident in Grumet's paper as it is in Wolcott's, though the strategy for keeping oneself and one's audience awake is markedly different in the two essays. Like Wolcott, Grumet also seems eager to get beneath the surface of things, even to the point of uprooting daffodils it seems, but the depths she seeks to plumb are more internal than those he explores. As a matter of fact, what Grumet does with the line about daffodils from Virginia Woolf's diary serves well to introduce the tactic she also applies to her treatment of the autobiographical accounts of her student, Kathy Farrar.

To refresh our memories, the excerpt from Woolf's (1953) diary reads as follows: "Art is being rid of all preaching: things in themselves: the sentence in itself beautiful: multitudinous seas; daffodils that come before the swallow dares" (p. 183). What I found initially interesting about Grumet's reaction to that excerpt was how quickly she turned away from the text, almost as though she had grasped its meaning at a glance, for in the very next line she writes: "Immediately I am convinced. Good-bye. I will go to Half Moon Bay, where I will walk on rocks and watch for whales." "Hey, wait a minute!" I wanted to yell after her, "there's more here than meets the eye." The ghost of Virginia Woolf, which had been reading over my shoulder and which now turned to face me head-on, nodded in agreement and blinked with surprise.

I needn't have reacted so swiftly myself it turns out, for Grumet does return to the excerpt and, almost immediately, twice repeats the isolated line "Daffodils that come before the swallow dares," but what she proceeds to make of that phrase puzzles me. Wrenched from the sentence in which it was lodged ("uprooted," one might say), the line no longer refers to the point about art being rid of all preaching, nor does it stand as an example of the dual beauty of language and of things in themselves. Instead, it becomes a kind of verbal Rorschach, a splotch of colorful imagery that lends itself to all kinds of hermeneutical ruminations. Grumet starts them off by claiming that the phrase is not what it seems to be. Its "semblance dissembles," she says. "It hides in what it reveals." What does it hide? Virginia Woolf's surprise and relief, we are told, "her despair of the long grey months, her doubt, her loss, her dread." In Grumet's view, Woolf's talk about daffodils is "a clever trick," a "sleight of hand," something for which poor Virginia is to be forgiven.

How Grumet comes to know all those things about the personal meaning those seven words must have had for its author remains a mystery to me, but to say that may only be to confess a kind of insensitivity that some critics may ascribe to my gender, I suppose. In any event, what is important to us here is not the validity of Grumet's interpretation of an isolated fragment from a writer's diary; rather it is her readiness to depart from whatever might be the initial object of her attention in order to explore the dimly lit world of *Sturm und Drang* that rumbles ominously just beneath the surface of things. That characteristic readiness to dig for worms, so to speak, is clearly evident in Grumet's treatment of the three autobiographical essays by her student, Kathy Farrar. Here, too, she quickly moves from a set of rather routine accounts of personal experience to a much darker interpretative terrain, a world of violence, struggle, abandonment, anxiety, and more. Although she never comes out and says so directly, I think the reader is supposed to conclude that her interpretive accounts penetrate to the deeper meaning of what the author was trying to say and thus come closer to the truth than do the author's words themselves.

Perhaps they do, but Grumet's descent into a kind of nether world of personal sorrows and passions leaves me feeling very uneasy all the same. I am quite willing to believe that there is more to what Farrar has written than meets the eye, but before I go reading a whole lot of symbolic meaning into her words, I would like to know a lot more than I am told about what was going on back in the classroom where these essays were generated. Grumet reports that this student was asked "to situate the experience of education among the relations within which it has come to form in her own world." What kind of an assignment is that? I wonder. Something about it does not sound right to me. Surely Farrar must have had more than that to go on before she set pen to paper. Were examples offered? Were personal accounts discussed in class? What was said about the purpose of the exercise? Did the teacher, either overtly or covertly, make clear what kind of essays she wanted, what kind would please her? Was Farrar graded for her performance in this class, or were no grades given? Were the accounts to be shared with other students or were they treated confidentially?

I raise these questions not to discredit the veracity of what Farrar has written but only to better understand what to make of her essays. To me, all three of them read like responses to homework assignments, which they apparently were. There is nothing wrong, of course, with a teacher trying to wrest symbolic meaning from what a student writes on demand, but it seems to me that its status as homework has to count for something in that interpretation. Moreover, what interests me fully as much as the essays themselves is what the teacher was trying to do and why. Presumably something educational was going on between Grumet and her student, but I am not exactly sure what it was, Farrar's testimony about the worth of the activity notwithstanding.

In sum, neither Wolcott nor Grumet seem terribly interested in what one might speak of as "the ordinary stuff" of schools and class-rooms. Both of them go looking for trouble, in a manner of speaking, though in vastly different ways, of course: Wolcott with his eye out for "system qualities," which become "handles" that potentially could be manipulated to make the world better; Grumet ever atune to the involuntary sighs and sidelong glances that signal private longings and thus invite imaginative entry into a person's inner world. If we were to exaggerate these tendencies to make them stand out even more than they do, we might say that Wolcott goes wide, whereas Grumet goes deep. By different routes, one horizontal, the other vertical, both manage to leave behind the nitty-gritty world of chalkdust, raised hands, late assignments, hall passes, posters, workbooks, bulletin boards, questions, answers, quizzes, and all of the remaining sights and sounds of a typical school day, including, of course, the suppressed yawns and heavy eyelids of late afternoon.

So what? Who can blame them? Aren't we glad to be free of that world ourselves, even as many students and their teachers would be if they had the chance? Of course we are. Thus we not only cheer Wolcott and Grumet on their way but want to shout after them, as a kid brother or sister might do, "Hey, Harry! Hey, Madeleine! Wait up for me! I'm coming too!" But even if we don't get to go along, we can be relatively sure that they will write to us before too long, and we will eagerly devour their words, find them entertaining, insightful, perhaps even wise.

Meanwhile, back in the classroom . . . What *are* we to make of that customary hum? Anything at all? I confess I am not sure. There are times when I so want to be rid of it myself that I actively search for signs of pathology, "personal malfunctions" Wolcott might call them—bizarre behavior on the part of students, twitches, blinks, nails bitten to the quick, thumbs sucked raw, masturbatory rubbings and scratchings, malicious gleams in teachers' eyes, even a dead gerbil would be a welcome sight at times—anything to keep myself awake. At such moments, and they are far more frequent than I would like them to be, I hanker for the life of a *real* anthropologist, one who goes off to Bali for years at a time and watches cockfights or even the kind that stays at home and studies carnival freaks. On those occasions I likewise envy the life of therapists and remedial specialists, including those who work in schools and whose job it is to probe what William James (1901) used to call "the curious inner elements of [the pupil's] mental machine" (p. 11). I have always liked that phrase. There is something dark and sinister about it. Its bony finger beckons, at least on my off-days.

There are other times, however, and thank heavens they have come to predominate of late, when the thought of escaping, even momentarily, from my perch in the back of the classroom or from my stroll through near-empty school corridors is the furthest thing from my mind. At such moments I *know* this is where I should be and this is what I should be doing. The purity of that conviction, however, is seldom unalloyed. It is almost always mixed with doubt of one kind or another, even on good days; doubt about how to proceed methodologically, doubt about what to look at, even, from time to time, doubt about what it is I am actually trying to do.

Insofar as those feelings of doubt extend to my abiding interest in the ordinary stuff of schools and classrooms, which they certainly do from time to time, I seek to quell them with a reaffirmation of faith in a fundamental principle, which says that if we look at and listen to almost any aspect of social reality long enough and closely enough, we begin to see nuances of meaning and significance that were not there before. This principle applies as much to what goes on in schools as it does to our experience of the world in general.

It does not always work, of course. Sometimes we can look and listen for quite a long time without our perception changing at all. We may even fall asleep in the process. When that occurs, however, when I come home completely empty-handed from a morning or an afternoon spent in the back of a classroom or wandering the corridors of a school, I usually suspect that the source of the difficulty resides fully as much within me as within the phenomena under investigation.

This principle may help to explain my poking around schools without much in the way of hypotheses to guide my observations, but it still does not come to grips with my penchant for exploring ordinary affairs. If anything at all becomes more interesting as we gaze upon it or think about it, why start with something dull? Why not begin with something that is already interesting in the hope that our reflection upon it will make it even more so? Why not start with a problem that educators are actually struggling with, for example, and see if we can shed new light upon it by our close examination? Though that is a perfectly reasonable thing to do and I am happy that others are doing it, I personally find it to be counterproductive. Those aspects of schooling that are naturally interesting—the bizarre behaviors of the "problem children," for example, or the funny or sad or gossipy events that keep the teachers' lounge abuzz—strike me as being too seductive somehow. They lead my thoughts *away* from schooling rather than toward it. They are certainly absorbing as topics of conversation, but I fail to find them very engaging, either aesthetically or philosophically.

Here I must recount a very recent experience. A few nights ago I attended a dinner meeting of school principals. The group was small, and the principals knew each other pretty well, so that the talk, which was about schools, soon became candid. One by one the principals began to share accounts of recent experiences. What struck me about the conversation was that almost all the anecdotes dealt with what I would call "horror stories," tales of students who had attempted suicides, or were neglected by their parents, or were strung out on drugs, and so forth. This was not at all surprising, of course. In fact, it was perfectly understandable, I suppose, given the difficulties and the temptations kids face these days and given also the responsibilities of these administrators. The content of what was being said, though quite depressing in many ways, was clearly interesting to all of us there. Yet as the talk continued I found myself thinking how little all these hair-raising stories had to do with what I normally see and think about as I walk the corridors and sit in classrooms of the very schools over which these administrators preside. It was as if they and I inhabited different institutions, almost different universes. "What shall we make of that difference?" I asked myself as I sauntered home that evening.

The fact that I as yet have no good answer to that question bothers me, of course, but not to the point of wanting to undertake a case study of an actual or potential school dropout, as Wolcott (1983, 1987) has done so skillfully. Instead, it has driven me to think even more intently than I had managed to do so far about the kind of looking I have been trying to do in those schools for the past several months. What am I looking for? I am increasingly coming to believe that that may be the wrong question to ask.

Perhaps the idea of looking *for* something is what is wrong. Perhaps we have become so intent in looking *for* that we no longer know how to look *at*. Perhaps looking *for* encourages us to look *past* things rather than *at* them. Looking *for* constricts awareness; looking *at* expands it.

What would it mean to look *at* a classroom or a school rather than looking *for* something that might be found there? Does it mean just factually recording what we see and hear, like a camera or tape-recorder? Of course not. There is no such thing as an innocent gaze, as those of today's social scientists who have taken "an interpretive turn" never tire of reminding us. We look and see with the language and concepts we possess. We also look through eyes that have seen before, that have a history. We come to our looking, in other words, with built-in biases that permit us to see some things quite easily and other things only with difficulty, if at all. We also create categories and concepts as we go along. These alter our future looking. What we see, in other words, changes us. We learn to look. We also *lose* old ways of seeing. We sometimes forget how to look.

But still, even if we give up looking *for* something, might we not yet *find* things through our looking? And, if so, what might we expect them to be? Here a form of Meno's paradox takes over, which says that if we knew what we would find by looking we would have already found it. But the situation is not hopeless. There is always a one-word answer to the question of what we might find by looking *at* rather than *for* things. The answer is: ourselves. I know that sounds awfully corny when stated so baldly, but it is true, isn't it? Look at what Wolcott and Grumet tell us. Aren't they clearly in the process of trying to figure out what their work and the observations it entails are doing to them as persons? It seems to me they are.

But there are problems with this answer, beyond its being corny. One is that I have already described Wolcott and Grumet as looking *for* trouble, but I have just been talking about the virtues of looking *at* rather than *for*. Can one look *for* something and still find oneself? That seems to be what I am now saying. Another problem is that the act of finding oneself sounds like a terribly narcissistic endeavor. Surely we don't want to say that the main reason for undertaking qualitative research in education is for researchers to find themselves!

To the first difficulty I would want to take a position that might be called an Aristotelian hardline. It says that everything we do is in some manner and in some degree constitutive of the self. We discover ourselves as easily in looking *for* trouble as in looking *at* things. What we discover, of course, is that we have become a person who chooses to look for trouble. Here I must interject yet another anecdote. An investigative reporter recently told me of a dream he had in which he was a solitary wanderer, prowling the streets at night, looking for clues associated with some crime, when it suddenly occured to him (in the dream) that the crime he was investigating had not yet been committed! The thought not only awakened him but caused him to reflect for quite some time on the kind of person he had become.

The second difficulty is somewhat harder to deal with, for it raises the question of what we actually hope to accomplish by what we are doing. "Finding ourselves" seems far too narcissistic a goal, I agree, even though it may turn out that we always do find ourselves in our work, whether we acknowledge it or not. But what else is there beyond that? What good does it do to mope around schools, looking in classrooms, following principals about, and so forth, especially when at the same time we are unable to say what it is we are looking for?

There are two answers to that question. One is that whatever we see may ultimately be helpful to others by enabling them to see the same thing themselves. Wolcott expresses this hope when he says, "The purpose I now reaffirm for my own orientation is to help us—myself and perhaps a few others—better to understand, to convey that understanding in a manner understandable to others and to have it lend helpful insight."[1] The benefit, in other words, comes in sharing our "findings."

The other is that our *way* of looking may also be shareable. Others may come to see *as* we do, as well as *what* we do. From a somewhat narrow point of view, this form of benefit might be looked upon as more methodological than substantive. From a broader perspective, what is being exhibited when we look *at* things is less a method than a basic orientation to the world, a way of life.

By now many will have sensed a family resemblance between the position taken in this essay and the larger intellectual tradition that is sometimes labelled "romantic." Those who discern me to be headed in that direction are correct in their surmise. My project to explore and even to celebrate the mundane aspects of school life partakes of the

---

1. This quotation is taken from the March 1988 draft of Chapter 4.

same spirit of investigation that animated the early romantics, particularly Wordsworth and Coleridge in England, Nietzsche in Germany, and Emerson in this country. To cite a few more modern examples from the many that could be named, it is also that same spirit that drives the poetry and prose of William Carlos Williams, the philosophy of the later Wittgenstein, the sociology of Erving Goffman, the history of Gertrude Himmelfarb, the anthropology of Clifford Geertz.

It was Wordsworth (1800/1961), we might remember, who dedicated his poetry (in the "Preface to the Lyrical Ballads") to the goal of "making the incidents of common life interesting" (p. 51). Actually, that is far too bland a description of what he was really up to. The philosopher Stanley Cavell (1986) comes closer to capturing the ambitiousness of the romantic project when he writes,

> Romanticism's work . . . interprets itself . . . as the task of bringing the world back, as to life. This may, in turn, present itself as the quest for a return to the ordinary, or of it, a new creation of our habitat; or as the quest, away from that, for the creation of a new inhabitation: Wordsworth and Coleridge would represent the former alternative; Blake and Shelley, I believe, the latter. (p. 190)

Some may read my declaration of allegiance to the romantic tradition as an abandonment of social science in general and of educational research in particular. They may see it as a form of "going soft," of giving in to sentiment, of saying farewell to reason and tough-mindedness. The crudest of my critics may even accuse me of being disloyal to my gender. I do not believe it need mean any of those things, even though I acknowledge that many people who do indeed seem to have given up on reason, and sometimes common sense as well, are often dismissed as being "mere romantics." I would prefer to call such persons "sentimental fools" or something like that in order to avoid giving romanticism a bad name. Like Cavell, I am happy to join what he calls "the romantic quest," and I further join him in saying:

> I accept the traditional rebuke of such a quest, that it is childish, or adolescent, or, well, Romantic; that peculiarly maddening rebuke, which casts those who would diagnose our solemn, universal destructiveness, as themselves the gloomy malcontents. It is to be expected. (p. 187)

In the final analysis, the point of view I have been arguing for comes very close, I suspect, to what Grumet believes as well, which is why my sympathy for her project overrides my objections to the strategies she has chosen to employ. Our chief difference may be that I take Virginia Woolf at her word even more readily than Grumet does. "Art is being rid of all preaching," Woolf reminds us. I heartily concur. "So is a certain kind of research," I would add. Not all of it, mind you, certainly not all of it. But a very large portion of what we refer to these days as qualitative inquiry, including most of what I try to do myself, seems to me to partake of that same spirit that Woolf ascribes to art—its abandonment of the preaching role, its absorption in the world as given us by our senses, even its surprise and delight in the unexpected beauty that so often breaks ground or sweeps into view before our very eyes.

REFERENCES

Cavell, S. (1986). In quest of the ordinary. In M. Eaves & M. Fisher (Eds.), *Romanticism and contemporary criticism* (pp. 183–239). Ithaca, NY: Cornell University Press.

James, W. (1901). *Talks to teachers on psychology: And to students on some of life's ideals.* New York: Henry Holt.

Wolcott, H. F. (1973). The man in the principal's office: An ethnography. New York: Holt, Rinehart and Winston. (Reissued, Prospects Heights, IL: Waveland Press, 1984)

Wolcott, H. F. (1983). Adequate schools and inadequate education: The life history of a sneaky kid. *Anthropology and Education Quarterly, 4*(1), 3–32.

Wolcott, H. F. (1987). Life's not working: Cultural alternatives to career alternatives. In G. W. Noblit & W. T. Pink (Eds.), *Schooling in social context: Qualitative studies* (pp. 303–325). Norwood, NJ: Ablex Publishing.

Woolf, V. (1953). *A writer's diary.* New York: Harcourt Brace Jovanovich.

Wordsworth, W. (1961). Preface to the lyrical ballads. In C. R. Woodring (Ed.), *Prose of the romantic period.* Boston: Houghton Mifflin. (Original work published 1800)

Response to the Commentary by Jackson

MADELEINE R. GRUMET

I am delighted to learn that Professor Jackson finds my citations edifying. Nevertheless, his enthusiasm for what he finds in the margins of my text goes too far when he marginalizes work that does not stay within the boundaries that he has set for his own enterprise. Jackson's praise of the ordinary and proscription of work that strays beyond its familiar limits would have, I suggest, serious implications for the study of education were we to heed his admonishments.

We must not be lulled into acquiescence by the familiar reassurances of the ordinary. This seemingly comfortable word has a past that is much less democratic than its current usage would suggest. It derives from order, the authoritarian imposition of regulation and rank. Order denotes a particular arrangement of persons in hierarchical categories. In *Discipline and Punish*, historian Michel Foucault (1979) has shown us how order—ecclesiastic, military, medical, or scholarly—separates, designates, and controls others so as to maintain the privilege of those who impose it. Order, naturalized over time, becomes the ordinary: a pattern of groupings, practices, and categories that seep into the ground of human experience and perception.

The authoritarian intention that hovers under the ordinary is revealed in the Oxford English Dictionary's listing of persons who themselves have carried *Ordinary* as their title: in ecclesiastical and common law, "One who has by his own right and not by special deputation, immediate jurisdiction in ecclesiastical cases . . ."; in civil law, "A judge having authority to take cognizance of cases in his own right and not by delegation"; "an officer in a religious fraternity having charge of the convent"; and here's my favorite, "The Chaplain of Newgate Prison whose duty it was to prepare condemned prisoners to death"; and finally, a stage prompter—"The players are prompted by one called the Ordinary, who followeth at their back with the book in his hand" (*Oxford English Dictionary*, 1982, p. 2006).

There I go again, sliding beneath the surface of common parlance. Is recourse to etymology looking for trouble, too?

Jackson's rebuke casts me as Hamlet to his Gertrude. Though by age and gender I more closely resemble the middle-aged matron than I do her rebellious son, I share his impatience with the normative demand that we stick to the surface of things.

> *Queen*: Good Hamlet, cast thy nighted color off.
> And let thine eye look like a friend on Denmark.
> Do not for ever with thy vailed lids
> Seek for thy noble father in the dust:
> Thou know'st 'tis common; all lives must die,
> Passing through nature to eternity.
> *Hamlet*: Ay, madam, it is common.
> *Queen*: If it be,
> Why seems it so particular with thee?
> *Hamlet*: Seems, madam. Nay, it is; I know not seems.
>
> *(Act I, Scene 2)*

More than a decade ago I referred to this battle of the generations as I argued for suspicion in educational research:

> Hamlet locates his motive for revenge not in the commonsense world that he shares with those around him but in the underworld, the dark, latent side of experience embodied in the Ghost. Hamlet finds his motive for action . . . by denying what is obvious to everyone else and by approaching the situation they accept as self-explanatory as mystifying. He practices the injunction of phenomenological bracketing that "helps us to see the ordinary as strange and in need of some explanation." His research is disconcerting to the court. (Grumet, 1978, p. 44; quoting Roche, 1973, p. 27)

So, it appears, is mine. Literally, disconcerting. It interrupts the concert of assumptions and methods of the good company of qualitative researchers that Jackson identifies with practice. Had he, indeed, looked *at* the argument of my paper, he might have attended to the distinction between epistemology and hermeneutics that, following Rorty, I bring to the study of validity. When Phil calls out both plaintively and disingenuously, "Hey, Harry! Hey, Madeleine! Wait up for me! I'm coming too!" he reveals the lock-step order that he would impose on this company of scholars, strolling arm in arm, walking to his stride, where "everybody agrees on how to evaluate everything everybody else says" (Rorty, 1979, p. 320):

> Epistemology views the participants as united in what interests in achieving a common end. Hermeneutics views them as united in what he calls a

societas—persons whose paths in life have fallen together, united by civility rather than by a common goal, much less by a common ground. (p. 318; emphasis in original)

It is the determination of what should constitute the common ground of qualitative research that Jackson is trying to establish here. Let me suggest another option. As critic of this study, Jackson might do what literary critics do, that is, interpret the material that has been presented in the work they are reading by presenting the context within which it makes sense to them. I think that is what *good* critics do. They take the work that is a result of selection and emphasis and exclusion and return it to a world, hopefully (said the author) but not necessarily a world within the same galaxy as the one from which it issued. This is the process that I nominated for qualitative research as I offered readings of the ordinary world of schooling as presented in Kathy Farrar's texts that returned her stories to a context related to but different from the explicit one she named.

But that is not what Jackson does. He eschews interpretation. His professed ambition to stick to the intent of the author dooms him to recover what he can never find.[1] His misreading of my paper is proof enough of that. He is not even able to discern the exaggerated flippancy of my escape to Half Moon Bay, so set is he on taking me—and Virginia and Kathy—at our words. Rather than paying attention to Kathy's texts and commenting on or joining our conversation, he says that we should not talk about such things. He balks at "reading a whole lot of symbolic meaning into her [Kathy's] words," and suddenly he slides from his association with Gertrude and reminds me of the kids who were also scared to look below, above, beyond the surface of the text in high school English classrooms. They, seventeen and terribly unsure of everything about their minds and bodies, had no tolerance for complexity, for mystery, for contradiction. Their passion for the ordinary, for conformity, was understandable, given their vulnerability. But what of Philip Jackson, an articulate and gifted ethnographer, an acknowledged leader in his field? Why does this work make Jackson so nervous and so intent on this normative definition of the field?

Gertrude had her reasons for wanting Hamlet to stay close to the surface of things. Whatever was rotten in the state of Denmark was no mystery to her. What does Jackson know that he does not want the rest of us to find out? Has he been co-opted by the very order that he por-

---

1. Paul Ricoeur's (1976) critique of the "intentional fallacy" is instructive here.

trayed so vividly for us in *Life in Classrooms* (1968)? Is that why he imagines that the rest of us are "finding ourselves" in work that is not intimidated and confined by the ordinary? That is the order that takes the longings and terrors that drive our lives and labels them *Verboten*. Repressed and denied in the culture of the school, they surface in the horror stories of the principals at play. And that, of course, is what I am getting at in my essay when I suggest that there is a dialectical relationship between the culture of schooling, between order, and between those disorderly cultures it contradicts. The autobiographical method presented here is designed to investigate how the order of school experience is invested with value and meaning that originates in another order, that of domesticity and family life. If that is trouble, then we are all in it, for it is the place we have all come from. I do not think this place of feeling is trouble. But I know we get into trouble when we forget where we have come from and wander through classrooms as if there were no fleet of yellow buses, no friendly crossing guards ready and waiting to take us home.

REFERENCES

Compact edition of the Oxford English dictionary. (1982). Oxford, UK: Oxford University Press.

Foucault, M. (1979). *Discipline and punish* (A. Sheridan, Trans.). New York: Random House.

Grumet, M. (1978). Curriculum as theater: Merely players. *Curriculum Inquiry, 8,* 37–64.

Jackson, P. W. (1968). *Life in classrooms.* New York: Holt, Rinehart and Winston.

Ricoeur, P. (1976). *Interpretation theory.* Fort Worth: Texas Christian University Press.

Roche, M. (1973). *Phenomenology, language and the social sciences.* London: Routledge and Kegan Paul.

Rorty, R. (1979). *Philosophy and the mirror of nature.* Princeton, NJ: Princeton University Press.

Part III

GENERALIZABILITY

One of the central aims of scientific inquiry is to create ideas that allow us to anticipate the future. Such ideas are typically referred to as predictions. Generalizations are not dissimilar. They consist of ideas—or images—that in some way allow us to understand or anticipate phenomena we have not yet encountered from phenomena we have encountered. Generalizations enable us to form expectations on the basis of prior experience.

As Robert Donmoyer points out, in conventional forms of statistically oriented research, the procedures through which acceptable generalizations are formulated are well defined: The random selection of a sample from a population is the cornerstone of inferential statistics. Inferential statistics, with the assistance of probability tables, tell us just how confident we can be about differences between groups and, through such analyses, how confidently we can generalize.

These procedures, so well defined in the empirical research community, are seldom particularly relevant for qualitative research efforts. First, case studies, one of the prime subjects of qualitative inquiry, are rarely randomly selected, and even if they were, given conventional assumptions, $n = 1$ is simply too small a sample. Second, since the data generated by qualitative inquiry into cases are never mainly quantitative, statistical treatment is not a viable option. Yet qualitative researchers are justifiably uncomfortable with the notion that the careful study of cases yields conclusions that pertain only to the cases studied and to no more. Life does not work that way. We do generalize all the time from individual, nonrandomly selected events; we do seem to learn valuable things from these events that help us cope with our respective futures. We were generalizing animals well before the birth of inferential statistics.

The aim of Donmoyer's and Janet Schofield's papers is to explore the meaning of generalization within the context of qualitative research. If conventional criteria for generalization are not appropriate for qualitative studies, what criteria are? How can one—if indeed one

can—make inferences about other situations from nonrandomly selected cases? What do we mean by generalization? Who generalizes?
On what grounds can claims about the generalizability of case
studies be justified?

Donmoyer and Schofield address these questions and others like
them in very different ways. Donmoyer leans toward the use of personal experience as a source of generalization. One of his major ideas
is that the practice of education as it unfolds in classrooms is inevitably focused, not upon aggregates (we are tempted to say faceless aggregates), but upon individual students. Hence the teacher must always adjust or fine-tune whatever generalizations he or she has that
might be relevant to a particular context or situation. Generalizing
for Donmoyer is mainly a personal, idiosyncratic effort. The products
of conventional research are, in essence, heuristic for the teacher, not
the probability statements they appear to be.

In Donmoyer's view, generalization emerges as a form of personal knowledge often revealed in the narrative of the parable or
story; we generalize each time we try to learn lessons from the past.
As a result, in Donmoyer's worldview, the meaning of generalization
broadens, and with the broadened view distinctions among types of
generalizations can be forged. Hence we have formal generalization,
the type most commonly produced through statistically driven research, and naturalistic generalization, the kind born of personal experience.

Schofield portrays another world. She, too, makes useful distinctions. She tells us that we can generalize through qualitative research by focusing on what is, what may be, and what could be. Each
type of generalization is made possible if one designs studies that are
appropriate for each aim. But Schofield goes well beyond making distinctions. She identifies the design features necessary to provide each
kind of generalization and offers us examples from her own work to
illustrate the ways in which potential generalizations can emerge.

There is an interesting difference in the spirits of Donmoyer's
and Schofield's chapters. Each addresses the issue of generalization in
qualitative inquiry. They have this aim in common. What differs is
the flavor of their work. Schofield's chapter participates in an insightful logic of inquiry. Donmoyer's argument moves into a more
phenomenological epistemology. Their aim is similar, but their trajec-
tories differ. This difference is, in our view, a healthy sign of the
richness of the issues. The scope for interpretation is wide, and
efforts aimed at addressing critical matters such as generalization

emanate from a very wide range of sources. Donmoyer's and Schofield's chapters are illustrations of such sources.

With Howard Becker's comments we get still another view. Why the fuss about generalization? he asks. Qualitative research abounds and has for years. Why yet another conference devoted to issues that in most fields have long been settled? The answer he offers relates to the naive expectations and standards concerning research held by educational practitioners. They have little background in research. What they have learned in their university studies has emphasized conventional, experimental forms, and hence when they apply the criteria they know to qualitative research, they find it wanting. In addition, the fact that qualitative researchers hang around, inspect everything, and often cannot tell the practitioners exactly what they are after makes their presence in schools troublesome.

Whether the standards held by practitioners reside at the root of skepticism about qualitative research methods is a question each reader will need to determine. It strikes us that the problems qualitative researchers face go much deeper and are far wider. Practitioners, in fact, seldom read educational research, and they often feel incompetent to judge its adequacy. For most practitioners in our experience, most conventional research is thought to be remote from practice, except, perhaps, when its conclusions confirm or support what they already believe.

Matters of method—and generalizability is central to method—have to do with matters of legitimacy. And matters of legitimacy have to do with matters of publication, appointment, retention, and promotion. Scholastic virtue is defined by fidelity to a set of norms that participate in a well-established tradition. Those attempting to introduce a new set of norms tacitly, if not explicitly, redefine the criteria for determining competence. Not everyone enjoys sharing turf.

In addition, the consequences of accepting new criteria for doing and appraising research are political as well as epistemological. The politics of status and legitimacy also defines what good work consists of and what generalizability requires. In technical terms, the "causes" of acceptability are multivariate. Which variables are relevant is a major part of the continuing debate. We invite you to join in.

5 Generalizability and the Single-Case Study

ROBERT DONMOYER

Language is a marvelous invention. It helps us think precisely and communicate our thoughts to others. It also helps create culture. A shared way of talking helps insure not only that the world will be characterized in a similar way but also that it will be perceived similarly.

This latter characteristic has negative as well as positive consequences, of course, for what we cannot say we often cannot see. Nelson (1969), for example, informs us that the Eskimo group he studied had a wide range of terms with which to distinguish different kinds of ice. Our language has no such discriminatory power, and, therefore, we cannot perceive characteristics of ice that Eskimos see clearly.

Our language *is* rich in terminology to characterize color and texture, however. In contrast, the Hanunoo people of the Phillipines have only four words to describe color, and each of these words also simultaneously refers to a texture (Conklin, 1955). An art critic in our society would have a considerable advantage over a Hanunoo art critic both because our critic has a richer vocabulary with which to communicate perceptions and because the language used to communicate also enhances those perceptions.

Of course, unlike Eskimos, our survival does not depend on the ability to distinguish different kinds of ice. Similarly, art criticism (as we know it, at least) is not a culturally significant activity for the Hanunoo. It would be wasteful for any society to develop ways of talking that serve no purpose, and should societal conditions change— should, for example, art criticism suddenly become a culturally significant activity among the Hanunoo people—new terminology could be invented and new ways of talking could be developed.

THE PROBLEM

Research communities have often been likened to exotic cultures, in part because researchers who work within such communities often employ a shared and highly specialized way of talking (Campbell, 1979). Most social scientists in North America, for instance, speak English, but when they are talking with their colleagues about their work, their English is often unintelligible to ordinary citizens.

The terms *generalize, generalization,* and *generalizability,* for example, are not completely alien to ordinary discourse, but when social scientists use these terms, they have highly specialized meanings: The terms become associated with notions of random selection and statistical significance. Although ordinary citizens might talk of generalizing from a single incident, social scientists would be unlikely to talk about such a thing. Indeed, as long as social scientists employ the cant of their "tribe," they *cannot* talk about such a thing.

In this paper, I want to suggest that social scientists' traditional, restricted conception of generalizability is problematic for applied fields such as education, counseling, and social work. I will first argue that thinking of generalizability solely in terms of sampling and statistical significance is no longer defensible or functional. I will argue, in other words, that applied social scientists are currently in the sort of situation that the Hanunoo people would be in should art criticism suddenly become a culturally significant activity for them; in both situations there is a need to expand the way of talking and thinking about a phenomenon. In the second half of the paper I will propose an alternative way of talking and thinking about generalizability, a way of talking and thinking that suggests that single-case studies may be far more useful than has traditionally been believed.

THE ARGUMENT

The argument can be stated simply: Social scientists' traditional, restricted conception of generalizability is consistent with traditional views of applied social science but inconsistent with more contemporary views. Furthermore, the traditional, restricted conception is not only out of sync with contemporary epistemology; it is also dysfunctional because it limits our ability to reconceptualize the role social science might play in applied fields such as education, counseling, and social work.

The Traditional View

Traditionally social scientists have viewed the social universe in a manner similar to the way physical scientists, before Einstein, viewed the physical universe: Both the physical and the social world were thought to be places where lawful regularities existed between causes and effects. The role of research, whether in physical science or in social science, was to discover and validate generalizations about these regularities. Practitioners could then link particular situations to general statements about causes and effects and know what to do to produce desired outcomes.

E. L. Thorndike summed up this orientation in 1910 in the lead article of the inaugural issue of *The Journal of Educational Psychology.* "A complete science of psychology," Thorndike wrote,

> would tell every fact about everyone's intellect and character and behavior, would tell the cause of every change in human nature, would tell the result which every educational force—every act of every person that changed any other or the agent himself—would have. It would aid us to use human beings for the world's welfare with the same surety of the result that we now have when we use falling bodies or chemical elements. In proportion as we get such a science we shall become masters of our own souls as we are now masters of heat and light. Progress toward such a science is being made. (p. 6)

Thorndike's views seem rather quaint and dated today. Two problems have arisen to challenge his conception of the role of social science in applied fields: One challenge relates to the problem of complexity; the other to the problem of paradigms.

The Complexity Challenge

One of the most convincing presentations of the complexity challenge was made by Cronbach in his 1974 Distinguished Scientific Contribution Award address to the American Psychological Association. In part, the presentation was convincing because of who was making it. Approximately twenty years earlier, Cronbach had stood before the same organization and suggested that Thorndike's dream of "a complete science of psychology" could be realized if researchers would stop looking at the effects of treatments generally and, instead, begin to study the effects of interactions between treatments and people with different aptitudes (Cronbach, 1957). In 1974, however, after years of frustration brought on by "inconsistent findings coming from roughly similar inquiries," Cronbach (1975) declared, "Once we attend to interactions, we enter a hall of mirrors that extends to infinity. However far we carry our analysis—to third order or fifth order or any other— untested interactions of still higher order can be envisioned" (p. 119).

A major part of the problem, according to Cronbach, involves the changeability of culture. He cited as an example Bronfenbrenner's historical look at child-rearing practices of middle- and lower-class parents. Class differences documented in the 1950s were often just the reverse of practices that had been observed in the 1930s. Cronbach concluded:

> The trouble, as I see it, is that we cannot store up generalizations and constructs for ultimate assembly into a network. It is as if we needed a gross of dry cells to power an engine and could only make one a month. The energy would leak out of the first cells before we had half the battery completed. So it is with the potency of our generalizations. (1975, p. 123)

More recently, Cronbach has taken an even more radical tack with respect to the cultural dimension of human action. Like the symbolic interactionists and ethnomethodologists discussed below, Cronbach has concluded that human action is constructed, not caused, and that to expect Newton-like generalizations describing human action, as Thorndike did, is to engage in a process akin to "waiting for Godot" (Cronbach, 1982).

Cronbach's arguments have not gone unchallenged, of course. Phillips (1987), for instance, has argued that social phenomena are no more complex than phenomena in the physical world. He notes, for example, that determining where a particular leaf would land when it falls off a tree would be a task no less complex than the tasks social scientists confront.

The problem with Phillips's analysis is that few physical scientists are interested in predicting, much less controlling, where a single leaf falls, just as no engineer employing quantum mechanics is interested in what happens to individual atoms or electrons. Teachers, however, are interested in individual students, and counselors and social workers are concerned with individual clients. Social phenomena may or may not be more complex than phenomena in the physical world. (Phillips's argument is hardly convincing on this point because he fails even to address the problem of culture raised by Cronbach both in his 1974 address and, even more forcefully, in his more recent and more radical work.) It is obvious, however, that even if social phenomena are not more complex, social purposes are. Given the complexity of social purposes—given the concern with individuals, not just aggregates—it is unlikely that we will ever even approximate Thorndike's (1910) dream of a "complete science of psychology" (p. 6).

Phillips also indicates that Cronbach overestimates the complexity problem because he adopts an "unduly inductivist" position and ignores the fact that *a priori* theories help focus social scientists' attention on certain variables while screening out others. While Phillips's criticism of Cronbach is undoubtedly correct, he ignores the fact that the *a priori* theories that inevitably simplify the research process also create a new challenge to the empiricist view of social research articulated by Thorndike. Indeed, because we cannot escape the influence of *a priori* theories or paradigms, because even the most rudimentary acts of perception are influenced by latent *a priori* assumptions about the way the world is and ought to be (see, for example, Neisser, 1976), a second challenge to Thorndike's conception of social science and its role in applied fields has emerged.

The Paradigm Challenge

The problem posed by paradigms can be demonstrated by considering a term such as *learning*. Few people would disagree with the proposition that schools should promote learning, but the term *learning* will mean different things to a kindergarten teacher influenced by Piaget, a process-product researcher, an art teacher who wants to promote productive idiosyncrasy, and a parent who wants the schools to go back to basics. Each of these meanings reflects a different conception of what learning is and what teaching ought to be. Each can be said to reflect a different paradigm of reality.

Before a researcher can determine whether Program A produces more learning than Program B, the researcher must choose one of the paradigms—that is, one of the meanings—alluded to above or one of the multitude of other meanings that could be associated with the term *learning*. The meaning selected will influence the researcher's findings at least as much as the empirical reality being described.

The situation is further complicated by the fact that, from certain paradigmatic perspectives, the whole quasi-experimental approach to research becomes problematic. Freire (1970), Buber (1947/1968), peace educators such as Galtung (1974), and a humanist reading of Dewey (see Kleibard, 1975), for example, suggest that educational practice should not be built around predetermined student learning outcomes, no matter what conception of learning the predetermined outcomes reflect. This position suggests that rather than attempting to control students, teachers should engage in dialogue with students, and rather than transmitting a predefined curriculum to students, teachers should work with students to construct jointly the curriculum for the class.

This perspective of what education ought to be is compatible with ethnomethodologists' and symbolic interactionists' view of how human understanding actually develops and how human action actually occurs. Blumer (1969), the father of symbolic interactionism, for example, not only argues that human beings act toward things on the basis of the meanings things have for them and that meanings are a product of social interaction rather than external causes; he also argues that meanings are not static but must constantly be constructed and reconstructed by actors during social interaction. In adopting this later position, Blumer rejects the notion that "thought objects . . . determine . . . behavior by motivating it." Rather, according to Blumer:

> A realistic analysis of the human act shows that the tendency to act cannot be taken as moulding or controlling the act. At best the tendency or preparation to act is merely an element that enters into the developing act—no more than an initial bid for a possible line of action. . . .
>
> Since the act, whether individual or collective, is fashioned, constructed, and directed by the process of definition that goes on in the individual or the group as the case may be, it is this process that should be the central object of study by the psychologist and the sociologist. A knowledge of this process would be of far greater value for prediction, if that is one's interest, than would any amount of knowledge of tendencies or attitudes. (p. 98)

Thus, even if meanings and reasons are allowed to substitute for causes in a cause-and-effect explanatory framework, Blumer is not satisfied. According to him, the explanatory framework itself sends an inaccurate message regardless of its substantive content. In adopting this position, Blumer sides with those continental philosophers who have argued that epistemology can never be completely severed from psychology. According to Blumer, the traditional cause-and-effect approach to explanation, which is at the heart of Thorndike's conception of social science and also at the heart of traditional conceptions of generalizability, carries with it a certain metaphysical model of human beings and human action. It is because of this implicit model and his rejection of it that Blumer refuses to phrase research findings in terms of cause-and-effect generalizations, even probabilistic ones.

Whether or not one accepts Blumer's conception of human action, this conception does provide an alternative to Thorndike's conception of how the social world operates, and, as such, it reminds us once again that Thorndike's conception of the social world is just that, an *a priori* conception. This *a priori* conception is not determined by the facts but rather determines what the facts are.

Furthermore, even if we accept Thorndike's explanatory framework, the words and meanings we fit into that syntax (e.g., whether we talk and think of learning in a manner consistent with the process-product researcher or as a Piagetian psychologist does) will still have as significant an impact on our perception and assessment of empirical reality as does the reality itself. Indeed, as Kant concluded long ago, it is impossible to talk of the nature of reality with any sense of certainty because we can never know reality independent of the cognitive structures that influence our perceptions.

Implications

Both of the problems outlined above have implications for the way we think about generalizability. The complexity problem, for example, suggests that it no longer makes sense to think of generalizability as synonymous with the use of large samples and statistical procedures designed to insure that the large samples accurately represent the population. In the applied fields, social science can never provide the sort of certainty envisioned by Thorndike. Even statistically significant findings from studies with huge, randomly selected samples cannot be applied directly to particular individuals in particular situations; skilled clinicians will always be required to determine whether a research generalization applies to a particular individual, whether the generalization needs to be adjusted to accommodate individual idiosyncracy, or whether it needs to be abandoned entirely with certain individuals in certain situations.

To be sure, research with large samples can provide clinicians with some idea of a certain strategy's probability for success—it can make teachers and other clinicians more informed gamblers, in other words—but even this advantage has a downside. Researchers' ideal types can easily become stereotypes (Donmoyer, 1987b), and stereotypes, when applied to individuals, can easily become self-fulfilling prophecies (Rist, 1973). For example, findings that poor children will probably have reading difficulties may cause teachers and administrators to behave in ways that will actually create reading difficulties for particular poor children (Heath, 1982).

Thus, for practitioners concerned with individuals, not aggregates, research can never be generalizable in the sense suggested by Thorndike. Research can only function as a heuristic; it can suggest possibilities but never dictate action. It may well be the case that case study research can fulfill this function as well, or possibly even better, than more traditional approaches to research.

While the complexity challenge suggests the need to reconceptualize the notion of generalizability and to rethink the utility of single-case research, the paradigm challenge suggests, in a general way, how the notion of generalizability might be reconceptualized and what the role of case study research might be. Discussion of the role of paradigms in research reminds us that researchers must inevitably rely on *a priori* conceptualization that is not determined by the data but, rather, determines what the data are. In Lather's (1988) words, research is inevitably ideological; it inevitably conceals even as it reveals.

When clinicians utilize social scientists' cause-and-effect findings, for instance, they also are influenced by social scientists' *a priori* conceptions of social action and social relationships. These *a priori* conceptions, these social constructions, can easily become reality for those who employ them. When this occurs, other conceptions of reality are not even considered; indeed, the possibility that alternative conceptions of reality exist is normally not even recognized.

The discussion of paradigms suggests a role that case study research might play: Case study research might be used to expand and enrich the repertoire of social constructions available to practitioners and others; it may help, in other words, in the forming of questions rather than in the finding of answers. This role, in turn, suggests that it may be useful to think of generalizability more in psychological terms than in terms of mathematical probability. This is the tack to be taken in the second half of this paper.

The Existing Literature

Most social scientists have come to accept both that social purposes and social phenomena are too complex for social science to provide definitive answers to practical problems and that *a priori* assumptions or paradigms inevitably influence the conclusions of empirical research. Social scientists, however, have not always thought through the implications of these ideas. From the perspective of history, conceptual shifts in academic disciplines and fields may look like revolutions (Kuhn, 1971); a close-up look at paradigm shifts normally reveals a far more incremental and evolutionary process (Carloye, 1985).

For instance, at the moment, few applied social scientists would disagree with the proposition that social phenomena and/or social purposes are too complex for social science to provide definitive answers to practical problems in fields such as education, counseling, and social work. Yet many social scientists continue to distinguish between hypothesis-generating research and verification-oriented research; qualitative studies—particularly qualitative studies of single cases—are relegated to the less prestigious former category. The classic hypothesis generation/verification distinction, however, ignores the fact that in fields such as education, social work, and counseling—fields in which there is a concern with individuals, not just aggregates—all research findings are tentative.

Similarly, Weiss (1982) tells us, on the one hand, that the role of social science is not to give policy makers answers but to help them frame policy questions; on the other hand, she recommends that social scientists continue to engage in business as usual. The only procedural change she recommends, in fact, is the allocation of more time, so that social scientists can do what they have always done more thoroughly. Because Weiss remains under the spell of tradition, she fails even to notice that the frames social scientists provide have as much to do with the *a priori* conceptions that make empirical work possible as with the empirical work itself (Gusfield, 1976) and even to consider whether the shift in social science's role from answer-giver to question-framer makes many traditional social science procedures irrelevant. Nor does Weiss consider whether less traditionally accepted forms of research— for example, single-case studies—might serve social science's newly defined purpose as well or even better than more established ways of doing things.

One reason that social scientists often cling uncritically to outdated notions is the absence of an alternative language with which to talk about phenomena. As I indicated earlier, what we cannot say, we often cannot see.

The absence of an alternative language has certainly inhibited our rethinking the notion of generalizability and, consequently, our valuing of single-case studies. For example, when qualitative research first began to be taken seriously in the field of education, Feinberg (1977), at a government-funded conference of researchers sympathetic to qualitative work, offered the following knee-jerk assessment of the limits of qualitative case studies:

Even though the information collected on a single classroom group over the period of a year or more is extremely rich, the basic fact remains that for a single-classroom study, N = 1. . . .

A study such as Rist's may help to generate hypotheses about urban or ghetto schools. It does not allow for generalizations or broad conclusions (perhaps not even narrow ones). (p. 53)

Feinberg's sentiments have been echoed by other advocates and practitioners of qualitative research, including Mishler (1979) and Jackson (1974).

Over the years, others have tried to move beyond the traditional conception of generalizability with varying degrees of success. Hamilton (1976), for example, has talked of creating a "science of the singular." Similarly, Stake (1978, 1980) has spoken of "naturalistic generalizations" that

develop with a person as a product of experience. They derive from the tacit knowledge of how things are, why they are, how people feel about them, and how these things are likely to be later or in other places with which this person is familiar. They seldom take the form of predictions but lead regularly to expectation. They guide action, in fact they are inseparable from action. . . . These generalizations may become verbalized, passing of course from tacit knowledge to propositional; but they have not yet passed the empirical and logical tests that characterize formal (scholarly, scientific) generalizations. (1978, p. 6)

Both the Stake and Hamilton discussions are useful for those who wish to rethink the traditional notion of generalizability, but their utility is limited for two reasons. First, both discussions refer to evaluation research. Stake, for instance, develops the notion of naturalistic generalizations in the course of making the case for qualitative case studies as the method of choice in evaluating a particular program. (Because qualitative case studies can provide vicarious experiences and, hence, be a source of naturalistic generalizations, Stake argues, ordinary people will be able to better understand evaluation reports and, hence, better understand what is going on in the particular programs being assessed.) Given this focus on evaluation, the traditional concern associated with the notion of generalizability (i.e., how does in-depth knowledge of a single case help us understand and act more intelligently in other potentially different cases) was not even addressed by Stake.

The second problem is that neither Stake nor Hamilton develops his alternative conception in much detail. Stake, for example, makes some quick references to Polanyi's (1958) notion of tacit knowledge and Dilthey's (1961, 1976) notion of experiential understanding, but he fails to develop a theoretical language adequate to talk and think with much specificity about an alternative to the traditional notion of generalizability.

Lincoln and Guba (1985) have been somewhat more specific in reconceptualizing the notion of generalizability. They have actually shifted terminology; they talk of *transferability* rather than generalizability. They start with the assumption that research findings will always be only working hypotheses, an assumption that, as the above analysis suggests, is defensible whenever the concern is with individuals. (As I have noted in my review of their book [Donmoyer, 1987a], Lincoln and Guba do overlook the possibility that policy makers may find aggregate data sufficient for certain purposes.) They go on to ask, "How can one tell whether a working hypothesis developed in Context A might be applicable in Context B?" and then answer this question by noting:

> The degree of transferability is a direct function of the similarity between the two contexts, what we shall call "fittingness." Fittingness is defined as the degree of congruence between sending and receiving contexts. If Context A and Context B are "sufficiently" congruent, then working hypotheses from the sending originating context may be applicable in the receiving context. (p. 124)

Later, they add:

> Transferability, far from being established once and for all because certain methodological tenets, such as careful control and random sampling, have been followed, must be reassessed in each and every case in which transfer is proposed. That is to say, an investigator can make no statements about transferability for his or her findings based solely on data from the studied context alone. At best the investigator can supply only that information about the studied site that may make possible a judgment of transferability to some other site; the final judgment on that matter is, however, vested in the person seeking to make the transfer. (p. 217)

Clearly Lincoln and Guba provide a less ethereal, more easily understood alternative to the traditional view of generalizability. The transferability alternative, however, is hardly a radical departure from the traditional view. Although the notion of transferability accommodates the problem of complexity, it still assumes that findings from one setting are only generalizable to another setting if both settings are very similar. My intuition suggests this need not necessarily be the case.

The research community does not currently have a language available to translate my intuition into linguistic form. Indeed, the point of the second half of this paper is to try to develop such a language, or, more precisely, to take an existing, widely accepted theoretical language and apply it to unfamiliar territory: the context of research utilization. Before proceeding with this task, however, let me try to give some sense of where I am heading by relating two personal anecdotes. As I will argue in the next section, stories can often serve as a half-way house between tacit personal knowledge and formal propositional thought.

The first anecdote dates back to the time when I was taking anthropology courses. In one course, I read Eggan's (1974) "Instruction and Affect in Hopi Cultural Continuity," a paper that contained a rich narrative description of Hopi education. This description of both formal and informal education in a culture radically different from my own provided tremendous insight into schooling in my own culture. Later, when I became a teacher in my own culture, I believe I acted more intelligently—I certainly behaved more thoughtfully—as a result of having read the initiation rite ethnography.

My second story takes us back even further. When I was in my early teens, I had an opportunity to see Arthur Miller's *Death of a Salesman*. Though the Willy Loman on stage and the adolescent who sat in the darkened theater had little in common, I learned a great deal about myself that night. Despite the many differences between Miller's aging salesman and the adolescent who watched him—or possibly because of these differences—something, which in ordinary parlance could be called generalization, occurred.

If the sense of generalization referred to in the previous paragraphs is really to impact our thinking, a new theoretical language must be found. This language must be both more detailed than earlier talk of naturalistic generalizations and more radical than Lincoln and Guba's notion of transferability. The next section of the paper presents such a language.

AN ALTERNATIVE CONCEPTUALIZATION

Like Stake's notion of naturalistic generalization, the conception of generalizability I will articulate here is rooted in a conception of experiential knowledge. I will begin this part of the discussion, therefore, at the experiential level; then suggest why talk of working hypotheses and transferability is inadequate to describe the experience; go on to propose a more adequate theoretical language; and, finally, indicate how all of this relates to questions about the utility of single-case studies.

An Experience

My starting point for this discussion of an alternative conception of generalization is the starting point for all inquiry: personal knowledge (Polanyi, 1958). The particular personal knowledge that is relevant here was gleaned from six years of experience as a classroom teacher. I began my teaching career in a ghetto school in the middle of Harlem. Later I taught in an affluent suburb, which was in many ways the antithesis of the ghetto community in which I began my career; my students reflected community differences. Still later I taught a different grade in a rural island community where, once again, my students were quite different from the students I had taught earlier. Despite the differences, however, each year teaching became easier; each year I could more easily anticipate the consequences of my actions; increasingly, I could even control events. Generalization, of one sort or another, occurred.

The Language of Working Hypotheses and Transferability

The situation described above is hardly unique; if it were, experience would not be so valued by employers. The sort of experiential knowledge alluded to above, however, could be described in terms of Lincoln and Guba's language of transferability: According to this characterization, an experience in one situation leads to the development of working hypotheses; when a person moves to a new situation, he or she simply compares the sending situation to the receiving situation, determines the degree of fit, and applies those hypotheses that appear to be applicable in the new situation. This way of characterizing the situation, however, seems less than adequate for at least four reasons.

First, as Stake has suggested, much of the generalizing that occurs at the level of experience occurs tacitly; that is, much experiential knowledge has not been translated into propositional form, the sort of form implied by the term *working hypotheses*. To be sure, it is certainly the case that language is a potent influence on understanding. As I noted at the outset of this paper, what we cannot say we often cannot see. But it is also the case that language—particularly the propositional language of hypotheses—is too gross a tool to encompass all that we learn from experience.

In addition, mere mortals could never consciously articulate (1) the working hypotheses generated by experience in one situation, (2) the multiple, interacting characteristics at work in that situation, (3) the multiple, interacting characteristics at work in a second situation, and (4) the similarities and differences between situation one and situation two.

One final point with respect to the tacit knowledge issue: Clinicians often encode experiential knowledge in stories and anecdotes, and once such encoding has occurred, tacit knowledge is no longer entirely tacit. We can probably even find hypotheses in embryo form in the stories and anecdotes clinicians use to guide their actions. Much of the understanding engendered by narrative modes of discourse is still at the tacit level, however (Bruner, 1986), and, therefore, it would be inappropriate to characterize even actions engendered by stories and anecdotes as a process of transferring working hypotheses.

There is a second reason why talk of transferring working hypotheses is inadequate for characterizing the sort of experiential learning that occurs when a teacher or clinician in human service fields moves from one setting to another: The relationship of teachers and students—like the relationship of counselors or social workers and clients—need not necessarily be similar to the relationship of scientist and subject. The relationship is often closer to that captured by Blumer's (1969) notion of "joint action." Blumer's notion of "joint action" refers to the creation, through interaction, of a common set of meanings to describe a situation. The creation of a common set of meanings requires that each participant in an interaction imaginatively "take on the role" of the other participants. From this perspective, in other words, teachers and clinicians would not be so much concerned with "acting on" students or clients as with "interacting with" them.

Please note, I am not suggesting that teachers, counselors, and social workers never behave like applied scientists, that their thoughts can never be characterized by talk of transferring working hypotheses from one situation to another. It is just that skilled clinicians in such fields often play the dual role Powdermaker (1966) defines for anthropologists: They must be not only the stranger who stands outside the action and analyzes and acts on subjects; they must also function as a friend who *interacts* with and, in the process, jointly constructs meanings with students or clients. The language of transferability and working hypotheses fails to capture this interactive aspect of experiential learning.

Third, it is not just that talk of working hypotheses and transferability fails to do justice to the process of experiential learning; such talk also provides an inadequate characterization of the knowledge generated by that process. The sort of knowledge gained from experience is not purely intellectual. It is often affect-laden. It is the sort of knowledge that Isaiah Berlin (1966) describes when he talks about the kind of understanding historians need to practice their craft. Berlin describes this sort of knowledge as follows:

> When the Jews are enjoined in the Bible to protect strangers "For ye know the soul of a stranger, seeing ye were strangers in the land of Egypt" (Exodus, 23:9), this knowledge is neither deductive, nor inductive, nor founded on direct inspection, but akin to the "I know" of "I know what it is to be hungry and poor," or "I know how political bodies function," or "I know what it is to be a Brahmin." This is neither (to use Professor Gilbert Ryle's useful classification) "knowing that" which the sciences provide, nor the "knowing how" which is the possession of a disposition or skill, nor the experience of direct perception, acquaintance, memory, but the type of knowledge that an administrator or politician must possess of the men with whom he deals. (p. 45)

The sort of knowledge that Berlin suggests is required of administrators, politicians, and historians is also required of teachers, counselors, and social workers. Experience can provide such knowledge. When we think of generalizability in terms of the transferability of working hypotheses, however, the sort of visceral knowledge of which Berlin speaks can easily be obscured.

Finally, even when a clinician is not interacting with others and/or attempting to understand others from an insider's perspective, much of the learning that develops experientially can be categorized more as meaning making than as hypothesis generation and testing. For instance, before I taught in the ghetto, I had been socialized to think of my students as deprived. When I began teaching, however, I discovered that the students I taught were rich in many ways; for example, when I visited my Hispanic students' parents and needed my bilingual students to serve as my translators, it was I who felt deprived. Such experiences forced me to rethink my notion of deprivation and to define it in more than economic terms.

This redefinition process prepared me to work with a very different population of students in affluent suburbia. Here I found children who economically wanted for nothing and who at a very early age had a wealth of mainstream cultural knowledge and skills. Yet some of these same children, these children whose lives were a constant journey from soccer practices to ceramic classes to violin lessons to special math tutoring sessions to library programs to who knows where, often had been emotionally neglected by professional parents who assumed other professionals (i.e., the soccer coach, the ceramics teacher, etc.) would do their parenting for them. I wondered what it was like to spend so much time with paid professionals rather than parents, and I also wondered how successful my students would be outside of class, without an instructor controlling and directing them. Life, after all, is not a series of classes, at least not for most people. These children, at times, seemed much less able than many of the children I had worked with in the ghetto to know their own minds, to direct themselves toward things they wanted, and to function together as a group without the benefit of an adult's direction.

My experience in suburbia, in other words, expanded even further the meaning I attributed to the term *deprivation*. The notions of working hypotheses and transferability hardly do justice to the sort of meaning-making process just described.

The Language of Schema Theory

A far more appropriate way of characterizing how generalizability occurs in experiential learning is provided by schema theory. Here I will employ the notions of assimilation, accommodation, integration, and differentiation from the schema theory of Piaget (1971), first to characterize the sort of generalization that occurs in experiential learning and then to rethink the notion of generalizability in the context of research utilization.

Before proceeding, let me acknowledge two caveats with respect to my use of Piaget's terminology. First, Piaget's theory is actually two theories: a stage theory of child development and a more general theory of cognitive functioning. Piaget's stage theory is probably better known; it is also the least defensible part of Piaget's work. In employing Piaget's concepts, I in no way endorse his stage theory. Rather, it is his more general description of cognitive processing that I am utilizing here.

Second, Piaget developed his terminology in the process of trying to explain the origin of what he termed "logico-mathematical knowledge." Piaget's way of characterizing cognitive functioning need not be limited to this narrow sphere of understanding, however (Cowan, 1978; Turner, 1973). Here I will employ the notions of assimilation, accommodation, integration, and differentiation far more liberally and relate schema theory to various sorts of social knowledge, including the sort of visceral, affect-laden knowledge discussed by Berlin.

With these caveats duly noted, let us proceed with a discussion of the notions of assimilation, accommodation, integration, and differentiation. According to schema theorists, all knowledge of the empirical world must be filtered through cognitive structures, which shape what we know. Piaget calls this shaping process *assimilation*. Piaget also describes a complementary process, which he calls *accommodation*. This process involves the reshaping of cognitive structures to accommodate novel aspects of what is being perceived. After the dual processes of assimilation and accommodation have occurred, Piaget's theory indicates, a cognitive structure will be both more *integrated* (a particular structure will accommodate more things) and more *differentiated* (a particular structure will be divided into substructures).

A simple example might clarify the Piagetian notions. When I was in graduate school, my oldest son was in kindergarten. He would ask me rather interesting questions. He would ask, for instance, how many recesses I had at my school and when my school had sharing time. In Piagetian terms, my son was *assimilating* my graduate school experience into his very limited cognitive structure of schooling. Over the years, my son's conception of schooling has expanded considerably. He has attended middle and senior high schools as well as elementary schools. He has attended schools throughout the United States and in a foreign country. He has accompanied me to many universities and heard many of my graduate students speak of their experiences. In the process, my son's cognitive structure of schooling has *accommodated* much of the novelty he has seen and heard. As a result, this cognitive structure is both more *integrated* (the terms *school* and *schooling* mean more things) and more *differentiated* (he can now talk about different kinds of school and different aspects of schooling, and he can think about more distinctions related to schooling that he cannot even articulate in language).

I believe I underwent a process similar to my son's when I moved from a Harlem school to schools with very different populations. The sort of generalization that characterized my movement from one school to another was not primarily mediated by working hypotheses transferred from one setting to the next. Rather, the mediating mechanisms are better characterized as cognitive structures that could only partially be coded into language and that, in fact, often functioned at the level of tacit knowledge.

It is important to note that when generalization is thought of in this way, the diversity between school settings becomes an asset rather than a liability: When diversity is dramatic, the knower is confronted by all sorts of novelty, which stimulates accommodation; consequently, the knower's cognitive structures become more integrated and differentiated; after novelty is confronted and accommodated, he or she can perceive more richly and, one hopes, act more intelligently.

Schema Theory and Case Studies

What does all of this have to do with the issue of generalizability and the single-case study? Stake's comment that case studies can provide *vicarious* experiences serves as the linkage.

Those of us who have lost ourselves in a powerful novel or who have been captivated by a superb storyteller around a campfire or who have been transported to another time and place by a powerful narrative history could hardly deny narrative's ability to provide vicarious experience. The following very brief excerpt from Eggan's (1974) ethnography of Hopi cultural life demonstrates how a skilled storyteller can use her direct experience to create a vicarious experience for her readers:

> If those who doubt that the forces of nature are powerful in shaping personality and culture were confined for one year on the Hopi reservation—even though their own economic dependence on "nature" would be negligible—they would still know by personal experience more convincing than scientific experiments the relentless pressure of the environment on their own reaction patterns. They would, for instance, stand, as all Hopis have forever stood, with aching eyes fastened on a blazing sky where thunderheads piled high in promise and were snatched away by "evil winds," and thus return to their homes knowing the tension, the acute bodily need for the "feel" of moisture. (p. 320)

Langer (1953) says that narrative can create a virtual reality, that is, a reality that exists within our imaginations. The above discussion of paradigms reminds us that scientific knowledge is also undergirded by imagination. Indeed, both forms of understanding require symbolic mediation; it is just that the symbolic form we call narrative allows us to symbolize and hence think and communicate about certain aspects of experience—those things Langer (1953) labels the "ineffable" and Mann (1969) and Vallence (1977) call the "lived-in" aspects of experience—better than does propositional language. There is a structural equivalence between narrative and real-world experience. Both unfold in time. Both can have multiple things happening simultaneously. Both integrate thought and feeling.

Three Advantages of Case Studies

But why should vicarious experience substitute for the real thing? What can case studies do that direct experience cannot? There are at least three answers to these questions. In the remainder of this paper, I will review each of these answers and, in the process, clarify some other related and salient points.

Accessibility. First, case studies can take us to places where most of us would not have an opportunity to go. As I noted above, my son has had an opportunity to experience schooling in a wide range of settings, and as a result he can now think of schooling much more complexly than he could when he was in kindergarten. It is not likely, however, that he will ever be able to experience a tribal society's approach to schooling. Yet he can read Eggan's (1974) compelling description of Hopi initiation rites and experience vicariously the Hopi process of formal education and the meanings the Hopi attach to this process. I suspect that after reading Eggan's case study, he would have an even more enriched conception of schooling than he has acquired through direct experience. This enriched conception would not only allow him to understand schooling in Hopi culture; it would also help him look at schools in his own society in a new way: He should be able both to see different things and to see differently things he has seen before.

This first benefit does not only apply to learning about exotic cultures. Case studies also allow us to experience vicariously unique situations and unique individuals within our own culture. They can help us overcome the problem caused by the fact that (1) many clinicians learn best by modeling, but (2) there are often not enough truly exceptional models to go around.

Several years ago the Rockefeller Brothers' Fund allowed me to experience (in the role of qualitative researcher) a truly unique and highly effective principal (Donmoyer, 1983, 1985a). One of the many things I learned while interacting with this man was that he and I interpreted his interactions with his staff very differently. My interpretation was influenced by behaviorist psychology and contemporary political science: I coded much of his behavior as positive social reinforcement and political favor trading. He (and, to a large extent, his staff) was influenced by his own folk paradigm, and he characterized his actions in terms of different kinds of "personal closeness," a term he had invented.

To the extent that I could understand the principal's perspective and communicate it in the narratives I wrote—and elsewhere, I believe, I have demonstrated the need to use narrative in reporting this particular case, at least (see Donmoyer, 1985a)—readers can experience vicariously an individual whom I had an opportunity to experience directly.

In the process, they, too, can begin to see staff relationships in a new light. Their staff relationship schema, in other words, can become enriched as they accommodate the novelty of this particular case.

I should emphasize two points here. First, it does not especially matter whether the principal's folk perspective is more correct than the social science perspectives I brought to the situation. Elsewhere I have suggested that the relative correctness of rival interpretations often cannot be determined (Donmoyer, 1985b). Rival interpretations often reflect the use of alternative theoretical languages, and languages are not true or false, only more or less adequate. Even adequacy can only be assessed in terms of particular purposes in particular contexts, and ultimately it must be the reader who decides whether the principal's interpretation of his interactions with staff serves the reader's purpose in the reader's particular situation.

When generalizability is viewed from the perspective of schema theory, in other words, the role of the research is not primarily to find the correct interpretation. Indeed, the search for the correct interpretation may well be a search for a Holy Grail. Rather, from the schema theory view of generalizability, the purpose of research is simply to expand the range of interpretations available to the research consumer.

The second point I want to make relates to the goal of expanding the range of interpretations available to research consumers. When this is our goal, when, in other words, generalizability is viewed from the perspective of schema theory, uniqueness is an asset rather than a liability. To be sure, it is certainly legitimate to ask questions about typicality—to ask what most principals normally do. When we are interested in expanding cognitive structures, however, this is not the question being asked. To the contrary, when we are interested in expanding cognitive structures, the outlier is prized, for the outlier has great heuristic value.

Seeing Through the Researcher's Eyes.   There is a second reason the vicarious experience of case studies might be preferred to direct experience: Case studies allow us to look at the world through the researcher's eyes and, in the process, to see things we otherwise might not have seen. When I read Lightfoot's (1983) description of St. Paul's School in her book *The Good High School,* I get to see what a private, elite school looks like from the perspective of a black female. When I read Wolcott's (1987) observer-as-participant study "The Teacher as Enemy," I get to view cross-cultural teaching from his highly unique vantage point. It is true that when I read Lightfoot and Wolcott I learn as much about Lightfoot and Wolcott as I do about the phenomena they studied.

This is not a liability, however, when our interest is in expanding the readers' cognitive structures. Indeed, given what we know about the mediating influence of cognitive structures on perception, a complete description of a phenomenon is impossible. The best we can hope for is that any individual will have a rich repertoire of schemata through which to view particular events. By viewing a situation vicariously through the eyes of a Lightfoot or a Wolcott, it is likely that a richer repertoire of schemata will develop.

Let me pause here to raise three additional points that are related both to what has just been said and also to one another. First, when we look through a researcher's eyes, we do not necessarily see the world through the researcher's personal, idiosyncratic perspective. The researcher's perspective might be the intersubjectively shared theoretical perspective of a discipline or field of study. When one reads Suransky's (1982) five case studies of early childhood programs in her book *The Erosion of Childhood*, for example, one does not so much see these programs through Suransky's eyes alone as through the lenses of the neo-Marxist and feminist theory that influences Suransky's perspective. In short, case studies can help those who are uninitiated into a particular theoretical viewpoint come to understand that viewpoint.

Second, case study narratives like Suransky's—that is, case study narratives influenced by the perspective of formal theory—are not only useful to those uninitiated in a particular theoretical viewpoint. If the theoretically colored case studies are well done, they can add depth and dimension to theoretical understanding. By definition, theory simplifies our understanding of reality. At least in this respect, the social scientist's ideal types are no different from stereotypes. Well-done case studies can add nuance and subtlety to the ideal-typical perspective of theory.

Third, let me confront the question that was begged in the previous paragraph: What constitutes a "well-done case study" when one is viewing generalizability from the perspective of schema theory? The answer to this question is not dramatically different from more traditionally oriented qualitative researchers' definition of quality work (see, for example, Miles & Huberman, 1984). To be sure, those who approach qualitative research from the perspective of schema theory will probably be more open to use of literary discourse, the sort of discourse championed by Eisner (1985) and Barone (1987). Because those influenced by schema theory recognize that all knowledge is symbolically mediated, they should be more receptive to the Eisner/Barone argument that certain aspects of experience can only be accommodated and communicated through literary modes of symbolism. The bottom line for assessing the quality of a case study, however, is still the richness of the data presented.

To be sure, given what has been said in this paper, we can no longer talk of raw data if, by that term, we mean data uncontaminated by the language and the anticipatory schemata of the researcher. We can, however, talk of data that are medium-rare, for example, low-inference descriptions of behavior and excerpts from transcribed interviews. There should be sufficient medium-rare data so that the reader does not simply assimilate the case being described into a theoretical ideal type; rather the reader should have an opportunity to enrich his or her understanding of an ideal type by accommodating the novelty of the particular case. Indeed I think it is reasonable to assume that case studies will provide sufficient medium-rare data so that a reader who starts from a different orientation from the researcher's could fashion an interpretation significantly different from the researcher's narrative.

To put this matter another way, good case studies employ theoretical constructs the way the historian of a particular revolution uses the construct of "revolution." In 1957, William Dray, a philosopher of history, noted that a historian who sets out to explain the French Revolution

> is just not interested in explaining it as a revolution—as an astronomer might be interested in explaining a certain eclipse as an instance of eclipses; he is almost invariably concerned with it as different from other members of its class. Indeed, he might even say that his main concern will be to explain the French Revolution's taking a course unlike any other; that is to say, he will explain it as unique in the sense distinguished above. (p. 47)

Decreased Defensiveness.   There is a third reason that the vicarious experience provided by case studies might be preferable to direct experience: Vicarious experience is less likely to produce defensiveness and resistance to learning. One flaw of Piaget's theory is that it assumes that accommodation will inevitably accompany assimilation. We know, however, that human beings socially construct reality and that those with power can often force their social constructions on others. They can—through the exercise of power—make the world change to conform to their conception of it rather than alter their cognitive structures to accommodate those aspects of the world that are disconcerting and threatening. The power of teachers to socially construct reality and create self-fulfilling prophecies, for instance, has been well documented (see, for example, Rist, 1973; Sharp & Green, 1975).

People, of course, can screen out disquieting and psychologically threatening aspects of vicarious experience, just as they screen out aspects of direct experience that make them uncomfortable. When the threat is merely psychological (which is the case when experience is merely vicarious), however, it seems reasonable to assume that resistance to accommodating novelty will not be as great as when a threat is experienced in real life. A teacher reading a narrative description of the self-fulfilling prophecy phenomenon at work in another teacher's classroom, for instance, will likely feel less threatened than if initially asked to confront that phenomenon in his or her own work. For that construct to have impact, of course, the teacher must eventually apply it to him- or herself. If the self-fulfilling prophecy construct is part of the teacher's cognitive repertoire, however, such self-analysis is at least possible.

CONCLUSION

Philosophers and historians of science talk about scientific revolutions, giant shifts in perspectives and procedures within particular disciplines and fields of study. For those in the midst of such a revolution, however, the "revolutionary" process can seem slow and labored, indeed. Giving up sacrosanct notions is a slow and painful process, and time is inevitably required to develop new ways of talking and thinking about the ideas that have guided our thinking and our actions in the past.

Here I have argued that social scientists' traditional way of talking and thinking about generalizability is no longer adequate. I have not suggested the traditional notion is useless. For policy makers who are interested only in aggregates, not individuals, and for whom questions of meaning and perspective have been resolved, the traditional notion of generalizability will do just fine. Practitioners in fields such as education, counseling, and social work, however, are concerned with individuals, not aggregates, and, for them, questions about meaning and perspective are central and ongoing. If research is to assist such clinicians, an alternative way of conceptualizing generalizability is required.

Here I have suggested that schema theory—in particular, the Piagetian notions of assimilation, accommodation, integration, and differentiation—provides an alternative way of talking and thinking about generalizability. I have also suggested that when we apply this way of talking and thinking to the area of research, qualitative case studies appear to have far more utility for applied fields such as education, counseling, and social work than was traditionally believed.

REFERENCES

Barone, T. (1987). Research out of the shadows: A reply to Rist. *Curriculum Inquiry, 17,* 453–463.

Berlin, I. (1966). The concept of scientific history. In W. Dray (Ed.), *Philosophical analysis and history* (pp. 5–53). New York: Harper & Row.

Blumer, H. (1969). *Symbolic interactionism: perspective and method.* Englewood Cliffs, NJ: Prentice-Hall.

Bruner, J. (1986). *Actual minds; possible worlds.* Cambridge, MA: Harvard University Press.

Buber, M. (1968). Education. In M. Buber, *Between man and man.* New York: Macmillan. (Original work published 1947)

Campbell, J. (1979). A tribal model of the social vehicle carrying scientific knowledge. *Knowledge: Creation, Diffusion, Utilization, 1,* 181–201.

Carloye, J. (1985). Normal science and the extension of theories. *The British Journal of the Philosophy of Science, 36,* 241–256.

Conklin, H. (1955). Hanunoo color categories. *Southwestern Journal of Anthropology, 11,* 339–344.

Cowan, P. (1978). *Piaget with feeling.* New York: Holt, Rinehart and Winston.

Cronbach, L. (1957). The two disciplines of scientific psychology. *American Psychologist, 12,* 671–684.

Cronbach, L. (1975). Beyond the two disciplines of scientific psychology. *American Psychologist, 30,* 116–127.

Cronbach, L. (1982). Prudent aspirations for social inquiry. In W. Kruskal (Ed.), *The social sciences: Their nature and lines* (pp. 61–82). Chicago: University of Chicago Press.

Dilthey, W. (1961). *Meaning in history.* London: Allen and Unwin.

Dilthey, W. (1976). *Selected writings.* New York: Cambridge University Press.

Donmoyer, R. (1983). The principal as prime mover. *Daedalus, 112,* 81–94.

Donmoyer, R. (1985a). Cognitive anthropology and research on effective principals. *Educational Administration Quarterly, 21,* 31–57.

Donmoyer, R. (1985b). The rescue from relativism: Two failed attempts and an alternative strategy. *Educational Researcher, 14,* 13–20.

Donmoyer, R. (1987a). [Review of *Naturalistic inquiry.*] *Teachers College Record, 88,* 470–474.

Donmoyer, R. (1987b). Why case studies? *Curriculum Inquiry, 17,* 91–102.

Dray, W. (1957). *Laws and explanation in history.* London: Oxford University Press.

Eggan, D. (1974). Instruction and affect in Hopi cultural continuity. In G. Spindler (Ed.), *Education and the cultural process* (pp. 311–332). New York: Holt, Rinehart and Winston.

Robert Donmoyer   199

Eisner, E. (1985). *The educational imagination*. New York: Macmillan.

Feinberg, S. (1977). The collection and analysis of ethnographic data in educational research. *Anthropology and Education Quarterly, 8*, 50–57.

Freire, P. (1970). *Pedagogy of the oppressed*. New York: Seabury Press.

Galtung, J. (1974). On peace education. In C. Wulf (Ed.), *Handbook on peace education* (pp. 153–172). Frankfurt/Main, FRG, and Oslo, Norway: International Peace Research Association.

Gusfield, J. (1976). The literary rhetoric of science. *American Sociologist, 41*, 11–33.

Hamilton, D. (1976). *A science of the singular*. Unpublished manuscript, CIRCE, University of Illinois, Urbana.

Heath, S. B. (1982). Ethnography and education: Defining the essentials. In P. Gilmore & A. Glatthord (Eds.), *Children in and out of school: Ethnography and education* (pp. 33–55). Washington, DC: Center for Applied Linguistics.

Jackson, P. (1974). Naturalistic studies of schools and classrooms: One reader's digest. In M. Apple, J. Subpoviak, & H. Lufler (Eds.), *Educational evaluation: Analysis and responsibility* (pp. 83–96). Berkeley, CA: McCutchan.

Kleibard, H. (1975). Reappraisal: The Tyler rationale. In W. Pinar (Ed.), *Curriculum theorizing: The reconceptualists* (pp. 70–83). Berkeley, CA: McCutchan.

Kuhn, T. (1971). *The structure of scientific revolutions*. Chicago: University of Chicago Press.

Langer, S. (1953). *Feeling and form*. New York: Scribner's.

Lather, P. (1988, April). *Ideology and methodological attitude*. Paper presented at the annual meeting of the American Educational Research Association, New Orleans, LA.

Lightfoot, S. L. (1983). *The good high school*. New York: Basic Books.

Lincoln, Y., & Guba, E. (1985). *Naturalistic inquiry*. Beverly Hills, CA: Sage.

Mann, J. (1969). Curriculum criticism. *Teachers College Record, 71*, 27–40.

Miles, M., & Huberman, M. (1984). Drawing valid meaning from qualitative data. *Educational Researcher, 13*, 20–30.

Mishler, E. (1979). Meaning in context: Is there any other kind? *Harvard Educational Review, 49*, 1–20.

Neisser, U. (1976). *Cognition and reality: Principles and implications of cognitive psychology*. San Francisco: W. H. Freeman.

Nelson, R. (1969). *Hunters of the northern ice*. Chicago: University of Chicago Press.

Phillips, D. C. (1987). *Philosophy, science and social inquiry*. Oxford, UK: Pergamon Press.

Piaget, J. (1971). *Biology and knowledge* (B. Walsh, Trans.). Chicago: University of Chicago Press.

Polanyi, M. (1958). *Personal knowledge*. Chicago: University of Chicago Press.

Powdermaker, H. (1966). *Stranger and friend: The way of an anthropologist*. New York: W. W. Norton.

Rist, R. (1973). *The urban school: Factory for failure*. Cambridge, MA: M.I.T. Press.

Sharp, R., & Green, A. (1975). *Education and social control: A study in progressive primary education*. London: Routledge and Kegan Paul.

Stake, R. (1978). The case-study method in social inquiry. *Educational Researcher,*
     7, 5–8.
Stake, R. (1980, April). *Generalizations.* Paper presented at the annual meeting of
     the American Educational Research Association, Boston.
Suransky, V. (1982). *The erosion of childhood.* Chicago: University of Chicago Press.
Thorndike, E. L. (1910). The contribution of psychology to education. *The
     Journal of Educational Psychology, 1,* 5–12.
Turner, T. (1973). Piaget's structuralism. *American Anthropologist, 75,* 351–373.
Vallence, E. (1977). The landscape of the great plains experience: An application
     of curriculum criticism. *Curriculum Inquiry, 7,* 87–105.
Weiss, C. (1982). Policy research in the context of diffuse decision making.
     Journal of Higher Education, 53, 619–639.
Wolcott, H. (1987). The teacher as enemy. In G. Spindler (Ed.), *Education and the
     cultural process* (pp. 136–150). Prospect Heights, IL: Waveland Press.

6 Increasing the Generalizability of Qualitative Research

JANET WARD SCHOFIELD

TRADITIONAL VIEWS OF GENERALIZABILITY

Campbell and Stanley (1963) laid the groundwork for much current thinking on the issue of generalizability just over twenty-five years ago in a groundbreaking chapter in the *Handbook of Research on Teaching*. They wrote, *"External validity* asks the question of *generalizability*: To what populations, settings, treatment variables, and measurement variables can the effect be generalized?" (p. 175; emphasis in original). They then went on to list four specific threats to external validity: the interaction of testing and the experimental treatment, the interaction of selection and treatment, reactive arrangements, and the interference of multiple treatments with one another. Although Campbell and Stanley specifically included populations, settings, treatments, and measurement variables as dimensions relevant to the concept of external validity, the aspect of external validity that has typically received the lion's share of attention in textbook and other treatments of the concept is generalizing to and across populations. This may well be due to the fact that, because of advances in sampling theory in survey research, it is possible to draw samples from even a very large and heterogeneous population and then to generalize to that population using the logic of probability statistics.

Campbell and Stanley (1963), as well as many others in the quantitative tradition, see the attempt to design research so that abstract generalizations can be drawn as a worthy effort, although issues connected with internal validity are typically given even higher priority. Thus researchers in the quantitative tradition have devoted considerable thought to the question of how the generalizability of experimental and quasi-experimental studies can be enhanced. Such efforts are

201

consistent with the fact that many quantitatively oriented researchers would agree with Smith (1975) that "the goal of science is to be able to generalize findings to diverse populations and times" (p. 88).

In contrast to the interest shown in external validity among quantitatively oriented researchers, the methodological literature on qualitative research has paid little attention to this issue, at least until quite recently. For example, Dobbert's (1982) text on qualitative research methods devotes an entire chapter to issues of validity and reliability but does no more than mention the issue of generalizability in passing on one or two pages. Two even more recent books, Kirk and Miller's *Reliability and Validity in Qualitative Research* (1986) and Berg's *Qualitative Research Methods for the Social Sciences* (1989), ignore the issue of external validity completely. The major factor contributing to the disregard of the issue of generalizability in the qualitative methodological literature appears to be a widely shared view that it is unimportant, unachievable, or both.

Many qualitative researchers actively reject generalizability as a goal. For example, Denzin (1983) writes:

> The interpretivist rejects generalization as a goal and never aims to draw randomly selected samples of human experience. For the interpretivist every instance of social interaction, if thickly described (Geertz, 1973), represents a slice from the life world that is the proper subject matter for interpretive inquiry.... Every topic ... must be seen as carrying its own logic, sense of order, structure, and meaning. (pp. 133–134)

Although not all researchers in the qualitative tradition reject generalization so strongly, many give it very low priority or see it as essentially irrelevant to their goals. One factor contributing to qualitative researchers' historical tendency to regard the issue of external validity as irrelevant and hence to disregard it is that this research tradition has been closely linked to cultural anthropology, with its emphasis on the study of exotic cultures. This work is often valued for its intrinsic interest, for showing the rich variety and possible range of human behavior, and for serving a historical function by describing traditional cultures before they change in an increasingly interconnected and homogeneous world. For researchers doing work of this sort, the goal is to describe a specific group in fine detail and to explain the patterns that exist, certainly not to discover general laws of human behavior.

Practically speaking, no matter what one's philosophical stance on the importance of generalizability, it is clear that numerous characteristics that typify the qualitative approach are not consistent with achieving external validity as it has generally been conceptualized. For example, the traditional focus on single-case studies in qualitative research is obviously inconsistent with the requirements of statistical sampling procedures, which are usually seen as fundamental to generalizing from the data gathered in a study to some larger population. This fact is often cited as a major weakness of the case study approach (Bolgar, 1965; Shaughnessy & Zechmeister, 1985).

However, the incompatibility between classical conceptions of external validity and fundamental aspects of the qualitative approach goes well beyond this. To give just one example, the experimental tradition emphasizes replicability of results, as is apparent in Krathwohl's (1985) statement: "The heart of external validity is replicability. Would the results be reproducible in those target instances to which one intends to generalize—the population, situation, time, treatment form or format, measures, study designs and procedures?" (p. 123). Yet at the heart of the qualitative approach is the assumption that a piece of qualitative research is very much influenced by the researcher's individual attributes and perspectives. The goal is *not* to produce a standardized set of results that any other careful researcher in the same situation or studying the same issue would have produced. Rather it is to produce a coherent and illuminating description of and perspective on a situation that is based on and consistent with detailed study of that situation. Qualitative researchers have to question seriously the *internal* validity of their work if other researchers reading their field notes feel the evidence does not support the way in which they have depicted the situation. However, they do not expect other researchers in a similar or even the same situation to replicate their findings in the sense of independently coming up with a precisely similar conceptualization. As long as the other researchers' conclusions are not inconsistent with the original account, differences in the reports would not generally raise serious questions related to validity or generalizability.

In fact, I would argue that, except perhaps in multisite qualitative studies, which will be discussed later in this paper, it is impractical to make precise replication a criterion of generalizability in qualitative work. Qualitative research is so arduous that it is unlikely that high-quality researchers could be located to engage in the relatively unexciting task of conducting a study designed specifically to replicate a previous one. Yet studies not designed specifically for replication are unlikely to be conducted in a way that allows good assessment of the replicability issue. Of course it is possible, even likely, that specific ideas or conclusions from a piece of qualitative work can stimulate further research of a qualitative or quantitative nature that provides information on the replicability of that one aspect of a study. However, any piece of qualitative research is likely to contain so many individual descriptive and conceptual components that replicating it on a piece-by-piece basis would be a major undertaking.

THE INCREASING INTEREST IN GENERALIZABILITY IN THE QUALITATIVE TRADITION

In the past decade, interest in the issue of generalizability has increased markedly for qualitative researchers involved in the study of education. Books by Patton (1980), Guba and Lincoln (1981), and Noblit and Hare (1988), as well as papers by Stake (1978), Kennedy (1979), and others, have all dealt with this issue in more than a cursory fashion. Two factors seem to be important in accounting for this increase in attention to the issue of generalizability. First, the uses of qualitative research have shifted quite markedly in the past decade or two. In the area of education, qualitative research is not an approach used primarily to study exotic foreign or deviant local cultures. Rather it has become an approach used widely in both evaluation research and basic research on educational issues in our own society. The issue of generalizability assumes real importance in both kinds of work.

The shift in the uses of qualitative work that occurred during the 1970s was rapid and striking. The most obvious part of this shift was the inclusion of major qualitative components in large-scale evaluation research efforts, which had previously been almost exclusively quantitative in nature (Fetterman, 1982; Firestone & Herriott, 1984). The acceptance of qualitative research as a valid and potentially rich approach to evaluation progressed to the point that Wolcott (1982) wrote, with only some exaggeration, "By the late 1970s the term 'ethnography' . . . had become synonymous with 'evaluation' in the minds of many educators" (p. 82). Evaluations are expensive and time-consuming undertakings. Although formative evaluations are usually site-specific, the worth of a summative evaluation is greatly enhanced to the extent it can inform program and policy decisions relating to other sites. In fact, as Cronbach (1982) points out, when summative evaluations are reported, no more than a fraction of the audience is interested primarily in the specific program and setting that was the object of the study. Even at the study site itself, by the time the evaluation is completed, changes may well have occurred that have important consequences for program functioning and goal achievement. Thus the question of whether an evaluation's findings can usefully be generalized to a later point in time at the site at which the evaluation was conducted is an issue that, although often ignored, requires real consideration.

The issue of generalizability is also salient for more basic qualitative research on educational issues in this country. Funding agencies providing resources for qualitative studies of educational issues are presumably interested in shedding light on these issues generally, not just as they are experienced at one site. For example, I am currently directing a qualitative study of computer usage in an urban high school. It is clear that the impetus for the funding of this study by the Office of Naval Research derived from concerns about the Navy's own computer-based education and training efforts, not from concerns about the public schools. Quite apart from the goals of funding agencies, many qualitative researchers themselves hope to accomplish more than describing the culture of the specific school or classroom that they have chosen to study. For example, Peshkin (1982) writes of his study of school and community in a small town in Illinois, "I hoped . . . to explicate some reality which was not merely confined to other places just like Mansfield" (p. 63), a hope tellingly reflected in the title of his book, *Growing Up American* (1978), as opposed to "Growing Up in Illinois" or "Growing Up in Mansfield." This desire to have one's work be broadly useful is no doubt often stimulated by concern over the state of education in our country today. It is also clearly reinforced by the fact that, unlike most readers of ethnographic reports of exotic cultures, most readers of qualitative reports on American education have had considerable exposure during their own school years to at least one version of the culture described. Thus, unless the researcher chooses a very atypical site or presents an unusually insightful analysis of what is happening, the purely descriptive value of the study may be undercut or discounted.

So far I have argued that qualitative research's shift in both purpose and locale in the last decade or two has contributed to an increased interest in generalizability among qualitative researchers. There is yet one other factor contributing to this trend—the striking rapprochement between qualitative and quantitative methodologies that has occurred in the last decade (Cronbach et al., 1980; Filstead, 1979; Reichardt & Cook, 1979; Spindler, 1982). Exemplifying this trend is the shift in the position of Donald Campbell. Campbell and Stanley (1963) at one point contended that the "one-shot case study," which is one way of describing much qualitative research, has "such a total absence of control as to be of almost no scientific value" (p. 176). However, more recently Campbell (1979) wrote a paper to "correct some of [his] own prior excesses in describing the case study approach" (p. 52) in which he takes the, for many, rather startling position that when qualitative and quantitative results conflict, "the quantitative results should be regarded as suspect until the reasons for the discrepancy are well understood" (p. 52).

One result of the rapprochement that has occurred is that qualitative and quantitative researchers are more in contact with each other's traditions than had typically been the case heretofore. As is often the case when a dominant tradition makes contact with a minority one, the culture and standards of the dominant group make a significant impact on the members of the minority group. This trend has most likely been reinforced by the fact that a great deal of the qualitative research on education conducted in the past fifteen years has been embedded within multimethod evaluation projects undertaken by private research firms that have traditionally specialized in quantitative research. Thus the concept of external validity and the associated issue of generalizability have been made salient for qualitative researchers, whose own tradition has not predisposed them to have given the issue a great deal of thought.

RECONCEPTUALIZING GENERALIZABILITY

Although many qualitative researchers have begun to recognize the importance of dealing with the issue of generalizability, it is clear that the classical view of external validity is of little help to qualitative researchers interested in finding ways of enhancing the likelihood that their work will speak to situations beyond the one immediately studied—that is, that it will be to some extent generalizable. The idea of sampling from a population of sites in order to generalize to the larger population is simply and obviously unworkable in all but the rarest situations for qualitative researchers, who often take several years to produce an intensive case study of one or a very small number of sites. Thus most of the work on generalizability by qualitative researchers in this decade has dealt with developing a *conception* of generalizability that is useful and appropriate for qualitative work.

A second approach to the issue of generalizability in qualitative research has been very different. A number of individuals have worked on ways of gaining generality through the synthesis of preexisting qualitative studies. For example, Noblit and Hare (1988) have recently published a slim volume on meta-ethnography. Substantially earlier, Lucas (1974) and Yin and Heald (1975) had developed what they call the "case survey method." Ragin (1987) has presented yet another way of synthesizing qualitative studies, one that employs Boolean algebra. I will discuss these approaches to generalizing from qualitative case studies briefly at the end of this chapter. At the moment, I would like to focus on issues connected with the first approach—that is, with transforming and adapting the classical conception of external validity such that it is suitable for qualitative work.

Important and frequently cited discussions of conceptions of generalizability appropriate in qualitative work can be found in Guba and Lincoln (1981, 1982), Goetz and LeCompte (1984), and Stake (1978). Guba and Lincoln's stance on the issue of generalizability is aptly summarized in two excerpts of their own words. Guba and Lincoln write:

> It is virtually impossible to imagine any human behavior that is not heavily mediated by the context in which it occurs. One can easily conclude that generalizations that are intended to be context free will have little that is useful to say about human behavior. (1981, p. 62)

They go on to say:

> The aim of (naturalistic) inquiry is to develop an idiographic body of knowledge. This knowledge is best encapsulated in a series of "working hypotheses" that describe the individual case. Generalizations are impossible since phenomena are neither time- nor context-free (although some transferability of these hypotheses may be possible from situation to situation, depending on the degree of temporal and contextual similarity). (1982, p. 238)

Given these views, Guba and Lincoln call for replacing the concept of generalizability with that of "fittingness." Specifically, they argue that the concept of "fittingness," with its emphasis on analyzing the degree to which the situation studied matches other situations in which one is interested, provides a more realistic and workable way of thinking about the generalizability of research results than do more classical approaches. A logical consequence of this approach is an emphasis on supplying a substantial amount of information about the entity studied and the setting in which that entity was found. Without such information, it is impossible to make an informed judgment about whether the conclusions drawn from the study of any particular site are useful in understanding other sites.

Goetz and LeCompte (1984) place a similar emphasis on the importance of clear and detailed description as a means of allowing decisions about the extent to which findings from one study are applicable to other situations. Specifically, they argue that qualitative studies gain their potential for applicability to other situations by providing what they call "comparability" and "translatability." The former term

> refers to the degree to which components of a study—including the units of analysis, concepts generated, population characteristics, and settings— are sufficiently well described and defined that other researchers can use the results of the study as a basis for comparison. (p. 228)

Translatability is similar but refers to a clear description of one's theoretical stance and research techniques.

Stake (1978) starts out by agreeing with many critics of qualitative methods that one cannot confidently generalize from a single case to a target population of which that case is a member, since single members often poorly represent whole populations. However, he then goes on to argue that it is possible to use a process he calls "naturalistic generalization" to take the findings from one study and apply them to understanding another *similar* situation. He argues that through experience individuals come to be able to use both explicit comparisons between situations and tacit knowledge of those same situations to form useful naturalistic generalizations.

Several major themes can be found in the work of qualitative researchers who have written recently on the concept of generalizability. Whether it is Guba and Lincoln (1981, 1982) writing of fittingness, Goetz and LeCompte (1984) writing of translatability and comparability, or Stake (1978) discussing naturalistic generalizations, the emerging view shared by many qualitative researchers appears to involve several areas of consensus. First of all, there is broad agreement that generalizability in the sense of producing laws that apply universally is not a useful standard or goal for qualitative research. In fact, most qualitative researchers would join Cronbach (1982) in arguing that this is not a useful or obtainable goal for any kind of research in the social sciences. Second, most researchers writing on generalizability in the qualitative tradition agree that their rejection of generalizability as a search for broadly applicable laws is not a rejection of the idea that studies in one situation can be used to speak to or to help form a judgment about other situations. Third, as should be readily apparent from the preceding discussion, current thinking on generalizability argues that thick descriptions (Ryle, cited in Geertz, 1973) are vital. Such descriptions of both the site in which the studies are conducted and of the site to which one wishes to generalize are crucial in allowing one to search for the similarities and differences between the situations. As Kennedy (1979) points out, analysis of these similarities and differences then makes it possible to make a reasoned judgment about the extent to which we can use the findings from one study as a "working hypothesis," to use Cronbach's (1982) term, about what might occur in the other situation. Of course, the generally unstated assumption underlying this view is that our knowledge of the phenomena under study is sufficient to direct attention to important rather than superficial similarities and differences. To the extent that our understanding is flawed, important similarities or differences may inadvertently be disregarded.

THREE TARGETS OF GENERALIZATION

Given the growing emphasis on generalizability in qualitative research and the emerging consensus about how the concept of generalizability might most usefully be viewed by qualitative researchers, two questions present themselves:

To what do we want to generalize?
How can we design qualitative studies in a way that maximizes their generalizability?

It is to these two questions that I will devote the majority of the rest of this chapter. Although I will use the term *generalize* here and elsewhere, it is important that the reader recognize that I am not talking about generalization in the classical sense. Rather, I use it to refer to the process as conceptualized by those qualitative researchers to whose work I have just referred.

I believe that it is useful for qualitative researchers interested in the study of educational processes and institutions to try to generalize to three domains: to *what is*, to *what may be*, and to *what could be*. I will deal with these possibilities one at a time, providing the rationale for striving to generalize to each of these kinds of situations and then suggesting some ideas on how studies can actually be designed to do this.

Studying What Is

From one perspective the study of any ongoing social situation, no matter how idiosyncratic or bizarre, is studying *what is*. But when I use the phrase *studying what is*, I mean to refer to studying the typical, the common, or the ordinary. The goal of describing and understanding cultures or institutions as they typically are is an appropriate aim for much current qualitative research on educational institutions and processes. If policy makers need to decide how to change a program or whether to continue it, one very obvious and useful kind of information is information on how the program usually functions, what is usually achieved, and the like. Thus the goal of studying *what is* is one important aim for many kinds of summative evaluations. It is also appropriate outside of the area of evaluation for researchers hoping to provide a picture of the current educational scene that can be used for understanding or reflecting on it and possibly improving it. Classic works of this type that focus primarily on *what is* are Wolcott's *The Man in the Principal's Office* (1973) and Jackson's *Life in Classrooms* (1968). If one accepts the goal of designing research to maximize the fit between the research site and *what is* more broadly in society, an obvious question that arises is how this can be accomplished within the context of the qualitative tradition.

Studying the Typical.   One approach sometimes used is to study the typical (Bogdan & Biklen, 1981; Goetz & LeCompte, 1984; Patton, 1980; Whyte, 1984). Specifically, I would argue that choosing sites on the basis of their fit with a typical situation is far preferable to choosing on the basis of convenience, a practice that is still quite common.

The suggestion that typicality be weighed heavily in site selection is an idea that needs to be taken both more and less seriously than it currently is. When I say that it needs to be taken more seriously than it currently is, I am suggesting that researchers contemplating selecting a site on the basis of convenience or ease of access need to think more carefully about that decision and to weigh very carefully the possibility of choosing on the basis of some other criterion, such as typicality. When I say that the strategy of selecting a typical site needs to be taken less seriously than it may sometimes be, I intend to point out that choosing a typical site is not a "quick fix" for the issue of generalizability, because what is typical on one dimension may not be typical on another. For example, Wolcott (1973) chose to focus his ethnographic study of a principal on an individual who was typical of other principals in gender, marital status, age, and so forth. This choice most likely substantially enhanced the range of applicability or generalizability of his study. Yet such a typical principal operating in an atypical school or an atypical system or even an atypical community might well behave very differently from a typical principal in a typical school in a typical system. The solution to this dilemma cannot be found in choosing typicality on every dimension. First of all, not too many typical principals operate in environments that are typical in every way. So this strategy gains less in the realm of generalizability or fittingness than it might appear to at first glance. More important, even if one could achieve typicality in all major dimensions that seem relevant, it is nonetheless clearly true that there would be enough idiosyncracy in any particular situation studied so that one could not transfer findings in an unthinking way from one typical situation to another.

Carried to extremes or taken too seriously, the idea of choosing on the basis of typicality becomes impossible, even absurd. However, as a guiding principle designed to increase the potential applicability of research, it is, I believe, useful. This is especially true if the search for typicality is combined with, rather than seen as a replacement for, a reliance on the kind of thick description emphasized by Guba and Lincoln (1981, 1982), Goetz and LeCompte (1984), and Stake (1978). Selection on the basis of typicality provides the potential for a good "fit" with many other situations. Thick description provides the information necessary to make informed judgments about the degree and extent of that fit in particular cases of interest.

In arguing that qualitative researchers would do well to seek to study the typical, I am not suggesting that we study the typical defined solely by national norms. Research that followed this prescription would greatly increase our knowledge of typical situations, but in a nation as diverse as the United States, it would provide too restricted, pallid, and homogeneous a view of our educational system. My emphasis on typicality implies that the researcher who has decided on the kind of institution or situation he or she wants to study—an urban ghetto school, a rural consolidated school, or a private Montessori school—should try to select an instance of this kind of situation that is, to the extent possible, typical of its kind. Such an approach suggests, for example, that a researcher interested in studying mathematics teaching choose to observe classrooms that use a popular text and generally accepted modes of instruction, rather than falling for convenience's sake into the study of classrooms that may well do neither of these. Furthermore, to the extent preliminary investigation of possible sites suggests that some or all are atypical in certain regards, careful thought about the possible implications of this atypicality for the topic under study may help to aid in site selection.

In sum, the point of my argument here is that choosing a site for research on the basis of typicality is far more likely to enhance the potential generalizability of one's study than choosing on the basis of convenience or ease of access—criteria that often weigh more heavily than they should. However, even if one chooses on the basis of typicality, one is in no way relieved of the necessity for thick description, for it is foolhardy to think that a typical example will be typical in all important regards. Thus thick description is necessary to allow individuals to ask about the degree of fit between the case studied and the case to which they wish to generalize, even when the fit on some of the basic dimensions looks fairly close.

Performing Multisite Studies. An alternate approach to increasing the generalizability of qualitative research was evident in the sudden proliferation in the 1970s of multisite qualitative studies. Such studies were almost always part of federally funded evaluation efforts focusing on the same issue in a number of settings, using similar data collection and analysis procedures in each place. Well-known examples of this approach include the Study of Dissemination Efforts Supporting School Improvement (Crandall et al., 1983; Huberman & Miles, 1984) and the study of Parental Involvement in Federal Educational Programs (Smith & Robbins, 1984). One of the primary purposes of conducting such multisite studies is to escape what Firestone and Herriott (1984) have called the "radical particularism" of many case studies and hence to provide a firmer basis for generalization.

The multisite studies conducted in the 1970s were extremely varied, although they were all quite expensive and tended to take several years to complete. At least two kinds of variation have special implications for the extent to which this approach actually seems likely to produce results that are a good basis for generalization to many other situations. The first of these is the number of sites studied. Firestone and Herriott's (1984) survey of twenty-five multisite case study efforts found major variation on this dimension, with one study including as few as three sites and another covering sixty. All other things being equal, a finding emerging repeatedly in the study of numerous sites would appear to be more likely to be a good working hypothesis about some as yet unstudied site than a finding emerging from just one or two sites.

A second dimension on which multisite studies vary, which is also likely to effect the degree of fit between these studies and situations to which one might want to generalize, concerns the heterogeneity of the sites chosen for study. Generally speaking, a finding emerging from the study of several very heterogeneous sites would be more robust and thus more likely to be useful in understanding various other sites than one emerging from the study of several very similar sites (Kennedy, 1979). Heterogeneity can be obtained by searching out sites that will provide maximal variation or by planned comparisons along certain potentially important dimensions. An example of the second strategy can be found in the parental-involvement study previously mentioned. The sites chosen for study were selected to allow comparison between urban and rural settings, between those with high and low reported degrees of involvement, and so forth (Smith & Robbins, 1984). This comparative strategy is potentially quite powerful, especially if there is heterogeneity among cases within each of the categories of interest. For example, if several rather different rural cases all share certain similarities that are not found in a heterogeneous group of urban cases, one has some reasonable basis for generalizing about likely differences between the two settings. Although the most obvious comparative strategy is to select cases that initially differ on some variable of interest as part of the research design, it is also possible to group cases in an *ex post facto* way on the basis of information gathered during the fieldwork. For example, if one were studying numerous very different classrooms and found that student achievement gains were quite high in some and quite low in others, one could compare these two sets of classrooms as a strategy for trying to suggest factors that contribute to high or low gains.

In sum, the possibility of studying numerous heterogeneous sites makes multisite studies one potentially useful approach to increasing the generalizability of qualitative work to *what is*. Yet I am very hesitant to see this approach as the only or even the best solution to the problem. First, such studies can be quite expensive, and the current lull in their funding highlights the extent to which such research is dependent on federal dollars that may or may not be forthcoming. Second, as Firestone and Herriott (1984) point out, budget constraints make it likely that studies including very large numbers of sites are less likely than studies of a relatively small number of sites to be able to devote intensive and prolonged care to studying the details of each site. Thus there is typically a trade-off to be made between the increased potential for generalizability flowing from studying a large number of sites and the increased depth and breadth of description and understanding made possible by a focus on a small number of sites. In suggesting that an increased number of sites leads to increased generalizability, I am assuming that enough attention is paid to each site to ensure that problems of internal validity do not arise. To the extent such problems do arise, generalizability is obviously threatened, since one cannot speak meaningfully of the generalizability of invalid data. The fact that roughly 40 percent of the multisite studies surveyed by Firestone and Herriott (1984) involved just one or two short visits to the research site raises serious questions about whether such studies can appropriately be categorized as qualitative research in the usual sense of that term. The term *qualitative research*, and more especially the word *ethnography*, usually implies an intensive, ongoing involvement with individuals functioning in their everyday settings that is akin to, if not always identical with, the degree of immersion in a culture attained by anthropologists, who live in the society they study over a period of one or more years (Dobbert, 1982; Spindler, 1982; Wolcott, 1975). Thus it is conceivable, though not logically necessary, that attempts to gain generalizability through studying large numbers of sites undercut the depth of understanding of individual sites, which is the hallmark of the qualitative approach as it has come to be understood.

Studying What May Be

The goal of portraying typical schools—or, for that matter, typical instances of federal educational programs as they now exist—is, I believe, worthwhile. Yet accepting this as our only or even primary goal implies too narrow and limited a vision of what qualitative research can do. I would like to suggest that we want to generalize not only to *what is* but also to *what may be*. Let me explain. Here I am proposing that we think about what current social and educational trends suggest about likely educational issues for the future and design our research to illuminate such issues to the extent possible. Let me use some of my own current research to illustrate this possibility, without implying that it is the best or only example of such an approach.

One very obvious and potentially important trend in education recently has been the increasing utilization of microcomputers in instruction. In fact, microcomputers are being adopted in schools at an almost frantic pace (Becker, 1986) in spite of tight educational budgets and a generally acknowledged tendency on the part of educational institutions to resist rapid change. There is a clear division of opinion about the likely consequences of this trend. At one extreme are those who see computers as having the capability to revolutionize education in absolutely fundamental ways. Proponents of this school of thought make the rather startling claim that "the potential of computers for improving education is greater than that of any prior invention, including books and writing" (Walker, 1984, p. 3). Others take quite a different stance, emphasizing the inherent conservativism of the teaching profession with regard to pedagogical change and the failure of other highly touted educational innovations to bring about far-reaching changes. Thus it seemed important to me to design a research project focused on understanding the impact of computer usage on students and classrooms (Schofield & Evans-Rhodes, 1989; Schofield & Verban, 1988). One could approach this issue with an emphasis on what is. For example, it would be possible to choose a school that is presently typical in terms of the uses it makes of computers in instruction. But this strategy encounters an immediate problem if one's goal is to speak to what may be. Changes in both microcomputer technology and in individuals' level of experience with computers have been so rapid in the past decade that a study of what is today could arguably be a study of primarily historical interest by the time it gets conducted, written, and published. In hopes of not just documenting the present, which is rapidly becoming the past, but of speaking to the future, I have made a number of methodological decisions that, in their abstract form, may be of use to others interested in making their work applicable to what may be.

Studying the "Leading Edge" of Change. First, since it is hard to know what kinds of computer usage will become most typical or popular in the future, I have made a point of studying a broad array of uses rather than just one particular kind. More important, I have not looked only for heterogeneity of usage but for types of usage that are now in their infancy but that many informed observers see as likely to be common in the future. Thus I consciously chose to study a school that not only uses computers as they are currently employed around the country to teach computer programming and word processing in fairly typical ways but that also was the field test site for the kind of artificially intelligent computer-based tutor that researchers in a number of centers around the country are currently developing for classroom use (Feigenbaum & McCorduck, 1983; Lawler & Yazdani, 1987.) I see this choice as a step in the direction of increasing the chances that this work will "fit" or be generalizable to the educational issues important at the time the work is published. But this is only a mere first step.

Probing Factors Likely to Differentiate the Present from the Future. One of the big problems in trying to make one's work applicable to even the fairly near future is, as Cronbach (1975) has so eloquently argued, that people and institutions change. Thus it is logically impossible to see the future even when studying futuristic uses of artificial intelligence, because one is studying that future technology in the context of a present-day institution peopled with individuals who are shaped by the era in which they live.

There is no completely satisfactory solution to this situation, but a partial one emerged as I grappled with the issue. It is to think through how the present and the future are likely to differ. Then the research can be structured in a way that explicitly probes the impact of things that are likely to change over time. Of course, if the analysis of the likely differences between present and future is wrong, this approach will not be particularly useful. But if the analysis is accurate, this strategy has the potential to enhance greatly the usefulness of the study.

Let me illustrate in concrete terms how I have done this. Given the rapidity with which computers are being adopted for use in widely varying arenas of life, especially in schools, it seems a reasonable expectation that one major difference between now and five to ten years in the future is what might be called the "novelty factor." Specifically, many of today's high school students are having their first real introduction to the computer, or at least to its use for educational purposes, in their high school classrooms. However, in ten years it is rather unlikely that high school students will be having their first exposure to educational computing in the tenth or eleventh grade. I have used this assumption, which is, I think, relatively uncontroversial, to influence the shape of my study in a way that will allow it to speak more adequately to the future. For example, in interviews students were specifically asked about the impact of novelty on their reactions to the computer and its importance in shaping their feelings about computer usage. Similarly, observers in the study carefully looked for reactions that appeared to be influenced by students' unfamiliarity with the computers. Moreover, I have been careful to find out which students have had prior computer experience and what kind of experience this has been in order to see as clearly as possible whether these students differ from those for whom computer use is a completely novel experience. The fact that students were observed during the full course of the school year allowed assessment of whether any initial differences in students' reactions due to prior experience were transitory or relatively long-lasting. To the extent that novelty is crucial in shaping students' reactions, I will be forced to conclude that my study may not help us understand the future as well as it might otherwise. To the extent that students' reactions appear to be more heavily influenced by things that are unlikely to change in the near future, such as adolescents' striving for independence from adult control, the likely applicability of the findings of the study to the near future is clearly increased.

Considering the Life Cycle of a Phenomenon. The preceding discussion of the possible impact of novelty on students' reactions to educational computing brings up an important point regarding qualitative

work and the issue of generalizability. The ethnographic habit of looking at a phenomenon over substantial time periods allows assessment
of one aspect of generalizability that quantitative research usually does
not—of where a particular phenomenon is in its life cycle and what the
implications of this are for what is happening. Qualitative research,
when studying a dynamic phenomenon, is like a movie. It starts with
one image and then moves on to others that show how things evolve
over time. Quantitative research, in contrast, is more typically like a
snapshot, often taken and used without great regard for whether that
photograph happened to catch one looking one's best or looking unusually disheveled. This point can be illustrated more substantively by
briefly discussing a study that I carried out in a desegregated school
during its first four years of existence (Schofield, 1982/1989). The
study tracked changes in the school by following two different groups
of students from the first day they entered the school to graduation
from that school three years later. Important changes occurred in race
relations over the life of the institution and over the course of students'
careers in the school. Such findings suggest that in asking about what
happens in desegregated schools and what the impact of such schools is
on students, it is important to know where both the students and the
institution are in their experience with desegregation. Yet virtually all
quantitative studies of desegregation, including, I must admit, some of
my own, tend to ignore these issues completely. In fact, as I discovered
in reviewing the desegregation literature (Schofield & Sagar, 1983),
many do not even supply bare descriptive information on the life-cycle
issue. Paying attention to where a phenomenon is in its life cycle does
not guarantee that one can confidently predict how it will evolve.
However, at a minimum, sensitivity to this issue makes it less likely
that conclusions formed on the basis of a study conducted at one point
in time will be unthinkingly and perhaps mistakenly generalized to
other later points in time to which they may not apply.

Studying What Could Be

As mentioned previously, I would like to argue that qualitative
research on education can be used not only to study *what is* and *what may
be* but also to explore possible visions of *what could be*. By studying what
could be, I mean locating situations that we know or expect to be ideal
or exceptional on some *a priori* basis and then studying them to see what
is actually going on there.

Selecting a Site That Sheds Light on What Could Be.   When studying what could be, site selection is not based on criteria such as typicality or heterogeneity. Rather it is based on information about either the *outcomes* achieved in the particular site studied or on the *conditions* obtaining there. Perhaps the best-known example of site selection based on outcomes is choosing to study classrooms or schools in which students show unusual intellectual gains, as has been done in the voluminous literature on effective schools (Bickel, 1983; Dwyer, Lee, Rowan, & Bossert, 1982; Phi Delta Kappan, 1980; Rutter, Maughan, Mortimore, Ouston, & Smith, 1979; Weber, 1971). For an example of site selection based on the conditions obtaining at the site, a less common approach, I will again make reference to my own work on school desegregation.

When thinking about where to locate the extended study of a desegregated school mentioned previously, I decided not to study a typical desegregated school. First, given the tremendous variation in situations characterized as desegregated, it is not clear that such an entity could be found. Second, there is a body of theory and research that gives us some basis for expecting different kinds of social processes and outcomes in different kinds of interracial schools. In fact, in the same year in which the *Brown* v. *Board of Education* decision laid the legal basis for desegregating educational institutions, Gordon Allport (1954) published a classic analysis of racial prejudice in which he argued that interracial contact can either increase or decrease hostility and stereotyping, depending on the kind of conditions under which it occurs. Specifically, he argued that in order to ameliorate relations between groups such as blacks and whites three conditions are especially important: equal status for members of both groups within the contact situation, a cooperative rather than a competitive goal structure, and support for positive relations from those in authority. A substantial amount of empirical and theoretical work stemming from Allport's basic insight has been carried out in the past three and a half decades, most of which supports his emphasis on the crucial importance of the specific conditions under which intergroup contact occurs (Amir, 1969; Aronson & Osherow, 1980; Cook, 1978; Pettigrew, 1967, 1969; Schofield, 1979; Schofield & Sagar, 1977; Slavin, 1980; Stephan, 1985).

It is clear that desegregating school systems often take little if any heed of the available theory and research on how to structure desegregated schools in a way likely to promote positive intergroup relations, perhaps at least partly because much of this work is laboratory based and hence may seem of questionable use in everyday situations. Thus selecting a site for study on the basis of typicality might be expected to yield a site potentially rich in sources of insight about the problems of desegregated education but weak in shedding light on what can be accomplished in a serious and sophisticated effort to structure an environment conducive to fostering positive relations between students. Since both scholars in the area of intergroup relations and the public are well aware of the potential for difficulties in desegregated schools, the task of seeing whether and how such difficulties can be overcome seems potentially more informative and useful than that of documenting the existence of such difficulties. Thus I chose to study a site that at least approximated a theoretical ideal. My goal was not to generalize to desegregated schools as a class. Rather it was to see what happens under conditions that might be expected to foster relatively positive outcomes. If serious problems were encountered at such a site, there would be reason to think that problems would be encountered in most places or, alternatively, to revise or reject the theory that led to the site selection. However, if things went well at such a site, the study would then provide an opportunity to gain some insight into how and why they go well and into what the still-intractable problems are.

Of course, the strategy of choosing a site based on some *a priori* theoretical viewpoint or, for that matter, any seriously held expectation about it raises a difficult problem. If one is unduly committed to that viewpoint, one's analysis of both what happens and why may be heavily influenced by it, and one may not ask whether other more fruitful perspectives might emerge from a more dispassionate approach to studying the situation. This is the very danger that has led to the development of such elaborate safeguards in the quantitative tradition as the double-blind experiment. Although such procedures are rarely used in the qualitative tradition, a substantial literature on the issue of internal validity in qualitative research offers assistance with this problem to the researcher who pays it close heed (Becker, 1958; Bogdan & Biklen, 1981; Glaser & Strauss, 1967; Goetz & LeCompte, 1984; Guba, 1981; Guba & Lincoln, 1981; Kirk & Miller, 1986; Miles & Huberman, 1984a, 1984b; Patton, 1980; Strauss, 1987). Furthermore, if one's purpose is not to support or reject a specific *a priori* theory but to discover, using an approach that is as open as possible, what is actually happening in a site that was chosen with the assistance of a particular theory, problems related to internal validity are somewhat mitigated. For example, the fact that I chose to study a school that theory suggested might be conducive to positive relations did not keep me from exploring in considerable depth problems that occurred there (Sagar & Schofield, 1980; Schofield, 1981, 1982/1989).

One characteristic of the school chosen for the study was especially helpful in assessing the degree to which the theory on which the site was chosen was useful. Specifically, for various reasons, conditions in two of the three grades in this school came much closer than conditions in the remaining grade to meeting those that theory suggests are conducive to producing positive relations. Thus it was possible to assess intergroup relations as the children went from one kind of environment to another within the school (Schofield, 1979, 1982/1989; Schofield & Sagar, 1977). This suggests one very useful strategy for studying what may be—selecting an "ideal" case and a comparative case that contrasts sharply on the relevant dimensions.

Generalizing from an Unusual Site to More Typical Ones.   Although I indicated above that my goal was to learn about the possibilities and problems associated with a *certain kind* of desegregated education, I would like to argue that studying a site chosen for its special characteristics does not necessarily restrict the application of the study's findings to other very similar sites. The degree to which this is the case depends on the degree to which the findings appear to be linked to the special characteristics of the situation. Some of the findings from the study I have been discussing were clearly linked to unusual aspects of the school and hence have very limited generalizability to other situations, although they may nonetheless be important in demonstrating what is possible, even if not what is generally likely. For example, I found very low levels of overt racial conflict in the school studied (Schofield & Francis, 1982). It would obviously be misguided to conclude on the basis of this study that intergroup conflict is unlikely in all desegregated schools, since the school's emphasis on cooperation, equal status, and the like did actually appear to play a marked role in reducing the likelihood of conflict.

However, other findings that emerged from the study and were also related to atypical aspects of the situation may have a greater degree of applicability or generalizability than the finding discussed above. For example, I found the development of a color-blind perspective and of an almost complete taboo against the mention of race in the school studied (Schofield, 1986, 1982/1989). Since the emergence of the color-blind perspective and the accompanying taboo appeared to be linked to special characteristics of the school, I would not posit them as phenomena likely to occur in most desegregated schools. But I feel free to argue that *when* they do develop, certain consequences may well follow because these consequences are the logical outcomes of the phenomena. For example, with regard to the taboo against racial reference, if one cannot mention race, one cannot deal with resegregation in a straightforward way as a policy issue. Similarly, if one cannot mention race, there is likely to be little or no effort to create or utilize multicultural curricular materials. Thus, although the taboo against racial reference may not occur in a high proportion of desegregated schools, when it does occur the study I carried out gives a potentially useful indication of problems that are likely to develop.

I would now like to turn to a third finding of the study, one so unrelated to the atypical aspects of the situation studied that it is a reasonable working hypothesis that this phenomenon is widespread. After I observed extensively in varied areas of the school and interviewed a large number of students, it became apparent that the white children perceived blacks as something of a threat to their physical selves. Specifically, they complained about what they perceived as black roughness or aggressiveness (Schofield, 1981, 1982/1989). In contrast, the black students perceived whites as a threat to their social selves. They complained about being ignored, avoided, and being treated as inferior by whites, whom they perceived to be stuck-up and prejudiced (Schofield, 1982/1989). Such findings appear to me to be linked to the black and white students' situation in the larger society and to powerful historical and economic forces, not to special aspects of the school. The consequences of these rather asymmetrical concerns may well play themselves out differently in different kinds of schools, but the existence of these rather different but deeply held concerns may well be widespread.

I have gone into some detail with these examples because I think they raise a crucial point for judging the applicability or generalizability of qualitative work. One cannot just look at a study and say that it is similiar or dissimilar to another situation of concern. A much finer-grained analysis is necessary. One must ask what aspects of the situation are similar or different and to what aspects of the findings these are connected.

GENERALIZING THROUGH AGGREGATION OR COMPARISON OF INDEPENDENT STUDIES

This paper has argued that it is possible to achieve greater generalizability of qualitative research to situations of interest than is often now the case by following some of the design suggestions discussed above. However, there is another approach to increasing the generalizability of qualitative case studies that should not be ignored. This other strategy aims not at increasing the generalizability of one study or a set of studies planned in conjunction with each other but at finding ways to aggregate, compare, or contrast already existing studies. One of these strategies was first laid out some time ago by Yin and Heald (1975). Another promising approach is suggested by Ragin's (1987) recent work on a strategy that he calls the "qualitative comparative method." A third very different approach has been outlined recently by Noblit and Hare (1988).

The Case Survey Method

Yin and Heald (1975) point out that case studies, whether qualitative or quantitative, are very prevalent in many fields. The nub of the problem from their perspective is that while "each case study may provide rich insights into a specific situation, it is difficult to generalize about the studies as a whole" (p. 371). Their solution to this problem is to propose a method for aggregating the information from separate studies. They call the method they developed the "case survey method." Basically this method consists of several steps. First, the literature relevant to one's interest is located. Then these studies are subjected to close scrutiny, so that those failing to meet certain crucial methodological requirements can be removed from the set to be analyzed. Then coders go through each of the remaining case studies with the goal of using the information contained therein to complete a set of closed-ended questions. These questions pertain to the topic of one's study and constitute the dataset ultimately used in the case survey approach. For example, Yin and Heald (1975) discuss a study of the effectiveness of urban decentralization efforts in which the closed-ended questions covered (1) the nature of the case study itself, (2) the context in which the decentralization effort occurred, (3) the characteristics of the specific effort at decentralization, and (4) five possible outcomes of decentralization. One then uses the material in the questionnaires to search for patterns on which generalizations can be based. The strategy for producing these generalizations is the use of statistical tests of association between different variables. For example, Yin and Heald report a statistically significant positive association between their judgments of the quality of specific case studies and the degree to which the study concluded that decentralization succeeded. The case survey procedure is parallel in some respects to the procedures suggested more recently by Miles and Huberman (1984a, 1984b) for aggregating data from multisite studies. However, Miles and Huberman tend not to emphasize statistical significance, perhaps because the number of studies in many multisite qualitative endeavors is so small as to preclude attaining statistical significance unless the effects are of extraordinary strength.

As Yin and Heald (1975) acknowledge, there are clear limitations to the approach they suggest. First, of course, there must be a substantial body of literature available relevant to a particular topic for this procedure to work well. For example, Yin and Yates (1975) aggregated data from more than 250 studies of urban decentralization. When the number of available cases is small, statistical techniques lack power, since each case study must be treated as a single observation. Also, in such cases the number of variables worthy of coding may well be large compared to the number of sampling points (i.e., case studies), which also poses statistical problems. Second, the case survey method, with its emphasis on reducing the rich descriptive material provided in many case studies to uniform quantifiable data, risks ignoring unique factors that may be crucial to understanding specific cases or kinds of cases. Third, as Yin and Heald (1975) note, the case survey method may be more suited to inquiries focusing on outcomes rather than on process. Because of the numerous limitations of the case survey method, Yin (1981) has concluded that the "case-survey method should be used in highly selective situations" (p. 63) and that other methods for comparing across cases may ultimately prove more fruitful.

Unfortunately, the development of other methods for comparing and aggregating across cases, especially cases that have not been planned as part of a unified multisite effort, are not well developed. Although the work of Miles and Huberman (1984a, 1984b) and Yin (1984) provides many useful design and analysis suggestions for investigators planning multisite studies, relatively little methodological guidance is available to researchers who wish to compare studies that were designed and executed independently. A crucial difference between these two cases, of course, is that in the former one can obtain some degree of uniformity in the information gathered. This is crucial for the kinds of pattern-producing techniques suggested by Miles and Huberman and by Yin. There are other important differences as well. For example, in a multisite study with central direction it is at least theoretically possible, if not eminently practical, for one individual to have access to the raw data from all the different sites. However, such is generally not the case when one is trying to conduct comparisons of previously published case studies or ethnographies. Thus, at this point in time, our ability to achieve generalizations through the comparison of independently conducted pieces of qualitative work on a particular topic is quite limited.

The Qualitative Comparative Method

One promising new strategy for aggregating case studies has recently been developed by Ragin (1987). Ragin starts with the premise that two of the distinctive traits of case studies, and of case-oriented comparative research more generally, are their attention to cases as wholes and to the possibility that several different sets of circumstances can lead to the same outcome. He argues that most attempts to aggregate numerous case studies using quantitative approaches tend not to make use of these strengths and thus do not make full use of the data bases on which they are built. To remedy this situation, Ragin proposes an approach that he calls the "qualitative comparative method." This approach is based on Boolean algebra, the algebra of sets and logic. Although a full discussion of this technique is beyond the scope of this paper, since it would require introducing readers to the basics of Boolean algebra, it is possible briefly to discuss Ragin's general approach without becoming unduly technical.

First, Ragin's techniques can be used with widely varying numbers of case studies as one's raw data. In this regard it is more flexible than the case survey method, which is suitable only when relatively large numbers of case studies are available because of its dependence on the concept of statistical significance. Second, the techniques can be used with either preexisting case studies or with multisite studies planned with the qualitative comparative strategy in mind. All that is necessary are data that allow one to build truth tables—that is, categorical information on the variables of major interest to the analysis. Ragin argues that his approach allows one to examine complex and multiple patterns of causation, to produce parsimonious explanations, to study cases both as wholes and as parts, and to evaluate competing explanations. Ragin presents several extended and sharply contrasting examples of the varied ways in which the approach he uses can be applied. Although his approach seems better suited in many ways to aggregating qualitative case studies than the case survey method, since a Boolean approach allows one to take better advantage of the characteristic strengths of case studies, it is too early to understand completely either its full potential or the various problems that individuals using this approach will face.

Meta-Ethnography

Consideration of the techniques discussed above suggests that both the case survey method and attempts at case comparison are often based on a logic that seeks to generalize by aggregating studies. Noblit and Hare (1988) suggest that such an effort is misdirected, arguing that efforts at aggregation tend to ignore the interpretive nature of qualitative research and to miss much of what is most important in each study. They believe it is possible to systematically compare very diverse cases in order to draw cross-case conclusions. However, they see such an effort as best conceptualized as the *translation* of studies into one another rather than as their aggregation. They call this translation "meta-ethnography."

Noblit and Hare argue that studies of similar topics can be seen as directly comparable, as essentially refutational, or as together suggesting a new line of argument. Once a preliminary look at the material to be synthesized suggests which of the above is the case, a translation and synthesis is attempted. This process may refute the initial assumption about the relation between the cases, but it would generally be expected not to do so.

In order to perform the translation and synthesis, Noblit and Hare suggest a focus on and a listing of the concepts, themes, and metaphors that the author of each study utilizes. The meta-ethnographer lists and organizes these themes and then attempts to relate them to one another. This somewhat abstract process is perhaps best clarified by a brief example. Noblit and Hare exemplify the idea of a reciprocal translation of studies by comparing Collins and Noblit's (1978) research in a desegregated school to Wolcott's study, *The Man in the Principal's Office* (1973). The comparison makes sense and, in fact, is only possible because Collins and Noblit's study laid great emphasis on the role of the principal in the desegregated school they studied. Noblit and Hare list the terms used in both studies to describe the context in which the principal functioned, the principal's behavior, and the like. The meta-ethnography then consists of a discussion of the ways in which the two situations and studies appear to be similar and different and, more important, of the extent to which the themes developed in each are adequate to handle the other ethnography as well. These judgments are based on attributes of the themes, such as their economy, cogency, and scope. For example, Wolcott describes the conduct of the principal he studied as characterized by patience and prudence. Collins and Noblit compare two different principals in a particular school. The first was said to have created negotiated order in the school. His successor, with a far different style, created what Collins and Noblit characterized as a bureaucratic order. After discussing the particulars of the two studies, Noblit and Hare (1988) conclude that a translation between them is possible but that Wolcott's metaphors are more adequate to this task than those of Collins and Noblit. This means that Wolcott's concepts were able to capture what occurred in the Collins and Noblit study in a fuller and more adequate way than the Collins and Noblit themes fit the Wolcott study. Of course, it is possible in a meta-ethnography that none of the studies compared will have characterized its themes in a way that adequately fits all others, even though there are many parallels. In such a case, the hope is that the individual doing the meta-ethnography may be able to produce new, more inclusive concepts that work better than those from any particular study.

SUMMARY AND CONCLUSIONS

Although qualitative researchers have traditionally paid scant attention to the issue of attaining generalizability in research, sometimes even disdaining such a goal, this situation has changed noticeably in the past ten to fifteen years. Several trends, including the growing use of qualitative studies in evaluation and policy-oriented research, have led to an increased awareness of the importance of structuring qualitative studies in a way that enhances their implications for the understanding of other situations.

Much of the attention given to the issue of generalizability in recent years on the part of qualitative researchers has focused on redefining the concept in a way that is useful and meaningful for those engaged in qualitative work. A consensus appears to be emerging that for qualitative researchers generalizability is best thought of as a matter of the "fit" between the situation studied and others to which one might be interested in applying the concepts and conclusions of that study. This conceptualization makes thick descriptions crucial, since without them one does not have the information necessary for an informed judgment about the issue of fit.

This paper argues that three useful targets for generalization are *what is*, *what may be*, and *what could be* and provides some examples of how qualitative research can be designed in a way that increases its ability to fit with each of these situations. Studying *what is* refers to studying the typical, the common, and the ordinary. Techniques suggested for studying *what is* include choosing study sites on the basis of typicality and conducting multisite studies. Studying *what may be* refers to designing studies so that their fit with future trends and issues is maximized. Techniques suggested for studying *what may be* include seeking out sites in which one can study situations likely to become more common with the passage of time and paying close attention to how such present instances of future practices are likely to differ from their future realizations. Studying *what could be* refers to locating situations that we know or expect to be ideal or exceptional on some *a priori* basis and studying them to see what is actually going on there. Crucial here is an openness to having one's expectations about the phenomena disconfirmed.

A very different approach to increasing the generalizability of qualitative research is evident in the work of some scholars who have focused on how to achieve generalizability through the aggregation or comparison of extant independently designed case studies or ethnographies. The case survey approach suggested by Yin and Heald (1975) is promising in a limited number of cases in which comparable information is available from a relatively large number of studies. Case comparison strategies, such as the qualitative comparative method suggested by Ragin (1987), may be more realistic and fruitful in many areas of research; but these comparative techniques are still in the early stages of development. Noblit and Hare (1988) suggest a kind of comparison they call "meta-ethnography," which focuses on the reciprocal translation rather than the aggregation of studies. Although such an approach may have promise, it is so new that its ultimate fruitfulness is still quite untested.

Acknowledgments

Much of the research on which this paper is based was funded by the Office of Naval Research, Contract Number N00 14-85-K-0664. Other research utilized in this paper was funded by Grant Number NIE-G-78-0126 from the National Institute of Education. However, all opinions expressed herein are solely those of the author, and no endorsement by ONR or NIE is implied or intended. My sincere thanks go to Bill Firestone and Matthew Miles for their constructive comments on an earlier draft of this paper.

REFERENCES

Allport, G. W. (1954). *The nature of prejudice.* Cambridge, UK: Cambridge University Press.

Amir, Y. (1969). Contact hypothesis in ethnic relations. *Psychological Bulletin, 71,* 319–342.

Aronson, E., & Osherow, N. (1980). Cooperation, prosocial behavior, and academic performance: Experiments in the desegregated classroom. In

L. Bickman (Ed.), *Applied social psychology annual* (Vol. 1, pp. 163–196). Beverly Hills, CA: Sage.

Becker, H. J. (1986). Instructional uses of school computers. *Reports from the 1985 National Survey* (Issue No. 1) (pp. 1–9). Baltimore, MD: Center for Social Organization of Schools, Johns Hopkins University.

Becker, H. S. (1958). Problems of inference and proof in participant observation. *American Sociological Review, 23*, 652–659.

Berg, B. L. (1989). *Qualitative research methods for the social sciences.* Boston: Allyn & Bacon.

Bickel, W. E. (1983). Effective schools: Knowledge, dissemination, inquiry. *Educational Researcher, 12*(4), 3–5.

Bogdan, R. C., & Biklen, S. K. (1981). *Qualitative research for education: An introduction to theory and methods.* Boston: Allyn & Bacon.

Bolgar, H. (1965). The case study method. In B. B. Wolman (Ed.), *Handbook of clinical psychology* (pp. 28–39). New York: McGraw-Hill.

Brown v. Board of Education (1954). 347 U.S. 483.

Campbell, D. T. (1979). Degrees of freedom and the case study. In T. D. Cook & C. S. Reichardt (Eds.), *Qualitative and quantitative methods in evaluation research* (pp. 49–67). Beverly Hills, CA: Sage.

Campbell, D., & Stanley, J. (1963). Experimental and quasi-experimental designs for research on teaching. In N. Gage (Ed.), *Handbook of research on teaching* (pp. 171–246). Chicago: Rand McNally.

Collins, T., & Noblit, G. (1978). *Stratification and resegregation: The case of Crossover High School.* Final report of NIE contract #400-76-009.

Cook, S. W. (1978). Interpersonal and attitudinal outcomes in cooperating interracial groups. *Journal of Research and Development in Education, 12*, 97–113.

Crandall, D. P., et al. (1983). *People, policies and practices: Examining the chain of school improvement* (Vols. 1–10). Andover, MA: The Network.

Cronbach, L. J. (1975). Beyond the two disciplines of scientific psychology. *American Psychologist, 30*, 116–127.

Cronbach, L. J. (1982). *Designing evaluations of educational and social programs.* San Francisco: Jossey-Bass.

Cronbach, L. J., Ambron, S. R., Dornbusch, S. M., Hess, R. D., Hornik, R. C., Phillips, D. C., Walker, D. F., & Weiner, S. S. (1980). *Toward reform of program evaluation.* San Francisco: Jossey-Bass.

Denzin, N. K. (1983). Interpretive interactionism. In G. Morgan (Ed.), *Beyond method: Strategies for social research* (pp. 129–146). Beverly Hills, CA: Sage.

Dobbert, M. L. (1982). *Ethnographic research: Theory and application for modern schools and societies.* New York: Praeger.

Dwyer, D. C., Lee, G. V., Rowan, B., & Bossert, S. T. (1982). *The principal's role in instructional management: Five participant observation studies of principals in action.* Unpublished manuscript, Far West Laboratory for Educational Research and Development, San Francisco.

Feigenbaum, E. A., & McCorduck, P. (1983). *The fifth generation: Artificial intelligence and Japan's computer challenge to the world.* Reading, MA: Addison-Wesley.

Fetterman, D. M. (1982). Ethnography in educational research: The dynamics of diffusion. In D. M. Fetterman (Ed.), *Ethnography in educational evaluation* (pp. 21–35). Beverly Hills, CA: Sage.

Filstead, W. J. (1979). Qualitative methods: A needed perspective in evaluation research. In T. D. Cook & C. S. Reichardt (Eds.), *Qualitative and quantitative methods in evaluation research* (pp. 33–48). Beverly Hills, CA: Sage.

Firestone, W. A., & Herriott, R. E. (1984). Multisite qualitative policy research: Some design and implementation issues. In D. M. Fetterman (Ed.), *Ethnography in educational evaluation* (pp. 63–88). Beverly Hills, CA: Sage.

Geertz, C. (1973). Thick description: Toward an interpretive theory of culture. In C. Geertz (Ed.), *The interpretation of cultures* (pp. 3–30). New York: Basic Books.

Glaser, B., & Strauss, A. (1967). *The discovery of grounded theory*. Chicago: Aldine Publishing.

Goetz, J. P., & LeCompte, M. D. (1984). *Ethnography and qualitative design in education research*. Orlando, FL: Academic Press.

Guba, E. (1981). Criteria for assessing the trustworthiness of naturalistic inquiry. *Educational Communication and Technology Journal, 29*, 79–92.

Guba, E. G., & Lincoln, Y. S. (1981). *Effective evaluation: Improving the usefulness of evaluation results through responsive and naturalistic approaches*. San Francisco: Jossey-Bass.

Guba, E. G., & Lincoln, Y. S. (1982). Epistemological and methodological bases of naturalistic inquiry. *Educational Communication and Technology Journal, 30*, 233–252.

Huberman, A. M., & Miles, M. B. (1984). *Innovation up close: How school improvement works*. New York: Plenum Press.

Jackson, P. W. (1968). *Life in classrooms*. New York: Holt, Rinehart and Winston.

Kennedy, M. M. (1979). Generalizing from single case studies. *Evaluation Quarterly, 3*(4), 661–678.

Kirk, J., & Miller, M. L. (1986). *Reliability and validity in qualitative research*. Beverly Hills, CA: Sage.

Krathwohl, D. R. (1985). *Social and behavioral science research: A new framework for conceptualizing, implementing, and evaluating research studies*. San Francisco: Jossey-Bass.

Lawler, R. W., & Yazdani, M. (Eds.). (1987). *Artificial intelligence and education: Learning environments and tutoring systems* (Vol. 1). Norwood, NJ: Ablex Publishing.

Lucas, W. (1974). *The case survey method: Aggregating case experience*. Santa Monica, CA: Rand.

Miles, M., & Huberman, A. (1984a). Drawing valid meaning from qualitative data: Toward a shared craft. *Educational Researcher, 13*, 20–30.

Miles, M., & Huberman, A. (1984b). *Qualitative data analysis: A sourcebook of new methods*. Newbury Park, CA: Sage.

Noblit, G. W., & Hare, R. D. (1988). *Meta-ethnography: Synthesizing qualitative studies*. Beverly Hills, CA: Sage.

Patton, M. Q. (1980). *Qualitative evaluation methods.* Beverly Hills, CA: Sage.

Peshkin, A. (1978). *Growing up American: Schooling and the survival of community.* Chicago: University of Chicago Press.

Peshkin, A. (1982). The researcher and subjectivity: Reflections on an ethnography of school and community. In G. Spindler (Ed.), *Doing the ethnography of schooling: Educational anthropology in action* (pp. 48–67). New York: Holt, Rinehart and Winston.

Pettigrew, T. (1967). Social evaluation theory: Convergences and applications. In D. Levine (Ed.), *Nebraska symposium on motivation* (Vol. 5). Lincoln: University of Nebraska Press.

Pettigrew, T. (1969). Racially separate or together. *Journal of Social Issues, 25,* 43–69.

Phi Delta Kappan. (1980). *Why do some urban schools succeed? The Phi Delta Kappa study of exceptional urban elementary schools.* Bloomington: Phi Delta Kappa and Indiana University.

Ragin, C. C. (1987). *The comparative method: Moving beyond qualitative and quantitative strategies.* Berkeley: University of California Press.

Reichardt, C. S., & Cook, T. D. (1979). Beyond qualitative *versus* quantitative methods. In T. D. Cook & C. S. Reichardt (Eds.), *Qualitative and quantitative methods in evaluation research* (pp. 1–33). Beverly Hills, CA: Sage.

Rutter, M., Maughan, B., Mortimore, P., Ouston, J., & Smith, A. (1979). *Fifteen thousand hours: Secondary schools and their effects on children.* Cambridge, MA: Harvard University Press.

Sagar, H. A., & Schofield, J. W. (1980). Racial and behavioral cues in black and white children's perceptions of ambiguously aggressive acts. *Journal of Personality and Social Psychology, 39,* 590–598.

Schofield, J. W. (1979). The impact of positively structured contact on intergroup behavior: Does it last under adverse conditions? *Social Psychology Quarterly, 42,* 280–284.

Schofield, J. W. (1981). Competitive and complementary identities: Images and interaction in an interracial school. In S. Asher & J. Gottman (Eds.), *The development of children's friendship.* New York: Cambridge University Press.

Schofield, J. W. (1986). Causes and consequences of the colorblind perspective. In S. Gaertner & J. Dovidio (Eds.), *Prejudice, discrimination and racism: Theory and practice* (pp. 231–253). New York: Academic Press.

Schofield, J. W. (1989). *Black and white in school: Trust, tension, or tolerance?* New York: Teachers College Press. (Original work published 1982)

Schofield, J. W., & Evans-Rhodes, D. (1989, May). *Artificial intelligence in the classroom: The impact of a computer-based tutor on teachers and students.* Paper presented at the 4th International Conference on Artificial Intelligence in Education, Amsterdam, The Netherlands.

Schofield, J. W., & Francis, W. D. (1982). An observational study of peer interaction in racially-mixed "accelerated" classrooms. *The Journal of Educational Psychology, 74,* 722–732.

Schofield, J. W., & Sagar, H. A. (1977). Peer interaction patterns in an integrated middle school. *Sociometry, 40*, 130–138.

Schofield, J. W., & Sagar, H. A. (1983). Desegregation, school practices and student race relations. In C. Rossell & W. Hawley (Eds.), *The consequences of school desegregation* (pp. 58–102). Philadelphia, PA: Temple University Press.

Schofield, J. W., & Verban, D. (1988). Computer usage in the teaching of mathematics: Issues which need answers. In D. Grouws & T. Cooney (Eds.), *Effective mathematics teaching* (pp. 169–193). Hillsdale, NJ: Erlbaum.

Shaughnessy, J. J., & Zechmeister, E. B. (1985). *Research methods in psychology.* New York: Knopf.

Slavin, R. E. (1980). Cooperative learning. *Review of Educational Research, 50*, 315–342.

Smith, A. G., & Robbins, A. E. (1984). Multimethod policy research: A case study of structure and flexibility. In D. M. Fetterman (Ed.), *Ethnography in educational evaluation* (pp. 115–132). Beverly Hills, CA: Sage.

Smith, H. W. (1975). *Strategies of social research: The methodological imagination.* Englewood Cliffs, NJ: Prentice-Hall.

Spindler, G. (1982). General introduction. In G. Spindler (Ed.), *Doing the ethnography of schooling: Educational anthropology in action* (pp. 1–13). New York: Holt, Rinehart and Winston.

Stake, R. E. (1978). The case-study method in social inquiry. *Educational Researcher, 7*, 5–8.

Stephan, W. J. (1985). Intergroup relations. In G. Lindzey & E. Aronson (Eds.), *The handbook of social psychology* (Vol. 2, pp. 599–658). New York: Random House.

Strauss, A. L. (1987). *Qualitative analysis for social scientists.* Cambridge, UK: Cambridge University Press.

Walker, D. F. (1984). Promise, potential and pragmatism: Computers in high school. *Institute for Research in Educational Finance and Governance Policy Notes, 5*, 3–4.

Weber, G. (1971). *Inner-city children can be taught to read: Four successful schools.* Washington, DC: Council for Basic Education.

Whyte, W. F. (1984). *Learning from the field: A guide from experience.* Beverly Hills, CA: Sage.

Wolcott, H. F. (1973). *The man in the principal's office: An ethnography.* New York: Holt, Rinehart and Winston.

Wolcott, H. F. (1975). Criteria for an ethnographic approach to research in schools. *Human Organization, 34*, 111–127.

Wolcott, H. F. (1982). Mirrors, models, and monitors: Educator adaptations of the ethnographic innovation. In G. Spindler (Ed.), *Doing the ethnography of schooling: Educational anthropology in action* (pp. 68–95). New York: Holt, Rinehart and Winston.

Yin, R. K. (1981). The case study crisis: Some answers. *Administrative Science Quarterly, 26*, 58–64.

Yin, R. K. (1984). *Case study research: Design and methods.* Beverly Hills, CA: Sage.

Yin, R. K., & Heald, K. A. (1975). Using the case survey method to analyze policy studies. *Administrative Science Quarterly, 20,* 371–381.

Yin, R. K., & Yates, D. (1975). *Street-level governments: Assessing decentralization and urban services.* Lexington, MA: D. C. Heath.

Commentary on the Papers
by Donmoyer and by Schofield
_____

Generalizing from Case Studies

HOWARD S. BECKER

WHY ARE WE HAVING THIS CONFERENCE?

When I was asked to participate in (yet another) conference on qualitative research in education, I wondered, "Why in the world are they having this conference?" I knew the answer, of course: Qualitative research is still somehow not respected as real science in education, so those of us who do it have to get together to answer those questions still one more time.

But why is qualitative work still not respected as real science in education? It's nothing new. For me, qualitative research on education starts with Willard Waller's *Sociology of Teaching*, published in 1932; others may want to start earlier or later, but the tradition is certainly at least fifty years old.

And the tradition thrives. A reasonably selective bibliography of solid qualitative studies of educational organizations and activities would include dozens, maybe hundreds, of items, many of them classics of social research. Such studies have added immeasurably to our understanding, not just of educational matters, but of social organization generally.

So what's wrong? There are several overlapping answers to that. One is that education, like other applied fields, is dominated not by sophisticated researchers but by laypeople who are the consumers of educational research. These consumers—teachers, administrators, and others—have had some training in research, but not very much. Often they have had just one course in which, since education is still dominated by models taken from psychology, they learn what "real research" looks like. It looks like experiments, with comparable data gathered in standardized ways from isolated subjects, summarized and tested with old-fashioned statistics. Since qualitative research—can I substitute "field research"?—doesn't look anything like that, these consumers don't recognize it as having any value.

More sophisticated research consumers have another complaint about qualitative research. Questionnaires and tests can be examined ahead of time and purged of dangerous material. Qualitative researchers, on the other hand, won't say what they are going to do, claiming they don't know for sure. They just hang around, poking into everything. No telling what they'll ask, what they'll stumble onto, what untoward events will happen when they happen to be there to see and hear the whole thing, what students and subordinates will tell them when you aren't looking. Canny administrators try to contain snoopy sociologists, but it isn't easy. No wonder some presidents of small colleges would not let David Reisman interview their faculty about civil liberties unless they were in the room!

Worse yet, good fieldworkers do not restrict themselves to studying the help but insist on treating administrators and other important people as objects of study, whose actions are to be investigated as skeptically and objectively as those of their underlings.

Finally, field research is fundamentally useless to people who run educational institutions, not because it cannot uncover solutions to problems but because the solutions it uncovers are too radical to be "practical." Field studies usually find the causes of educational problems in the basic character of the organizations in which they arise. That inevitably suggests that the problems cannot be solved without making changes administrators cannot or do not want to make. Quantitative studies that don't look so deep make less trouble.

Here's a simple example. When my colleagues and I discussed a draft of our study of medical students (Becker, Geer, Hughes, & Strauss, 1961) with the faculty of the school we had studied, they wanted to know what our recommendations were. We said we didn't have any but would suggest solutions to particular problems they described. They said they didn't like the way students crammed for exams by memorizing stuff from books and lecture notes.

"Well, what skill do you want to test students for?"

"We'd like students to be able to examine a patient, take a history, order appropriate lab work, make a reasonable diagnosis, and suggest a plan of treatment."

"Fine. Give each student two patients to work up, then check their findings against yours."

They looked glum when we said that. "That's all very well in theory, but it's not practical."

"Why not?"

They had their own practices to attend to, their research to do, their papers to write; there was no time for such an elaborate testing procedure, not without giving up things clearly more important to them. They wanted a solution to the problem, but not at that price. We could solve the problem as originally stated, but not with those additional constraints.

But those are all reasons why the typical nonresearcher consumers of research on educational organizations don't like qualitative research and attack it by calling it unscientific. We, who are researchers, have to deal with that, but we don't have to believe that it poses deep epistemological problems. Our epistemological problems are no worse than those of social scientists working on any other kind of social organization. If we think that, say, William Foote Whyte (1943) had it more or less right when he did *Street Corner Society* (and who doesn't?), then we don't have anything special to worry about.

Nevertheless, people are worried about this problem of generalizing. I'd like to propose a diagnosis and a remedy, not because I'm sure I'm right, but provisionally, as a way of opening another perspective on the topic.

WHOM ARE WE GENERALIZING FOR?

We can agree with Donmoyer that human activity ought to be seen, à la Blumer (1969), as collective action. We can push that a little further, and perhaps avoid some of the confusions surrounding the idea of generalization, by seeing making generalizations as something social scientists do together, as a routine part of their work activity.

That view of generalizing lets us take advantage of recent work by sociologists of science (e.g., Latour, 1987; Fujimura, Star, & Gerson, 1987, and the literature cited there), who have begun to look at science not as a form of knowledge but as a kind of work. Such a view does not canonize any one form of generalization as The Right Way to do it. Rather, we can look and see what kinds of generalizations the people doing this kind of science would like to make, what kinds their situation makes possible, and what they have to do to get those generalizations.

Consumers' responses, a major aspect of the situation researchers work in, help shape the work product. Educational researchers usually make their generalizations for multiple audiences of consumers: for social scientists and theorists of education, to be sure, but also for educators, administrators, and the lay public. Each audience wants a somewhat different kind of generalization, some of which are more possible than others.

Since, of course, we are not just studying this form of science-making, but are also engaging in it, we cannot be satisfied with that kind of neutral, detached observation. We need to go beyond analysis of the problem and find some sort of solution.

WHAT ARE WE GENERALIZING ABOUT?

Applied academic fields have their subject matter defined for them by the institutions for which they work. So the subject matter of the field of education is schools, and what educational researchers want to generalize about is schools. What I find out by studying *this* school, on this view, ought to apply to *all* schools, or all members of some subclass of schools.

We might try to redefine the subject matter as education, wherever it happens and by whomever it is carried on. We might study the way thieves teach one another the latest techniques of their trade, or the way young people teach one another to use drugs or engage in sexual activity. But that's just cheap irony, because everyone knows that those activities are not education, at least not what any reasonable layperson means by education. When we study education, we want to study schools in order to find out about all schools.

Generalization becomes a problem because, if we think of education and learning as generic social processes, there is no reason to think that those processes take place only in schools. There is no reason, for that matter, to think they take place in schools at all, even though that is the story schools tell about themselves and the story well-socialized members of our society believe or, at least, pretend to believe so that they won't appear to be nuts.

Generalization is a problem, too, because schools are not all alike in the way they are organized, so that there is no good reason to think that what we find in one will be found in any others. Both of these problems make it difficult to see what you can generalize about if the subject of your generalizations has to be schools.

Where Does Education Take Place?

If we want to generalize about education, we might just ignore schools and study the generic social processes of teaching and learning, wherever they occur and whoever is involved. This enterprise quickly runs afoul of conventional, strongly entrenched ideas of what these words refer to. We can, of course, make words mean just what we want them to mean, and some of us could get away with this, but I doubt we could do it in any organization that claimed to be dealing with education as ordinarily defined and tried to raise money on that basis.

The word *education* assumes that people learn by being taught, that it consists, as a social enterprise, of knowledgeable people teaching people who are less knowledgeable, and typically, not surprisingly, less powerful and less well placed (children or immigrants, for instance), and that this activity goes on in schools. That's what education *is*. You can study, as a number of people have, how youngsters learn to use marijuana. You may find, as Schaps and Sanders (1970) did, that young women typically learn from their boyfriends, while the boyfriends learn from one another. You cannot, however, call that education and expect anyone to take you seriously.

But suppose that the process by which boyfriends teach girlfriends to smoke dope has a lot in common with other activities in which knowledge, skill, and ideas are passed on. It might, for instance, resemble the system described by Gagnon and Simon (1973), in which young women teach their boyfriends to engage in romance, which they have been practicing by themselves for quite a while, while the boyfriends are teaching them to engage in sex, which *they* have been practicing by *them*selves for a similar period of time. If the process works, and each learns what the other knows, they can manage to fall in love in the more or less standard way.

We might find, further, that these processes of peer teaching and mutual learning have their counterparts inside schools and other so-called educational institutions. It has certainly been true for some time that personal computer users have taught one another how to use their machines, despite or because of the more conventional standardized instruction available here and there. And it has been demonstrated in a variety of studies that students in conventional institutions teach one another how to deal with the constraints, requirements, and opportunities those places embody.

To take another variation on the standard model of education, some kinds of teaching and learning are, unlike the elementary and secondary education that form the core of interest for educational researchers, totally voluntary: Lessons in piano playing, tennis, and French are all like that. They take place in profit-making establishments, are often if not always individual, and have no fixed term, no credits, and no degrees. Students just take lessons until they feel they aren't getting anything out of it any more. The distribution of power between student and teacher is so different from the stereotypical school that this is bound to be a somewhat different generic type. (See the discussion in Becker, 1986.)

We can very likely make generalizations about phenomena so defined, that is, phenomena defined as being alike in ways we think central to the way collective activity is carried on in them. A good example would be Erving Goffman's analysis (1961) of what places having the generic features of "total institutions" had in common with respect to the way their inmates (be they nuns, sailors at sea, or mental patients) had to live and the kinds of adjustments they made to living that way. Another would be his analysis of the characteristic social forms that grew up around people who had stigmas of various kinds (Goffman, 1963). The brilliance of his analyses was that you could see that, in the generic sense he had in mind, everyone had some sort of stigma, not just people who were blind or missing a limb, and every institution was, in some respects, a total institution. Understanding a generic phenomenon let you generalize about some large area of social life.

Generalizing this way is something like the Lincoln-Guba model Donmoyer finds inadequate (which I've always interpreted to be a lot more like what he recommends than he thinks it is). His changes seem to be mostly in the direction of finding ways for practitioners to apply knowledge and to take advantage of the kind of learning that comes from experience, the case study then playing the role of provider of vicarious experience.

I'd put it this way: Researchers cannot avoid devising working hypotheses about what they study and, having done that, will of course revise and amplify them to take account of further findings (as Donmoyer's schema theory suggests). But the hypotheses and ideas they develop in this way will probably be about things that are not related in any clear way to schools. If, however, you don't generalize about schools, in some crucial respect you haven't solved the problem most educational researchers have in mind when they talk about generalizing.

Schools Are Not Alike

Researchers who work in the field of education run afoul of one of the great scams of our society: the notion that things called by the same name are the same in other respects. Maybe. Maybe not. The most direct answer to the question of what all organizations called schools have in common is that they are called "schools." Whether that regularity entails any other regularities is problematic or, as we like to say, an empirical question.

It is possible that the people who assign such names do it by looking for just the regularities we would require before we would say that members of that class are alike. That isn't silly, but it certainly isn't guaranteed to be the way things are done. In fact, that usually isn't how people assign such names, although the mechanisms for doing that— for example, certification by the state—probably keep the assignments from being totally unrelated to some set of criteria.

It is also possible that, once an organization is called a school, it comes to resemble the ideal type. If you have the name, you probably have acquired an obligation to live up to the legal or commonsense requirements that go with it. If you don't you may not have any students, may be sued by the state's attorney or the U.S. Postal Service for fraud, or just be laughed at by the people you wanted to impress by taking the name. So, once you have the name, your organization may end up looking quite a bit like the ideal type.

Nevertheless, the name and the reality are at best loosely connected, and some things called schools may actually resemble places that go by other names more than they do other places called schools. Edgar Friedenberg (1959), for instance, had great fun talking about schools as prisons. Of course, he was being ironic, and many thought he was just plain snotty. But few doubted that he was talking about a real enough aspect of contemporary American schools, though many thought he was "going too far," leaving out more favorable aspects of the schools that would balance off the bad stuff he insisted on talking about. Some critics conceded that some schools were prisonlike but thought that it wasn't that many.

The example makes clear why we have trouble generalizing. If schools are supposed to be a certain way, and in reality they ain't the way they spozed to be, the people who run them are falling down on the job. But we ordinarily give such respectable people the benefit of the doubt, not requiring them to prove that their organization is what they say it is. It is one of the several privileges of respectability. That is a bad habit we have, taking the classifications and ideas of the people we study as though they were the way things really are, instead of just more data about what we are studying.

HOW CAN WE GENERALIZE?

Another complication of generalizing arises from the notion that we do not have a valid generalization unless we get the same result in every organization that fits our definition. But that's not true. You can develop generalizations by seeing how each case, potentially, represents different values of some generic variables or processes.

The study of prison cultures furnishes a nice example. Students of prisons (e.g., Sykes, 1958) had demonstrated that, in the men's prisons they studied, inmates developed an elaborate culture. They created a convict government that took over many of the functions of keeping order in the joint; they developed quasi-markets in cigarettes, drugs, tailor-made clothing, and a variety of personal services; they organized sexual activity; they enforced a strict code of convict behavior emphasizing the necessity of never giving information about other prisoners to prison guards and officials.

Analysts of prison culture attributed these inventions to the deprivations of prison life: Deprived of autonomy, prisoners carved out a governmental structure that got some autonomy back for them and a convict code that preserved that autonomy; deprived of drugs, sharp clothes, and other goods they were used to in civilian life, they organized markets to provide those things; deprived of sex, they improvised prison-specific homosexual relationships that did not threaten their self-conceptions as macho men. The generalization was, prisoners develop a culture that solves the problems created by the deprivations of prison life.

So far, so good. Ward and Kassebaum (1965), with this theory in mind, studied a women's prison. They didn't find any of that. Quite the opposite. Even the officials of the prison complained about the lack of a convict code: The women were forever snitching on one another in a way that made a lot of trouble. There was no underground market in much of anything. Sex life was not organized in the predatory style of the men's prison; instead, the women developed pseudo-families, with butches acting as the husbands and fathers of a collection of wives and daughters. (See also Giallombardo, 1966.)

Do these differences invalidate the generalization that the deprivations of prison life lead to the creation of a prison culture? Do they mean that no generalizations about prisons are possible? Not at all. They mean that the generalizations are not about how all prisons are just the same, but about a process, the same no matter where it occurs, in which variations in conditions create variations in results. That's actually a classier form of generalization anyway.

In this case, the theory wasn't wrong, but you had to put in the right values of the variables to see how it was right. You could still say that the deprivations of prison life led to the creation of prison culture, but that this was true only if you understood that prison deprived women of different things than men. Women were not deprived of autonomy because, on their own testimony, they had never had it; they had always lived under the protection of a man—a father, husband, or lover. They were, however, deprived of exactly that kind of protection. So they didn't develop a convict government, but they did develop a system of homosexual relationships in which one woman stood in as the masculine protector.

New women prisoners were especially afraid because, due to variations in the gender distributions of crime, men's prisons have a lot of professional criminals serving time for robbery, burglary, and other less violent crimes, while most women prisoners are in for drugs, prostitution, and typically amateur crimes of passion. There are, thus, more murderers in women's prisons, which as a result sound like more dangerous places, even to the murderers who know themselves as nondangerous (they just wanted to kill that one person who done them wrong). So even the murderers are looking for someone to take care of them.

Similarly, women's prisons typically allow inmates to buy things they want, like cosmetics and clothes, so that there is no need for the development of an underground market.

In short, women are deprived of different things, both because their lives on the outside and, therefore, their needs on the inside differ, and because the prison is run differently for them. Their culture responds to that difference. The generalization is still true, even though the results are quite different.

That's how we might go about generalizing about schools. In fact, I think we could reasonably say that it *is* how we go about generalizing about schools, whether we admit it or not. All that remains is to accept that as what we're doing and recognize it as a perfectly OK way to do it.

REFERENCES

Becker, H. S. (1986). A school is a lousy place to learn anything in. In H. S. Becker (Ed.), *Doing things together* (pp. 173–190). Evanston, IL: Northwestern University Press.

Becker, H. S., Geer, B., Hughes, E. C., & Strauss, A. L. (1961). *Boys in white: Student culture in medical school.* Chicago: University of Chicago Press.

Blumer, H. (1969). *Symbolic interactionism.* Englewood Cliffs, NJ: Prentice-Hall.

Friedenberg, E. (1959). *The vanishing adolescent.* New York: Dell.

Fujimura, J. H., Star, S. L., & Gerson, E. M. (1987). Méthodes de recherche en sociologie des sciences: Travail, pragmatisme et interactionnisme symbolique. *Cahiers de Recherche Sociologique, 5,* 65–85.

Gagnon, J. H., & Simon, W. (1973). *Sexual conduct: The social sources of human sexuality.* Chicago: Aldine.

Giallombardo, R. (1966). *Society of women.* New York: Wiley.

Goffman, E. (1961). *Asylums: Essays on the social situation of mental patients and other inmates.* Garden City, NY: Doubleday.

Goffman, E. (1963). *Stigma.* Englewood Cliffs, NJ: Prentice-Hall.

Latour, B. (1987). *Science in action.* Cambridge, MA: Harvard University Press.

Schaps, E., & Sanders, C. R. (1970). Purposes, patterns and protection in a campus drug-using community. *Journal of Health and Social Behavior, 11,* 135–145.

Sykes, G. (1958). *The society of captives.* Princeton, NJ: Princeton University Press.

Waller, W. (1932). *The sociology of teaching.* New York: Wiley.

Ward, D. A., & Kassebaum, G. G. (1965). *Women's prison: Sex and social structure.* Chicago: Aldine.

Whyte, W. F. (1943). *Street corner society.* Chicago: University of Chicago Press.

Part IV

ETHICS

As in the case of our opening part on subjectivity and objectivity, in this part on ethics in qualitative research we have juxtaposed a philosopher, a fieldworker, and a constructivist scholar. Jonas Soltis, a philosopher, develops his conceptions of ethics from a schema formed by four qualitative research types (description, evaluation, intervention, and critique) and three "intuitively heuristic" perspectives (personal, professional, and public); Louis Smith draws his notions of ethical behavior from the many research projects he has conducted; and Yvonna Lincoln creates a response to each from a constructivist paradigm that she and Egon Guba have been explicating for some years. To all three, ethical conduct is not just the simple matter of avoiding placing at risk those whom in our research projects we variously call the researched "others," "subjects," and "respondents." It is the infinitely more complex challenge of doing good, a consideration that places researchers at odds with one another as they raise entirely different quetions about the location of good in the conduct of research. And it is, as well, the identification of what constitutes proper behavior in the range of roles, settings, and circumstances where qualitative researchers are apt to find themselves. Smith's paper definitely suggests this range, though neither he nor Soltis nor Lincoln consider how the diversity of ethical crossroads that researchers traverse might vary with factors such as their age, gender, race, ethnicity, status, and occupational expertise.

We find in these papers a blend of the general and the specific that can be used to instruct novice researchers who, unlike Smith, do not have an abundance of practical experience and concomitant wisdom to draw upon. Either directly or by inference we know that Soltis, Smith, and Lincoln are concerned about what we teach our students about ethical behavior. Of course, our personal examples as researchers most powerfully communicate our own code of ethics in practice. Since not all students, however, have the opportunity to be research assistants, many will hear about ethics, if at all, under the more formal circumstances of the classroom. To be sure, the various statements on ethics prepared by professional associations are useful instructional materials, but most essentially as points of reference. They miss the type of anchoring that we think the three writers here provide in the form of general questions, actual cases, and philosophical orientation.

At the very least, Soltis, Smith, and Lincoln provide valuable starting points for what our students should know. More than this, we see in Soltis's matrix, which Lincoln, not Soltis, presents in her text; in Smith's many concrete cases, with their accompanying questions and dilemmas; and in Lincoln's critique, plus her notable delineation of the broad ethical principles of the "categorical imperative" and the "practical imperative," a contribution to what researchers who are well beyond the dissertation stage should know. If there is much already written about ethics in research, and much that all experienced researchers already know, we still find most sensible the conclusion that all researchers must be continually open to the prospect of learning about ethical practice. We believe this because of the considerably diverse ways qualitative researchers may be present in the lives of the researched and because of the changing currents of thought about what is ethical practice.

Clearly, researchers need both cases and principles from which to learn about ethical behavior. More than this, they need two attributes: the sensitivity to identify an ethical issue and the responsibility to feel committed to acting appropriately in regard to such issues. Cases and principles are meaningless without these attributes, and all three are meaningless unless they are embodied in persons who are disposed to be ethical. For is it not true that we are unlikely to behave any more ethically as researchers than we are inclined to behave as nonresearchers? But granted that persons mean to do right, we know that different persons will locate what is ethical in very different behaviors. Lincoln is particularly concerned to make this clear when she elaborates on the researcher's conduct she sees associated with positivist and nonpositivist paradigms. And Soltis, in his rejoinder to Lincoln (Smith chose not to prepare one), provides a sharp example of such behavior with his reference to the researcher's dependence upon "the *using* of others as a means to the researcher's ends" (emphasis in original). Lincoln perceives such positivist-type conduct as contrary to her constructivist outlook.

Indeed, much of what is most controversial with regard to ethical practice follows from the researchers' conception of how they should relate to those who join them in their research projects as the researched. Surely few researchers, especially in the field of education, would take issue with Soltis's designation of education as a "moral enterprise." Few researchers, therefore, would fail to hope that something that is good for the researched would be the outcome of their research. Doing good, however, is increasingly contested by writers who believe that empowerment and praxis should be essential attributes of the researcher-researched relationship. Our writers in this section, each in his or her own way, have something of value to say about this and, accordingly, about the enactment of doing good. Of course, as with the writers in previous sections, they do not leave us with cases settled, dilemmas resolved.

Smith's many field-based questions demonstrate the unexpected variety of ethical instances that may arise in the course of a research career; his reactions to them demonstrate the necessary place of good judgment in research—the sort that emerges, one hopes, from the convergence of principle, experience, and reflection. Since we believe that ethical conduct is a matter of neither the generalized principle uniformly applied nor of the particularized advice to "do what you think best," we envisage ample scope for considerable, continuing debate. Soltis, Smith, and Lincoln herein advance the cause of productive debate.

7 The Ethics of Qualitative Research

JONAS F. SOLTIS

The question guiding my writing of this paper was, How can we best conceptualize the ethics of qualitative research as researchers and as the teachers of educational researchers? Ethics is ubiquitous. It permeates all aspects of our lives. For example, fairness is required of us both as professors and as parents. Honesty is essential to research quality as well as to our everyday dealings with others. A promise of confidentiality is as binding when given to unsavory informants as when given to friends.

When Kenneth Strike and I set about writing *The Ethics of Teaching* (1985), it became clear to us that the ethical principles undergirding professional decision making were generic ones not unique to teaching. Our task was primarily one of applying ethics to teaching situations and showing others how to do so themselves.

However, it also seemed clear to us that the unique relationship of teacher to student created a specific moral situation, one in which the student placed trust in the teacher and had a legitimate expectation of being taught a true version of the subject matter, of not being taken advantage of or harmed in any way, and, in general, of having his or her own well-being, not the teacher's, function as the guiding value of the enterprise. This suggested to us that certain sorts of ethical issues are more likely to arise in educational than in other settings. Our case study approach was designed to take advantage of this supposition.

It seems to me that the same is true of the qualitative research enterprise. General ethical principles are applicable across the board. They may achieve a pungency in certain research settings, but the principles of honesty, justice, and respect for persons, for example, are not unique to qualitative research. However, there may be typical, repeated sets of qualitative research circumstances that give rise to

247

research-specific ethical dilemmas regarding such things as deception, the propriety of intervention, possible harm to participants, contract obligations, informed consent, and even social rights and wrongs. Some of these are more general and no doubt occur across many qualitative research settings. Others may be more likely to arise only in special settings.

In this paper I would like to sketch a very broad overview of the ethics of qualitative research by exploring four major purposes to which qualitative research in education has been put and by showing how each of these gives rise to both generic and specific types of ethical issues. The four purposes of research I am referring to are qualitative description, qualitative evaluation, qualitative intervention, and qualitative critique.

Before I begin, I would like to make clear an assumption that undergirds my thoughts about the ethics of qualitative research; all readers may not share this assumption with me, but I think they should. It is that education is, at base, a moral enterprise. Education is ultimately about the formation of persons. It is about developing and contributing to the good life of individuals and society. Even though we may disagree about the specifics of what constitutes the educated person and the good life, it is toward these high moral ends that the human enterprise of education in a democratic society is negotiated and directed. We lose our moral direction when this ultimate end is forgotten in the pursuit of more immediate and pressing ends, or hidden by the facade of value-free research, or overlooked through a lack of attention to the ethical dimension of what we are about.

One argument for qualitative research has been that it has the potential to capture more of the human dimension of educating than does the quantitative approach. What could be more human than the moral sphere? What purpose could be more worthy than to include in our educational research a concern for the good and the rights of those we investigate and the society of which we and they are a part? At base, my assumption is that qualitative educational research cannot be value-free; it must be ethically conducted and ethically concerned.

But how shall we conceive of qualitative research? While the tendency has been to treat qualitative research as all of a piece, usually in contrast to quantitative research (Eisner, 1981; Shulman, 1981; Smith, 1983; Smith & Heshusius, 1986), it has recently become fashionable to attempt to categorize internal differences. For instance Jacob (1987) sees considerable variety in qualitative approaches and would sort them out by linking them to one of six basic social science research traditions: human ethology, ecological psychology, holistic ethnography, cognitive anthropology, ethnography of communication, and symbolic interactionism. Others, like Fetterman (1988), classify different methodological approaches along the lines of ethnography, naturalistic inquiry, generic pragmatic qualitative inquiry, connoisseurship/criticism, and phenomenography. The editors of two special issues on qualitative research in the *Journal of Thought* (Sherman & Webb, 1986) remark that "there still is a need to ground all qualitative methodologies in some general, logical scheme" (p. 6).

This situation, wherein qualitative research is at once taken to be a generic posture different from quantitative research and yet presumed to contain within it many different approaches and methods, makes problematic any attempt at specifying a representative group of qualitative research settings. Nevertheless, I think a look at the major purposes to which admittedly different approaches to qualitative research have been put offers one way to capture a general view of the ethical aspects of the field. So I have looked at qualitative developments in educational research in the recent past and classified them in terms of what researchers have tried to do.

The classic and pervasive purpose of qualitative research has been to adopt, create, and use a variety of nonquantitative research methods to describe the rich interpersonal, social, and cultural contexts of education more fully than can quantitative research. In one sense, this is the major purpose of all qualitative research—to inform our deep understanding of educational institutions and processes through interpretation and narrative description. With the enormous growth of the field of educational evaluation, however, qualitative researchers have added another purpose in attempts to provide richer and wider-ranging assessments of educational processes, products, and projects. This second purpose is to add qualitative judgments of goal attainment to quantitative ones. Beyond this, there have also been attempts to use qualitative research to bring about and document change. The rationale for this third purpose, intervention, is obvious—to change and understand the effects of change on the human beings involved. And, finally, critique through research of the educational effects of such concepts as gender, class, and race, as well as such practical matters as textbooks and school organization, has served a fourth purpose of bringing qualitative methods to bear on our critical understanding of the politics and ideology of education in our time. Of course, it is possible to find a mix of all these purposes in a single research endeavor. The point here is not to suggest their exclusivity but to suggest that in serving these different purposes, qualitative researchers may face a range of different ethical issues.

PERSONAL/PROFESSIONAL/PUBLIC PERSPECTIVES

In what follows, I will illustrate typical ethical problems and issues that seem to arise naturally across as well as within each of these purposes of qualitative research. Some of the issues identified will be more research purpose–specific than others, but all will be part of the broad description of the ethics of qualitative research.

I am also going to make use of an intuitively heuristic threefold set of philosophical/ethical/educational perspectives that I have used elsewhere in a different context (Soltis, 1983). Like the four purposes described above, these perspectives are not mutually exclusive. In fact, as clear and separate categories, they may be logically suspect. Nevertheless, they do provide me with a way to suggest that sometimes ethical issues are seen differently because they take on different quality tones for individuals, depending upon which perspective they have assumed. I call these perspectives the personal, the professional, and the public. I will briefly describe each in turn.

There surely is a sense in which we take ethics to be a very personal matter. It is I myself and each of you as individuals behaving as responsible moral agents who ultimately make decisions, act, and are held ethically accountable. Ethics is also personal in the sense that dilemmas arise in interpersonal contexts. When doing qualitative research, I may worry over such things as violating a person's privacy, or not keeping a promise of confidentiality, or harming others by my actions and even by my inactions. When I do so, I realize that in my research I have been dealing not with "subjects" but with real people who deserve respect as persons and who require me to recognize their claims for ethical treatment. I also may wrestle with my internally developed ethical code as I try to navigate the world of persons in face-to-face situations. This is part of what it means to experience ethical issues from a personal perspective.

The shift of focus when taking the professional perspective involves moving from the personal to the communal point of view. The key characteristic of this shift is an implicit recognition and acceptance of the shared obligations of a community of practitioners. The "I" of the personal perspective becomes the "we" of the professional perspective. Whether codes of proper professional conduct are made explicit or remain implicitly embedded in the practices of the group to which one belongs is not the point, even though making such norms explicit may be desirable. The point is that membership in a professional community carries with it binding collective obligations and forces us to view ethics from a shared perspective. Professional ethical standards may or may not square with one's personal sense of the ethical, but group norms and sanctions become relevant to one's decision making and conduct as a practitioner in a way not experienced by nonpractitioners. The professional perspective on ethics carries with it a special sense of obligation inclusive of but also going beyond the personal in a collective way.

As persons and professionals, we also operate in the public domain. When we take the public perspective, we realize that there is a broader community than our own community of practice in which ethics is relevant. In one sense, of course, ethical obligations are set in the context of the entire universal community of all human beings in all times and places. But the public domain in which we live, work, and exist is a particular one situated in a particular historical time and a particular sociocultural place. When we see our actions as educators and researchers having an impact on this public sphere, we need to shift focus again to raise ethical questions of how we advance or diminish the rights or wrongs of our society by means of our work within it. The serious consideration of public ethics forces us to look beyond the personal and professional perspectives to the moral issues of our socially constructed and publicly shared lifeworld. This is taking the public perspective.

Let me turn now to sample some typical ethical issues and problems that seem to arise in the four purposes of qualitative research that I have identified, making use of the personal, professional, and public perspectives wherever they may be helpful.

PURPOSES OF QUALITATIVE RESEARCH

Description

Descriptive research in education has as its primary purpose a revealing of the human dimensions of some educational phenomenon. This sort of description ordinarily calls for face-to-face involvement with other persons in which both the personal and professional ethical perspectives may come into play. In these settings, while the quality or "fit" of description is clearly uppermost on the researcher's agenda, problems regarding such things as privacy, deception, and confidentiality can become key personal and/or professional ethical concerns.

For example, it is not hard to imagine scenarios in which the identity of those studied and reported on in articles and books can only be thinly disguised. The ethically sensitive researcher would worry over his or her personal invasion of the privacy of others. From the professional perspective, the ethical dilemma might be seen as the right of privacy versus the obligation to publicly disseminate research, but ultimately the rights of those being researched should be honored.

In other cases, it might be highly advantageous to a researcher seeking an insider's uncontaminated description of a school, for example, to consider a participant-observation strategy that deceives all or most of those observed. Is deception ever justified? If deception is personally abhorrent, might the professional purpose of good description override it? The issue of deception is a complex one, but in the main, a research methodology based on deception would have little to professionally recommend it on ethical grounds.

Or consider confidentiality. The key to securing the aid of reliable informants may cry out to be discarded when a researcher is informed of or directly witnesses illegal activities, for example, school dropouts mugging people and buying drugs. What mixed obligations does the researcher have? To break confidence and lose research? To maintain confidentiality and let the authorities handle things? Ethical dilemmas like these abound in the real-world settings of qualitative inquiry.

These sorts of issues have been given thoughtful and thorough examination by others (e.g., Klockers & O'Connor, 1979; Reynolds, 1979; Rynkiewich & Spradley, 1976). They are also treated, along with other principles of professional ethical conduct, in the codes of ethics of the American Anthropological Association (1971), American Psychological Association (1972), and American Sociological Association (1971), as well as in *Standards for Evaluation of Educational Programs, Projects, and Materials* (1981). These codes do not provide answers for all situations, but they do provide important professional guidelines and standards.

The point that I would like to make here is that doing qualitative descriptive research places the researcher in face-to-face relationships with other human beings, and ethical problems of a personal as well as a professional nature are bound to arise. Description is not neutral. It is the interpretive result of an interpersonal engagement with others and as such has the potential of being ethically sensitive, especially with regard to the principle of respect for persons, that Kantian ethical imperative to treat persons as ends in themselves and not as means to our ends.

Evaluation

If the purpose of research shifts to evaluation, other, more purpose-specific, issues might be identified besides those already mentioned. Judgment of others, by its very nature, would seem to carry with it a heavier ethical burden than description. Fairness, for example, would seem to be a key ethical concern in any evaluation. Issues of justice might arise in evaluative research that uses control groups, denying valuable services to some and allocating scarce resources to others. To complicate matters even more, I am going to treat evaluative research primarily as a part of funded-project research. This will allow me to introduce contract obligations into the discussion here, even though this could have come in other places as well.

There is no doubt that funded-project research has been the major stimulant to evaluation in recent years, and qualitative researchers have cogently argued that for evaluation to be fair and thorough it must include more than quantitative measures. In one sense, quantitative evaluation is less problematic than qualitative evaluation. There are a number of recognized standard achievement tests and other common forms of evaluation available to the quantitative researcher. This does not mean, however, that they are ethically unquestionable. They may be racially, culturally, or sexually biased, for example.

Qualitative measures, to the contrary, are not uniformly agreed upon or as easily administered. Moreover, the measuring instrument of qualitative research is often the researcher himself or herself. There is obviously greater potential for personal biases to enter into evaluation in qualitative than in quantitative research. Honesty and fairness then would seem to be among the most relevant personal and professional ethical principles in evaluation.

In contracted evaluative research there also might come into play a professional commitment to freedom to pursue description, interpretation, and evaluation, wherever it may take one. A research contract might specify dimensions of evaluation that limit that freedom and thereby create situations in which the qualitative researcher might feel obligated to breach the contract. Moreover, the contractor may even seek to suppress negative findings. Other conflict-of-interest issues such as confidentiality and the contractor's right to know might also arise.

Perhaps one of the most common ethical problems of evaluative research is the use to which results are to be put. Here a public perspective on the ethics of qualitative research is essential. Honestly critical evaluations may bring about a cessation of public funding to a group in need of help. The negative research evaluation of project Head Start in its early years did just this. But looking only for good results, while it may maintain a helping posture toward those in need, might ultimately result in the funding of an ineffective program for them and be a waste of the taxpayers' money to boot.

In fact, in contracted and funded research, wherever dollars and one's expanding academic research *vita* are at stake, there is always a danger that the personal self-interest of the researcher will get in the way of ethically responsible decisions. Hence the addition of external funding, contracts, and potential political outcomes, as well as judgments of good-bad, desirable-undesirable, and helpful-unhelpful, makes contemporary qualitative evaluation research ethically complex not only from the personal and professional perspectives but also from the public perspective.

Intervention

Interventionist research raises other basic issues. What right does a researcher have to try to change others? Might some of the changes actually secured bring with them unanticipated harm to those being studied? How does the interventionist researcher know that he or she is right? As in evaluative research, there is a presumption that the one doing interventionist research knows what the good is. In evaluation one judges the achievement of some presumed good; in intervention one tries to bring about a good and document it. This brings up the ticklish ethical issue of treating people as means to our ends rather than as autonomous human beings who should be free to choose their own ends. Paternalism in the worst sense of the term is always potential in interventionist research. Of all the purposes to which research on human beings is put, intervention raises ethical issues of manipulation and control to the highest level.

The National Commission for the Protection of Human Subjects of Biomedical and Behavioral Research (1978) has identified three centrally relevant principles for all researchers to use to guide their ethical deliberations. These principles, which seem most apt when considering interventionist research, are beneficence, respect, and justice. They embody the professional ideals of doing good, not harm, to those studied, of recognizing their human dignity, and of being fair to all concerned. Each of these principles is clearly in danger of violation when research is carried out in the interventionist research mode.

Critique

Finally, we come to qualitative research carried out for the purpose of political, social, cultural, or ideological critique. The presumption of knowing the evil is as important a guiding principle in critique as is knowing the good in evaluation and intervention. How you come to know either is the basic ethical question that must be asked by critical researchers, who often assume a morally superior stance toward other researchers. When critical researchers try to penetrate our taken-for-granted personal and professional points of view, they are raising ethical questions from the public perspective in a very special way. They ask questions such as, Are we the servants of class interests? Do we perpetuate an unjust social system? Are we the slaves of technological consciousness and scientism? From the public perspective, these questions require deep and serious reflection. The posture of critical researchers when raising questions of this sort may seem to put them above the fray; but it is important that critical qualitative researchers be sensitive to many if not all of the ethical issues we have raised so far in the actual conduct of their own research. They must be equally sensitive to their assumption of an ethical position that calls out for some form of explicit justification.

Are there any unique, purpose-specific ethical issues in critical research? I am not sure. There does seem to be a crucial and fundamental difference between qualitative research carried out for this purpose and that carried out for the other purposes examined. In critical research there seems to be the presumption that the very purpose of all human research is to raise our consciousness regarding ethically suspect arrangements embedded in the structure of our sociocultural world. This requires that researchers be ethical in the *purpose* as well as in the *processes* of doing research. Perhaps this raises the most fundamental ethical question of all: Should the fundamental purpose of human inquiry be directed primarily at securing the good of human beings?

Clearly this crucial and fundamental issue can only be raised but not settled here. So perhaps I would do well to end this wide-ranging reflection on the ethics of qualitative research by remarking on what the conceptualization I have offered suggests regarding the teaching of ethics to students in apprenticeship to us as coresearchers.

IMPLICATIONS FOR TEACHING

Certainly our students come to us with a personal ethical point of view. It is not as if they must learn ethics from the beginning, as they in fact need to learn how to do qualitative research from scratch. This is not to say that we cannot or should not help them further their development as ethical persons, however. On the contrary, their personal ethical codes can be challenged and expanded, their justificatory arguments enhanced by both rationality and empathy, and their sensitivity to ethical issues strengthened by our overt attention in their training and education to ethical questions that arise in qualitative research.

Moreover, if they come to us as naive ethical relativists, we must tell them they cannot become qualitative educational researchers and maintain that ethical position as professionals. We must show them that there is a set of ethical principles, values, and ideals that they must accept and commit themselves to if they are to be members of the educational research community. This is what constitutes membership in our guild. Our professional ethical values include honesty, fairness, respect for persons, and beneficence. They are nonnegotiable. There are also a number of other professional ethical issues, standards, and norms, some of which were treated briefly in this paper, that we must help students to see from the professional point of view. These include privacy, avoidance of deception, confidentiality, contractual obligations, and informed consent. Our students must be shown that ethics is an important part of the work of our professional community and not just a struggle of a personal sort.

And finally we must enlarge their horizons of public consciousness. What they will do as individual and professional researchers may have far-reaching impact on unnamed and unknown individuals and subgroups in our society. Education is a public trust. All who are given the power to shape and direct it have a great responsibility for the way that the lives of numerous human beings turn out.

My assumptions seem to be showing. I hope I have persuaded you to believe that education is a moral enterprise. I also hope that I have persuaded you to believe that qualitative research cannot be value-free and that it must be an ethically conducted and ethically concerned endeavor. At the present time, a new and powerful form of research on human beings and human affairs is taking shape in the educational community. I believe that we who have a major role to play in its direction and development also have a moral obligation to see to it that not only does research do good but also it is done ethically.

REFERENCES

American Anthropological Association. (1971). *Principles of professional responsibility.* Washington, DC: Author.

American Psychological Association. (1972). *Ethical principles in the conduct of research with human subjects.* Washington, DC: Author.

American Sociological Association. (1971). *Codes of ethics.* Washington, DC: Author.

Eisner, E. (1981). On the differences between scientific and artistic approaches to qualitative research. *Educational Researcher, 12,* 5–9.

Fetterman, D. M. (1988). *The silent scientific revolution: Qualitative approaches to evaluating education.* Berkeley, CA: McCutchan.

Jacob, E. (1987). Qualitative research traditions: A review. *Review of Educational Research, 57,* 1–50.

Klockers, C. E., & O'Connor, F. W. (1979). *Deviance and decency.* Beverly Hills, CA: Sage.

National Commission for the Protection of Human Subjects of Biomedical and Behavioral Research. (1978). The Bellmont report: Ethical principles and guidelines for the protection of human subjects of research (DHEW Publication OS 78-0012). Washington, DC: U.S. Government Printing Office.

Reynolds, P. D. (1979). *Ethical dilemmas and social science research.* San Francisco: Jossey Bass.

Rynkiewich, M. A., & Spradley, J. P. (1976). *Ethics and anthroplogy: Dilemmas in field work.* New York: Wiley.

Sherman, R. R., & Webb, R. B. (Eds.). (1986). Qualitative research [Special issue]. *Journal of Thought, 21*(3).

Shulman, L. S. (1981). Disciplines of inquiry in education: An overview. *Educational Researcher, 10,* 5–12.

Smith, J. K. (1983). Quantitative vs. qualitative research: An attempt to clarify the issue. *Educational Researcher, 12,* 6–13.

Smith, J. K., & Heshusius, L. (1986). Closing down the conversation: The end of the quantitative-qualitative debate among educational inquirers. *Educational Researcher, 1,* 4–12.

Soltis, J. F. (1983). Perspectives on philosophy of education. *Journal of Thought, 18,* 14–21.

Standards for evaluation of educational programs, projects, and materials: Developed by the joint committee on standards for educational evaluation. (1981). New York: McGraw-Hill.

Strike, K. A., & Soltis, J. F. (1985). *The ethics of teaching.* New York: Teachers College Press.

8 Ethics in Qualitative Field Research: An Individual Perspective

LOUIS M. SMITH

A PERSPECTIVE: DEFINITIONS, BELIEFS, AND ASSUMPTIONS

It seems appropriate to begin an essay on the ethics of field research by situating the discussion within the context of a personal perspective. This should lead to increased meaning of the more general and abstract discussion.

I work in a department of education, in contrast to a disciplinary department of anthropology, psychology, or sociology. Most of the individuals I teach are preservice teachers, inservice teachers, and Ph.D. students who will return to public school positions or enter departments of education in colleges or universities. For a variety of reasons I have remained at Washington University for more than thirty years. I find this work both important and satisfying and not in need of further justification.

Most of the inquiry I do is qualitative field research. I expect it to enrich and contribute to the teaching I do, at one or the other levels of experience of the students (Elliott, 1978). I believe educational research in general is important and that the subcomponent of qualitative research also is important. In general, qualitative research, or "naturalistic research" as it is sometimes called, is "noninterventionist" in form, in contrast to experimental inquiry. Events such as schooling, curricular approaches, or classroom interaction occur "normally," and the investigator observes and interprets them.

A number of colleagues have commented on a draft of the essay. Many of the ideas grew out of earlier joint work with these colleagues.

Most of the research I have done in this qualitative or naturalistic mode has been published in technical reports, journal articles, or books and monographs. It is available for scrutiny by other researchers, by students and colleagues, as well as by teachers and administrators. There exists an open quality in the reporting and availability of research findings. Parenthetically, it might be noted that there are national differences in government reports in the United States and the United Kingdom. In the former case any American citizen can obtain a copy of any Office of Education or National Institute of Education (NIE) final report. In the United Kingdom, one of the major problems is getting final reports released for public scrutiny.

Much of the content of what I teach, at all levels, involves students in learning to do qualitative field research. I believe that such inquiry is or can be part of being a creative and reflective scholar-teacher, which, in turn, is part of my definition of being a professional teacher. This is a strong personal value commitment (Smith, Cohn, & Gellman, 1987).

Most of my research has been done within elementary and secondary schools, mostly public schools but some private schools as well. Each of these organizations has its own forms and procedures for legal and ethical relationships.

Much of the teaching and the research that I do is collaborative; that is, it directly involves colleagues, often in quite close but varied relationships. Some of these colleagues are students; some, former students now teaching in the public schools; and some, part of education departments at Washington University or other institutions in the metropolitan St. Louis area or around the country. Most of these relationships also involve friendships, some of several decades' standing. I value these relationships highly. They are part of a more general personal and professional lifestyle.

Washington University has a strong tradition of academic freedom. It does not set research agendas for its faculty members, beyond expecting that each faculty member have an active program of inquiry under way. The university, and the department, allocates time for inquiry and on occasion supplies additional support in summer research grants and paid leaves of absence during the academic year. I have found these arrangements to represent a shared value commitment and to be very supportive and helpful to me over the years.

Most of the research I have done has been supported by grants and contracts: the Office of Education, NIE, the local regional educational laboratory (CEMREL, Inc.), and several private foundations. Each of those relationships has involved a variety of legal and ethical ties. Tax dollars, especially, have their own kind of ethical imperative.

I am a member of a number of professional organizations (APA, AAA, AERA), each of which has its own ethical code. AERA has been my focal organization for attendance, presentation, and participation.

This preliminary perspective has attempted to show the particularities and complexities of one individual researcher's beliefs and entanglements surrounding qualitative inquiry in order to set the stage for a consideration of their interplay with research ethics. I see this as an extension of Kaplan's (1964) point of "autonomy of inquiry" of individual scientists and communities of scientists (p. 3).

AN INITIAL VIEW OF ETHICS IN INQUIRY

Ethics has to do with how one treats those individuals with whom one interacts and is involved and how the relationships formed may depart from some conception of an ideal. At a commonsense level, caring, fairness, openness, and truth seem to be the important values undergirding the relationships and the activity of inquiring.

At a more technical level, inquiry is supposed to increase knowledge—in this instance about teaching, learning, and schooling. In recent years the nature of knowledge, understanding, and truth have all become problematic as debates and controversy in education and the social sciences have increased in scope and intensity. Also, at a technical level, inquiry should not harm the subjects of that inquiry. In recent years discussions of research implications and practices regarding the rights of human subjects have become more central and debated within the several disciplines and professions. The two most important principles for the protection of human subjects are informed consent and anonymity. They are and have been central to my thinking about ethics in qualitative inquiry. They will become clarified and differentiated below in discussion of the particulars of several major projects.

PROJECTS AND ISSUES

The Complexities of an Urban Classroom

Surprisingly, even in long retrospect, the first of my qualitative field studies, the study of an urban seventh-grade classroom, published as *The Complexities of an Urban Classroom* (Smith & Geoffrey, 1968), involved an ethical stance, a resolution of a number of difficult ethical choices in a manner that was as ideal as any project I have done since. A description of the origin and the implementation of the project and an accent on the ethical implications of the decisions will clarify a move toward a more general statement. Geoffrey was a graduate student in one of my classes. We had been reading George Homans's book *The Human Group* (1950). One of the issues under discussion was the need for an educational case study to go along with the other half-dozen case studies Homans reported on and analyzed. Geoffrey asked me if I would be interested in coming to the school where he taught, to see what "it was really like" in an urban school. From the very beginning of the project, the investigator-subject relationship was collegial. The widely held hierarchical view of the university professor and the public school teacher did not disappear overnight, but without really realizing it we were working on the dissolution of that hierarchy.

The formal responsibility of the school district was upheld by the principal. Geoffrey paved the way for my conversations with his prior discussions with the principal. Later I talked with the principal about the project and what I hoped to accomplish. Interestingly, this conversation was monitored by the clerk who occupied part of the same office space. Part of our agreement was that I would stay in Geoffrey's classroom and only go into the classrooms of other teachers if they invited me. With that agreement in hand, he said that it was fine with him if it was all right with the district superintendent. I made an appointment with the superintendent and told him of my relationship with Geoffrey as well as the provisional agreement of the principal and its conditions. The district superintendent saw the acceptance of the project to be within his sphere of authority, and he agreed to it. Informally, after his own discussions with her, Geoffrey had me meet the eighth-grade teacher whom he perceived to be the informal leader of the faculty. We had a general conversation, a part of which involved the project per se. Later I met the teachers at his end of the building and those who were part of his coffee klatch. At the first staff meeting I was introduced to the faculty. Here, too, I explained briefly what we hoped to do. In a sense, then, they could interact with me as much or as little as they desired.

This beginning with the staff and with the district hierarchy, which had formal, legal responsibility, was as open, clear, and honest as I could make it. We were engaging in what later became known as "informed consent."

At that time, *in loco parentis* still had both legal and ethical status as a principle. I still believe that it is an important principle. To Geoffrey's pupils, I was introduced as a teacher from "City University" who was going to be with them, trying to understand how teaching and learning goes: what they find difficult and easy, interesting and uninteresting. There was no vote or choice involved. As best as I could determine, to them I was sort of like a student-teacher. No parent was contacted. In a sense, and in retrospect for better or worse, I was just another part of the school program. To have behaved differently would have violated all kinds of unwritten rules or norms about the behavior of educational adults in the school. From my position, I was not going to try to change anything in the Washington School; rather I was to observe and to think about what was going on. Later, in my own teaching, using the information and ideas garnered from the Washington School experience, a more general commitment to a set of values, goals, and objectives would become a part of my own teaching. I am not sure in what ways I would alter the ethical arrangements in the situation now.

From the start, I had strong beliefs on another point: Every proper name in the story would be coded for anonymity. In this way, no harm could come to anyone connected with the research. The most difficult decision involved coding the teacher, William Geoffrey. We talked at some length about this. Ultimately, he decided that he would go with a pseudonym. I wrote a letter of recommendation for his file explaining "who he was" for those occasions when he might seek a new position. In recent years, particularly as I have added a historical dimension to my research, considerable debate has occurred over the counterargument that it is impossible for others to check one's work if no one knows exactly who is who, and when and where the events took place. That is an issue needing discussion.

Another set of events has helped with the anonymity issue. It is usually three to five or more years after a project is complete that a book is published. By this time, a number of personnel changes have occurred, pupils have graduated and moved on, faculty have retired or moved. Sometimes the school itself has undergone major transitions. Further, I have been very hesitant to have the books I have done reviewed in the local community. For most of the local educators it was a few years longer, if at all, before they knew about the Washington School. In classes I teach I continue to maintain the code of anonymity.

Other aspects of the research warrant an ethical comment or two: We, Geoffrey and I, jointly engaged in data collection, analysis, writing, and authorship. Our inside-outside stance generated an amazingly powerful set of data. Regularly we met at 7:00 A.M. for coffee, donuts, and conversation at a local restaurant. Mostly I was trying to pick Geoffrey's brain for the whys and wherefores of what was going on. I was trying for a nonevaluative, empathic if you like, stance for understanding him and his actions. I was still trying to be "an objective outsider," but obviously stretching that stance. Alternatively, I did not take the perspective of either a central office advocate or a child advocate, positions others have taken in their work. Becker (1970) has raised the broader implications of this stance in his provocative paper "Whose Side Are You On?" Ethical issues merge into political issues.

In the analysis and the writing I tended to take the lead. Neither of us at the time quite knew how to proceed. Geoffrey was still more of a "subject" than I now would argue for. Using his framing of his class, rather than my framing of his views and of his classroom behavior, might have created differences in parts of the book. Some of our recent, extended conversations around a possible "revision" and reprinting of the book have suggested possibly major alternative reorganizations of theoretical contexts, but not much has changed in the actual conceptions and miniature theories we worked toward then, twenty-five years ago. The fact that we could meet last year for a semester and coteach a seminar on the issues suggests some of the long-run implications of the ethical nature of our shared qualitative fieldwork.

Finally we coauthored the book, splitting the royalties fifty-fifty. The perquisites of a more general sort have fallen disproportionally on me rather than him. I believe these would have been more equal if he had elected to pursue a university career rather than become a highly respected principal and later a public school superintendent. On several occasions I urged him to think of pursuing a career that could lead to a deanship in a school of education. In my view, good administrators in the public schools and the universities are rare and valuable people.

Anatomy of Educational Innovation

The second project I undertook had a different ethical aspect from its very inception: The Milford School District administrators came to me through the Graduate Institute of Education's (GIE) Bureau of Consultant Services. The district wanted an outsider to study their creation of a uniquely designed school building and its uniquely designed program and organization. As I perceived it then, and now, the issue was not the possibility of my exploiting them but rather of protecting myself from being co-opted by them. The superintendent, the curriculum director, and the principal were not innocent "babes in the woods." They were Ph.D.'s, trained at major universities, with considerable experience in education, teaching, and administration. I was on my second field project and was feeling my way along. Part of my image then of social science research was that the researcher was an independent, objective outsider seeking some "vision of impartial truth." I was a part of multiple, collegial groups, the GIE at Washington University, AERA, and APA, all of whom held expectations about the "proper" behavior of a researcher. One's scientific reference groups, I felt then and feel now, are an important part of the context of ethical decisions and actions. At the time, I had a more absolutist view of these groups, whereas now I see them as socially constructed, evolving and changing, and often in considerable conflict with one another as to norms, values, and perceptions of what is "legitimate" in the nature of educational inquiry and its multiple practices. Relativism, even "committed relativism," to use William Perry's (1970) conception, is a slippery slope for everyone.

From the Kensington School's inception, and from the interviews they had in the hiring process, the teachers knew that they were to be a part of a special school situation, one having aspects of a "fishbowl." At the school's first staff meeting, my research assistants and I were on the agenda early. We explained our plans and procedures and the agreements we had with the administration and the Office of Education (OE). For the teachers, the research was a *fait accompli*. In a sense it was part of the "normal" bureaucratic and authoritarian nature of the public schools. No one raised objections or concerns, formally or informally, at the time. Rather, they seemed eager to find out who we were and how we would carry out our task. Again, within the context, I tried for a kind of collegiality. But as participant an observer as I was, I was still an outsider.

The relationship of the professional staff to the pupils, parents, and patrons had its own intriguing and sometimes tragic story, which I and my colleagues have tried to sort out in several books (Smith, Dwyer, Prunty, & Kleine, 1988; Smith & Keith, 1971; Smith, Kleine, Prunty, & Dwyer, 1986; Smith, Prunty, Dwyer, & Kleine, 1987). The situation was further complicated in that the district supplied some minimal funds for the project and I prepared a proposal for a small contract from the U.S. Office of Education. Drafts of this were discussed, rewritten, and cleared with the principal and the superintendent. In turn, the superintendent took the research project to the Milford Board of Education for discussion and formal approval. He made the presentation. I did not attend the meeting. At the time all this sort of "made sense." I had no clear notion of "negotiation" and all of what later would arise as "ethical issues in rights of human subjects." I worried more about protecting my independence and the kind of "objectivity" that my earlier training in psychology had indicated was part of being a "scientist."

One of the major consequences of receiving a government contract was that, at a minimum, I "owed" the Office of Education a final report.

"Inadvertently" the district and I had brought a third party into the relationship, and, in ethical terms, a very powerful party, for I could not avoid writing some kind of a report on the project, and the district could not suppress whatever kind of report was submitted. The contract, I see now, created a major set of ethical issues, issues at best dimly perceived then. Deadlines were also included. And we had difficulties in meeting them, much to the consternation of the people at OE, since they were being criticized by Congress for the number of overdue and unfinished projects. I remember some angry telephone calls from project officers at OE, some guilt on my part, and an even greater reluctance to submit the final report until it said what I wanted it to say. Mixed in were images of some level or standard of quality that I wanted in the report before I would send it on its way to live the kind of life of its own that project reports tend to lead.

Drafts of the final report were neither negotiated nor cleared with anyone in the district. At the time, I perceived these tasks to be my responsibility. (Now, I try to build in time for a round of discussions with appropriate persons on early drafts of reports.) Everyone received a copy of the report. The book that Pat Keith and I (1971) wrote did attend to the few comments we received on the report. We did not, however, try to clear the book contents.

In sum, we tended to be outsiders. We "fiddled while Rome burned," in the words of one enraged reviewer. Nor, to take an alternative stance, did we write an exposé of "wasted" taxpayers' money for the local newspapers, for which some citizens might have argued. In some significant sense we did not appreciate the political context of schooling and the role that research could play in political processes, if not, indeed, political wars, given that views of education are highly disputed among interested parties. Then and, still on occasion, now, we think there is a role for "relatively" detached, nonpartisan observers and interpreters of educational events. For, as I will soon consider, my colleagues and I, in our teaching, take strong value stands and argue for particular positions on action research, scholar-teachers, and inquiry-oriented teaching and learning in preschools and elementary and secondary schools. This orientation is a very significant part of the overall puzzle, if not pattern, of the ethical image I want to create.

One of the most difficult issues we live with from the original Kensington study is the knowledge that some of our portraits of people in the school and the district did not match their own perceptions of themselves; they were less than pleased with the images we reflected back to them. These images of persons and practices seemed important for our story and seemed to be as well grounded in the data as we could make them. We had no special malice toward anyone; we did our best to see the world from their perspectives. Yet somehow, from their point of view, we had come up short. Even now I do not see any easy resolution to this dilemma.

The CEMREL Experience

For a decade, roughly 1966 to 1976, I worked part time for CEM-REL, Inc., the regional educational laboratory whose central offices were in St. Louis. My job titles varied from project director to senior research associate, with most of the time spent as an "evaluator" doing qualitative field studies on one or another of CEMREL's curriculum-development projects. In this setting the ethical issues took on a special character and meaning.

First, and very significantly, the director of the laboratory thought that the kind of work I was doing was generally important and could specifically enhance the curriculum-development thrust of the lab. I saw our "understanding" this way: From my point of view they are supporting my research, and from their point of view I am doing curriculum evaluation. My informal charge was "Do what you think best, and try to be relevant to the programs." That kind of freedom and responsibility I found to be congruent with some major part of my personality. I thrived under it. And I believe I made a major contribution to the work of the organization.

Ethically, that general stance put almost full responsibility upon me. There was no place to hide. In addition, it gave me enormous power vis-à-vis the program directors and the evaluation staff. Mostly it meant that all assignments were discussed and negotiated "among equals" out of interest and good conscience on the part of all the parties. And mostly it went very well, I believe, for all of us and for the work of the organization.

When I was a member of a team of people working on programs such as the Computer Assisted Instruction project (Russell, 1969; Smith & Pohland, 1974) or the Statewide Extended Pilot Trials of the Aesthetic Education Program (Smith & Schumacher, 1972), most of the overall issues regarding the rights of human subjects (e.g., informed consent and anonymity) were handled at the "upper levels" of the organization and in consultation with state departments of education, regional agencies, and local school districts, not to mention schools and classrooms. This is a world of agreements by elected and appointed authorities that seems very important for the ethics of research but is little discussed. At my "level" I tried to keep the CEMREL officials informed of my preferred style of work and the ethical implications of that style. Also at my "level," I recall on one occasion using a Howard Becker approach. Since I was in the getting-acquainted stage, I took to the field site a book or report that I had written and said something to the effect that we were supposed to have a product something like this when we were finished. This was part of the informed if not the consent half of a general position of being as clear and frank as possible about what we planned to do. It implied that the individuals in our field setting could do within their organizations whatever they thought necessary to protect themselves. Consent is not notoriously high on the agendas of some schools and educational organizations. In keeping with our important second principle (the first is informed consent), we coded all proper names of people, places, and organizations so as to protect anonymity. In the large CEMREL projects, the coding also kept people inside the project unknown to each other, something very difficult, if not impossible, to do if there is only one principal or one superintendent.

The CEMREL work involved a particular set of dimensions of people and ethics. Usually my agreements with this laboratory were simple: half of me (on a reduced load at the university), a half-time assistant (usually a Washington University Ph.D. student), part of a secretary, and some travel money. All moneys went directly to the university, which saved me from the ethical issues relating to university policies on moonlighting, overload, and violation of outside work arrangements. But the "outside money" with its reduced load also carried another set of ethical issues, those vis-à-vis one's university colleagues. Insofar as one has time and resources to do work that results in creative activities—and publications, which deans and university promotion committees see as important—one performs fewer and fewer other university activities—committee work, advising, undergraduate service teaching, and so forth. Thus another kind of ethical problem arises. One can argue the case for pluralism in university activities. I believe pluralism is appropriate and desirable and would so argue, but if review committees tend to be simplistic and single-priority bodies, and ours at Washington University are this way, then the demands of the department create an ethical problem that has not been well addressed.

Having a half-time assistant raised additional ethical issues. How to "chunk" a portion of the project so that it became a dissertation problem that really belonged to the student was both a conceptual and an ethical issue. I do not believe in "assigning" pieces of a project to students. I try to be helpful as adviser and colleague, and yet I want problems to remain "theirs" in the fullest and best sense of the word. We worked hard on this issue. Students at this level, I have hoped and I have found, contribute their best ideas to the overall effort as well as their particular "chunks." Qualitative fieldwork, as we practice it together, is not typical graduate student "scut" work done just to make some income. If ideas are to be contributed and discussions to be freewheeling in the best creative and critical sense and to result in some writing also, then it seems obvious that one's colleagues should share in the publications as well. This continues a tradition begun with Geoffrey and carried on ever since. From my point of view, and I believe from the point of view of most of the students, this kind of relationship during the graduate student years has led to continuing professional collegiality and long-term friendships. Such relationships have been a very important aspect of the way I want to live my life. In this context, ethical dimensions of research take on a very different meaning from what is sometimes presented in textbooklike accounts.

The CEMREL decade of experience, and the accompanying large number of curriculum-development, research, and evaluation projects I was able to share in, was a major part of my professional life. It gave me opportunities for developing naturalistic methods, for raising substantive issues in educational theory and practice, and for "complexifying," to use a label of one of my colleagues, my views of the ethical issues in qualitative research.

Recent Studies and Their Ethical Issues

One of the practices in research planning that I have fallen into is the phasing of work into an overlapping of projects. Essentially it involves being in the final phases of one project while in the beginning phases of another. On occasion opportunities arise that make me move more quickly than I desire into a new project. The ethical problem thus created is that some projects do not get finished as early as expected, and colleagues, funding agencies, and publishers are left waiting while I work on other activities. At its worst, I have had a project or two that never were finished with the level of quality I had hoped for. Others literally dragged on for years in a form that left me and my coworkers dissatisfied with the final product. In a sense this is relative, for each of the projects I have undertaken seems at the outset to have the potential of becoming a "classic." Not to reach that level, or at least as close to it as I am capable of getting, seems an injustice to everyone concerned.

One illustration of this occurred in a project we called *Federal Policy in Action: A Case Study of an Urban Education Project* (Smith & Dwyer, 1979).

Just as we were about to start our Kensington Revisited project, I was asked to do a history and analysis of a large urban education project that was in deep difficulty and that later, and independent of our study, was to have its substantial funds cut off midway into its efforts. We ended up with a long, 500-page final report full of data and ideas. We thought we had a book contract but eventually did not. Two editors fought over its appropriateness, and the editor with the power decided that it did not fit the company's series of books. By the time all that was clear, I was already into the beginnings of a project that was to consume me for a full decade. I was not able or did not find the time to return to the federal policy study and to provide the publications that it warranted. We did meet the letter of our contract in that we wrote a final report for NIE that appeared as a technical monograph, but the project and the findings did not receive the attention we and the agency people thought it deserved. At this late date I still do not know what to make of the ethical problem. Even for one who works hard, as I believe I do, there are not enough hours for finishing in a way I would like all of the intellectual activities that I am involved in and feel are important. So I am left with some guilt for not having done things as well as they should have been done for some people who have invested in me and my colleagues and our projects.

The *Federal Policy in Action* project had another ethical wrinkle or two that seem important in retrospect. The actors in the project were well-known social scientists, "our betters," as we phrased it at the time. This posed a problem as to how to code and make anonymous these individuals and the array of problems that they ran into in the process of trying to carry out an "inquiry and assistance project." My relationship to the project and its multiple classes of participants—the funding agency, the principal investigators, the advisory board, and the institutions from which they came—was varied and also evolving. We threaded our way through that with great care, trying to behave ethically and responsibly, while also trying to tell the stories that needed telling and trying to make the interpretations and analyses that seemed relevant and important. All that is in the report, but little of it has gotten into the discussion of the problems, difficulties, and possibilities in improving urban schools and linking research, theory, and practice in that effort. Not having gotten that done is an injustice to some of the most important problems facing contemporary education. For the moment the resolution is that I live with some guilt. Funding agencies do not seem keen on eradicating the guilt of unprincipled principal investigators.

The *Case Studies in Science Education* project (Stake & Easley, 1978) involved a number of separate studies of school science programs. I did one on the Alte School District (Smith, 1978). It was carried out in a local school district in which I had many former students, colleagues, and friends. These people knew me and knew qualitative research from the inside, as they had done work with me in earlier days. The ethical problem that I came to call "the two-edged sword problem" arose in discussions with the superintendent of the Alte Public Schools. I had commented that one of the practical reasons for wanting to work in his district was that I knew a number of teachers and administrators. The project was under impossible timelines, portal to portal in one semester, and knowing people would make the project move so much faster than if one had to build the kind of trust that field research requires. He was concerned about the negative half of the acquaintance, the second edge, that is, the possibility that the relationships could be exploitative. We talked our way through the issue, and almost from the first day I ran into it. It was well illustrated in my first interview about the project with one of the involved individuals, a principal, a former student and good friend who had worked with me on a field study. On his desk he had a stack of documents a full eight or ten inches high. He commented, "Lou, I think you will find these of some use." They were varied— curriculum guides, committee reports, district memoranda, and so forth. In a sense I could have written a reasonable report from those alone. I raised the "two-edged sword" discussion with him. Because of our close relationship, he saw no problem. And so the project went.

Our Kensington Revisited project and its trilogy of books (Smith et al., 1986, 1988; Smith, Prunty, Dwyer, & Kleine, 1987) raised two additional and special ethical issues. In the course of doing the initially planned revisit of the Kensington School and the follow-up of the original faculty, I discovered a closet full of school board minutes and got caught up in the sixty-five-year history of the school district. These minutes seemed to have potent things to say about innovation, the key concept in our investigation. But using them amounted to a considerable expansion of the original project; it would add a couple of years to the activities and demand a renegotiation of the entire affair. The expansion of the project became an ethical issue, for it influenced everyone connected with the project: my co-investigators Dwyer, Kleine, and Prunty, all of whom had other career issues and agendas in their minds and on their calendars; the project people at NIE, who were cooperative and helpful but who also had other demands on their time and resources; my colleagues at Washington University, who had to live with my obsessions and part-time absences; and, most of all, the faculty of the Kensington School and the administration of the Milford

Schools, who had me around for a longer time than anticipated. The along-the-way discussions of substantive issues that I had hoped for never materialized to the degree that had been planned. The historical dimension seemed so important that it overrode all the other issues. In retrospect I still believe it was important enough to warrant the effort. Whether it would have been possible to have split it off as a later project and renegotiate on those terms, rather than along the way as we did, is still debatable in my own mind. At the time the practical problems of resources and squeezing the work into busy schedules loomed larger than the ethical issues. In retrospect the final research product, a trilogy of books, seems to be a much more powerful statement on the issues of innovation and school improvement over the long haul than would have been the case had the pieces been split off and treated separately. It seems to me other alternatives are arguable and possibly better than the one we chose. The complexity of the ethical issues involved in such midstream major project redefinition seem worthy of extended discussion.

A second major ethical issue arose during the course of the project. It was one I had never faced before. While we were in the mid to later part of the study, the district became entangled in a widely publicized desegregation lawsuit. Since I knew more about the history of the school district than anyone else, the school lawyer wanted me to testify as an expert witness. At one extreme, such testimony would reveal the name of the district and the school and in effect violate all my commitments to maintaining the anonymity of the participants, those of the present and those from fifteen years before. At the other extreme, refusing a subpoena, if it came to that, left me with the possibilities of a fine or a prison sentence. If I hadn't known about the ethical principle of dialogue before, I discovered it then. I talked with my wife and my brother, a nonacademic, among other family members. I talked with my colleagues in the department. I talked with the university lawyers. I raised the issues with my qualitative research methods seminar. I telephoned my project officer at NIE. And I talked with the teachers at Kensington, the superintendent of the Milford Schools, and the district lawyer. The key actor, among several, was Ron George, the Milford Superintendent of Schools. To him it was simple: "You can't violate your commitments to the staff, teachers, and administrators of Kensington. We'll solve our court problems without involving you." And that was that. As always, I kept copious notes on all of those conversations. To this point I have never tried to write about the experience or raise it publicly as I am doing now. In part the experience and the story got caught up in the prior issue of being too busy with a project that had expanded beyond all reason. But it, too, is an ethical issue worthy of more extended discussion.

CONCLUSION

In this paper, I have not tried for a large theoretical justification of the positions presented here. Rather, I have attempted to draw in some detail the way I conducted a series of qualitative studies in schools and classrooms. Along the way, I have commented on some slightly more abstract statements, ones that might be seen as general ethical principles yet that seem reasonably close to the settings, the decisions, and the actions I have taken. In summary form, they seem relatively simple but important.

Some Concrete Principles

In every project the special circumstances always made me pause and try to think through what was happening and how I should behave ethically in that special set of circumstances. These idiosyncratic and often unexpected circumstances seem to argue for beginning with an ethical perspective close to one's general personal ethical position.

Frequently, I seemed to be starting from a general commonsense position and set of considerations. Conscience, Judaic-Christian tradition, and more rationalized secular humanism seem the sources and substance of that "common sense" (e.g., Haydon, 1937). In retrospect, I would argue that that collage of one's personal background and experience is where each individual must start.

Fairly early on, the protection of the rights of human subjects led me to concerns with two significant mediating principles: coding for anonymity, thereby protecting the privacy of individuals who participated in the research, and informed consent, telling the people involved as clearly and as honestly as possible what I was about in the project.

I extended and generalized the informed consent principle into one of dialogue. From the beginning to the end of each project, I try to keep talking with the individuals involved. I keep the inquiry goals not only in my own mind but also in front of all research participants. As the goals elaborate and differentiate into subgoals and new goals, I keep talking about those changes. I try to listen to the ideas and sentiments of the various groups and individuals in the setting and reach agreements on how to incorporate those ideas into what I do. Further, as I invent ways of garnering information about those elaborations, I keep talking to individuals about the reasonableness of those goals and the reasonableness of the strategies and tactics for reaching them. Concerns and hesitations from all parties become opportunities for creative, mutual problem solving. All differences do not evaporate, but many if not most seem to be open to discussion and finding alternatives. In terms of personal items and agendas, persistence without arm twisting seems to capture some of the flavor of the temperamental stance I favor. I have never been on a project that I did not think was highly important and really worth doing, and hence worth arguing and working creatively for. Were I to feel the study to be unimportant, this would change much of the motivational and convictional quality. I would not like to be in that situation.

And all the foregoing seems to be arguing for another general principle: The inquiry has to be something that is worth doing. For me, research is not just a simple technical exercise. It becomes part of a larger scheme of ideas worth exploring. Always there is an element of personal choice on my part with any project I do, even when the initiation comes from outside. Saying no early on to projects with marginal interest and importance in my own eyes seems, almost unexpectedly, a major ingredient in the ethics of research. As part of the ethics of research, we need further discussion about what kinds of projects one turns down. For instance, the availability of funds for some activities and the lure of fame and fortune for others can be very seductive tempters into projects that one cannot defend on grounds of importance or significance.

In turn, having a head full of interesting and important problems that are looking for times, occasions, and resources becomes another part of the ethics of important and significant research. The intake manifold of abstract theoretical problem possibilities in my life seems very broad and open-ended, so that almost any concrete problem that comes floating by immediately gets placed into a context of relevance and importance. "Creative rationalizing" may be a mixed metaphor of how I evaluate those tendencies and this principle.

As I string out this list of principles, I am struck with another one. At the most microlevel, every decision and every act in a qualitative research project can be placed against one's ethical standards. From the very conception of the problem to the entry procedures to the kind and place of sampling and data collecting on through to publication—the entire research process can be viewed in terms of its implications for the people involved. Or, at another level, larger patterns of behavior and action can be isolated and compared to one's general ethical standards. Either way, micro or macro, that becomes a heady, necessary, and potentially onerous agenda.

Some Abstract Principles

When pushed hard for a more general statement of ethical principles, I tend to fall back on statements of several kinds drawn from political science, philosophy, and psychology.

First, in perhaps an oversimplified manner, I have had a long commitment to the values of what is sometimes called "secular humanism" or "democratic liberalism." When I ask myself what kind of society I want to live in and foster, I return to the very broad ideals of "liberty, equality, and fraternity." When I find puzzlement in the ethical issues in how I relate to the people in the setting I am facing in fieldwork, I ask myself how the issues play against these very broad abstract ideals articulated two centuries ago in the French Revolution. In some fundamental sense, my commitment to the knowledge being generated is that it will contribute to the emancipation, to the empowerment if you like, of the individuals in the setting and of the teaching profession at large. Even though social distinctions exist in all of the groups in which I work, I always try to minimize them in order to move toward equality in interpersonal relations. Further, I have a vision of an educational community of people working together in some kind of a fraternal or caring fashion. Obvious problems occur among individuals and subgroups within schools and the profession; at different points in time, they hold different views and give different priorities to the values they cherish. Finding creative, integrative solutions through dialogue and discussion in such problem-filled circumstances is no mean accomplishment. And, equally obvious, the solutions one finds never work perfectly and often work badly. But that does not destroy the ethical point of having a model of a liberal society to help guide the quality of the decisions and the judgments that one tries to make.

The best guide I have found for thinking through the issues of the trade-offs among values is the account by Oliver and Shaver, *Teaching Public Issues in the High School* (1966). As a first step, they argue for separation of definitional issues, factual issues, and value issues. The core of the resolution of value conflicts is to treat the values as dimensional concepts and ask oneself how much of one value one is willing to give up for how much of another value. And that is a very difficult intellectual process in complex practical situations. As educators, they suggest a variety of teaching techniques, such as role playing, selecting extreme examples, and small-group discussion, as ways of improving one's ability to deal with value issues.

Second, the picture of ethical issues I have tried to paint involves the social-interactional context of inquiry. The number of people involved is larger than the dyad of researcher and subject, as it is traditionally argued. Justice and caring have to enter into one's thinking and action in quite concrete but complex ways, as Kohlberg (1971) and Gilligan (1982) have argued.

Third, I would argue for what Perry (1970) has called "committed relativism." In agreement with him, I personally do not believe, as I hope the extended illustrations indicate, that there is a simple, absolutist set of values to undergird the ethics of fieldwork. But a commitment is necessary nonetheless. And this pushes me toward one final general philosophical statement, the "decision of principle" as developed by the philosopher R. M. Hare (1952). He comments that when one has said all there is to say about a decision or course of action, that is, one has made a full justification of the decision or action, placing it into a total way of life, then there is nothing more that can be said. If the critic still asks, "But why should I live like that?" the answer is that, by definition, there is no more that can be said. In Hare's words: "He has to decide whether to accept that way of life or not; if he accepts it, then we can proceed to justify the decisions that are based upon it; if he does not accept it, then let him accept some other, and try to live by it. The sting is in the last clause" (p. 69). Part of my intent has been to gradually extend and indicate, through the illustrations and the arguments, where the fieldwork inquiry I do fits into the more general professional and personal lifestyle I have constructed and want to lead. I see that as everyone's necessary challenge in a discussion of ethics in qualitative inquiry in education.

REFERENCES

Becker, H. S. (1970). *Sociological work: Method and substance.* Chicago: Aldine.

Elliott, J. (1978, July). *What is action research?* Presentation to CARN Conference, Cambridge, UK.

Gilligan, C. (1982). *In a different voice.* Cambridge, MA: Harvard University Press.

Hare, R. M. (1952). *The language of morals.* London: Oxford University Press.

Haydon, A. E. (1937). *Man's search for the good life.* New York: Harper & Brothers.

Homans, G. (1950). *The human group.* New York: Harcourt, Brace.

Kaplan, A. (1964). *The conduct of inquiry.* San Francisco: Chandler.

Kohlberg, L. (1971). The concepts of developmental psychology as central guide to education: Examples from cognitive, moral and psychological education. In M. C. Reynolds (Ed.), *Proceedings of the Conference on Psychology and the Process of Schooling in the Next Decade* (pp. 1–55). Minneapolis: University of Minnesota Press.

Oliver, D. W., & Shaver, J. P. (1966). *Teaching public issues in the high school.* Boston: Houghton Mifflin.

Perry, W. G. (1970). *Forms of intellectual and ethical development in the college years.* New York: Holt, Rinehart and Winston.

Russell, H. (Ed.). (1969). *Evaluation of computer assisted instruction program.* St. Ann, MO: CEMREL.

Smith, L. M. (1978). Science education in the Alte Schools: A kind of case study. In R. Stake & J. Easley (Eds.), *Case studies in science education* (pp. 1–143). Washington, DC: National Science Foundation.

Smith, L. M., Cohn, M., & Gellman, V. (1987). The reconstruction of educational psychology. In B. Somekh (Ed.), *Action research in development #8* (pp. 219–227). Cambridge, UK: Cambridge Institute of Education.

Smith, L. M., & Dwyer, D. C. (1979). *Federal policy in action: A case study of an urban education project.* Washington, DC: NIE.

Smith, L. M., Dwyer, D. C., Prunty, J. J., & Kleine, P. F. (1988). *Innovation and change in schooling: History, politics, and agency.* London: Falmer Press.

Smith, L. M., & Geoffrey, W. (1968). *The complexities of an urban classroom.* New York: Holt.

Smith, L. M., & Keith, P. (1971). *Anatomy of educational innovation.* New York: Wiley.

Smith, L. M., Kleine, P. F., Prunty, J. J., & Dwyer, D. C. (1986). *Educational innovators: Then and now.* London: Falmer Press.

Smith, L. M., & Pohland, P. A. (1974). Education, technology and the rural highlands. In D. Sjogren (Ed.), *Four evaluation examples: Anthropological, economic, narrative, and portrayal* (pp. 5–54). Chicago: Rand McNally.

Smith, L. M., Prunty, J. J., Dwyer, D. C., & Kleine, P. F. (1987). *The fate of an innovative school: The history and present status of the Kensington School.* London: Falmer Press.

Smith, L. M., & Schumacher, S. (1972). *Extended pilot trials of the aesthetic education program: A qualitative description, analysis, and evaluation.* St. Louis, MO: CEMREL.

Stake, R., & Easley, J. (Eds.). (1978). *Case studies in science education.* Urbana, IL: College of Education, University of Illinois.

Toward a Categorical Imperative for Qualitative Research

YVONNA S. LINCOLN

The task here is to make some sort of sensible response to the very fine papers by Jonas Soltis and by Louis Smith. That is no mean feat, simply because the papers are, at one level, incommensurable; that is, there is no common basis of comparison, since Soltis and Smith have entered the topic from two very different perspectives. One could, I suppose, force the two papers together, and, indeed, I tried that. But it seems that a more profitable route might simply be to aid and abet the reader in seeing what the papers offer and attempting to understand what they might still be missing.

Thus I have set myself three tasks: first, to try to capture what I believe the Soltis paper offers; second, to do the same with the Smith paper; and finally, to offer some analysis of where we are now, metaphorically and practically. The last word has not been written, of course, just as the last word on ethics has not been written for experimental, conventional, or quantitative inquiry. But the two papers taken together offer sound guidelines for where profitable discussion might begin.

PRESENTATION BY JONAS SOLTIS

In some ways, the Soltis paper fails to live up to its abstract.[1] The paper offers a map of types of ethical issues and types of research contexts, which may be displayed as they are in the table on the next page (for which Soltis bears no responsibility). For each of the cells of the table, Soltis says he will consider a total of six sets of ethical decisions that must be made: privacy, confidentiality, contractual obligations, institutional mores, social and cultural power, and relativism.[2] That is not

A Matrix or Map of Potential Ethical Issues
in Contemporary Forms of Qualitative Research

Purposes of Qualitative Research	Ethical Issues: Perspectives Brought to Bear		
	Personal	Professional	Public
Description			
Judgment, Evaluation			
Intervention, Change Agentry			
Social Critique			

done very clearly or completely in the paper, although it can and probably should be done. However, I am not convinced that these are the only issues (as you will see from the later analysis of the Smith paper). Nevertheless, it would be helpful to see those issues (as sub-issues in each cell) debated by the larger profession.

There are, however, two problems with his discussion. First, these items might not be the entire subset. But whether or not they are the subset, the paper needs to look for examples and to discuss each issue as it might arise within each cell. I am not unaware that this means six times twelve short discussions, but it would help to clarify the range of potential ethical issues existing in the map or matrix. It would also aid and abet in clarifying where, when, or whether certain forms of qualitative research typically bring certain ethical issues to the fore more often than do other forms of qualitative inquiries. This would be useful to know, particularly in teaching our students about qualitative research in general or different strands (types) in particular.

Second, it is also not clear from his discussion how the problems of qualitative research are distinct from those of quantitative research. He does not conclude, as some might, that dimensions of ethics are type-specific (that is, belong solely to a qualitative inquiry). Neither would I. I strongly believe that each of the items has to be considered as part and parcel of the total ethical decision-making arena for whatever kind of research in which we might engage. The privacy and confidentiality issues, for example, are attenuated, but this has always been the case in qualitative research. The main difference, it seems to me, is that we are rarely talking about those living oceans away, who cannot assert that they have confidentiality and privacy rights and whose identities are not likely to be known to any save other anthropologists and sociologists who have traveled to far-flung lands to engage in research.

Now it is the case that we engage in inquiry close to home, not for the sake of pure curiosity, or for understanding other lifeways, but for the sake of description, evaluation, intervention, and social-consciousness raising (which he terms "critical research"). The problem here is not that we face what Soltis labels "different ethical issues" but that we have brought the same issues home as we became introspective about our own social functioning, intervention, and ideologies. We should have guessed that our philosophical, epistemological, and methodological chickens would come home to roost.

The issues of privacy and confidentiality are indeed a problem compounded by high interaction and typically not faced in the same manner by those who bury identities under numbers and aggregated sums, means, and distributions. We know that privacy, anonymity, and confidentiality are virtually impossible to guarantee in qualitative case studies that are of high fidelity (Lincoln & Guba, 1989). What we do not know is how the social contract must be renegotiated so that parties to the inquiry, whether research, evaluation, or policy analysis, understand that they retain and indeed acquire other forms of power within the setting as a result of making a trade-off with privacy. We do understand, however, that there is a trade-off and that that trade-off may be in fact more important to respondents than privacy (Guba & Lincoln, 1988). We know, for example, that respondents value the power to negotiate inquiry questions in a cooperative manner with the inquirers. Moreover, they see having both a high degree of input in framing the focus of the study and coequal power in determining agendas for negotiation as powerful and desirable trade-offs in the balance between privacy and agency. It may well be that the social contracts between researchers and respondents should be written to consider more heavily those ends that are *more desirable* to research participants. It must be remembered that laws and regulations regarding confidentiality, privacy, and anonymity for research respondents were framed under epistemologies and ontologies (i.e., logical positivism and post-positivism) that are now believed to be *inadequate* and, indeed, *misleading* for human inquiry (Lincoln & Guba, 1985).

To sum up this argument, several things are now clear: First, privacy, confidentiality, and anonymity regulations were written under assumptions that are ill suited to qualitative and/or phenomenological, constructivist philosophies; second, from some small and preliminary studies, we now understand that respondents may be willing to give up strict privacy and anonymity rights for the larger right to act with agency in participating in the research efforts as full, cooperating agents in their own destinies; third, we have not, as a profession, considered carefully enough either how we explain this trade-off to respondents or what the trade-offs might be in our own professional lives. On the third point, it seems clear that we must trade the role of detached observer for that of professional participant. But, clearly, the issue is far more complex than simply fretting about privacy, anonymity, and confidentiality.

Soltis also broaches the topic of deception. He notes that "it might be highly advantageous to a researcher seeking an insider's uncontaminated description of a school . . . to consider a participant-observation strategy that deceives all or most of those observed." I have argued strenuously in other places that deception, based as it is in a realist ontology that presumes there is a "real" reality "out there" onto which "scientists" must converge, makes deception possible, and even desirable, in some instances. But the conviction that there *is* no reality "out there" (the phenomenological and constructivist posture) militates against deception and, in fact, specifically makes such a decison inimical to the research effort. It is subversive to the research effort to search for the *multiple social constructions* that individuals hold and, at the same time, deceive them regarding the purposes of the research. It leaves respondents, at best, confused, and, at worst, unable to make informed consent decisions or to act in what they might consider their own best interests under the law or under their own human dignity. How are respondents to tell inquirers about the meaning attribution, or sense-making, in which they engage if the researcher deceives them regarding the *meanings for which he or she searches?*

There simply is no such thing as an "uncontaminated description" of a setting. Again, the ideas of contamination and noncontamination require a belief in a realist ontology that presumes the existence of a value-free set of natural laws that govern human behavior. Such a thing has yet to be found (and will not be). All human behavior and, consequently, all human settings and organizations are constructed around human values, whether tacit or propositional. The idea of an "uncontaminated description" bears witness to a belief that the organization (setting, project, program, and so forth) exists outside of the humans who populate it. Science is now beginning to understand that such is and never was the case.

With respect to evaluative qualitative inquiry, Soltis raises another set of issues, those that he terms "contractual." These likewise are not new problems; they existed when evaluators used primarily or only quantitative methods for evaluation studies. It has always been the case that evaluation sponsors, funders, or clients have occasionally sought to limit distribution of findings and results, have sought to control tightly the range of information (and, therefore, power) available to less powerful groups, and have sought to stifle the spread of negative findings. That continues to be a contractual-ethical issue, although it is probably true that qualitative studies—by virtue of their implied hermeneutic, dialectic format for data collection and analysis, and the validity checks contained in member checking—militate *against* information's being concentrated in the hands of a relatively few powerful sponsors. In short, the methods themselves, and the means by which validity and construction fidelity is established and achieved, act to prevent some of the larger abuses of the information-as-power game often played by funders.

Intervention research carried out with qualitative methods, Soltis points out, may raise "other basic issues," among which are the "presumption that the one doing intervention research knows what the good is" and "paternalism," including "manipulation and control." Again, I would assert that paternalism, manipulation, control, and the presumption that the "scientist" knows what the good is are not new to qualitative research. They are among the rankest abuses of the logical positivist paradigm. More so than the constructivist paradigm, logical positivism sets up a cycle wherein the researcher, whether implied or announced, is always the person(s) adjudged to know "the good." After all, in the conventional paradigm, it is the inquirer who seeks funding, who frames and bounds the questions, who designs the overall inquiry strategy (methodology), and who makes all decisions regarding appropriate manipulation and control that he or she believes will enable him or her to finally assert that the study was "contamination-proof" (Lincoln & Guba, 1985). This problem is not new to qualitative research; it is merely exacerbated by the high face-to-face interaction and levels of trust that researchers may need to engage in fruitful inquiry.

I do not believe that I give away the farm to say that it is possible to have, in some instances, more manipulation and control present in qualitative studies, depending on the philosophical system that guides the framing and design of the study. But I know for a fact that it is possible to have less manipulation and control present, to have less paternalism. This is achieved by having more participation by respondents, wherein respondents are themselves responsible for determining what they believe to be good for themselves. This is enabled and facilitated by inviting respondents to be conjoint framers of the problems under investigation and by having them fully participate in determining methods for data collection and analyses that they believe are noninjurious to themselves as human or political beings. Often logical positivism demands the very paternalism that Soltis abhors, while phenomenological constructivism can avoid the problem altogether. The methods, after all, whether quantitative or qualitative, act in the service of a larger paradigm. The *paradigm* itself determines whether the inquiry will be based on human dignity or on paternalism.

This by no means exhausts the kinds of problems that Soltis raises, and, in fact, I have skipped a crucial one, that of critical research, or research whose presumption is "to raise our consciousness regarding ethically suspect arrangements embedded in the structure of our sociocultural world." It should, however, be clear to the reader from the foregoing discussion that qualitative inquiry carries with it some ethical problems (as do all forms of human inquiry). What is not clear from the Soltis discussion is how those problems differ substantially from those associated with quantitatively oriented inquiry. Although it is not my place to do so here, elsewhere I have undertaken a discussion of problems that I believe are *unique* to phenomenological inquiry (Lincoln & Guba, 1989). It is those that seem to be the likeliest to provide subtle opportunities for unethical behavior on the part of researchers.

It is also not clear from Soltis's paper how the purposes of inquiry (i.e., description, judgment/evaluation, intervention/change agentry, and social critique) fit with other analyses of the forms of qualitative research (i.e., ethnomethodology, ethnography, ecological psychology, cognitive anthropology, and such other traditions as symbolic interactionism [Fetterman, 1988; Jacob, 1988; Smith, 1987; Smith & Heshusius, 1984; Wolcott, unpublished handout, 1981]). Different traditions, it is argued (Smith, 1987), produce very different products or expected products, different conclusions, and, presumably, different judgments regarding their adequacy (goodness and trustworthiness) as inquiries. If that is the case, then, ought not judgments of ethical decisions also abide within traditions, so that appropriate decisions regarding ethical stances can be made? Focusing on purpose is useful and, indeed, serves good utilitarian and heuristic ends, but some consideration of tradition—and therefore, of intended method, analysis, perspective, and product—ought also to generate its own unique set of ethical deliberations.

Soltis's description of the types and purposes of qualitative inquiry misses the point in that his four purposes are also those to which nonqualitative inquiries have been put: description (as, for instance, in classical anthropological or sociological monographs that seek to shed light on radically different folkways); judgment/evaluation (as, for instance, in the evaluation mounted in the federal curriculum initiatives in the post-Sputnik era); intervention/change agentry (as, for instance, in the Great Society programs mounted under Lyndon Johnson's presidency); and social criticism (as, for instance, in the ongoing Marxist or critical theorist traditions). It may have heuristic value for inquirers to think in some conscious way about their purposes in conducting a given inquiry. In fact, such reflection ought to make it more difficult for inquirers to be co-opted by persons in traditional positions of power and authority. But the fact that qualitative methods are now being brought to bear on the same kinds of inquiries in which we once used quantitative methods does not help as much as it should in predicting ethical dilemmas that might arise and projecting how we might avoid them or confront them with integrity.

What we are missing from this discussion is a set of examples that might permit the reader to see some ways in which qualitative research poses different, unique, or more difficult dilemmas. What we have is a kind of ethical "periodic table" of possible concerns, which should allow us to predict and contemplate the kinds of problems that we might encounter in the four arenas in which qualitative research is commonly used. By looking at the *types* of ethical decisions, the *perspectives* one might bring to bear, and the *arenas* in which they operate, Soltis suggests, we should be able to do something very like a chemist in predicting possible problems and solutions that represent the best of ethicality in that situation (a relativist decision, in any event). My own problem with this way of approaching ethics in qualitative research is that it may not prove as useful as the table of chemical elements proved to chemists. This is the case for two reasons: First, we do not know if the prediction of ethical dilemmas is as orderly as the prediction of available electrons or the properties of inert gases appeared to be (and we suspect that it is not), and second, we suspect (and have argued earlier) that it is indeed the case that each age redefines ethical problems anew, taking into account a changing technology and context. Therefore the prediction of ethical dilemmas cannot readily proceed from such a table. It is also the case that while such a table might provide much fodder for discussion and, therefore, for teaching purposes, it would hardly suffice for addressing the kinds of concerns raised, for example, by the Smith paper.

PRESENTATION BY LOUIS M. SMITH

It may be helpful to turn to the Smith paper at this point to demonstrate the kind of argument I am making. What Louis Smith has tried to do is to re-create for the reader some situations he has found troublesome in his life as a qualitative researcher. He has outlined a half-dozen historical, first-hand vignettes that have given rise to his own personal ethical crises and ruminations. Embedded in those experiences are more than a dozen ethical issues, which I have extracted and abstracted below for several reasons. They are real, were unexpected, and have no firm resolution, even now. They give some feel for the kinds of issues that tend to arise willy-nilly to blindside us. Finally, they provide an indication as to why a periodic table of ethical considerations is inadequate to the problem of forecasting what we might encounter in the complex arena of human affairs.

1. Should sites and people—whose identities are usually concealed—be public? If they are not, how can our research results be checked by other researchers?
2. When our respondents choose up sides, or when thorny issues arise, how do we answer the question, "Whose side are you on?" The ethical issue becomes merged into a political one. Advocacy roles, particularly in qualitative studies, are hard to avoid.
3. When people and agencies come to you for service and/or research, how do you protect yourself from being co-opted?
4. How do ethical responsibilities change when a third party—say, a funder—is brought into a research arrangement?
5. Who negotiates the study with those who will be respondents—those who are doing the research or those to whom the respondents owe their ongoing work contracts?
6. What are the ethical ramifications of the world of agreements formulated by elected and appointed authorities? When the boss tells you to "cooperate," are you free not to? After all, "consent is not notoriously high on the agendas of some schools and educational organizations."
7. What happens when researchers' portraits of people do not match their own perceptions of themselves?
8. What is the ethical price to pay of failing to appreciate the political context of schooling and the role research might play in the political process?
9. What are the ethical considerations vis-à-vis one's own university colleagues, when you are off doing university-prized outside con-

tract research while they are performing the lion's share of student advising, committee work, and other less rewarded and less glamorous (but necessary) university chores?

10. When you have a graduate assistant on a research project, how do you see to it that a chunk of the project really belongs to the student for a dissertation and that you are not simply passing off some uninteresting but necessary task that you would not consider doing yourself?

11. What are the ethical implications of the overlapping of projects? What happens when "opportunities arise that make me move more quickly than I desire into a new project"? How do you finish each project in a reasonable time so that all researchers are satisfied with the quality of the final product or products? Where is the time found for sober and careful reflection on *each* project?

12. Is it ethical to fail to do the publication that a given study really warrants (either because of the intrinsic importance of the questions, or because of the significance of its findings, or both)?

13. How do you make certain that what is in the report becomes a part of the larger national debate and discussion on schooling (for instance, on improving urban schools)?

14. When arranging for site work, is it better to know the people on site, or better that they be strangers (the "two-edged sword" problem)?

15. What do you do about a "midstream major project redefinition"? What is the ethical fallout when new information or issues arise that necessitate a major project redefinition? Who gets to negotiate?

16. What are your ethical responsibilities when the project site finds itself in the middle of a lawsuit—especially when you have information that could be useful to both sides?

I have repeated in shortened form the dilemmas Smith presented to indicate just how few of them could be predicted—and, therefore, resolved—from the table generated from the Soltis paper. My guess is that fewer than half could even be generated from the table, let alone resolved satisfactorily from it. In many instances, the dilemmas are unresolvable, save in a case-by-case, personal way, by a researcher making a decision based upon personal convictions, the larger good, or the least harm. These issues are subtle and, to some extent, serendipitous. They occur mainly as the "interaction effect"—if you will pardon my quantitative usage—of particular persons in particular contexts at particular times, with many persons acting on different sets of personal and professional principles, depending on who they are and where they "sit" in the context.

What Smith has tried to do is to formulate some general ethical principles that would enable a person such as himself to address the dilemmas with which he has struggled. Those, too, deserve some discussion, since they could not easily be formulated from the Soltis discussion. Six "ethical guideposts" constitute Smith's "general ethical principles."

First, Smith suggests that a researcher must enter his or her work with an ethical perspective that is very close to (if not coterminous with) one's own personal ethical position; that is, the professional and the personal positions ought to coincide at many, or most, points. This personal ethical position ought to be formed from "a collage of one's personal background and experience." In other words, if it would not be appropriate ethical behavior in your own personal life, with family, friends, relatives, and neighbors, it would likely be inappropriate and unethical behavior with funders, colleagues, and respondents.

Second, Smith suggests that we extend and generalize the principle of informed consent to a principle of "dialogue," by which he means (I believe) the negotiation of research processes and products with one's respondents, so that there is mutual shaping of the final research results. This is fully consonant with emerging discussions of qualitative research and the proposed treatment of respondents as agents with dignity and self-determination rights (see, e.g., Heron, 1981). "Dialogue" suggests a mutuality in the interaction between persons, an egalitarianism that has been distinctly lacking in experimental models of research. In part, it has been this lack, and the imbalance it has brought about between researcher and researched, that has prompted both a move to more qualitative forms of inquiry and, concomitantly, a reexamination of the ethical issues raised in social science (despite professional association standards and federal laws regulating research relationships).

The third principle that Smith would urge to guide research is what I have termed "the passionate principle": The inquiry itself must be something well worth doing. A researcher must be able to defend the project to anyone on the grounds of its importance and significance and, consequently, is ethically bound to reject projects of only marginal interest or importance. This, I fear, would leave many federally funded projects undone, if my own experience is any guide. I have known literally dozens of colleagues who commented, "This is a dumb project, but I guess I'll put in a proposal, since it's what they're funding this year." My guess is that this principle has been violated more in recent years because of the reversal of the proportion of agency-initiated funding priorities versus field-initiated priorities.

The fourth general principle is that every decision and every act in a piece of qualitative research can be judged according to an ethical procedure. The ethical procedures that ought to be used to judge are not specified, but emerging debates regarding qualitative research, or naturalistic inquiry, would agree that each and every act, and each and every decision point, has embedded within it a set of moral considerations that may be examined apart from the rest of the research acts and decisions. This, too, is in keeping with emerging definitions of qualitative research as *participative, cooperative,* or *experiential,* terms that reflect the dialectical, dialogical, social, interactive, and moral dimensions of social science (Reason & Rowan, 1981). Qualitative research is increasingly seen not simply as a set of findings that reflect nonnumerical or quantitative data but, rather, as a set of social processes characterized by fragile and temporary bonds between persons who are attempting to share their lives and create from that sharing a larger and wider understanding of the world. (In that sense, the "lover model" of research first proposed by Shula Reinharz, 1979, is a most appropriate one, since qualitative research takes on many of the characteristics of lovers' creation of a mutual world.) If research is a set of social—and, therefore, political—processes, then its separate acts and decisions are indeed subject to judgment according to ethical canons.

The fifth principle is that for individual researchers, broader social principles dictate ethical stances. In its more generic sense, this can be translated to mean that a researcher's social and political lives are entwined with his or her research life. For Smith, this means that his research is governed by four broad social principles, namely secular humanism, democratic liberalism, emancipation, and empowerment. But for different individuals, the meaning is that one's social and political ethics are merged with one's research ethics, that is, that social and personal and political ethics are in some sense reflections of the same moral position. The moral stance does, and should, dictate decisions that are consonant with one another across the spheres of one's life—the personal, professional, and public, as Soltis would label them.

The final ethical principle offered by Smith is that of committed relativism, a concept borrowed from Hare (1952). The principle in effect states that ethical principles are chosen, and, once chosen, the best one can do is to live within the precepts of the principle. If one is unable to do that, then another principle must be chosen, and one must try to live within the confines of that principle. Whatever the choice of principles, once it is chosen, it must either be lived or rejected in favor of another.

It is not insignificant, then, that what the new generation of qualitative researchers calls for is, in part, the explication of principles under which research processes are conducted and toward which the findings are socially formulated and conceived. The point, made over and over (e.g., Guba & Lincoln, 1981; Lincoln & Guba, 1985) is not simply that values undergird our research regarding choice of problem, choice of context, choice of interpretation, and choice of patterns of behaviors toward research participants. The point is also whether or not those values *escape debate* when science falls back on the value-free claim. Under the claim of value freedom, public policy analysts are left with the hollow argumentation over implementation strategies, themselves seemingly void of groundedness and therefore chosen for reasons of cost, expediency, convenience, comfort of delivery personnel, or the cult of efficiency. Increasingly, however, social science has returned to richness and to recognition that richness involves both exploring contextual values and grounding public policy initiatives in implementation strategies chosen for their complementarity to target population values.

Thus Smith's call for making a decision about principles and then trying to live by those principles is clearly consonant with the reexploration of qualitative methods and inquiry. Additionally, committed relativism is a principle with which Soltis would have no quarrel, recognizing that there are more greys than either black or white on the ethical palette.

As a way of summarizing the first two sections, let me try to capture the several central points I have been trying to make. First, the crossing of concerns proffered by Soltis gives us a way of thinking about potential ethical problems but does little to help students, or researchers new to qualitative inquiry, formulate their own ethical postures or stances needed for guidance in the grey areas. The Smith paper goes a bit further, in that it tries, using real events, persons, and situations, to explain just how difficult it is to predict events that bring about moral and ethical quandaries. And a careful reading of the latter paper will prompt many readers to review incidents in their own professional lives, some of them resolved well, if not with clearly formulated and explicated principles, and some of which have left the same discomfort that Smith feels. In response to that discomfort, Smith has attempted to describe a half-dozen principles for guidance in the dilemmas he encounters. The question arises: Would all of us feel the same confidence in passing those principles along to each and every one of our students as we feel in allowing Louis Smith to operate on them? I believe the answer—for me, at least—would have to be no. My long experience with Louis Smith has left me with every confidence that the research carried out by him is as honest, as whole, and as careful as any human being is capable of making it. But I cannot say the same for my students, whom I do not know as well and who are new to naturalistic inquiry, qualitative methods, and research processes in general. If long years of experience with another professional are not possible, and if we are responsible for shaping those professional years in such a way that they will reflect well on the students, the teachers, and the profession in general, we have the very practical problem of, what can we give them?

A RELATIVIST'S ANSWER
TO A RELATIVIST PHENOMENOLOGY

Elsewhere I have argued (Lincoln & Guba, 1989) that different philosophical systems, particularly those under which we typically conduct disciplined inquiry (that is, the positivist and the phenomenological), give rise to starkly different ethical concerns, a situation previously largely unmarked, but one that should have been self-evident. It is argued by Christian theologians that the Judaic law, upon the coming of Christ, was superseded by the New Testament; it was, in a sense, "updated." The analogy here is similar: A new paradigm for inquiry demands a rethinking of the rules lodged in the old paradigm.

In the logical positivist system, the subject-object dualism demanded as firm a separation between researcher and researched as was possible to achieve in the face of human reactivity. That distancing (thought, *inter alia*, to help in avoiding contamination of research results) allowed and, indeed, required that professional standards and federal regulations be constituted that protected the research "object"—a human being—from being permanently harmed or from having his or her constitutional rights violated. Between these two considerations—the obligation to avoid harm and the right to retain constitutionally guaranteed rights—research subjects were treated as something between priceless Ming vases sent for cleaning, and children. Responsibility for their protection rested with researchers, whose "moral boiling points" (Webb, Campbell, Schwartz, and Sechrest, 1966, p. vi) varied from cool-to-the-touch to scalding. Reality belonged to the researcher to create; objectivity was an ideal situation; distance from the object of the research (and, therefore, contamination of research results) was to be sought with whatever means; and research results were to be as free from bias, prejudice, and researcher values as the "cool, stripped-down language" (Firestone, 1987, p. 17) of science would permit. Thus it is no particular surprise that both professional codes of conduct and federal law assume the posture that researchers are in the best position to determine, within certain guidelines, what constitutes ethicality in social science research. Logical positivism prescribes a set of attitudes toward research subjects[3] that fosters believing—on both sides—that researcher knows best.

Phenomenological systems, however, begin with a different set of premises and, consequently, demand ethical restraints that are not currently prescribed by law. The system undergirding most of what researchers are talking about here is premised on rather radically different presumptions and assumptions regarding reality, the nature of the researcher-researched interaction and relationship, the possibility of generalization, the possibility for linearly causal statements, and the possibility of a value-free science (Lincoln & Guba, 1985). Beginning with the premise that reality is a socially constructed entity, the phenomenologist looks in natural contexts for the ways in which individuals and groups make sense of their worlds. The collection of those intact realities (or constructions), and the interpretation of how those realities got constructed (the understanding of meaning making), is the main point of the phenomenologically oriented inquirer. The shift in focus from the inquirer's reality as the only one of importance, to the realities of many individuals as equally important, represents a major philosophical shift. That shift is supported by a switch from quantitative methods, which act to reduce constructions to readily manipulated numeric representations, to qualitative methods, which have as their methodological base an expansionist epistemology grounded in holism. The shift not only represents an attempt to find out about the world in a radically different way than has been conventional. It also thrusts upon the respondent two new roles: that of agency, self-determination, and participation in the analysis and reconstruction of the social world; and that of collaborator in both the processes and products of inquiries. The transformation of the researched from "object needing protection" to "person empowered to determine the direction and focus of participation" requires a transformation in axiology.

That is where we are now: struggling with a set of professional standards and values that belong to a predecessor paradigm, a separate ontological, epistemological, methodological, and axiological system that is rapidly being replaced by naturalistic inquiry.

As nearly as one can tell, the conversation about ethics is a logical step in the explication of the paradigm supplanting scientific method. If we see research participants in a vastly different way, ought we not generate new rules that cover the new relationships between researcher and researched, among professionals engaged in research, and among researchers and their audiences and the public? I believe the answer is yes.

Pieces like the Soltis and Smith papers, as well as earlier works on ethics (Lincoln & Guba, 1989; see especially more current works in the bibliography to that article), might best be thought of as dialogue in a long, leisurely, and penetrating conversation among sets of friends and colleagues. But in the meantime, we must guide those we teach and mentor in the research process, and we need to have some preliminary agreements among ourselves about what constitutes ethical behavior in a revisionist and revolutionary research world. Toward that end, I would like to offer a set of principles—with some sense of apprehension and a strong caution to regard my offering for what it is: a raw first attempt at a more appropriate and fitting ethical principle for qualitative researchers. I would suggest that both the Soltis diagram and the small, succinct Smith cases might be fruitfully explored in the context of two Kantian ethical principles: the *categorical imperative* and the *practical imperative*.

The categorical imperative was expressed in many ways by Kant himself, but its basic form is this: "Act as if the maxim of thy act were to become by thy will a universal law of nature" (Reese, 1980, p. 279). For Kant, this was the "imperative without condition" (p. 279). A rough and modern translation would read something like this: Behave as if the principle underlying your action were to become—by your will alone—a universal law of nature. That is, act in such a way that you would not be distressed to discover that the principle undergirding your own action were now a law that could be enacted by others upon you.

The categorical imperative is often deemed the "golden rule" of philosophical systems, since its sense is very like the dictum to do unto others as one would have them do unto oneself. The ethical criterion here, again in simplistic form, is judged by whether one would wish the principle guiding his or her own actions to become law that would guide the actions of others toward him or her. Is what you are doing now something you would wish done to yourself? Your spouse? Your minor children? Your aging parents? Your best friend? If it is not, then it is probably something you ought not to be doing; it is a principle that you cannot, ethically, support. A brief example will demonstrate what I mean. Reese comments, in his *Dictionary of Philosophy and Religion* (1980), that the categorical imperative is exclusionary of all actions devoid of integrity, forcing one into duplicity, or inner inconsistency. The paradigm case of unethical behavior from this standpoint is the lie. The lie is an instance of duplicity; it throws one into an essential inconsistency. The nature of a lie requires one to except oneself from the principle one's act requires of others. The only way to universalize behavior in this situation is to eliminate the lie. (p. 279)

I have elsewhere argued (Lincoln & Guba, 1989) that deceptive research practices (that is, deception of research respondents) would be expressly forbidden in naturalistic inquiry and phenomenological philosophical systems (because of deception's inherent contradictions with the axioms of naturalistic, or phenomenological, inquiry). Invoking the categorical imperative as a guiding ethical principle for qualitative research would prohibit any and all deception of subjects/respondents, as deception requires the universalization of deception—a practice no lawful society could long withstand. Thus the categorical imperative is fully consonant with the philosophy of phenomenological inquiry.

The categorical imperative carries with it another strength, in that the private, or personal (as Soltis terms it), becomes the standard for the professional and the public alike. Acting on the categorical imperative demands an end to divided consciousness on the part of researchers ("I wouldn't do this to my friends, but this is my *research project!*") and forces each research act to be judged on the strength of whether that act, or the maxim undergirding it, should be a universal law. For healthy persons, that is a powerful constraint.

The *practical imperative* is a corollary to the categorical imperative. Briefly stated, it is, "*Treat every man as an end in himself, and never as a means only.* In other words, never use another as an instrument" (Reese, 1980, p. 279; emphasis in original). Were we to legislate the practical imperative today, clearly half or more of the social science projects currently underway would fail the standard and lose their funding. Since ethical principles are inevitably human principles, all systems are "flawed" in some sense; they are social constructions that allow given societies to retain some sense of public and private civility while ensuring that rights rest with individuals the society deems responsible enough to handle them.

Of course, having a universal principle is no guarantee that others will adopt it, apply it as we might ourselves, or even respect our right to hold it. There is no principle on earth that can protect the innocent from the unprincipled or that can, for that matter, protect the principled from being taken advantage of by those less scrupulous. What I am suggesting is that we must give guidance, and Kant's categorical imperative (or the New Testament's "do unto others as you would have them do unto you") is about the best of the ethical guidance we can give.

There do exist, however, systems of inquiry (for example, naturalistic, phenomenological, or constructivist models) wherein the researcher's ends are only one set of needs that are fed into the inquiry and wherein the *inquiry's ends* are jointly, democratically, and cooperatively determined by both inquirers and respondents who act as co-inquirers. When this form of inquiry takes place, the situation created is less one of satisfying the inquirer's needs for publication and more a trade in which both researcher and participant get something powerful and important from the process. The inquirer gets his or her data and publication. But the co-participants in the process have access to information and power that they did not have before and are free to use that knowledge, improve practice, or improve their own lives in any way they deem fit. That is a far cry from the systems that proceeded on what Reinharz (1979) called the "rape model" of research (where the inquirers took what they wanted, leaving respondents defenseless, vulnerable, and perhaps wounded).

What I mean to suggest is that it is not *necessary* to *use* others. We can engage them, and invite them to engage us, in determining *what needs to be researched*, *why*, and *how we should go about that*. It is quite possible to move away from a model of inquiry that demands that we use our respondents and to adopt one that permits egalitarian and authentic exchanges. Our respondents are not naive. They know that we need to publish, as academics and social scientists. We can fulfill the corollary to the categorical imperative, however, by (finally) giving them back something they can use: information, power, the tools to exercise that power, and the rights to say in what way the information and power surrounding them will be used.

Smith has suggested several principles that ought to guide qualitative researches. I am suggesting two more. Why? Because those principles, while accommodating themselves comfortably to a relativist ontology and to a constructivist epistemology without providing absolutist and realist rules, nevertheless demand standards of behavior fitted to the hardest of all sciences, the human sciences (Diamond, 1987). The two Kantian principles are also appropriate in that they force examination of personal ethical principles with virtually every act "committed" in the name of science. Searching self-examination is an excellent path to united consciousness as well as to the value clarification and explication demanded by a new generation of qualitatively oriented researchers. And, finally, they are appropriate because as teachers we are often asked what ought to be the ultimate rules that guide our actions as researchers, rules to which we can appeal when examining and justifying our research processes and products. I can think of no sterner standards.

NOTES

1. *Editors' note*: The Soltis paper (Chapter 7), as it was reviewed by Lincoln, was prefaced by an abstract. We decided not to include any abstracts in this collection.

2. *Editors' note*: The sentence from Soltis's abstract to which this comment refers reads as follows: "Issues raised in the inchoate matrix created by considering each of these dimensions include privacy, confidentiality, contractual obligations, institutional mores, social and cultural power, and relativism."

3. When talking about logical positivism, I use *subjects*, and when talking about phenomenological, or naturalistic, systems of inquiry, I use *respondents*. The late Robert L. Wolf, of Indiana University, often pointed out to his students the Latin roots of these two terms: *subject* is from the Latin *sub jugere*, to place under the yoke, or to enslave, while *respondent* is from the Latin *respondere*, to answer back (as an equal).

REFERENCES

Diamond, J. (1987, August). Soft sciences are often harder than hard sciences. *Discover, 4,* 34–35, 38–39.

Fetterman, D. M. (Ed.). (1988). *Qualitative approaches to evaluation in education: The silent scientific revolution.* New York: Praeger.

Firestone, W. A. (1987). Meaning in method: The rhetoric of quantitative and qualitative research. *Educational Researcher, 16,* 16–21.

Guba, E. G., & Lincoln, Y. S. (1981). *Effective evaluation.* San Francisco: Jossey-Bass.

Guba, E. G., & Lincoln, Y. S. (1988). The countenances of fourth-generation evaluation: Description, judgment and negotiation. In D. Cordray & M. Lipsey (Eds.), *Evaluation studies review annual* (Vol. 11, pp. 70–88). Newbury Park, CA: Sage.

Hare, R. M. (1952). *The language of morals.* Oxford, UK: Clarendon Press.

Heron, J. (1981). Philosophical basis for a new paradigm. In P. Reason & J. Rowan (Eds.), *Human inquiry: A source-book of new paradigm research* (pp. 19–36). New York: Wiley.

Jacob, E. (1988). Clarifying qualitative research: A focus on traditions. *Educational Researcher, 17,* 16–24.

Lincoln, Y. S., & Guba, E. G. (1985). *Naturalistic inquiry.* Newbury Park, CA: Sage.

Lincoln, Y. S., & Guba, E. G. (1989). Ethics: The failure of positivist science. *Review of Higher Education, 12*(3), 221–240.

Reason, P., & Rowan, J. (Eds.). (1981). *Human inquiry: A source-book of new paradigm research.* New York: Wiley.

Reese, W. L. (1980). *Dictionary of philosophy and religion.* Atlantic Highlands, NJ: Humanities Press.

Reinharz, S. (1979). *On becoming a social scientist.* San Francisco: Jossey-Bass.

Smith, J. K., & Heshusius, L. (1984, March). *Closing down the conversation.* Paper presented at the annual meeting of the American Educational Research Association, San Francisco.

Smith, M. L. (1987). Publishing qualitative research. *American Educational Research Journal, 24,* 173–183.

Webb, E. J., Campbell, D. T., Schwartz, R. D., & Sechrest, L. (1966). *Unobtrusive measures: Nonreactive research in the social sciences.* Chicago: Rand McNally.

Wolcott, H. (1981). Unpublished handout. UCEA Career Development Seminar, University of Alberta, Alberta, Canada.

Response to the Commentary by Lincoln

JONAS F. SOLTIS

Lincoln's "periodic table" extrapolation of my attempt to cast a coarse heuristic net into the ocean of qualitative research ethics misconceives and misdirects the project I had hoped to initiate with my paper. Perhaps that is because I am a philosopher and she is a researcher.

I had hoped to help qualitative educational researchers see that there is a multifaceted, overlapping complex of potential ethical issues in every dimension of their work that they need to become sensitive to if they are to be true to their commitment to a *human* science. I sought to locate some typical issues by fashioning a crude net that looked as if it might at least capture some of the bigger ethical fish in the sea of qualitative educational research to serve as examples. I did not try to produce a framework for prediction and the testing of hypotheses. I am not a researcher who is driven to find out all I can about the world. I am a philosopher, a gadfly who seeks, for himself and for others, ways of thinking about the world that will lead all of us to live the examined life together. I wanted to sensitize, not rationalize. I wanted to suggest, not discover.

Spending years trying to fill in a periodic table of ethical issues in qualitative research would not necessarily advance or insure the ethical behavior of researchers. It might inform us, but it also would divert our attention from the "ought" to the "is." Creating a sensitivity to the ought and encouraging researchers' recognition of obligations in many different moral situations are what I tried to do.

Professor Lincoln ended her response humbly though triumphantly with a proclamation of the ought. That is not what I tried to do, either. Her ending is as troublesome to me as her beginning; not because we ought not to seek the ought, but because she seems to assume that the project is to *find* the ought. Once that is done, you only need to adopt it as *the* principle (or two) for the profession and then the job is complete.

What if, as I have tried to show, there are numerous ethical principles we already accept as persons, as professionals, and as members of our shared public world, principles such as the ones sprinkled through-out my paper—honesty, equity, truth, justice, confidentiality, fairness, respect for others, and so on. They are not always easy to apply. They often conflict, and sometimes we overlook them as researchers. What we need to find and be sensitive to, then, are not universal principles but research situations where numerous moral obligations need serious tending to. My project was to create ethical awareness and sensitivity to moral situations in research settings and to suggest that we need to include this sort of consciousness raising in our research training pro-grams.

I am not against Lincoln's (read Kant's) principles. I am only urging that we do not misconceive the project of the ethics of qualitative research. It is neither to fill in a table of all possible ethical situations nor to find the most basic principles that qualitative researchers should use to guide their work. Rather it is, as Lincoln herself seems implicitly to recognize in her response to Smith's paper, to see in the richness of doing research a multiplicity of unanticipated ethical situations that call for sensitivity and integrity in dealing with them—in ways, moreover, that sometimes result in less than our full satisfaction with their reso-lution. Finding ethical principles does not solve real ethical problems. In fact, Lincoln's ethical principles themselves are questionable.

As a professional philosopher, I subscribe to my tribe's view that there are no ethical principles that cannot be challenged by reason or by some difficult dilemma. This is not to say that a telling challenge will make a principle untenable. However, given certain circumstances, it may make it doubtfully universal. Let me illustrate by taking the two principles Lincoln offers as a basis for the ethics of qualitative research.

Consider the categorical imperative's being used at this conference on qualitative research. Let us suppose that Lincoln gave me a copy of her response in advance and I saw in it that she had caught me in some serious logical lapses and omissions of crucial examples. Ethically, I suppose, I am bound to read my original, flawed paper at the conference to provide the honest context for the response she worked so hard and skillfully on. Otherwise, had I repaired my paper in advance, her re-sponse would have looked foolish.

Now, do I will that all paper writers refrain from repairing their papers in fairness to respondents? Why not will the opposite? Having compassion for all the less-than-perfect paper writers in academia, and with an eye toward improving the quality of work in the field, I could will that it become a universal law that the critique of respondents prior to a public conference be used by paper writers to improve their papers.

In this way, the public role of respondents at conferences would be changed to a pedagogical one of telling how well the paper writer learned from their critique so that we might all learn how to teach others to repair faulty papers. Not a bad universal, I would say! We should note, though, that we could will either way for good reasons. Having a good fundamental principle is not even half the battle, it seems. One needs to use it thoughtfully, compassionately, intelligently, and creatively, and even then one still may not make the wisest choice.

The real problem with the principles Lincoln chose as basic for qualitative research is the second one: Do not treat people as means to our ends but as ends in themselves. This most important ethical principle is related to others many of us hold dear—respect for persons and the grounding of morality in an individual's freedom, rationality, and autonomy. But think with me a minute. There is something about qualitative research that singularly depends upon the *using* of others as a means to the researcher's ends. No matter how much researchers rightly respect their respondents' personhood and rationality and do not impede their freedom or autonomy, researchers still use others as a means to their own ends—to produce knowledge or improve practice, for example. How could it be otherwise? This seems to be part of the *raison d'être* of doing research about the human condition. Thus, how could qualitative researchers logically and without qualification accept the universal principle to *never* use others as a means to our ends?

This is not to suggest that Lincoln's principle is wrong or untenable. It is a very sound ethical principle that we all should worry over and try to follow as fully as possible, given the circumstances. What my discussion of it does, however, is to force us to see a potentially basic ethical problem permeating all of qualitative research. Once again, since I take my project to be the consciousness raising of sensitivity to potential ethical issues among researchers, I take this disclosure to be a step in the right direction. I thank Lincoln for conceiving the project of ethics in qualitative research in a way that seeks more closure. It has helped me make my conception of the project clearer and its open-ended inconclusiveness more apparent.

I cannot end, however, without at least offering a stab at the question I have just raised regarding the ethics of means and ends. We at this conference believe that qualitative research can do good. It can change our conceptions of what we take to be meaningful research and what we need to know and understand to be better educators. It can restore the human and moral dimension to legitimate knowledge claims about human beings in educationally relevant settings. It can provide knowledge and perspective that can be used by educators to improve the education of many. These benefits, I would argue, justify the entry of ethically sensitive researchers into the lives of others, using them as a means to improve the education of many, but only doing so with a keen awareness of their participants' personhood and autonomy and of the many ethical dimensions that need to be tended to in working for the good.

Part V

USES OF QUALITATIVE INQUIRY

On the face of it, the topic of the uses of qualitative inquiry might well be expected to turn to mundane cases, such as informing educational policy makers or clarifying and illuminating the impossible complexity of the phenomena of social research. Indeed, these are worthy instances of using the products of qualitative inquiry. Far from mundane, however, our "cases" in this section relate to conspiracy—in a manner of speaking—at the hand of Thomas Barone, and applesauce making, at Christopher Clark's. They are ample testimony to the diverse forms that the products of qualitative inquiry—our books, dissertations, and journal articles—may assume.

We begin with surprise: conspiracy and applesauce, indeed! With judgment rightfully suspended until we get past title, introduction, and other preliminaries, we conclude with respect earned and extended to two unexpected products and uses of qualitative inquiry. Discussants Matthew Miles and Michael Huberman bring critical scrutiny to bear on the papers from a philosophical stance to which they give no name but which is located somewhere between the extremes of causal realism and causal idealism. They, like Guba and Lincoln before them, are identified with a particular tradition in qualitative research; accordingly, they have an established frame of reference that not only directs their own robust research efforts but also gives them a perspective for assessing the work of their colleagues.

Barone's paper, a bonanza of linguistic elegance, is appropriately steeped in literary allusions, for it is in narrative text, most particularly in fiction, that he finds the occasion for conspiracies of beneficence. We learn that Barone seeks "positive options for the future"; he finds them most to his taste in the "verbal imagery" of literature. These images are the stuff of "utopian" visions fashioned by active readers into conspiracy that they can direct toward the educational status quo. His own utopic enactments are illustrated by his use of two texts, one, a play by Julian Mitchell, the other, a short story by

John Updike. Barone is a practitioner of what he proposes in his
paper. Whether, in fact, he is more than an armchair plotter of conspiracy, a spinner of fine utopic webs that do not advance beyond the
words with which they are spun, we do not learn. That is another
story that he can tell at another time. But we do learn that his conspiratorial plots are to be directed "against inadequate present conditions in favor of an emancipatory social arrangement in the future."

At the heart of Clark's paper is a long account of an elementary
school classroom of twenty-one first- and second-graders with whom
he participated in making a pot of cinnamon-spiced applesauce. Clark
creates a vividly rendered text; we are there in the classroom, as he
means for us to be—and as he meant the forty or so persons to
whom he sent a copy of his tale to be. They were invited to respond
with accounts of their use of his applesauce experiences. Thus, when
he elaborates on the uses of his product of qualitative inquiry, he
combines his own experiences with those of a range of different
types of persons. While Clark nowhere refers to conspiracy, he explicitly—by his many invitations—provides occasion to others for
possible reflection and possible action. He concludes with reference
to "qualitative accounts" having "profound and unpredictable effects
on human thought and action." Educational researchers are disposed
to wanting good to be done.

Miles and Huberman are refreshed and disarmed by Clark's felic-
itous account—warm applesauce could do that to the most hardened
of us, but not beyond the point of at least mild critique. They find,
as they say, that five questions "lingered on after our reading." Their
questions relate to Clark's methods of inquiry, analysis, and finding
of conclusions. Clark worked as a connoisseur and thereby risks
making "hair-raising errors." He worked alone and, as participant-
observer, was himself the "instrument" of data collection, while
Miles and Huberman advocate multiperson research and some use of
codified instruments. Moreover, they want the products of qualitative research to be connectable to those of our "nonqualitative colleagues." For this connection to occur, they specify that Clark, and
the rest of us, must clarify "what kind of knowledge" we have
created, "how we came by it, why it is trustable," and whether it can
be applied beyond the settings in which it was found.

Miles and Huberman do not get past their first page of their
reaction to Barone's paper before they show their hand: It is held
palm up in Barone's direction, the physical indicator of their stated,
"Not so fast, Barone." In his paper, so they elaborate, they found six
"unquestioned assumptions," a more serious matter than the linger-

ing questions they direct to Clark. These six points are the structure of what they conclude is an "elegant" but deeply flawed presentation of the use of qualitative inquiry. Miles and Huberman are committed to "trustable" information. Barone, they feel, in his attraction to fiction, plays too loose with veracity for their comfort. They, in contrast, admire the "methodological toughness" of their "nonqualitative colleagues," while their own stance in qualitative methodology is eclectic, pragmatic, and, though they do not say so explicitly, appropriately tough and therefore trustable. Their own position contrasts with Barone's presumed commitment to the qualitative tradition designated "educational criticism," which, in Barone's construal, they condemn as "epistemological purity and methodological monism." Barone's orthodoxy—"the One True Way"—leads to "a sort of epistemological terrorism."

Unsurprisingly, Barone writes a rejoinder to Miles and Huberman. Clark, whose paper they question but treat more in cautionary than in severely critical terms, does not. Cast as villain against the white-hatted Miles and Huberman, he turns their frequent charge of "straw-manning" back at them, while systematically addressing what he sees as their unsubstantiated charges about his assumptions. The strong exchange between Miles/Huberman and Barone is not of the puerile "you did"/"I didn't" type. It is about fundamental distinctions that midway through his reply Barone characterizes as their preferred "denotative, analytical forms of discourse" over his preferred "metaphorical, evocative, suggestive language."

Unlike East and West, the terrains of Miles/Huberman and Barone do meet, as in the forum provided by the conference that brought all of us together and in this volume that contains its formal proceedings. And the terrains will continue to meet whenever we instruct and train our students, hold forth at conferences, and write our books and articles. Clearly, we are well past the point where our adversaries are the fellows conducting surveys and doing path analysis. No longer need we look over our shoulders to find antagonists; just looking around us in the qualitative camp suffices to identify sufficient spurs to reflection and debate to inspire a whirlwind of intellectual robustness. Let the winds blow!

⑨ Using the Narrative Text as an Occasion for Conspiracy

THOMAS E. BARONE

A Sunday morning should be the occasion for a sabbatical.[1] On most Sunday mornings, the closure of a cycle has been, once again, achieved, and preparations for the next one can be momentarily deferred. A Sunday morning, therefore, should never be needlessly disturbed. It is a time for congenial gatherings of family and friends, not a time for contentious challenges to comfortable beliefs. Or maybe you try, as I often do when I am home next to my stereo, to reserve your Sunday mornings for engaging in a musical kind of concelebration, for listening to the contrapuntal harmonies of a fugue. Alas, how I would have enjoyed leading you into one today!

Now, my assigned topic may seem, at first glance, suited for a Sunday, fit for the back of the book. A text of qualitative inquiry ready for use implies a previous resolution of nettlesome questions, including questions of epistemology and ethics, that might have arisen during its preparation. We might, therefore, be expected merely to imagine appropriate contexts for their application or consumption. We would thus confine our attention to the most obvious sense of *use*, the one in which the verb rubs elbows with the name of an implement. I use a handkerchief. You use a lawn mower. The educational policy maker uses research findings. Subject uses object. This sense of *use* denotes the employment of the research text as a tool. It implies a text designed in accordance with one of two modes of thought (discussed in Bruner, 1987) that guide projects of social inquiry. This mode is the paradigmatic or logico-scientific (Bruner, 1987).

But I wonder about the appropriateness of this metaphor, educational-inquiry-text-as-tool. Fortunately, as a participant in other predicates, *use* acquires a second sense, one only marginally related to the first. How, for example, does one use an occasion? What does it mean to use time? In what sense is an opportunity used? *Occasion, time,* and *opportunity* are abstract nouns, not concrete persons, places, or things. Despite our impulse to reify, to think of *occasion* as if it were a physical object, the verb *to use* is now only nominally transitive. In the sentence "I use this occasion," the subject precedes a kind of objectless verbal unit. I, the subject, employ no thing. I, the subject, engage in an experience.

When used for *educational* purposes, a text of qualitative inquiry is, I propose, better viewed as an occasion than as a tool. It is, more precisely, an occasion for the reader to engage in the activities of textual re-creation and dismantling. These activities require a mode of thinking fundamentally different from the paradigmatic. Bruner (1987) calls it the "narrative mode." The primary form of written narrative discourse—and therefore of qualitative texts about human experience—is literature.

This, in barest outline, is my thesis. It suggests a reordering of the totem pole of qualitative inquiry genres, a challenging of important premises of the educational research establishment. In my defense of it I must occasionally return across the borders to earlier topics in this conference and disturb the finality of Friday's and Saturday's agreements to disagree. It may appear rude to offer, on a Sunday morning, Bartók instead of Bach. So I devote the remainder of this paper to an earnest explanation of why it had to be done.

USING THE LITERARY TEXT

How does a reader use a literary text? Two dimensions of the reading act demand our attention. In the first the reader constructs the reality of the text, a reality that resides neither in the literary work as object-in-the-world nor in the subjective "mind" of the reader, but within a continuous field of experience between the two. The text, that is, is given a place among the contents of consciousness. What occurs there is not, strictly speaking, a reader's response to the text. Although *reader response* names a school of theorists who have shifted the focus onto the literary experience and away from the "text itself," the term connotes to me a reader passively reacting to cues that emanate from the text. Instead, it is the reader who moves *toward* the text, exploring, while traversing, the landscape of meaning that Ricoeur (1976) calls the "sense" of the text.

When the text is perceived as literary, this sense is a formal reconstruction. Dewey (1934/1958) explains:

For to perceive a beholder [of a work of art] must *create* his own experience. And his creation must include relations comparable to those which the original producer underwent. They are not the same in any literal sense. But with the perceiver, as with the artist, there must be an ordering of the elements of the whole that is in form, although not in details, the same as the process of organization the creator of the work consciously experienced. Without an act of recreation the object is not perceived as a work of art. (p. 54)

In this reordering, elements of experience are recast into a form that is analogous to but does not replicate an actual experience. A work of art, says Langer (1957), is a semblance, a composed apparition. In experiencing this semblance the reader lives vicariously in a virtual world, only temporarily bracketed off from the mundane, the nearby. What he experiences there is an idea of a piece of subjective life. In this reconstructive process, I mean, the self of the reader discovers an "otherness" (Poulet, 1986). Awareness arises of an alternate consciousness, a "mind" behind the effect, a fellow being responsible for the virtual event now formally re-created. The reader hears the voice of another subject offering the fruits of her inquiry into the qualities of lived experience.

But there are *two* dimensions to this offering, dialectically intertwined within an aesthetic whole. These are the coequal, mutually supportive constituents of the literary text: aesthetic form, which embodies a personal vision, and aesthetic content, or evidence of the seriousness of that vision. Danger arises when either establishes dominance over the other, disallowing the aesthetic tension that characterizes the dialectic in good art. In some texts the bully is form.

Pure form is pure fancy. It is imagination roaming untethered in a nether realm, a world where the self can reside in solipsistic harmony, undisturbed by thoughts of the other. The thoroughly formal text is self-contained, rigid, closed. It can merely be overheard by the worldly reader, for its elements speak only to one another within the beautiful universe they comprise. Some, like the formalist critics, see *all* literature thusly, fallaciously equating the entire event of using fiction with the construction of illusion. And illusion, as the formalist Northrop Frye (1967) puts it, is "fixed and definable, and reality is best understood as its negation" (p. 169). If the formalists were correct, then the exclusion of all fictional literature from the club of qualitative inquiry would be justified. Who, after all, seeks the advice of the schizophrenic, the lonely madman whose texts are so long on visions but so short on evidence? Of course, not only schizophrenics imagine impossible worlds. Some works of fiction (I refuse to call them literature) also offer escape into fantasy. For evidence, visit the Gothic novel section of your local bookstore. Or watch "Dallas" on a Friday evening, followed immediately by "Falcon Crest." Bereft of credible evidence, such fiction is ill equipped to inform the reader about "reality." It remains harmlessly self-contained, lounging forever within that fantastic realm we sometimes call the "aesthetic remove." Using this kind of fictional text, the reader engages in a process of "psychical distancing" (Bullough, 1957). This is the occasion for romance, for contemplation free of impulses to action or thoughts of the practical.

Romantic visions are, interestingly, also the stuff of classical utopias. Hansot (1974) has noted the obsession with transcendent, atemporal form evident in most pre-Kantian utopian texts. The *Utopia* of Thomas More, the *Christianopolis* of Johann Valentin Andraea, and the *Republic* of Plato are self-contained entities, each static and nondevelopmental in its perfection. The notion of social change, of a more fully realized political arrangement, is rendered absurd in these ethereal worlds. Their imagery represents the desirable-but-*impossible*: It aims to show us ideology alienated from history.

To frustrate the totalitarian tendencies of sublime illusion, and otherworldly romance, and unalloyed subjectivity, and transcendent ideology, the reader must turn to truly literary texts. Since I want to highlight their qualifications as texts of social inquiry, I introduce the antithesis to aesthetic form. This is the historically undervalued dimension in art, aesthetic substance.

Not even poets, certainly not good ones, spin their imaginary webs from within a realm of pure fantasy. But novels and plays are often more obviously drenched in social realism. At least since Fielding, novelists have attended to specific characters in particular sociohistorical milieus, acutely observing the minutiae of human activity. "The basic talent of the novelist," Cook (1960) notes, "is to observe social behavior—the way a person furnishes his house or makes love or reacts to death or folds an envelope or constructs his sentences or plans his career" (p. 84). The writer of fiction fishes for this empirical evidence to be shaped into aesthetic content in the ongoing stream of everyday life. Although the autobiographical novel, which aims to transmute the essence of a lifestream into words, may best illustrate this point, all fiction is bathed in, or at least splashed by, personal experience. Roiphe (1988), for example, reminds us that Bernard Malamud's father owned a store, Chekhov was a doctor, Hemingway ran bulls, and Erica Jong was married to a psychoanalyst. Sometimes, however, the writer purposely diverts that lifestream into unfamiliar territory. She moves "into the field," if you will, intending to position herself effectively for a bestowal of meaning on a strange and distant landscape. This was Dickens's strategy as, in preparation for writing *The Life and Adventures of Nicholas Nickelby* (1839/1950), he gained admittance to several notorious Yorkshire boarding schools by assuming the false identity of someone seeking a school for the son of a widowed friend (Wolfe, 1973). Occasionally, an author's fascination with the particulars in the research setting causes the line between reportage and literary fiction to become blurred. For example, which of the following literary works, each crafted upon intense investigative research, shall we label "novelistic"? Hersey's *Hiroshima* (1946)? Capote's *In Cold Blood* (1965)? Twain's *Innocents Abroad* (1869/1899)? Michener's *Texas* (1985)? Haley's *Roots* (1976)? Orwell's *Down and Out in Paris and London* (1933/1961)?

The history of literature is replete with examples of elaborate, if nonsystematic, investigative efforts aimed at increasing the array of perceptions available to the author for arrangement into a plausible story. Upon that arrangement, however, the individual knowledge claims are transformed into what Ingarden (1968) has called "intentional sentence correlatives" (p. 32). These are component parts of the text, but as contributors to a fashioned totality their specific content is immediately qualified. Similarly, Pepper (1945) labels these pieces of aesthetically fashioned evidence "danda," to distinguish them from nonfictional "data." Both Ingarden and Pepper understand that to construe narrative meaning the reader must focus away from individual statements as claims of factuality and toward the insinuations in their interactions as correlatives. The particulars are arranged to foreshadow that which is to come: the central insights acquired within the whole experience of using the text.

Of course, in a good marriage of aesthetic form and substance, the "whole" of the story is, in turn, conditioned by the particulars that comprise it. For the reader of literature who demands edification and not merely good feelings, aesthetic content will provide the ballast that grounds the lofty formal text. Aesthetic content opens up the text to the multiplicities of experience, conditions it, plants it specifically in virtual space and time, and provides (in Ricoeur's term) a reference for the sense of the text.

This view of the function of aesthetic content offers an answer to Miller's (1976) rhetorical question, Why is there criticism instead of silent admiration of the text? The reader uses aesthetic content to avoid entrapment in her own re-creation. In the literary text ambiguity displaces both propaganda and literality, for multiple interpretations, even conflicting ones, become possible. The once seamless illusion is interrupted and disturbed, and associations alien to the sealed-off world of the text can be imagined. It is at that moment, with the text off its pedestal and in hand, that the reader finds his own voice as observer/ critic. The dimension of textual usage antithetical to reconstruction is entered. The text can now be *dismantled*.

I might have said "deconstructed," but I shrink from the intimations of finality in that term now identified with the likes of deMan and Derrida. It is difficult to return to a text that has been mocked, derided, trashed. Some texts may indeed invite such a fate, but others offer a hope undeserving of such cynicism, and so return to them we must. Still, even these worthy texts must be opened to the continuous processes of reconstruction and dismantling (and reconstruction and dismantling . . .) that constitute their very existence. These two dimensions in the use of literary texts are at once anatagonistic and mutually nurturing. Only in the tension emanating from the pull toward a closed meaning and the countervailing enticements of indeterminate significance is the relationship not merely sustained but enhanced, as described here by Iser (1980):

> The text provokes certain expectations which in turn we project onto the text in such a way that we reduce the polysemantic possibilities to a single interpretation in keeping with the expectations aroused, thus extracting an individual, configurative meaning. The polysemantic nature of the text and the illusion-making of the reader are opposed factors. If the illusion were complete, the polysemantic nature would vanish; if the polysemantic nature were all-powerful, the illusion would be totally destroyed. Both extremes are conceivable, but in the individual literary text we always find some form of balance between the two conflicting tendencies. The formation of illusion, therefore, can never be total, but it is this very incompleteness that in fact gives it its productive value. (pp. 59–60)

Iser sees a balancing operation as the reader oscillates between these poles. Ironically, the dynamism and buoyancy of the literary experience can be maintained only if this balance is never quite achieved. Instead, the balance is elusive, remaining always tantalizingly ahead but out of reach. The text engages the reader by continuously offering surprising, even shocking, revelations that confound literary clichés and formulae but that also avoid arbitrariness and implausibility.

This, then, is the readable text, inviting literature, the useful piece of social inquiry in narrative form. Its allure derives not merely from the elemental (or eidetic) nature of its dynamic form, which (as Langer,

1957, has noted) mimics the rhythms of human physiology, the ebb and flow of life itself. Nor does its attractiveness stem solely from a desire to experience vicariously a cycle completed. Of course each of us is, as Kermode (1967) has suggested, "in the middest" (p. 7), in the middle of history, in the middle of life—in the process, that is, of authoring our own autobiographical text. And while we seek a meaningful orientation in the world, from our finite perspective the full meaning of events eludes us. We do hanker for release from the tension between the actual and the potential that pervades our lives. But it is not simply to feel an ersatz resolution to this tension that we commit the act of reading literature. The most useful literary texts offer more: They suggest, through their verbal imagery, plausible options for the future; that is, the configuration of images in a good story comprises a vision of what might be called a *concrete utopia* (Hansot, 1974).

Concrete utopic imagery differs in kind from the idealized imagery that haunts transcendent, classical utopias. The ethereal beauty of the latter, we recall, is privately contemplated from a psychic location safely distanced from the potentially corrupting presence of empirical phenomena. The aesthetic remains aloof from the everyday world. Concrete utopias, on the other hand, are located in that imaginary space where a seriously deficient here-and-now meets a desirable, but possible, future. Concrete utopias thrive on the tension between the goodness of their formal aspirations and the viscous contingencies of the formless mundane world. This kind of imagery serves, that is, as a social critique. Like the classical utopia, the concrete utopia defies the moral imperialism of the present by offering a sharp contrast for its inadequacies. But unlike the former, which "often locates the ideal future at too great a distance to be functional" (Goodwin & Taylor, 1982, p. 26), a concrete utopia proposes an accessible replacement. These utopian images are therefore provisional, for the critique itself is necessarily open to criticism and reconstruction.

Of course, a good story is sometimes cautionary. The reader may be distressed by the plight of the characters in the virtual world he has re-created. Then the imagery is anti-utopian, functioning much like negative space in a painting. In dismantling the textual illusion, the reader attempts to imagine its preferable reverse. That is how I use a pair of texts, a historical drama entitled *Another Country* (Mitchell, 1982) and a short story by John Updike (1959).

The play by Julian Mitchell is about dropping out of school and society. The protagonist, Guy Bennett, is based upon the life of Guy Burgess, an infamous British spy who defected to the Soviet Union in 1955. The script recounts certain key incidents in Bennett's youth in an uppercrust public school. Despite his awareness of his homosexual tendencies, Bennett is initially devoted to the acquisition of status within the rigidly hierarchical school system. He craves membership in the ruling student elite, called the "demigods." Bennett's ultimate aspirations are even grander, for "life is ladders. That's all. Prepper to here. First form to sixth. Second assistant junior Undersecretary to Ambassador in Paris" (p. 45). But Bennett's aspirations crumble when his liaison with a schoolmate for whom he cares deeply is revealed. Disillusioned and embittered, he ponders the apparent futility of further participation in a hypocritical way of life. Suddenly Bennett resembles what we nowadays awkwardly refer to as an "at-risk" student, a potential dropout. Ultimately he does indeed leave the school and the sociopolitical system that feeds and is fed by it. The last lines of the script suggest Bennett's embrace of a drastic alternative to that system. He finally succumbs to the Marxist ideology of his heterosexual friend, Tom Judd, and sets about living a life of revenge through total indiscretion.

Through re-creating the illusion of this text, I understand the alienation of one student trapped in an institution that demands loyalty to repressive features of the larger culture. I directly apprehend Bennett's desire to honor, instead, loyalty to his own authenticity as a human being. I feel his despair and anger that he would later assuage through a flight to another country and a vengeful act of treason. Now I carry this configuration of meanings I have re-created to my professional life outside of the text. I search out the undergrounds to which adolescents with stifled aspirations might nowadays retreat—places where they engage in risky business, whether seething in silence, or plotting strategies of resistance, or simply melting away. The adolescents in the Cincinnati area schools that I visit seem quite unprepared for conducting international espionage. But evidence of Bennett-like resentment abounds, from the flagrant vandalism of school property to the subtleties within a surly and insolent demeanor. When weariness overtakes defiance, the vanquished may simply regress to form, relinquishing all hopes of authoring their own lifetexts for the privacy of romantic daydreams, or the blank stare of the tube, or the abyss of chemical dependency, or even abandonment of life itself. My exploration of the geographies of these "other countries" helps to heighten my sensitivity to schooling conditions that may serve as breeding grounds for these acts of vengeance or resignation.

Using the second text requires less travel. I am not William Young, the protagonist in Updike's short story "A Sense of Shelter" (1959), but I admit to occasional jolts of self-recognition as I confront this character. Young is an academically capable but socially awkward adolescent who will *never* leave school. Fearful of life in the unfamiliar and uncertain realm outside, he resembles only the early Guy Bennett in his vow to remain sealed in and secure forever,

> high school merging into college, college into graduate school, graduate school into teaching at a college—section man, assistant, associate, *full* professor, professor of a dozen languages and a thousand books, a man brilliant in his forties, wise in his fifties, renowned in his sixties, revered in his seventies, and then retired, sitting in the study lined with acoustical books until the time came for the last transition from silence to silence, and would die, like Tennyson, with a copy of *Cymbeline* beside him on a moon-drenched bed. (pp. 73-74)

The use of Updike's text can sensitize the reader to the presence of the school "shut-in," the student for whom school offers easy passage through safe if narrow corridors that emancipate by providing direction but that simultaneously limit possibilities. Who among us, and our students, are the William Youngs, the human hothouse plants who thrive only in the rarefied atmosphere of the classroom? "A Sense of Shelter" points out qualities of school life that tend to reinforce the isolation of at least a certain type of student from the larger world.

Like *Another Country*, this text thus reorganizes my experiences of familiar commonplaces by challenging a tired, habitual response to them, offering a strange new way of perceiving and interpreting their significance. Now more "wide-awake" (thank you, Maxine Greene, 1977), I attempt to imagine a landscape of learning that offers the reverse of the dismal landscapes re-created in this pair of texts: a concrete utopia where personal growth is affirmed rather than stifled or narrowly channeled. And then, having listened (as Barthes, 1975, would say) to this "something else" (p. 24), I reenter, in each case, the world of the text to find that its configuration of meanings, now set against the backdrop of these newfound references, is itself enhanced. Upon my return, the voice of the other in the text grows more articulate, its insinuations about the shortcomings of the world-at-hand more obvious and persuasive. Suddenly my act of reading is achieving its end: I am using the text as an occasion for conspiracy.

I propose that the will to interpret a narrative text can arise from a desire for conspiracy. I do not mean conspiracy in the obvious, shallow, political sense. Nor do I acknowledge connotations of evil or treachery as inherent in an act of conspiracy. Quite the contrary, conspiracy can be a profoundly ethical and moral undertaking. "Conspiracy: combination or union of persons for a single purpose or end" (*Webster's New Collegiate Dictionary*). From the Latin, "*con* plus *spirare*, to breathe together," or better, from the Old French, "*conspirer*, a learned borrowing" (*World Book Dictionary*). A conspiracy, thus, is a conversation about the relationship between present and future worlds. The reader, a historically situated self, learns from the re-created other in the text to see features of a social reality that may have gone previously unnoticed. And if the reader, although cautious and wary, ultimately resonates with the interior vision of the text and is persuaded of its usefulness, he borrows it for his own. There is a "breathing together," a sharing of ideas and ideals for the purposes of an improved reality. This conspiracy is a plot against inadequate present conditions in favor of an emancipatory social arrangement in the future.

In a useful act of narrative reading, the conspiratorial discourse is pregnant with images of a proximate future. These are utopian visions, but never hapless ones immaculately conceived through mere wishful thinking. The visions are substantial, concrete in their attentiveness to current conditions. The most useful accurately diagnose social maladies and suggest potential cures. They are offsprings of a potent union of the virtuous and the feasible.

I suggest that such images can contribute to an educator's professional platform, the web of personally held beliefs and values that, like a good novel, recognize these established realities of the common order even while calling them into question.[2] This platform is provisional in that it must undergo continuous critical reexamination. Educators, as professionals, engage in an ongoing process of reconstructing what they hold to be the educationally good, true, and beautiful. Still, educational decision making is contingent upon this professional platform, no matter how fragile and tentative its nature. We carry it with us as we enter into political deliberations with others in our professional communities. A professional platform provides the space from which we launch the educational projects that aim to change what is into what ought to be.

USING THE PARADIGMATIC TEXT

Good narrative texts, therefore, offer an occasion to conspire about, and so make visible, new worlds that are both desirable and possible. A paradigmatic text, on the other hand, possesses the characteristics of what Illich (1973) would call an "industrial tool" (p. 33). Flowing out of the familiar creation-diffusion-dissemination pipeline, these texts are commodities designed upon utilization to produce systematically "knowledge" and "decisions." As social devices these texts are deliberately shaped to achieve this end. Their elements of design are selected to fulfill paradigmatic purposes. Polanyi (1962, 1964, 1966) has been especially helpful in illuminating the subjective elements of the scientific research process. Choice points pervade that process—in the selection and conceptualization of the research question, in the preference for particular methods and strategies for securing information, in the opting for a propositional form of language to represent that information, in the selection of a linear format for disclosure (Allender, 1986).

The text-as-tool, it seems, is "something fashioned," which is coincidentally, as Geertz (1973) reminds us, the original meaning of the word *fiction*. In a basic sense, therefore, *all* texts, including paradigmatic ones, are fictional. Of course, the manner of fashioning, or *modes of fiction*, favored by the author will vary greatly in accordance with purpose. A novelist with a narrative purpose will select different modes of fiction from, say, the emic-oriented anthropologist who aims to fashion a "correct" actor-oriented interpretation. As Geertz (1973) notes:

> In the former case, the actors are represented as not having existed and the events as not having happened, while in the latter they are represented as actual, or having been so. This is a difference of no mean importance . . . but the importance does not lie in the fact that [one] story was created while [the other] was only noted. The conditions of their creation, and the point of it (to say nothing of the manner and the quality) differ. But the one is as much a *fictio*—a "making"—as the other. (pp. 15–16)

The modes of fiction closest to the paradigmatic ideal disallow the aesthetic structuring of details that promotes the re-creation of an illusory world. They also bar (as do the antithetical modes of fashioning preferred by romantic novelists) the presence of aesthetic substance and the attendant ambiguity of meaning. Banished are what Iser (1980) calls "gaps, . . . the unwritten part [of the text], . . . elements of indeterminacy [without which] we should not be able to use our imagination" (p. 58). The text-as-tool is not meant to be dismantled and reconstructed. Its modes of fiction call for a seamless, denotative, linear discourse that rearranges the relationship among complex phenomena into propositional form. This promotes the logical deduction of suitable contexts for the application of the tool.

The text-as-tool does not prize metaphorical aptness; it offers technical precision. It is not designed to surprise the reader-as-user. Its modes of fashioning are not selected to challenge the common order.

As an object of craft rather than art, a tool is fashioned for use within that order, tacitly bestowing legitimacy upon it. Illich (1973) notes that industrial tools do not give the user much "opportunity to enrich the [social] environment with the fruits of his or her [personal] vision" (p. 21). As I use a tool, my images of the desirable should conform to the technical possibilities offered by its design. I become implicated in a taken-for-granted notion of the ideal. The text-as-tool is designed to mask any sense of values beyond the apparent value inherent in its utilization. No human agent, the text implies, guided its production; no utopian visions attend its utilization. This text offers one verbal version of reality, meant to be taken literally, taken for the only world that can be represented, the real one.

So the modes of fiction used to fashion the text-as-tool ironically deny its fictional status. They are selected for their effectiveness in misrepresenting a fashioned reality as objective, impersonal, and formless. Take the design element of language. We have all heard the detached, passionless textual voice that strives toward the impossible language "which the universe uses to explain itself to itself" (Rorty, 1982, p. 130). A closer monitoring reveals not the homogeneous hum of a universal language but a bewildering cacophony of idioms. These are the various tongues of the research communities or (borrowing Toulmin's, 1953, term) the "participant languages" (p. 13) of those who work in specialized fields. Each has been developed to further a paradigmatic purpose. One may even stand in contradistinction to another. The grammar and vocabulary of the Freudian text may, for example, compete with that of the Skinnerian text to channel the vision of the reader in accordance with the preferred interpretive framework. Each tool, moreover, is infatuated with the possibility of its own use. Or as Buchmann (1985) has written:

> Using one's resources is taken so readily to be a good thing because value and utility are equated. One's tools should not lie idle: Where knowledge is valued for its instrumental qualities the charge to use it is almost implied. (p. 156)

Accompanying these imperious demands for attention and use is an advertisement for a kind of safety in a correct, if theoretically framed, interpretation of how things really are. The use of a text-as-tool implies deliverance from a dread first sensed by Heidegger as pervading Western philosophical tradition: the awful anxiety that the "manifold possibilities offered by discursive thought will play us false, will make us 'lose contact' with the real" (Rorty, 1982, p. 130). Feeling anxious about the responsibilities inherent in personal judgment, the user of the paradigmatic text may succumb to this false offer of security in the technically correct, the conventionally valid. Thus anesthetized, he avoids the difficult assessment of the relative worth of visions that lie beyond the mere utility of the text.

Texts fashioned to provide knowledge within a particular theoretical framework may, therefore, be readily welcomed and eagerly consumed by a researcher already initiated into that paradigm. His purpose and vision are, after all, in accord with the paradigmatic mandate: to accumulate "objective" knowledge and to use it for prediction and control. He is "a truth-seeker . . . who deems himself to be faced with a problem which has one right answer. His business is . . . to converge upon . . . the truth-to-be-found" (Shackle, 1966, p. 767). But how to explain the widespread research aliteracy, the reluctance of educational practitioners to use the paradigmatic text? Perhaps these tools are too narrow, too specialized for the educational lay reader whose purposes and visions and decision-making process must transcend paradigmatic boundaries. If only education were not a profession. If only educating were synonymous with instructing or training, then educators might find the apparently nonproblematic technologies of paradigmatic texts more useful. But the languages of these texts conceal too much. The visions they offer are too restricted for engaging in an enterprise such as education, whose value-saturated subject matter must inevitably roam the broad expanses of life. The educator is more like the "poet-architect-adventurer [who] sees before him a landscape inexhaustibly rich in suggestions and materials for making things, for making works of literature or art or technology, for making policies and history itself" (Shackle, 1966, p. 767). Educators, in this sense, are not truth-seekers. They are *truth-makers* who engage in "originative" acts, creating the social worlds in which they will live (Noblit, 1984).

Truth-makers, I suggest, relate more readily to texts composed in forms of language that eschew the parochial dialects of paradigmatic texts, for example, the vernacular language of characters in the modern drama or the robustly evocative language of the novel. Barthes (1975) reminds us of the seductive quality of narrative texts so fashioned. The hopeful reader will, in Barthes's playful phrase, "cruise" the literary text seeking a pleasurable occasion. He desires, I believe, the opportunity to re-create a virtual world that stands against, and comments upon, the qualities of life-at-hand. Anticipation of a climax in the interplay between the actual and the potential, between aesthetic form and content, impels the reader to remain engaged in the textual act. This anticipation, not a compulsion to know and utilize a literal version of the truth, explains the allure of a good story.

Because the narrative will be riddled with gaps in meaning, fraught with ambiguity, the educator-reader must expect to face the anxieties inherent in the use of personal judgment. But because she understands the nature of the educational enterprise, she will not choose to work at it with implements fashioned for narrow utilitarian purposes. She will not surrender a rigorous consideration of goals and visions for the anarchy of values implied in the facile application of any tool at hand. Instead, the educator will seek out texts that are occasions for a critical reexamination, for a dismantling and reconstruction, of her professional platform. She will then stand ready to take responsibility for the educational decisions that platform inspires and supports.

CONSPIRATORIAL TEXTS AND THE EDUCATION OF EDUCATORS

I am optimistic about the future of educational inquiry, for its recent history reveals a steady recovery of the human voice. Only decades ago virtually all educational researchers were quantitatively oriented social scientists praying in silence to what Langer (1957) has called the "idols of the laboratory." The high priests Campbell and Stanley offered holy communion in strict accordance with paradigmatic canons, and *every day was Sunday*. Who could have imagined the heresies about to be uttered?

Educational ethnographers, members of one of the earliest sects of *qualitative* educational inquirers, would never stray too far from the fold. Most have remained afflicted by what Finn (1988) recently called "status envy" (p. 5), strongly desiring for their own work the respect accorded the confident knowledge claims of the so-called hard sciences. Oblivious to the inevitably ideological nature of all methodology, they still seek to fix their texts under a halo of literal truth. But even qualitative research classics, such as *Life in Classrooms* (Jackson, 1968) and *The Complexities of an Urban Classroom* (Smith & Geoffrey, 1968), exhibit a curious mixture of narrative and paradigmatic design features. And in more recent works, such as *Schooling as a Ritual Performance* (McLaren, 1986), the language of disclosure swings back and forth from dense theoretical analysis to storytelling that approaches the grace and evocative force of literature. Listen to the voice of Peter McLaren in the final paragraph of that text, an excerpt from one of his remarkably eloquent and illuminating "field notes." It captures the texture of life outside of a Portuguese middle school in Toronto:

Wednesday, 28 June
The school stands empty. The doors are bolted and the grounds are bare. Yet nearby the sidewalks are alive with people. With brisk strides, they make their way from the subway exits and disappear down the narrow streets. Several girls from the Hairdressing School, resplendent in their stained white smocks and overly rouged faces, order coffees and cigarettes at the donut shop. Rust-splotched cars with metallic impressions of Senhor Santo Cristo dangling from the mirrors wind their way through the growing traffic. In the distance the procession of Mary, Queen of Angels, solemnly wends its way to the Iglesa Santa Cruz, led by an out-of-tune brass band. The statue of Our Lady is reverently held aloft on the shoulders of stocky men in oversized grey suits. At the far end of the procession the madman begins to howl, then stumbles and falls to the ground. And all around the pilgrims, children cry and tyres screech and sirens wail. And church bells sound the mass. (p. 256)

Ethnography remains the dominant form of qualitative educational inquiry, but during the last decade we have been introduced to a new generation of approaches to storytelling about lived experiences, including phenomenological writing, biography and autobiography, and educational criticism. In the best examples of these genres the reader is greeted by a voice that conveys, more strongly and consistently than in most ethnography, a sense of personal authorship. Still, some of the compunctions of a literal mode of rhetoric linger. For example, in my own efforts at educational criticism, I have felt a tension between my pledge to refer adequately to qualities located within the research setting and the enticements of novelistic modes of fiction. Genre-related constraints against composite characters and invented dialogue have unduly restricted the process of truth-making. They have prevented the fashioning of phenomena-at-hand into a story of even greater power and usefulness.[3] The text would be no less empirical (based, that is, upon experience) and, at least in Geertz's sense, no more fictional, but who (I admit to fretting about this) would bless it?

So this present paper temporarily serves as testimony to my resolve for making truths about educational research, and I suggest that future truths include these: that editors of prominent journals of educational inquiry will publish the most accomplished pieces of literary fiction with educational themes; that reading a doctoral dissertation will mean entering a virtual world that offers a fresh perspective on the reader's own *Lebenswelt*; that, therefore, graduate research classes . . . well, *you* imagine the desirabilities!

What kind of utopian vision is this? It is dismissible as idle daydream only by ignoring the history of the last quarter-century. More and more, qualitative educational inquirers are finding their own voices, and soon the most resolute among us may follow the lead of anthropologists such as Bowen (1964) and Bandelier (1898) who chose to novelize their texts. Meanwhile, educators and educators of educators need not sit idly by waiting for the millennium, the time when the literary works of a reformed research establishment pour out of the pipeline. A pool of useful novels and short stories about life in schools already exists.[4] Moreover, literary texts that speak to broader concerns can also contribute to the education of professional educators. Literature has only one theme, Eudora Welty notes, human life. The reading list for Professor James March's "Issues in Leadership" course at Stanford has included Cervantes's *Don Quixote*, Shakespeare's *Othello*, Shaw's *Saint Joan*, Tolstoy's *War and Peace*, Ibsen's *The Wild Duck*, and Stoppard's *The Real Thing* (Kurovsky, 1986). Robert Jennings of the State University of New York at Buffalo has used Wouk's *Caine Mutiny* to examine the problem of the organizational man and radical change, and Ibsen's *A Doll's House* on the clash between societal and personal values (Williams & Willower, 1983).

Students in my own curriculum courses read not only texts by Mitchell and Updike but ethnographic works by, among others, Rist (1970) and Anyon (1980), as well as educational criticisms I have written (1983, 1987). I encourage the use of these texts, not as tools, but as occasions for conspiracy. Together we attempt to lift the veils of objectivity to see the face of an author making choices about method, language, plot. We seek evidence of visions of educational significance that have inspired and guided the fashioning process. We strain to hear the personal voice that research conventions may have tended to muffle. "What is the author's story?" we ask. "Who are the characters? What is the nature of their plight? How is the central dilemma (as *our* dilemma) to be resolved?" Since we will not be making decisions affecting the lives of these characters, we re-create them as illusory inhabitants of virtual worlds. We attempt to use even the nonnovelistic texts *as if* they were pieces of novelistic fiction.

Of course, this attempt increases in difficulty as paradigmatic modes dominate the fashioning of the text. Thin description and systematic methods are features that are generally debilitating to the process of sharing useful stories. But while the narrative character of the autobiography, or the critique, or the novel may recommend these genres in principle, each text, regardless of genre, must be judged according to its individual merits. A text fashioned ethnographically may offer a less than ideal mixture of paradigmatic and narrative features but may be preferable to a novelistic short story that is poorly researched, unimaginatively plotted, and uninspiringly written. Indeed, I do not disagree with Williams and Willower's (1983) observation that, with the possible exception of Siegel's *The Principal* (1963), no existing novel provides a more insightful characterization of the work of the modern school principal than does the ethnographic *The Man in the Principal's Office* (Wolcott, 1973). But, I wonder, would this still be so, had Sinclair Lewis put a school administrator into his portrait gallery of professional figures that includes the physician Arrowsmith, the real estate salesman Babbitt, and the preacher Elmer Gantry?

Still, we do not take the words of *any* author, once heard, as final. Not Wolcott's or McLaren's or Anyon's. Not even Dickens's or Updike's or Lewis's. Even the most radical of artists cannot completely escape the prejudgments inherent within the cultural traditions upon which they comment. No understanding, Gadamer (1975) reminds us, is free of all prejudices, and so the literary text must be greeted with a spirit of skepticism. One voice does not a conspiracy make. The reader is obliged to speak. Lest he become enraptured in a "close reading," unable to move beyond the private universe of textual meaning, the reader must cast a suspicious eye on all texts. This may be especially difficult with a curriculum of literary masterworks, the intricacies of their formal beauty so dazzling and intimidating. But the reader must inquire about historical limitations; the voice in the text, no matter how mellifluous and seductive, must be questioned, perhaps even, as the post-structuralists would have it, interrogated.

Educational practitioners may need encouragement and guidance in overcoming habits of passive response to the literary text. But this gives the teacher-educator something to do: She will work to facilitate the conditions for an act of conspiracy. Part of her task is, indeed, to aid in a reconstruction of the formal illusion, to help make more audible the nuances of meaning in the textual voice. But she must not treat the text like a cognizable object, a tool that is privately owned. She is not the final judge of interpretive rectitude. Instead, the teacher-educator should act as "critical co-investigator" (Freire, 1970, p. 68), serving as leader of a discursive community of professionals in which each member shares responsibility for critical reflection and discussion. The "student" is encouraged to intervene in the reconstructed imaginary world of the text to tell about his particular approach to its dismantling, to speak of perceived strengths and limitations in the vision it proffers, to describe its place within his own personal/professional landscape.

Perhaps in this and other kinds of discursive gatherings we can begin to redress the sense of alienation pervading Western culture that Walker Percy (1986) suggests is partially traceable "to the surrender, albeit unconscious, of valid forms of human activity to scientists, technologists, and specialists" (p. 43). Language and meaning, he says, have largely disappeared, leaving a "great gap in our knowing" (p. 43). Modern man is like Robinson Crusoe on his island, a castaway. "He does not know who he is, where he came from, what to do, and the signs on his island are ambiguous. If he does encounter another human, a man Friday, he has trouble communicating with him" (p. 44). Many of the encounters portrayed in modern literature, Percy notes, "in novels and plays from Sartre to Beckett to Pinter to Joseph McElroy" (p. 45), consist of quasi-conversations or nonconversations between two who are suffering from the common complaint of our age: the loss of meaning, of purpose, of identity, of values, of vision, of voice. They are like "prisoners who find themselves in adjoining cells as a consequence of some vague, Kafka-like offense. Communication is possible only by tapping against the intervening wall" (p. 45).

I am personally acquainted with schoolpeople who have been reduced to tapping messages on the walls between their classrooms. Many teachers and administrators who are also my students and friends speak bitterly of limited opportunities for substantive conversations with colleagues and supervisors. Extrainstitutional mandates for "skills curricula" and standardized tests even reduce possibilities for critical co-investigations with their students. Add to the list of debilitating conditions a heavy workload that squeezes out time for personal reflection, for meaningful dialogue with oneself. And as we include professional norms such as institutional loyalty, dependence on authority, and harmonious pseudocollegiality—norms that dampen hopes of sparks generated from ideas rubbing together—it begins to appear that the modern technocratic institution of the school abhors conspiracy.

Denied the possibilities of formulating and progressing toward concrete utopian visions, educational practitioners may, like their students, become "at risk." They may exhibit the extremist tendencies of the moral dropout, their personal notions of the educationally desirable torn asunder. One part is chained to the conventional, forced to work toward technically virtuous, institutionally sanctioned ends-in-view, using any tool available. The other part flies off in frustration or outrage to search for "another country" on a magic carpet of utopian daydreams. There is nostalgic pining for impossibly perfect worlds that never really were. Or like the co-conspirators in *Another Country*, one imagines alien ideologies that can never be. Bennett and Judd, the homosexual and the communist, occupants of adjoining cells, are appalled at the distance between their ideals and the oppressive realities of life-at-hand. Tapping against the intervening wall, they finally learn each other's language. But their conversation is merely self-defeating pseudoconspiracy. Bereft of all hopes for making concrete, incremental improvements in the educational and political status quo, they can only plot its annihilation. So texts of inquiry into the quality of educational life must offer more than the documentation and cataloguing of its impoverishment, on the one hand, or abstract theorizing about it, on the other. Instead, they must participate in the larger project of serious fiction in our age, the aim of which, Percy (1986) insists, is nothing less than "an exploration of the options of postmodern man" (p. 44).

I have been arguing that the aesthetic episodes wherein we use serious literature—or even use essays, such as this one, that discuss serious literature—are occasions for tense negotiations between the self of the reader and the contents of the experienced world. Of course, in a good story the resulting growth of meaning gradually culminates in a harmonious resolution that, placed against the ongoing drama of life, appears as merely provisional. Such conspiratorial episodes are like acts in that drama, their resolutions temporary at best. Still, like Bennett and Judd, we all need what has been achieved upon the conclusion of a successful story: a sense of progression toward a concrete utopian vision and ideas about desirable possibilities for approaching the next chapter of our autobiographies. We also need to feel the special mixture of fatigue and fulfillment associated with the closure of an aesthetic experience, the kind of wearied elation that lingers after, say, a round with Dickens or with Bartók. It is the feeling that accompanies the true sabbatical, the intermission between the phases in our explorations of options. It is how we should feel on a Sunday morning.

Now, having offered this exploration of our options as educators and inquirers into the qualities of educational experiences, I at last find myself at such an intermission—and to the degree that we have achieved conspiracy, perhaps you do, too. So maybe it is time for us to lower our voices, put on some Bach, and, before the next cycle of exploration commences, together call it a week.

NOTES

1. This paper was presented on a Sunday morning, at the final session of the Stanford Conference. In composing this paper I used its assigned position in the conference schedule as a central metaphor in critiquing the usual view

of the implementation of research findings as the culmination of the inquiry process. In order to maintain the integrity of the text and to provide the reader with a fuller sense of the occasion for which it was prepared, I have chosen not to delete references to the context in which its original presentation took place.

2. This concept of an "educational platform" is borrowed from Walker's (1971) discussion of a curriculum platform. For Walker, "the word [platform] is meant to suggest both a political platform and something to stand on. The platform includes an idea of what is and a vision of what ought to be, and these guide the curriculum developer in determining what he should do to realize his vision" (p. 52).

3. There are, of course, different kinds of constraints inherent in the use of novelistic modes of fiction. Working successfully within these constraints requires a qualitative problem-solving process that is as rigorous, in its own way, as science-based research processes. See Ecker (1966) for a discussion of the artistic, qualitative problem-solving process.

4. Authors who have identified and discussed examples of fictional school characters include Bass (1970), Kramer (1981), and Williams and Willower (1983). An updated anthology of good stories with educational themes is sorely needed.

REFERENCES

Allender, J. S. (1986). Educational research: A personal and social process. *Review of Educational Research, 56*(2), 173–193.

Anyon, J. (1980). Social class and the hidden curriculum of work. *Journal of Education, 162*(1), 67–92.

Bandelier, A. (1898). *The delight makers.* New York: Dodd, Mead.

Barone, T. (1983). Things of use and things of beauty: The Swain County High School Arts Program. *Daedalus, 112*(3), 1–28.

Barone, T. (1987). On equality, visibility, and the fine arts program in a black elementary school: An example of educational criticism. *Curriculum Inquiry, 17*(4), 421–446.

Barthes, R. (1975). *The pleasure of the text* (R. Miller, Trans.). New York: Hill and Wang.

Bass, A. T. (1970). The teacher as portrayed in fiction. *Contemporary Education, 42*(1), 14–20.

Bowen, E. S. (1964). *Return to laughter: An anthropological novel.* Garden City, NY: Doubleday.

Bruner, J. (1987). *Actual lives, possible worlds.* Cambridge, MA: Harvard University Press.

Buchmann, M. (1985). What is irrational about knowledge utilization. *Curriculum Inquiry, 15*(2), 153–168.

Bullough, E. (1957). *Aesthetics: Lectures and essays.* Stanford, CA: Stanford University Press.

Capote, T. (1965). *In cold blood.* New York: Random House.

Cook, A. (1960). *The meaning of fiction*. Detroit, MI: Wayne State University Press.

Dewey, J. (1958). *Art as experience*. New York: Capricorn Books. (Original work published 1934)

Dickens, C. (1950). *The life and adventures of Nicholas Nickelby*. Oxford: Oxford University Press. (Original work published 1839)

Ecker, D. (1966). The artistic process as qualitative problem-solving. In E. Eisner & D. Ecker (Eds.), *Readings in art education* (pp. 57–68). Waltham, MA: Blaisdell.

Finn, C. (1988). What ails education research. *Educational Researcher, 17,* 5–8.

Freire, P. (1970). *Pedagogy of the oppressed*. New York: Seabury Press.

Frye, N. (1967). *Anatomy of criticism*. Princeton, NJ: Princeton University Press.

Gadamer, H. (1975). *Truth and method* (G. Barden & J. Cumming, Trans. & Eds.). New York: Seabury Press.

Geertz, C. (1973). *The interpretation of cultures*. New York: Basic Books.

Goodwin, B., & Taylor, K. (1982). *The politics of utopia: A study in theory and practice*. London: Hutchinson.

Greene, M. (1977). Toward wide-awakeness: An argument for the arts and humanities in education. *Teachers College Record, 19*(1), 119–125.

Haley, A. (1976). *Roots*. Garden City, NY: Doubleday/Anchor Press.

Hansot, E. (1974). *Perfection and utopia: Two modes of utopian thought*. Cambridge, MA: M.I.T. Press.

Hersey, J. (1946). *Hiroshima*. New York: Modern Library.

Illich, I. (1973). *Tools for conviviality*. New York: Harper & Row.

Ingarden, R. (1968). *The cognition of the literary work of art*. Evanston, IL: Northwestern University Press.

Iser, W. (1980). The reading process: A phenomenological approach. In J. P. Tompkins (Ed.), *Reader-response criticism: From formalism to post-structuralism*. Baltimore: Johns Hopkins University Press.

Jackson, P. W. (1968). *Life in classrooms*. New York: Holt, Rinehart and Winston.

Kermode, F. (1967). *The sense of an ending: Studies in the theory of fiction*. New York: Oxford University Press.

Kramer, J. (1981). College and university presidents in fiction. *Journal of Higher Education, 52*(1), 81–95.

Kurovsky, R. (1986). Novels, plays, poetry help aid leadership development. *Stanford Observer*.

Langer, S. (1957). *Problems of art*. New York: Scribner's.

McLaren, P. (1986). *Schooling as a ritual performance*. London: Routledge and Kegan Paul.

Michener, J. A. (1985). *Texas*. New York: Random House.

Miller, J. H. (1976). Stevens' Rock and criticism as cure, II. *Georgia Review, 30,* 330–348.

Mitchell, J. (1982). *Another country*. Ambergate, UK: Amber Lane Press.

Noblit, G. W. (1984). The prospects of an applied ethnography for education: A sociology of knowledge interpretation. *Educational Evaluation and Policy Analysis, 6*(1), 95–101.

Orwell, G. (1961). *Down and out in Paris and London*. New York: Harcourt Brace Jovanovich. (Original work published 1933)

Pepper, S. C. (1945). *The basis of criticism in the arts*. Cambridge, MA: Harvard University Press.

Percy, W. (1986). The diagnostic novel: On the use of modern fiction. *Harper's Magazine, 272*(1633), 39–45.

Polanyi, M. (1962). *Personal knowledge: Toward a post-critical philosophy*. Chicago: University of Chicago Press.

Polanyi, M. (1964). *Science, faith and society*. Chicago: University of Chicago Press.

Polanyi, M. (1966). *The tacit dimension*. Garden City, NY: Doubleday.

Poulet, G. (1986). Phenomenology of reading. In R. C. Davis (Ed.), *Contemporary literary criticism: Modernism through post-structuralism* (pp. 350–362). New York: Longman.

Ricoeur, P. (1976). *Interpretational theory: Discourse and the surplus of meaning*. Fort Worth: Texas Christian University Press.

Rist, R. (1970). Student social class and teacher expectations: The self-fulfilling prophecy in ghetto education. *Harvard Educational Review, 40*(3), 411–451.

Roiphe, A. (1988, February 14). This butcher, imagination: Beware of your life when a writer's at work. *New York Times Book Review*, pp. 3, 30.

Rorty, R. (1982). *Consequences of pragmatism*. Minneapolis: University of Minneapolis Press.

Shackle, G. L. S. (1966, December). Policy, poetry and success. *The Economic Journal*, pp. 755–767.

Siegel, B. (1963). *The principal*. New York: Harcourt, Brace and World.

Smith, L. M., & Geoffrey, W. (1968). *The complexities of an urban classroom: An analysis toward a general theory of teaching*. New York: Holt, Rinehart and Winston.

Toulmin, S. (1953). *Philosophy of science*. London: Hutchinson University Library.

Twain, M. (1899). *The innocents abroad*. New York: Harper. (Original work published 1869)

Updike, J. (1959). A sense of shelter. In J. Updike, *Pigeon feathers and other stories* (pp. 63–74). New York: Fawcett Books.

Walker, D. (1971). A naturalistic model for curriculum development. *School Review, 80*(1), 51–65.

Williams, R. H., & Willower, D. J. (1983). The school administrator in fiction. *The Educational Forum, 47*(3), 353–363.

Wolcott, H. F. (1973). *The man in the principal's office: An ethnography*. New York: Holt, Rinehart and Winston.

Wolfe, T. (1973). *The new journalism*. New York: Harper & Row.

10 What You Can Learn from Applesauce: A Case of Qualitative Inquiry in Use

CHRISTOPHER M. CLARK

I want to share with you the short history of a little report called "What You Can Learn from Applesauce." I wrote it in October 1987 to describe an afternoon in an elementary school where I had been working as a "professor in residence" for the whole school year. The short version of the story goes like this:

1. I was a participant-observer in a fascinating classroom experience.
2. I wrote a description and analysis of my experience.
3. I gave copies of that text to twenty-five or thirty friends and acquaintances.
4. I have heard from ten or fifteen of these individuals about how they have responded to or used the paper.
5. Now, I want to come to an understanding of how qualitative inquiry *can* be used by describing how this case *has* been used.

Before I get into responses and categories, let me show you what my friends were responding to. Here is the text of "What You Can Learn from Applesauce." As you read it, think about how you might make use of this example of qualitative inquiry.

WHAT YOU CAN LEARN FROM APPLESAUCE

In mid-October I spent a couple of fall afternoon hours helping twenty-one first- and second-graders make a pot of applesauce. The day climaxed with the great moment of tasting, when the contents of the pot, spiced with cinnamon and divided into twenty-two portions, was consumed with delight. Children and teacher alike declared that this was a fine and magical afternoon—one of those memorable high points that we cherish as examples of the way education should be all of the time.

At the risk of spoiling the magic by too much analysis I would like to reflect on what was learned (or could have been learned) in this classroom on an October afternoon. What can you learn from applesauce? This question applies not only to the learning of the six- and seven-year-olds, but also to the teacher and to me.

I've divided the list of what was learned from applesauce into those learnings intended or anticipated by the teacher, followed by surprises and subtle side effects of the activity. Since I did not interview the teacher in advance about her plans and expectations, the line between intentions and surprises is not definitive, but rather suggestive. This would remain true even after a post hoc interview, since her direct experience of the afternoon powerfully influences recollection and reconstruction of her plans and expectations. Hopes and fears about what might happen in the future (the stuff of planning) disappear like smoke in hindsight.

Anticipated Learnings and Conditions Supportive of Them

Simply put, the two most obvious academic learning goals of applesauce making were for the children to learn about the concept of orderly sequencing of steps in a moderately complex process and to practice expressing (through writing and drawing) an understandable description of their own activities. The former is a specific objective of the first-grade mathematics curriculum; the latter is a general aim of the language arts curricula for both grades. They were jointly pursued through teacher-led instruction about the sequence of steps to be followed and through the children's alternately acting out steps in the sequence and creating individual booklets describing and depicting the process. Seven children at a time peeled and cut apples with the help and supervision of two adult volunteers, while the remaining fourteen children drew pictures and wrote captions describing five steps in the applesauce-making process. After each child finished operating on one apple, he or she washed hands and returned to recipe-booklet making, being replaced at one of the seven cutting boards by a classmate. During the hour or so of apple cutting and peeling, the teacher was involved in helping children (especially first-graders) spell words for their booklet captions and in directing the flow of children between their writing desks and the cutting-and-peeling stations. The first hour and a quarter ended with slices and chunks of twenty-one apples simmering in a cinnamon-spiced pot, twenty-one recipe booklets nearing completion, and a great wad of newspaper, peelings, and apple seeds in the wastebasket. This might have been enough learning to satisfy most educators, but there was much, much more learned from applesauce.

Part of what else was anticipated and learned from applesauce falls under the heading "continuity of experience." First, the experience of food preparation constituted a link between home and school. Young children daily see, smell, and sometimes participate in food preparation in their own kitchens. Their prior out-of-school knowledge and experiences were drawn upon in this in-school project. More proximately, the applesauce-making activity drew on two recent school activities. The most immediate and direct connection was to a field trip to Uncle John's Cider Mill, where the children saw recently harvested apples by the bushel, saw and smelled the process of large-scale cider making in action, and obtained apples to bring back to school. The teacher saw an opportunity for children to mentally connect their visit to orchard and cider mill with their own transformation of apples into applesauce.

The second connection was to a prior field trip to a farmers' market, where the children purchased a variety of vegetables, brought them back to school, and made "stone soup." The applesauce-making project was structurally quite similar to the stone-soup project (with the important difference that there was no children's literature story or folk tale around which to organize the applesauce making, as there was with stone soup).

In sum, this second set of intended learnings had to do with the idea (and experience) that life outside school is (or can be) connected to life in school; that school learning activities need not be segregated from one's taken-for-granted everyday knowledge and learning; and that transformations of a grand scale (bushels of apples transformed into gallons of cider) can be effectively modeled on a manageably small scale. But this was not the whole story.

The probably anticipated but secondary student learnings from the applesauce project had to do with safety, sanitation, and satisfaction of two kinds. Learning to use a paring knife safely was intended, taught directly by modeling, tried empirically, and then backed away from when, in the judgment of the teacher, the risk of self-inflicted wounds appeared too high. (We switched to using plastic knives after the first few exciting minutes.) Nonetheless, the points were made: Safety is important, sharp knives must be handled with care, and relatively mature fine-motor coordination is required to peel an apple safely with a sharp knife. The role of sanitation in food preparation was emphasized by having the children wash their hands before and after food handling. Satisfaction as an outcome of this learning activity was intended to come both from the delicious and immediate tasting of the fruits of one's own labors and from having a booklet to take home that would serve as a prop and support for a "show-and-tell" conversation with parents. A subtle characteristic of these satisfactions is that they do not depend on competitiveness for success. Rather, there was "equity of outcome," in that everyone got to contribute, everyone got to taste from the pot, and everyone got to take home a booklet. The underlying message here is that learning can be fun, delicious, and communicable to an absent audience through the magic of writing. Again, for most of us, this would have been enough. But there was more to this applesauce than is usually the case.

Applesauce, unsurprisingly, is not all academic. The teacher intended (at least implicitly) that this set of activities would serve some social-learning functions as well. First among these was the idea that *cooperation* within the classroom social group could produce a delightful product that no one individual or small group could have produced. *Patience* in letting the project take as long as it needed to and the twin pleasures of *task ownership* by the children ("I'll cut *my* apple *my* way") and *active, multisensory participation* in a learning activity ("This is messy." "That smells good." "Look, I cut a seed in half!") were required, or at least encouraged, by the structure of the tasks and also hoped for as enduring, transferable, long-term outcomes of the process. Making applesauce may have served to make this classroom social group happier, more cohesive, more patient, and more confident. ("If we can make applesauce together, perhaps we can make a newspaper in the spring.")

Perhaps more could have been made of the math and science learning potential of applesauce. We could have weighed the apples, weighed what went into the pot, and weighed the contents of the pot after an hour of simmering, then hypothesized about how to account for the differences. We could have carefully emphasized how halves, quarters, eighths, and sixteenths are related to the whole. We could have counted seeds, dissected seeds, planted seeds, talked about nature's "intended" role for seed and fruit. We could have demonstrated bilateral and cross-sectional symmetry. (Have you ever cut an apple in half the "wrong" way? Try it: there is a delightful surprise within.) We could have taught juggling or given examples of the role of the apple in religion, myth, literature, and the economy of Michigan. We did none of these things, although I would not be surprised if the apple example arises again when large fractions are studied in math.

Surprises and Side Effects

What did the teacher learn more generally about herself and about teaching from applesauce? From her response to seeing the apparent danger of sharp knives in little hands, she learned something about her own tolerance for risk in the name of learning. In this case, the risk of injury appeared substantial, the particular learning aim of successful use of paring knives was marginal, and a safer alternative (plastic knives) was at hand. But it is interesting that the need for revision of this important detail of the applesauce-making plan did not arise during preactive planning, but only in the vividness of action. Perhaps this was a case of overgeneralization from the accident-free stone soup project, in which various vegetables were sliced and diced using the same sharp set of paring knives. What became clear as the first seven children began to work on their apples was that it is considerably easier to slice a celery stalk or a carrot than it is to peel an apple.

The teacher and I also learned something about the necessity of detailed planning of a complex activity. In this case, the planning challenge was to design a pair of activities that were substantively connected, academically defensible, and robust enough to be sustained in the face of internal interruptions (i.e., the children's continually shifting from drawing and writing to apple peeling and then back again to drawing and writing). It was also crucial to carrying out this plan that the teacher have one or two adult helpers, and the manifest success of the activity confirmed (for the teacher) the wisdom of seeking help in this kind of teaching. A final lesson learned (or reconfirmed) by the teacher was that, especially with young children, resolution of a cause-and-effect process during a single afternoon is quite satisfying. Beginning the afternoon with a bag of apples and ending the day with one's own recipe booklet and the taste of warm applesauce fits the attention span of six- and seven-year-olds quite nicely. Multiday projects may make sense later in the year.

Two subtle but important lessons about individual student differences and about gender roles were learned from applesauce. Some children who had various difficulties with reading or with verbal participation in group activities positively shone at apple cutting and peeling. They acted confidently and competently, even helping classmates learn how to cut and peel. The activity structure made it possible for them to thrive in the same classroom and group in which they typically struggle. Teacher, adult volunteers, and children noticed these individual differences to different degrees, and the consequences of this consciousness raising will take time to manifest themselves. But for now, it is worth noting that these insights would not have arisen in the context of more verbally loaded classroom activities. The issue of gender roles was subtle in that the question of whether it was appropriate for boys to be so involved in food preparation never came up. Boys and girls together pitched in and got the job done. One can only hope that this egalitarian approach will continue throughout the children's school experiences.

Conclusion

In conclusion, more was learned from applesauce than at first meets the eye. The planning, acting, revising, and happy resolution of the applesauce-making activity affected everyone involved. Academic, social, and professional-development learning potentials were realized in subtle and obvious ways. Reflection on the experience suggested additional curriculum potential that may be realized next year by this teacher and her students, or at any time by other teachers and students. And learnings about teaching, activity structures, and individual students may continue to influence this teacher's planning for the remainder of the school year. General abstract principles—such as continuity of experience, equity of outcome, multiability task demands, comprehensive planning, flexible revision of plans, and sensitivity to developmental capabilities of school children—take on vividness and new meaning when depicted in the garb of a concrete, visualizable classroom activity. And I, for one, will never be able to see a MacIntosh in quite the same simple light as I did in the days before learning from applesauce.

RESPONSES

So what do you think? How did this account connect with your background experiences? What uses might *you* make of it? I do want to hear your answers, but first, let me share with you some answers that I have already heard from others: the teacher and the principal, teacher-educators, researchers, and civilians.

Teachers and Teacher-Educators

I want to begin by describing how the teacher of the applesauce episode, Ms. Anderson, responded to the case description. Emotionally, she was flattered and pleased. She also expressed delight that so much could be made of what was, for her, a relatively ordinary set of events. She was eager to show the draft document to the school principal. Most significant, I think, was her wish to keep a copy on file in the school office as a preemptive response to parents who might question the academic value of enjoyable and practical activities such as applesauce making. That is, Ms. Anderson held an intuitive conviction that such activities are of value but did not feel confident that she alone could defend applesauce making on academic grounds. Now she had both the language and the authority of a professor to support her belief in the good of the work she was doing. Interestingly, the challenge never came—no parent lodged a complaint to which the applesauce case served as a response. But the support and affirmation that Ms. Anderson felt as a result of reading this description and analysis of her own teaching seemed to be important to her confidence and morale. To be known and to be appreciated are two of the psychic rewards of teacher participation in qualitative inquiry.

The school principal, Ms. McClintock, made use of the applesauce case with several different audiences. First, with the teachers and instructional aides she used the case study at a staff meeting to demonstrate that valuable learning can take place as a result of activities that fall outside the scope of published curriculum materials. The principal reported that this was received as an important message of encouragement to the staff, who were feeling a bit overwhelmed by central office expectations that they should literally implement a new science curriculum and a new spelling program. The principal also reported that having a professor's endorsement of the importance of such activities made the case more credible to teachers.

A second way in which Ms. McClintock made use of the case study was to add to the local language of practice. She now uses the expression *an applesauce event* to refer to school activities that combine elements of fun, teamwork, practical activity, and many social and academic learning opportunities. She has used (and explained) this language in conversations with teachers, individual parents, and members of the school parents' council to make a case for how teachers at Whitehills School sometimes go beyond the published curriculum to promote a wide range of valued kinds of learning and development. She also plans to begin the next school year, when several new teachers will join the staff, with a challenge to teachers to develop and share "applesauce activities" of their own.

Finally, Ms. McClintock sent a copy of the applesauce case to the superintendent, curriculum director, and each member of the school board at the end of the school year. Her cover letter introduced the case as an example of the good things that had happened at. Whitehills School during the year. A more subtle, implied message was that educationally rich and exciting things have been taking place at this school, outside the limits of published and mandated curricula. The underlying theme here is promoting and defending teachers' autonomy in deciding the "what" and the "how" of classroom teaching.

Let me now move 700 miles east from Ms. Anderson's classroom to the world of another teacher who is also a teacher-educator in a small church college. Ms. Potter, a veteran of twenty years of teaching multi-grade classes in church schools, has been education department chair at a church college for about five years. Her personal response to reading "applesauce" was nostalgic: "It took me right back to my own elementary teaching days; to the kinds of projects I loved to do with my kids. But while I was *doing* all that, it wasn't possible to sit back and *see* all the learning, all the complexity." One way, then, that Ms. Potter used this example of qualitative inquiry was to remind herself of the difficulty, perhaps impossibility, of acting and reflecting simultaneously. And in teaching, the demands of action often crowd out reflection.

In her role as teacher-educator, Ms. Potter used this case to show her students how many of the skills and dimensions of teaching and school learning fit together. Her students had been chafing at the reductionistic way in which their texts treat teaching and learning. Reading "Applesauce" aloud in class gave her students hope and optimism that all the pieces of teaching studied separately can come together again. This case study provides a visualizable context for novices to see how abstract ideas from educational psychology, curriculum theory, and methods courses look and feel and interact.

At another college of education, another teacher-educator read "Applesauce" aloud to his section of twenty prospective math teachers. In this instance, the intended purpose of so doing was to provide an example, if not a model, of how the undergraduate listeners could write about their own field observations of teaching and learning. These students, who had visited classrooms twice earlier in the term, were working on an assignment that called for describing an episode of teaching and learning by using concepts and ideas from their university coursework. Hearing the applesauce text helped them see one way in which literal description of teacher and student behavior could be interwoven with hypotheses, analysis, speculation, and interpretation. And, as important, the case supported the professor's claim that there is much more to teaching and school learning than meets the eye; that the extraordinary and complex lurk just below the surface of the ordinary and commonplace.

A teacher of elementary school mathematics who is also a teacher-educator read the applesauce paper and immediately mailed it to her stepdaughter. The stepdaughter was a first-year elementary school teacher and had intended to keep a written record of her experiences as a novice teacher. Her stepmother thought that the voice and form of the applesauce paper made it helpful as a model or example of how to write about one's own practice.

A final example of use by teacher-educators took place at a small college in North Carolina. The department chair in education was eager to encourage her faculty to do more research while at the same time maintaining the high quality of a labor-intensive teacher-preparation program. The applesauce paper was offered to faculty as one example of how qualitative or interpretive research could be done on a small scale while pursuing other ends and practical activities (e.g., supervision of student teaching). Beyond serving as a possible model for research in practice, the circulation of the applesauce paper also stimulated faculty deliberation about what counts as "real" research. That discussion, in turn, broadened the way in which this faculty thought about qualitative research in education.

The teachers and teacher-educators who made use of "What You Can Learn from Applesauce" used it primarily as an *example*: an example of a way of describing teaching, an example of how a practical activity can promote academic learning, an example of how the elements of teaching can all fit together again, an example of how the extraordinary and complex underlie the commonplace, an example of small-scale research on teaching. Each teacher and teacher-educator seized on this example to fill a practical pedagogical need—to teach or show something to an audience of parents, faculty colleagues, a stepdaughter, or prospective teachers. The need, the audience, and the principles to be taught were all in place before "Applesauce" came along. Teachers are always on the lookout for fresh, compelling examples, and qualitative research is a rich source of such examples. But as researchers, we cannot predict or control just how our cases will be used, for that is the task of the teacher.

Researchers

How did my colleagues and friends who are researchers make use of this example of qualitative research? Their responses ranged from the romantic to the revolutionary, and, as with teachers, it seemed that at least some of the researchers' goals, intentions, and audience were already in place before "Applesauce" came along.

Three researchers were moved to nostalgia by reading this case. They wrote me that they were reminded of times when they themselves had pursued fieldwork of the kind that I have been doing, and they took the occasion to thank me for reminding them of those days and to encourage and assure me that this is a good thing for me to be doing. Two other researchers responded by sharing with me their current work in progress and making a case that what they were doing had much in common with the spirit and direction of the work from which "Applesauce" developed. In all five of these instances the primary uses of the case study were to come to know me (as author) better and to come to be known better by me. These are personal and social functions that strengthen the community of educational research.

One researcher responded somewhat like a teacher—she used "Applesauce" as an example of a practical case in which "higher-order learning" could be pursued with young children. The research group that she leads had been discussing abstract theoretical ideas about higher-order learning for some time, and she felt a need to ground those ideas in a real, visualizable classroom situation. Reading "Applesauce" provided a way to put their theorizing to a small test and to bring a kind of practical balance to their decisions about research design, instrumentation, and methods of inquiry.

Still another researcher got an idea for a paper that he might write from reading the applesauce case. He is an instructional designer, and he saw in this case a starting point for a piece tentatively titled "Experience in Search of Objectives." The depth of curriculum potential revealed by the case study moved him out of the familiar ends-means paradigm for teacher planning and instruction. For a time, at least, he saw and appreciated how and why teachers do not always begin their plans by specifying measurable learning outcomes. Practice confronted theoretical prescription, and theory blinked first. My own habitual ways of seeing teaching and learning have been challenged and stretched by the direct experience of working in classrooms. Apparently, reading a case description can also raise fundamental questions in a thoughtful researcher's mind about his teleological orientation and perceptual framework.

This leads to my final example of researchers' responses to the applesauce case. A newly met friend, himself a leader in the qualitative tradition, encouraged me to use this case as the basis for a fundamental epistemological challenge to the field of educational research. He saw in this case an opportunity to show that researchers of every tradition systematically undercomplicate the educational settings under study. To fit the constraints of research design, time, language, theory, expectations, convenience, and preordained forms for reporting our work, we find ourselves studying cleaned-up, stripped-down caricatures of reality. Small wonder, then, that practicing educators rarely find realistically helpful support, enlightenment, or guidance from the research community. This is not the time or place to pursue this line of thought to conclusion. Rather, it serves as one example of how a specific case of qualitative research can connect with the philosophical project of a scholar and encourage him to enlist another in the cause.

Civilians

I have two responses to "Applesauce" to share from people who are neither teachers nor researchers. One of these readers did teach for two years in the early 1970s and is the mother of two school-aged children. The other is a nineteen-year-old college sophomore who is also my daughter. I think it is significant to note that the particular example of qualitative research under consideration here was understood and responded to by this lay audience. Some forms of qualitative inquiry can be used to open communication about education with the public. In this instance, the young student reported that reading this piece showed her that elementary school teaching demands a kind of sustained attention and "thinking on your feet" that she was not aware of. The former teacher told me that she was reminded of and reexperienced the intensity of her days teaching second grade, years ago. My daughter has since decided to become an elementary school teacher, and the former teacher has since taken steps to renew her teaching credential and seek a position teaching French to elementary school children. I am not claiming that reading "What You Can Learn from Applesauce" was the major influence in these two career decisions, but I do claim that picturing oneself in a new professional role is an important element in the personal decision-making process. Reports of qualitative inquiry can help people to imagine themselves in the place of the teacher; to simulate how that would feel and be; to take account of such a vicarious experience in deciding on a career in teaching.

CONCLUSION

What have we learned about qualitative inquiry in use? First, that reports of qualitative inquiry *can* be used and *are* being used by teachers and principals, teacher-educators, researchers, and civilians. This is encouraging to me, and I hope it is encouraging to others who pursue this form of scholarship. Second, the accounts of how people responded to the applesauce case remind us that people make sense of text in relation to their own past experiences, their beliefs and expectations, and their present needs and aspirations. While most reports of qualitative inquiry steer clear of making prescriptions for specific action, people can and have been moved to take specific action, advocate change, and make consequential decisions inspired or influenced by reports of qualitative inquiry. Like art, literature, poetry, and music, qualitative accounts of the drama of teaching and learning can have profound and unpredictable effects on human thought and action.

Third, several of the accounts of response to the applesauce case suggest that qualitative inquiry can fill a felt need to understand how teaching and learning fit together in context. The narrative-analytic form of this case helped readers see the flexible and uncertain yet real ways in which teaching skills, strategies and style, practical experience, knowledge of children, and more played parts in support of learning. Yes, teaching is complicated; no, teaching is not impossible.

Finally, qualitative inquiry can be used to explore the boundaries, limits, and possibilities of our own learning from experience. I have been surprised and delighted by what I have learned from "Applesauce." And I suspect that I am not finished learning from "Applesauce," as I look forward to the response of those who read these words and join the conversation.

Animadversions and Reflections on the Uses of Qualitative Inquiry

MATTHEW B. MILES and A. MICHAEL HUBERMAN

We found the papers by Thomas Barone and Christopher Clark by turns infuriating, seducing, monolithic, plausible, opaque, illuminating, misty, narcissistic . . . and so on (as Korzybsky was fond of pointing out, a list of properties of an object can never be exhaustive). In these remarks we want to summarize the reasons for these reactions as clearly as we can and suggest some alternative perspectives on the authors' comments—and indeed on the domain suggested by the label "uses of qualitative inquiry."

PAPER BY THOMAS BARONE

First the Barone paper. Just after its closing remarks, a strong association leaped to mind. It is cast in an ancient qualitative form: the joke.

> We are on a battleship, steaming along in an unnamed ocean. The captain has received a radio message that the mother of one of his men, Seaman Abernathy, has just died. The captain, a decent man, thinks about how to break the news. Next we hear the public address system: NOW HEAR THIS! ALL HANDS ON DECK IMMEDIATELY! The captain, faced with the assembled multitude of his crew, gives an order: "All men with living mothers, one step forward." Then: "NOT SO FAST, ABERNATHY!"

As with all qualitative texts, multiple conclusions can be drawn. What is the moral of this story? That tender-heartedness defeats itself? That human dilemmas are easiest solved through blunt instruments?

That hierarchical thoughtways never die? That abstract categories are cruel? Or only that we wanted to say, "Not so fast, Barone"?

In fact, that is what we do want to say. We think the paper contains a number of unquestioned assumptions, all of which deserve some unpacking. In brief, they are (1) that literature is a nonproblematic model for qualitative inquiry; (2) that "instrumental" knowledge and its use are by definition *bad*; (3) that only one pure epistemology—and its associated methodology—deserves our fealty; (4) that the label "conspiracy" is a good one to describe the relationships among producers and users of qualitative studies; (5) that in qualitative inquiry, and its use, we need not be especially concerned with such matters as truth, validity, verification, and cumulation of knowledge; and, finally, (6) that the methods the qualitative analyst employs do not matter much. Not so fast!

Literature as a Model for Qualitative Inquiry

Barone makes an elegant case for the literary experience of the author and the reader as a model for the production and "use" of qualitative studies. He speaks of the reader's "reconstructing" and "dismantling" the narrative text, of the development of multiple meanings and interpretations, and of "utopian visions"—alternative future worlds that the reading of the text opens up.

But this way of thinking, attractive as it may be, is problematic in four different senses we can think of. First, it emphasizes the communication between author and reader via the text and ignores the reality of qualitative studies: that the field worker who visited the site and collected reams of notes is in fact the author who erects the bulk of the text *and*, somehow, the reader who reconstructs and dismantles it. (Cf. Tesch's [1988] comments on decontextualizing and recontextualizing as typical processes in qualitative data analysis.) In short, initially at least, there are not two persons connecting through the (evolving) text, but one. Under these circumstances, the sense of "discovering otherness," or, as Barone puts it, "the voice of another subject offering the fruits of her inquiry into the qualities of lived experience," simply disappears. We can solve this sophistically by saying that the people the researcher is studying are "authors," but that is a great stretch. Tom Wolfe's landlady was not an author. When one met her, she seemed like an interesting human being, but that is another thing.

Second, there are definitional ambiguities. We never quite get a clear feeling of what a "novelistic" text is (it's presumably one where the text is not required to match something called "the facts"), but the label remains unclear. So does the idea of a "worthy text," a "readable text," a "good story." Does anything that has not been "mocked, derided, trashed" qualify as Good Stuff?

Third, the idea that the experience of reading a literary text necessarily leads to "utopian visions" that defy "the moral imperialism of the present" and offer "an accessible replacement" seems hortatory and forced. Lionel Trilling once said that the novel is a way of finding out how other people live. But the experience of diversity, or even of options, is a long way from the discovery of utopia. Much of the time we are reading for sheer novelty, so to speak. Somehow Barone seems to expect literary experience to be tremendously melioristic, contributing to a "professional platform . . . the space from which we launch the educational projects that aim to change what is into what ought to be."

Finally, even if we acknowledge that stories and novels let us generate new configurations of meaning that can be carried to our "professional life outside of the text," how does this "carrying" occur? It's hard enough to transfer technology. Perhaps the story has created a "lens" through which to look at our own reality. But (to use Barone's example of his use of Bennett's feelings as he understood them in the Julian Mitchell play), how can one assess the alienation, resentment, withdrawal, or vandalism of Cincinnati school students with any confidence that the dynamic is not something *other* than institutional entrapment? Or how come they don't become Marxists like Bennett? Or do espionage?

The Value of "Instrumental" Knowledge

Here we must simply be peevish. The paper denounces the "text-as-tool," asserting (without any exemplars) that it "does not prize metaphorical aptness . . . is not designed to surprise the reader-as-user . . . is fashioned for use within [the common] order, tacitly bestowing legitimacy upon it . . . [has a] detached, passionless textual voice . . . is infatuated with the possibility of its own use." We are warned that the user may "succumb to this false offer of security in the technically correct, the conventionally valid . . ." and is "thus anesthetized." Wow. Instrumental knowledge is BAD, because educators are "'poet-architect-adventurer[s]' . . . not truth-seekers . . . [but] *truth-makers* who engage in 'originative' acts" (note the normative/stipulative definition here). Instrumental knowledge will supposedly block creativity. But that is sheer nonsense. Architects need to know about capacity of bearing walls, and Scott's absurd failure in the Antarctic flowed directly from his lack of interest in available information about how to survive in polar climates. Knowing what leads to what in life is not a disadvantage for anyone, poets included. Educators included.

Further, we are not impressed with the distinction drawn between "use" of a text as "tool" (BAD) and as an "occasion" (GOOD). When one's language is of the form, "I used the occasion . . . ," there is almost always a following preposition: "I used the occasion to deliver some pointed remarks . . . I seized the opportunity to set them straight . . . I used the time for learning more about literary criticism." These "uses" are just as reasonable as the statement, "It was a wonderful occasion," made without any instrumental overtones.

Instrumental knowledge is a good thing, and aesthetic knowledge is a good thing. Why engage in this sort of straw-man exercise?

More explicitly: Real people (who have both work and personal lives) can use qualitative knowledge to set new policies, to steer their day-to-day work, to decide where to allocate energy and resources, to justify their work, to get added resources. *And* they can use qualitative knowledge to illuminate their own worlds, explore other worlds, delight themselves, reconsider who they are, fight off boredom, or lull themselves to sleep. All legitimate.[1]

Epistemological Purity and Methodological Monism

A good deal of the paper is devoted to attacking "paradigmatic" (read logical positivist or realist) ways of knowing and to proposing a "narrative" (read idealist/phenomenological) epistemology as the One True Way.

Of course it's true that the traditional scientific research process is riddled with arbitrary decisions on all points: the object of study, how it is represented conceptually, which tools are used, and how measures or observations deriving from those tools are to be interpreted. How could it not be so? And it is legitimate for Barone to criticize the tendency to represent findings derived this way as "objective, impersonal, and formless" and offering "one verbal vision of reality, meant to be taken literally."

As several people (most recently, Michel Foucault) have pointed out, a professional field of study is actually a loosely associated collec-

---

1. Instrumental and aesthetic uses are not exhaustive categories. As Jennifer Greene (personal communication, 1988) reminded us, the evaluation utilization literature also invokes "enlightenment" or conceptual use, as well as "symbolic" (persuasive, political, mobilizing) use. Cf. Weiss (1988); Knorr (1977).

tion of communities of discourse—"speech communities" (Foucault, 1982). It's also fair to claim that the educational research community has been dominated by the scientific or pseudoscientific mode of discourse that Barone calls "paradigmatic."

At one classical epistemological extreme, there are causal realists or logical empiricists who believe that there is a truth out there to be uncovered—and that, once uncovered, it can be used cumulatively to predict future occurrences of the same phenomena (correspondence theory). At the other extreme are causal idealists, for whom all social reality is constructed arbitrarily, believing that no lawful statements can be made that are independent of individual cognition: We put the meaning into the data.

But this is a continuum, not a choice between two pure types. The choice made in the Barone paper feels like a sort of epistemological terrorism, which typically involves straw-manning the adversary, usually with little or no supporting evidence.

As we have said elsewhere (Miles & Huberman, 1984a), epistemological purity doesn't get research done. There are few working researchers at the extremes. The social phenomenological research derived from Husserl and Schutz has always contained some systematic, inferential procedures for determining lawful constructs, such as typification or reflexivity. And most major neopositivist methodologists (see Cook & Campbell, 1979; Cronbach, 1975) have shifted toward more perceptual, context-embedded, interpretive inquiry.

We, for example, subscribe to a middle-ground epistemology of causal realism that does not believe in correspondence theory but does posit lawful relationships among social phenomena—yet relationships that can be deeply affected by local history, different contexts, and the perspectives of the researcher (Huberman & Miles, 1985; cf. Manicas & Secord, 1982, on "transcendental realism").

The idealist position is that theory has no uses. There is no need to stand on the shoulders of analysts, observers, and conceptualists who have studied similar phenomena and, gradually, come to collective understandings. There's little acknowledgement that such understandings are likely to be more powerful (more illuminating, more differentiated, more parsimonious, more credible to a wider variety of judges using other angles of vision) than the analytical Lone Ranger who rides into a novel universe and generates insights.

Thus one problem with inquiry seen in Barone's terms is that it can generate a methodological community, but it cannot, by itself, advance understanding of a substantive issue. It needs other approaches, including the "paradigmatic" ones derided in the paper, to be of use to either practitioners or to the community of researchers in the field being critiqued. This is due, in part, to the norm for uniqueness of vision built into the approach itself by *its* community of discourse. But, at worst, isn't there a kind of *tabula rasa* arrogance in this approach, as if prior generations of analysts and local actors were essentially myopic fools?

The main point is that approaches to educational inquiry vary, and vary legitimately. Clandinin and Connelly (1984) suggest six major perspectives on inquiry into schooling: *analytic* (something like the paradigmatic approach denounced by Barone); *portrait* (description of a working whole, à la Lightfoot (1983); *intentional* (are goals being accomplished?); *structural* (what regularities and patterns exist, serving what functions?); *societal* (what correspondences and linkages do social values and school experience have?); and *narrative* (what happened historically, both personally and socially?) Whether one feels, as Clandinin and Connelly do, that such diversity should be maintained and pursued, or, as we do, that eclectic, ecumenical stances are preferable, there is clear agreement that efforts at epistemological monolithism (read imperialism), even though they may be directed at earlier monopolies, don't help. Perhaps it is unreasonable to ask for epistemological tolerance from people who feel their positions have not been tolerated, but . . .

Methodological monism tends to follow from adherence to a single best way of knowing. Construing qualitative inquiry as a choice between classical ethnography and naturalistic novel-writing is a travesty of the field. Here again, we are at the extremes, being told that one genre is vastly superior to the other. But even within classical ethnography we have virtually dozens of approaches (cf. Jacob, 1987; Tesch, 1987). Some are heavily theory-driven, others strongly "emic" or perceptual. There is "ethnoscience," and there is a wide range of phenomenological approaches with more and less structured forms of inquiry. And many working researchers use instruments that span the epistemological spectrum. Where, for example, do you put Spradley (1979), who is an ethnographer but uses some classic phenomenological devices? Or Glaser (1978)? Or Giorgi (1970, 1987), who comes out of the Husserl/Merleau-Ponty school, but whose research entails structured observations, diaries, *and* narratives?

When Oscar Lewis (1966) novelizes urban poverty in Mexico, he is trying for a way to represent and illuminate social determinisms that differs from the conventional ethnographic bag of tools. Both sorts of attempts complement one another, because both sets of methods allow the researcher to capture a social universe that illustrates—or revises—conceptual notions of the parameters and dynamics of that universe.

That is what multimethod research is all about: the use of a variety of descriptive and analytic tools, and the attempt to find their intersections. A naturalistic novel and a set of field notes relating to the same social universe yield different kinds of information in different ways, and, above all, make different claims about the universality of the approach used. Flaubert and Zola were explicit about the need to include in their naturalistic novels oversized characters, extreme situations, and unobserved events in order to depict more dramatically, more "theatrically," the social mechanisms lying beneath everyday life. (In this respect, by the way, they were positivists writing novels, just as, say, Norris and Dreiser in the United States or Fontane in Germany were.) An ethnographic field study makes other claims in light of the kinds of tools it uses.

So, being methodologically ecumenical, either within a study or across different intellectual work modes (including educational criticism), is likely to be more fruitful than being monolithic. As it turns out, most working researchers doing qualitative work *are* methodologically ecumenical, but they don't talk about it in their methods section in epistemological terms.

The Concept of Conspiracy

Though Barone aims for a "neutral" meaning of the "conspiracy" label ("a conversation about the relationship between present and future worlds"), it seems he does not fully succeed, getting trapped in the cuteness of the label and segueing quickly to the idea of a "plot against inadequate present conditions in favor of an emancipatory social arrangement in the future." We'd favor more direct language.

Constructivists taught us long ago that cognition is an invention, not a reproduction. We reassemble (construct) information taken from the outside world in ways that allow us to make personal sense of it. So, too, with reading text. That information also makes us RE-construct our mental frames—progressively, we fashion a more integrated and differentiated vision of the information. And when a community of constructing/reconstructing people interacts, there tends to be increasing uniformity in the ways they process the new information generated among them. They have built shared meanings.

When mainstream educational researchers want to reach colleagues, they employ a language and forms of discourse that make for easier sharing—notes, papers, articles. When these researchers try to reach a public of practitioners, they often shift to forms of discourse that reduce social distance, or are more congenial to practitioner styles of exchanging evidence about the truth and meaning of their work. So a researcher-practitioner project may entail fewer technical reports and more case study materials, anecdotal accounts, or face-to-face talks about observations made by researchers.

It's not clear in the Barone paper just who the "co-conspirators" are in educational criticism, and whether there is any real concern to reach them. It seems to us that anthologies of educational criticism are not easily assimilable by either the researcher or practitioner community. We found parts of this paper itself rather opaque and vague:

> Pure form is pure fancy. It is imagination roaming untethered in a nether realm, a world where the self can reside in solipsistic harmony, undisturbed by thoughts of the other.

> "Intentional sentence correlatives" . . . are component parts of the text, but as contributors to a fashioned totality their specific content is immediately qualified. . . . These pieces of aesthetically fashioned evidence [are labeled] "danda," to distinguish them from nonfictional "data." . . . To construe narrative meaning the reader must focus away from individual statements as claims of factuality and toward the insinuations in their interactions as correlatives.

What we miss in this paper and in other educational criticism is any sense of a convivial attempt to facilitate what Barone calls "breathing together" by moving to the form or level of discourse used by the reader. There is more than a little unconscious irony in the suggestion that educators will "relate more readily to texts composed in forms of language that eschew the parochial dialects of paradigmatic texts."

As a nonconvivial example, the language in Barone's (1983) study of a high school arts program is compelling, evocative, and expressive, but written in such a way as to render descriptions opaque, fluid, impressionistic. The reader has to do a good deal of filling in, that is, a heavy amount of textual re-creation. In some cases, the barrage of metaphors can be outright distracting: One senses the author horning into his own prose and calling out, "Look at this. Look at how beautifully I rendered that apparently banal rural school district, how I made a conventional educational setting into an archetype." Similar accounts by, say, John McPhee (1977) are equally distinctive and illuminating, without continuously pulling the reader back from the text to admire its artistry.

In other words, there's a danger of the qualitative narrative's lapsing into a gentle solipsism, a comfortably narcissistic exercise of celebrating (as in Barone's *Daedalus* piece) or damning (as in other anthologies of educational criticism) a variety of educational settings. And there is a risk of its doing so in a form of discourse that does not communicate easily, conceptually or practically, either to a community of researchers or practitioners. The reader is forced into an enormous amount of textual re-creation simply to enter into a minimally intelligible common frame of meaning.

We qualitative researchers working in a more "rigorous" vein of field research have often been reminded of Campbell and Stanley's admonitions about the "misplaced precision" attendant upon the non-experimental, nonrandomized designs that we chronically use in case study work. We represent, it seems, the worst of both worlds: looseness in experimental design where controls are called for, and rigorous models of analysis where, in the social anthropology community at least, softer and less codified modes are more typical.

Is educational criticism vulnerable to a similar charge, of "misplaced fiction"? Not fictional enough to profit from the full range of rhetorical devices for whose use poets and novelists have full license; not "valid" or "reliable" enough (in terms of conventional canons among the research community); not "useful" enough to practitioners seeking straightforward, often anecdotal prose to explicate their everyday settings and suggest guidance for good action? Who, Barone asks, will bless this sort of work? Who, indeed?

Truth, Validity, Verification, and the Like

Though Barone acknowledges that the "reader must cast a suspicious eye on all texts" and suggests that internal coherence is insufficient for judging truth ("Who, after all, seeks the advice of the schizophrenic, the lonely madman whose texts are so long on visions but so short on evidence?"), the paper is generally free of ideas on how, or even whether, to judge the closeness of linkage between a text and what happened. Of course, that is irrelevant for the novel.

But it is highly relevant for something called "inquiry," which purports to produce something beyond Mr. Dooley's "knowledge that ain't so." We have a right to ask whether things happened as they are painted (do statements fit observations?), whether conclusions were tested or strengthened rather than simply being asserted, whether another analyst would draw a reasonably similar picture given the same set of field notes, and whether the text is totally idiosyncratic or builds on prior knowledge about the same phenomena.

Are matters of truth and validity relevant to *use* of qualitative findings? Of course they are: Shaky or false results give wrong instrumental guidance, and they do not really "enlighten" but rather put noise in the user's conceptual reframing efforts. Furthermore, even where use is symbolic or political, the user wants information that has *credibility*, that will be convincing to various audiences.

To anyone who thinks that correspondence between text and events is a minor issue, we commend a reading of Clifford's (1988) article "The Historical Recovery of Edyth Astrid Ferris." With great care and coherence, she describes the career of an Iowa woman who received her M.A. in education in 1926. She also details with extreme specificity all the sources of evidence consulted, from newspaper accounts and college records to state archives. The story is coherent and well linked to historical developments in the developing educational research infrastructure. A good, illuminating text, in short. Then we learn in the last paragraph of the article that Edyth Astrid Ferris never existed. She is a fictional composite.

Clifford's intent was to illustrate historical methods, suggest how a "biographer might think about the meaning of life history data" (p. 4), and sensitize the reader to the unacknowledged role of women in educational research. Yet we find the article both infuriating (how easy it is for the reader to be manipulated by a text and its legitimating devices) and revealing (how dreadfully easy it is for the writer to be plausible, without connection to what actually happened).

We certainly are not reassured by Barone's complaint that "genre-related constraints against composite characters and invented dialogue have unduly restricted the process of truth-making," even though he acknowledges "a tension between my pledge to refer adequately to qualities located within the research setting and the enticements of novelistic modes of fiction."

A last point here: The many examples in the paper of the use of literary materials as sensitizing and training devices are unexceptionable, if hardly new on the educational scene. Why not? We need all the vividness we can get. But reading fiction, or writing it, is not the same thing as doing research, where we want to tell a *true* story, not just a vivid, "plausible," "coherent" one. Furthermore, as the Clifford piece illustrates, "interrogating the text" has terrible limits. The text by itself cannot inform us of just how it is connected to the events it purports to portray. We need methodological accounts; we need the possibility of an "audit trail" (Guba, 1981; Miles & Huberman, 1984b) more than we need a conspiracy. We want a workmanlike sense that the researcher was *there* and came back with something we can trust. We need some backstage information, not just the text.

The Importance of Methods

Barone says little about *how* a researcher proceeds to develop a "good" narrative. That omission is perfectly natural if we use the metaphor of the researcher as artist or appreciative critic. Yet, as the saying goes, God is in the details. Unless we can develop more of a tradition of making our methods explicit—most notably our procedures for analysis—it will keep on being hard to trust the results of qualitative inquiry, to have anything like cumulation of knowledge, or to "use" the results for coherent purposes.

Never mind the epistemological position from which that complaint is perceived to come. We are all in the business of producing something like valid, usable knowledge. Just how we get to that knowledge is of major interest.

Elsewhere (Miles & Huberman, 1984a, 1984b) we have stressed the importance of three interrelated aspects of qualitative data analysis:

1. *Data reduction*—selecting, focusing, simplifying, abstracting the raw data from field notes
2. *Data display*—arraying reduced data in a compressed, organized form
3. *Conclusion-drawing/verification*—drawing meaning from reduced, organized data in the form of regularities, patterns, explanations, and testing them for plausibility, robustness, sturdiness, and validity

Intuitive analysts use these processes—they are inescapable—but ordinarily leave them inexplicit and uncommunicated. Hence the problem of reader ("user") mistrust—which is sometimes handled by efforts to make the text "plausible," "undeniable," "coherent," "readable," and so forth. We believe that qualitative researchers are coming out of the closet in increasing numbers, making their implicit methods increasingly explicit. That's what we need.

In sum, our animadversions have been directed against monolithism and straw-manning, and our reflections have emphasized the importance of ecumenical, pragmatic approaches that lead to trustable information that can be used by people other than the researcher, for their own—or shared—purposes.

PAPER BY CHRISTOPHER CLARK

Now we turn to the Clark paper. This is a refreshing, disarming, upbeat piece: a pleasure to read and reread and to hand around to one's friends. But just because of these characteristics, it's a piece to look at with a more critical eye. What's going on here? Why do we feel seduced, disarmed, buoyant when we've finished it? Why do our critical faculties recede when they run into pieces written this way, this well, and containing this kind of message?

We want to discuss five questions that lingered on after our reading: (1) What kind of qualitative inquiry is this? (2) What happened that afternoon? (3) How did Clark come to know that it did? (4) What is "use," anyway? (5) What "ought" to happen, our normative advice?

What Kind of Qualitative Inquiry Do We Have Here?

One of the intersections between our work and that of the "educational criticism" community is that we share an interest in connoisseurship. We have taken the position in several places (Huberman & Miles, 1985; Miles & Huberman, 1984b) that qualitative research is an offshoot not only of ethnography and social phenomenology but also of analytic induction. One major school in that tradition is that of clinical and expert judgment. The idea is that people with highly differentiated and integrated schemata of the field they operate in and/or study will identify more meaningful and robust information, will process or "encode" it more efficiently, and will be less subject to distortion and bias. Much of the burgeoning literature on experts versus novices lends support to this view of things, although it's not yet certain that what "experts" DO with this information is necessarily more conclusive than what the rest of us less exalted mortals do.

But parts of this literature also show that "experts" can make some hair-raising errors of judgment and inference that standardized instruments or statistical/actuarial analyses manage to avoid. Essentially, these biases involve faulty heuristics for selecting information from a complex stimulus field (e.g., overreliance on vivid data), for judging the frequency and probability of an event (e.g., overdependence on cognitively "available" information), for classifying persons and objects (e.g., ignoring base-rate information), and for revising initial judgments (e.g., succumbing to an "anchoring" effect). Nisbett and Ross (1980) provide a good overview of this literature.

Often, the connoisseur or the ethnographer or the educational critic operates alone in the field. He or she devises the instruments, collects the data, analyzes the data, interprets the data—a one-person research project. Typically, there are few codified instruments in use; the field researcher IS the instrument. How *good* an instrument depends on the degree of "connoisseurship" and on the quality of protection against different kinds of bias, including self-delusion.

We have devoted a lot of space in our sourcebook (Miles & Huberman, 1984b) to this issue and have tried to devise ways of limiting the damage to the robustness of the data collected in the field. But remember that our heuristics are not premised on the notion that there is the truth of the Lord out there in the field waiting to be disclosed. Rather, we think there are more and less compelling accounts of social phenomena to be had and that the less-compelling ones are typically those riddled with the kinds of biases described above.

Clark is clearly a connoisseur of the learning process and of some of the more subtle socioemotional dimensions of school life, to the point where he sees gold where others—including Ms. Anderson—may only see dross. It's less clear that he's a connoisseur of the classroom as a social surround, day-to-day, so that he might be tempted to see more there than is actually going on.

What Happened That Afternoon?

Given the thinness of Clark's methodological description (to which we'll return), we are obliged to make a leap of faith, at least in this piece, that what Clark saw and inferred from what he saw was real rather than surreal. No problem here, but just let's be clear that we're in the leap-of-faith business in this case.

But how much of a leap of faith? Clark is a bit disingenuous. He talks in his title about "what you can learn from applesauce." But later he cheers us up some more by assuring us that "there was much, much more learned from applesauce" than what was apparent from the summary description of the activity.

And as the piece goes on, he slips fluidly to and from "anticipated learnings" and "intended learnings" to just plain "learnings." Is he telling us that these things happened? Or that the environment was fashioned deliberately so as to allow these learnings to occur, whether they did or not? Or that, from his perspective as a psychologist, this kind of interactive, materials-rich experience, coupled with a shot of spatial and linguistic formalization (the booklets), is bound to have multiple effects that are probably not measurable in the short term but, in a more structural sense, will contribute developmentally to cognitive, social, and conative growth? Possibly most to the last one, in the best Deweyan (and Piagetian) tradition.

But at several points he wants us to believe, as he does, that these learnings are "happening." And he sees a lot of evidence for that claim, although we don't know from the piece itself just HOW he knows that. As devil's advocate, we might object that he sees too much of one kind of evidence. What about nonlearning? What about distractions, or learning that stopped at the monosensory? What about social dominance in the groups? What about instances of task nonownership? Note that being a devil's advocate here is hard sledding; we come on as spoilers, cynics, nay-sayers, closet child-haters . . .

This is a clue that we're probably in a normative universe here, not a descriptive or even an analytical one. What happened in and around making applesauce is something we want to happen more in classrooms. And when it happened while we were pupils, teachers, teacher trainers, even researchers, we resonated to it and were only sad it happened so seldom. So that when we get an account such as this one, we produce the kind of feedback Clark describes in the second part of "Applesauce." We melt. We project achieved learnings on desired ones. If we're psychologists, we KNOW that this kind of activity, in this kind of environment, has the potential of a high payoff, cognitively speaking. We begin to fill in the blanks that might not warrant filling in if we were a more dispassionate, detached clinician (or possibly a wise old skeptical fox of a teacher) watching the same events from a greater observational distance. If we are educators, we hear the ring of truth in the vividness and immediacy of the account, and we may well suspend disbelief, forgetting that vividness and immediacy can be the single greatest source of bias for both the perceiver and the observer. It's probably the educator—as opposed to the social scientist—in us that vibrates, and that explains why we got into this game in the first place, rather than into the mainstream experimental or survey game. Deep down, we are meliorists first and researchers second.

How Did Clark Come to Know What He Did?

What we don't know is how he actually went about making and recording his observations that October afternoon. He was a "participant-observer," but how much deliberate or systematic observing did he do that afternoon? It sounds from the paper as if he had his hands full with the children, the booklets, the cutting boards, the knives, the apple peels, and, most of all, the delicious anticipation of getting a taste of what was in the pot. As the social perception literature keeps reminding us (cf., for a recent and powerful reminder, Gilbert, Jones, and Pelham, 1987), active perceivers can make inferential errors that passive observers avoid.

So, to respond to Clark's warm invitation ("So what do you think? How did this account connect with your background experiences? What uses might *you* make of it?"), we want to use the account as an occasion to ask about *methods*.

We don't know very much about the data collection: when it happened, in what form, with which devices. We don't even know what the data looked like or how they were stored (as is, in the form of raw notes, or transformed, annotated, or coded in some way?). And we don't know much more about the analysis, except that there was one and it was based on a "description." But how did Clark choose his *level* of description (a sort of thin, arm's-length account of procedures followed, with few episodes, vignettes, or direct quotes)? Or his tactics of analysis, which seem to have been (though we do not know) what we have called "subsuming particulars into the general" and "making conceptual/theoretical coherence"? Just how did he make the leap from his "data" to the metaconclusions that Ms. Anderson was so surprised and delighted with because "so much could be made of what was, for her, a relatively ordinary set of events"? We cannot dismiss the skeptical thought that some of the conclusions were emerging during the afternoon and that the description we see was partially fashioned to be congruent with them. But we do not know.

Did Clark make any effort to test or verify his conclusions? Did he check for effects of his own presence, do any internal contrasts, look for deviant cases among the children, consider rival explanations? Again we don't know. It doesn't seem as if there was much exchange on the spot or soon thereafter with Ms. Anderson, a likely source of corroboration or of additional insight. She is, after all, the local connoisseur. Presumably, she has had several cohorts of first- and second-graders and, through a process of trial and error refined through reflective abstracting, has evolved her own differentiated, integrated ideas of which learnings are likely to occur in which settings.

What Is "Use"?

There is a wide range of "use" types among the people to whom Clark sent the account. We counted sixteen grouped below according to the roles of the users:

Teachers/Teacher-Educators
- Increasing sense of legitimacy in one's activities; supporting, affirming (Ms. Anderson)
- Increasing reflection on and understanding of the difficulty in simultaneous action and reflection (teacher-educator)
- Teaching novices about the complexity of teaching/learning (teacher-educator)
- Providing exemplar of self-documentation for reflection by students or teachers (second teacher-educator, math teacher)
- Providing model of research in practice (department chair)

School Administrator
- Demonstrating to teachers that learning can take place outside the official curriculum; tacitly encouraging staff
- Adding to "local language of practice" (the applesauce concept)
- Promoting and defending teacher autonomy in curriculum decision making; justifying to next-level authorities

Researchers
- Nostalgically evoking past field work; supporting Clark
- Sharing current work; strengthening collegial ties
- Testing theory and revising design in another research project
- Shifting framework; self-questioning
- Connecting with prior belief in need for epistemological shift in educational research; "enlisting" Clark in this cause

Students/Civilians
- Enlarging concept of teaching (student)
- Reexperiencing intensity of teaching (former teacher)
- Picturing self in professional role; aiding career decision (former teacher)

Several remarks here. As with any inductively drawn conclusion, one risk is that of forcing. For example, Clark construes the first set (teachers/teacher-educators) as all having to do with "examples," when the first two items do not seem like that at all.

Another risk is missing types of use that exist conceptually or in alternative contexts. For example, our earlier advice to Clark was to get some "use" feedback from school administrators and "policy makers"; one might well expect new sorts of uses (and/or bewilderment about use) to appear. (The school administrator's uses in fact turned out to be quite different from those made by people in other roles.)

Perhaps more crucially, the social relationship of Clark as inquirer with his "use" respondents is probably a strong influence on conclusions. All were friends, relatives, or acquaintances. It is probably not a coincidence that one "use" outcome is increased friendship and interpersonal support. What would happen if Clark had consulted some strangers or some enemies of this sort of inquiry? Note that we—who are far from enemies—have now made a rather different sort of "use" of the paper: an occasion for the skeptical inquiry called for by the role of "discussant."

What "Ought" to Happen, Our Normative Bias?

In this paper, we can see both the real rewards and potential limits of qualitative inquiry. It's because Christopher Clark is who he is that he can identify sources of growth and stimulation in the classroom that many educational researchers wouldn't dream of looking for or that many teachers (such as Ms. Anderson) apparently have come to take for granted or aren't convinced about. Another educational "critic" of the same level of connoisseurship but wearing another pair of conceptual lenses would see something else. This is cause for celebration, in that each vision enriches and stretches our perception of the classroom. But before we get too heady, we should remind ourselves that this kind of inquiry may be noncumulative, in the conventional social scientific sense of that word. It may also be fundamentally private, in a more phenomenological sense, both for the inquirer and the reader.

If we want to encourage "use" of such knowledge in an instrumental way—for example, as a fulcrum to shift the ways that classroom environments are built—we are probably going to have to be much clearer about what kind of knowledge this is, how we came by it, why it is trustable, and whether someone else can take it into a different setting than the one we found it in. And as we have suggested, the same requirements are present for "enlightenment" and even "symbolic" uses.

Being clearer about these matters, it seems to us, is one of the best ways to connect this kind of inquiry to the kinds of research our nonqualitative colleagues have traditionally done. They need our work to enlarge their perception of what school learning is or can be; their work, as one of Clark's respondents says, is horribly undercomplicated. And we qualitative researchers can use some of their methodological toughness without its corrupting the quality of our insights. Such a connection, we would argue, is neither a sellout, a perversion, nor an epistemological impossibility.

With that connection, we can avoid straw-manning and sterile, defensive debate. Even better: We can increase the insightfulness we relish
in the best work produced within the educational research community.
That is what ought to happen, and that is what we are working for.

REFERENCES

Barone, T. (1983). Things of use and things of beauty: The Swain County High
   School Arts Program. *Daedalus, 112*, 1–28.
Clandinin, D. J., & Connelly, F. M. (1984). *Perspectives on inquiry into schooling.*
   University of Calgary and Ontario Institute for Studies in Education.
Clifford, G. J. (1988). The historical recovery of Edyth Astrid Ferris. *Educational
   Researcher, 17*, 4–7.
Cook, T. D., & Campbell, D. T. (1979). *Quasi-experimentation: Design and analysis
   issues for field settings.* Chicago: Rand McNally.
Cronbach, L. (1975). Beyond the two disciplines of scientific psychology. *Ameri-
   can Psychologist, 30*, 116–127.
Foucault, M. (1982). *The archaeology of knowledge.* London: Tavistock.
Gilbert, G., Jones, E., & Pelham, B. (1987). Influence and inference: What the
   active perceiver overlooks. *Journal of Personality and Social Psychology, 52*, 861–
   870.
Giorgi, A. (1970). *Psychology as a human science.* New York: Harper & Row.
Giorgi, A. (1987). *Phenomenology and psychological research.* Pittsburgh, PA: Du-
   quesne University Press.
Glaser, B. (1978). *Theoretical sensitivity.* Mill Valley, CA: Sociology Press.
Guba, E. (1981). Criteria for assessing the trustworthiness of naturalistic
   inquiries. *Educational Communication and Technology Journal, 29*, 75–92.
Huberman, A. M., & Miles, M. B. (1985). Assessing local causality in qualitative
   research. In D. N. Berg & K. K. Smith (Eds.), *Exploring clinical methods for social
   research* (pp. 351–382). Newbury Park, CA: Sage.
Jacob, E. (1987). Qualitative research traditions: A review. *Review of Educational
   Research, 57*, 1–50.
Knorr, K. D. (1977). Policymakers' use of social science knowledge: Symbolic or
   instrumental? In C. H. Weiss (Ed.), *Using social research in public policy making*
   (pp. 165–182). Lexington, MA: Lexington Books.
Lewis, O. (1966). *The children of Sanchez.* New York: Random House.
Lightfoot, S. (1983). *The good high school.* New York: Basic Books.
Manicas, P. T., & Secord, P. F. (1982). Implications for psychology of the new
   philosophy of science. *American Psychologist, 38*, 390–413.
McPhee, J. (1977). *Coming into the country.* New York: Farrar, Straus & Giroux.
Miles, M. B., & Huberman, A. M. (1984a). Drawing valid meaning from qualita-
   tive data: Toward a shared craft. *Educational Researcher, 13*, 12–30.
Miles, M. B., & Huberman, A. M. (1984b). *Qualitative data analysis: A sourcebook of
   new methods.* Newbury Park, CA: Sage.

Nisbett, R., & Ross, L. (1980). *Human inference: Strategies and shortcomings of social judgment.* Englewood Cliffs, NJ: Prentice-Hall.

Spradley, J. (1979). *The ethnographic interview.* New York: Holt, Rinehart and Winston.

Tesch, R. (1987, April). *Comparing the most widely used methods of qualitative research: What do they have in common?* Paper presented at the meeting of the American Educational Research Association, Washington, DC.

Tesch, R. (1988, April). *The impact of the computer on qualitative data analysis.* Paper presented at the meeting of the American Educational Research Association, New Orleans, LA.

Weiss, C. H. (1988). Evaluation for decisions: Is anybody there? Does anybody care? *Evaluation Practice, 9,* 5–19.

Response to the Commentary by Miles and Huberman

THOMAS E. BARONE

Miles and Huberman's critique prompts me to extend a metaphor. My critics appear as mates in a cell unable to clearly decipher the sounds emanating from an adjacent cubicle. Nevertheless, they respond. But the prison guards need not be overconcerned, for the exchange has fallen far short of conspiracy! Perhaps this was inevitable, since my respondents and I have indeed been professionally socialized into different "communities of discourse." Their unpacking of my message, therefore, itself begs to be unpacked, a task that will, given editorial constraints, require much concision.

Miles and Huberman's harshest accusations are ironic, for they concern monolithism and straw-manning, precisely the quality and ploy that I find in their response. Let me elaborate. There are characters inhabiting their critique. Living in and between its lines are heroes and a villain, representing, respectively, them and me. *They* are the magnanimous ecumenicals, sensible nonextremists who "subscribe to a middle-ground epistemology." I am the radical, the purist, the "epistemological terroris[t]" with a "*tabula rasa* arrogance," the narcissistic "analytical Lone Ranger." I, of course, find these characterizations unconvincing. Indeed, I do not even recognize several of the "unquestioned assumptions" supposedly undergirding my positions. I see them as the assumptions of a straw-man.

Take supposed assumption number two, concerning "'instrumental' knowledge . . . [as] *bad*." I did (necessarily) devote much space to an explication of how Bruner's two fundamental modes of inquiry guide the formation of research texts. But a careful reading reveals a strong indication of what I have elaborated upon more extensively elsewhere (Barone, 1987, 1988): the existence of a continuum, rather than a simplistic dichotomy, of educational research genres. These walls between us, I understand, are thick, but at several points in this present text I did indeed suggest that most qualitative texts (e.g., McLaren, 1986; the early educational ethnographies; my educational criticisms) are complex composites, exhibiting, I said, "curious mixtures" of narrative and paradigmatic design features. Each text would lie somewhere along the paradigmatic/narrative continuum. So Miles and Huberman's examples are welcomed, but still additional, illustrations of the richness and diversity of the modes by which texts of qualitative inquiry are fashioned.

My belief that the selection of an appropriate text from this array depends on the purposes of the reader is consonant with my epistemological views (supposed assumption number three). While not uncomfortable with much phenomenological writing, I usually feel most at home when reading epistemological pragmatists like Dewey and James and neopragmatists like Richard Rorty. For them, the extreme positions of the idealist and realist are untenable. Reality resides in the interactions between the knower and the known. Each simultaneously conditions the other. Moreover, what is true for the pragmatists is that which is, in a very broad sense, useful. What is useful will obviously vary in accordance with the user's purpose. When, therefore, one's question about a facet of schooling is technical in nature, one appropriately looks toward the paradigmatic end of the continuum. Indeed, the horizontal continuum may then become a vertical one, the familiar totem pole in which the "harder" scientific genres sit atop the "softer" artistic ones. But we should not confuse all of the activities of schooling with education. The latter, like teaching and curriculum making, is a fundamentally value-laden enterprise, a moral craft.[1] For purposes of educational decision making, therefore, the totem pole is reversed. Texts with narrative design features now tend to be more useful, especially literary texts offering a virtual world that encourages the reader to reflect upon and critique the one at hand.

Even when used for appropriate purposes, however, literary texts are hardly nonproblematic (supposed assumption number one). The last section of my paper contains a discussion of potential problems as readers confront this kind of text. One problem for Miles and Huberman is the notion of conspiracy. For once, their statement of an assumption (number four) is correct! I do indeed believe that the term *conspiracy* aptly describes the potential relationship between text and reader. Among literary critics the notion of a conversation between reader and text is by now a familiar one. To suggest a conspiratorial element is to highlight the moral and political dimensions of that conversation. But early on, Miles and Huberman complain that my

---

1. Other writers have discussed more fully the notion that moral commitments should support these activities. They include Freire (1973), Giroux (1983), Huebner (1975), Kerr (1981), Macdonald (1977), Peters (1965), Tom (1984), and Van Manen (1982).

advocacy of novelistic literature as a research genre "ignores the reality of qualitative studies" and "emphasizes the communication between author and reader via the text." For them, conspiracy occurs "somehow" between the fieldworker and himself, who is both author and reader. Later they claim, however, that "mainstream educational researchers" are better at doing precisely this: convivially facilitating "what Barone calls 'breathing together'" between researcher and practitioner. Why? Because mainstreamers' language is more "direct." I suggest that complaints of opacity and vagueness are most likely to be lodged by readers such as Miles and Huberman who harbor strong preferences for denotative, analytical forms of discourse, over the metaphorical, evocative, suggestive language of the novelist or literary critic. At any rate, I am content to let other readers who are overhearing this quasi-conversation between prisoners judge for themselves the degree of clarity in my own textual voice. I also invite readers to assess the degree to which my educational criticism cited (Barone, 1983) communicates easily. But I find both their comments about that piece and their discussion of educational criticism generally to be highly gratuitous. I mention educational criticism briefly, only once, in the last section of my paper, clearly focusing instead on novelistic forms of literature. Nevertheless, Miles and Huberman manage to misconstrue my concerns about the need for enlightenment within the established research community regarding the potential of serious educational fiction as worries about the future of educational criticism. But I would suggest that the latter form of inquiry has already made its way into the church, even if usually forced to sit in a back pew. My attempt at truth-making here was aimed toward an act of legitimation that formalist aestheticians and positivist epistemologists may find truly outrageous, namely, the blessing of the former.

Are the "good guys" in the Miles and Huberman melodrama ready to bestow their blessings? Early on, in their espousal of multimethod research, the critics adopt a stance of benign catholicity, even accepting the naturalistic novel as a vehicle for depicting "the social mechanisms lying beneath everyday life." The reader is left unprepared for the drastic qualification to come later in a discussion of supposed assumptions five and six. There Miles and Huberman repudiate literature as a legitimate form of qualitative inquiry in its own right. Their objections, it turns out, are the tired, usual ones. Real researchers, they contend, do what novelists cannot (presumably, not even supposedly "positivist" ones such as Flaubert, Norris, and Dreiser). They speak the literal truth, provide the valid, verifiable kind of text that is above interrogation. Novelists, on the other hand, offer no final account of "*what actually happened"* (emphasis added). Moreover, they do not explicate their methods. One must conclude, therefore, that we can learn nothing from, say, a *Grapes of Wrath*, for it contains no array of "reduced data in a compressed, organized form." (Of course, I would contend that Steinbeck [1939] offers the reader trustworthy aesthetic content, new meaning to be shared, in a form that is magnificently organized and so "reduced" and "compressed" that nary a superfluous sentence is to be found.) Melville (1851/1967), another methodological Lone Ranger, would seem to fail us in his omission of "backstage information." Where is the possibility of an "audit trail" to reassure us of the verifiability of those intricate details of the whaling industry?

Novelists, as inquirers into the human condition, have long found it pointless to explicate their methods. And if current literary figures such as Updike and Mitchell are therefore still in my two critics' imagined closet, they might stumble upon none other than Miles and Huberman, presumably *temporary* occupants, dressed up like "intuitive analysts" rather than "real researchers" while composing this present critique. Performing much like literary critics, they have here left their analytical processes "uncommunicated." Does it follow that readers will find the content of their critique less than trustworthy and hard "to 'use' . . . for coherent purposes"? Or are Miles and Huberman, like other qualitative inquirers, aiming here for plausibility, striving to persuade readers to view a set of phenomena as they, after careful observation and reflection, view it?

Still, Miles and Huberman expect that, when costumed as *real* researchers, we establish clear "correspondence between text and event" and so arrive at a standardized, conventional account of reality that *is* the truth. But any such account is, of course, merely another version of events, one fashioned in accordance with the methods *valued* by the researcher. These values adhere to the perspective of the researcher and, as Miles and Huberman admit (at least at one point), "deeply affect" relationships among social phenomena. While Miles and Huberman believe that methods should be explicated, they see them as value-neutral. They are, therefore, blind to the values, interests, and, yes, the idea of educational virtue implicated in the design and use of their own research tools. Indeed, engaging in introspection about the personal interests and motivations (such as countervailing psychological needs for certainty and risk taking) that undergird one's methodological preferences may be seen as an act of narcissism, and so to be avoided, rather than as the potentially enlightening exercise that it can be.

So it is self-deluding to claim that one's preference for systematic, analytical methods is beyond the realm of preference and that those methods therefore yield findings beyond the realm of "mere" plausibility and coherence. Only when we finally see that, as Gouldner (1982) aptly put it, "methodology *is* ideology" (p. 343; emphasis added) can we begin to critique the nature of the educational vision implicit in a research text. Indeed, only as we promote a mind-set that enables readers with *educational* purposes in mind to view qualitative texts as fictional (i.e., fashioned) will we more fully honor the fragile, tentative, even ambiguous nature of the meanings to be gleaned from our value-saturated stories. We thereby enhance the possibility that readers will be afforded the very luxury of textual dismantling that Miles and Huberman have afforded themselves as they place their own vision of methodological virtue up against mine.

Or else we continue to attempt to sell those readers that which is useful only technically: texts containing facts apparently unadulterated by values and data seemingly uninformed by a vision of what is educationally significant. Such texts falsely promise nuggets of truth that are as unconditional and final, as hard, solid, and impenetrable as, well, pieces of a monolith. And monolithism is the very tendency that I thought I heard being deplored by the voices in the cubicle next to mine.

REFERENCES

Barone, T. (1983). Things of use and things of beauty: The Swain County High School Arts Program. *Daedalus, 112*(3), 1–28.

Barone, T. (1987). Research out of the shadows: A reply to Rist. *Curriculum Inquiry, 17*(4), 453–463.

Barone, T. (1988). Curriculum platforms and literature. In L. Beyer & M. Apple (Eds.), *The curriculum: Problems, politics, possibilities* (pp. 140–165). Albany: State University of New York Press.

Freire, P. (1973). *Education for critical consciousness.* New York: Seabury.

Giroux, H. A. (1983). *Theory and resistance in education: A pedagogy for the opposition.* South Hadley, MA: Bergin & Garvey.

Gouldner, A. (1982). Sociology: Contradictions and infrastructure. In E. Bredo & W. Feinberg (Eds.), *Knowledge and values in social and educational research* (pp. 324–354). Philadelphia, PA: Temple University Press.

Huebner, D. (1975). Poetry and power: The politics of curricular development. In W. F. Pinar (Ed.), *Curriculum theorizing: The reconceptualists* (pp. 271–280). Berkeley, CA: McCutchan.

Kerr, D. H. (1981). The structure of quality in teaching. In J. F. Soltis (Ed.), *Philosophy and education.* Chicago: University of Chicago Press.

Macdonald, J. B. (1977). Value bases and issues for curriculum. In A. Molnar &
    J. A. Zahorik (Eds.), *Curriculum theory* (pp. 92–107). Washington, DC: Asso-
    ciation for Supervision and Curriculum Development.
McLaren, P. (1986). *Schooling as a ritual performance.* London: Routledge and Kegan
    Paul.
Melville, H. (1967). *Moby Dick: Or the whale.* New York: Bantam. (Original work
    published 1851)
Peters, R. S. (1965). Education as initiation. In R. D. Archambault (Ed.), *Philoso-
    phical analysis and education* (pp. 7–48). London: Routledge and Kegan Paul.
Steinbeck, J. (1939). *The grapes of wrath.* New York: Viking Press.
Tom, A. R. (1984). *Teaching as a moral craft.* New York: Longman.
Van Manen, M. (1982). Edifying theory: Serving the good. *Theory into Practice,*
    21(1), 44–49.

CLOSING COMMENTS ON A CONTINUING DEBATE

ELLIOT W. EISNER and ALAN PESHKIN

It should be clear that the issues addressed in the previous pages have had no short history. It should be equally apparent that the prospects for reconciling different beliefs about the conduct of educational research are not high. Even among scholars who are sympathetic and experienced in qualitative inquiry, important disagreements exist: Witness the views of Thomas Barone as contrasted with those of Matthew Miles and Michael Huberman or those of D. C. Phillips and Egon Guba. From our perspective, such contrasts contribute to the intellectual vitality that a growing form of research needs. What would be unfortunate is a premature codification of "the right way to do qualitative work." Professors and students are tempted—all too tempted—to locate, or better yet, to formulate canons of methods that will give them handles for guiding and appraising qualitative research. We find it seductively reassuring to know the rules. They comfort the novice, add legitimacy to the work of the experienced scholar, give everyone the sense that things are known and in order. After all, rules embody standards and standards define the criteria for both consensus and quality.

We believe that all forms of inquiry, but particularly qualitative inquiry, necessitate openness to make its practice viable, that is to say, to make it capable of growth. For example, there is no reason, at least in our minds, why in the future the academy might not accept Ph.D. dissertations in education that are written in the form of novels. We know that there is likely to be considerable resistance to the idea that novelistic accounts of human affairs can yield knowledge of the type that one can trust. Yet we hasten to remind readers that for centuries novels have helped people more sensitively and insightfully understand the world in which they and others live. It is our current methodological traditions in education and the social sciences that leave us uncomfortable with a form of inquiry that yields products we regard as fiction. Fiction, we are taught to believe, is the antithesis of truth.

Our point here is not to push the novel but to make it clear that what we consider legitimate research procedure is a product of our judgment and our judgment is influenced by our professional socialization. One of the most exciting aspects of the current debate is the willingness to explore methodological issues that, inevitably, lead to epistemological ones: Can fiction be true? Can generalizations be drawn from case studies? Must knowledge be limited to claims about the world? We believe that the papers, commentaries, and responses to matters of validity, generalization, objectivity, ethics, and the like, which constitute the major substantive categories of this volume, exemplify the vitality that exists in the field. We see virtue in the disagreements that stimulated rejoinders; we see promise in the divergent perspectives on the same general point. Disagreement and divergence testify to the openness that serves well the cause of increasing understanding.

We hasten to add that our receptivity toward openness does not lead us to believe that nihilism is acceptable, that anything goes, or that solipsism must reign. We have not given up either human rationality or informed judgment as a basis for assessing our own work or the work that others in our field create. What we argue is that the way we do educational research ought not be restricted to a few traditional, institutionalized procedures and, moreover, that a willingness to explore the possibilities of forms of inquiry that typically do not appear in the conduct of educational research is precisely what creative scholarship requires.

Although most of the chapters in this volume relate directly to educational research, it is very important to note that qualitative inquiry is in no way limited to the conduct of research. Qualitative inquiry is exercised in all forms of human activity, in the creation of salads and symphonies, in the design of schools and sanctuaries. The art of teaching, at its best, exemplifies the use of what John Dewey referred to as qualitative thought. The fine-grained adjustments that good teachers make in speaking to individual children, their vision of options that can be pursued in a classroom, their assessment of levels of student interest and motivation, and their appraisal of student comportment as well as their written and verbal expression—all require the use of qualitative thought.

It would be unfortunate if qualitative inquiry were restricted to the conduct of research in education, regardless of how broadly research practices were conceptualized. Qualitative inquiry pervades human life, and qualitative thought is a requirement for maintaining one's humanity.

This volume provides a picture of the current debate as it unfolds among some of the nation's leading educational scholars. It seems to us that while their work advances the conversation, it does not close it. Indeed, the proper contribution of this volume is to open the issues even further. We believe that it is in the exploration of new possibilities and the development of an appetite for such exploration that educational life becomes more promising—and interesting, as well. We believe this volume contributes to that end.

The newest frontier, perhaps, is the study of the qualitative judgments that teachers and students make in the classroom. How do teachers and students fine-tune their interactions? How do teachers keep classroom momentum moving forward? How do children know just how hard to push their teacher or their friends? The rendering of classroom life may very well require forms of inquiry that make use not only of literary description but also of film media. Film, arguably the most interesting and far-reaching invention of the twentieth century, has barely been explored in education. It, too, provides a new sea upon which researchers and evaluators might sail.

Under the best of circumstances, our readers will find challenges both in works they find cogent and lucid and in those they find cloudy and incomplete. It is relatively easy to find value in that which is understood sufficiently well to be articulated with ease. Though less easy, there also may be occasion for useful provocation in thinking that is incipient and whose ready articulation is elusive. A salient need of qualitative inquiry, as we see it, is to keep the debate hot and continuous, so that our conventions avoid canonization, so that we avoid settling into standardized procedures. To be sure, inquiry continues in the meantime; it is not on hold awaiting the settling of the dust of discourse. It should incorporate the best of what we know from within—and from across—the several traditions of qualitative research that already have emerged, traditions that are variously known as connoisseurship, constructivism, critical theory, ethnography, phenomenology, and others. But we suggest that appraising the products of our scholarly effort should be not in the spirit of "This is it," but rather, in that of "What have we here?" and "If this, then what possibilities are next?" We look for intellectual ferment because we see it as an indicator of seeking and of concomitant growth in our capacity to conceptualize, investigate, conduct, draw meaning from, and present our studies. The intent of all this, lest we forget, is to enhance what we do in our scholarly pursuits, so that, in turn, we can enhance the educational process. In the end the differences we seek to make are located in schools, those social institutions in which children and adolescents spend so much of their lives.

ABOUT THE EDITORS
AND THE CONTRIBUTORS

INDEX

About the Editors
and the Contributors

ELLIOT W. EISNER is Professor of Education and Art at Stanford University. His major interests focus upon the educational uses of the arts in their own right and in the study of educational practice.

ALAN PESHKIN is Professor of Education at the University of Illinois in Urbana. His interest in qualitative inquiry has been directed to a series of ethnographic-type studies on the school-community relationship in different settings, including rural, fundamentalist Christian, and most recently, multiethnic. In regards to qualitative methodology, he has explored the issues of subjectivity.

MICHAEL W. APPLE is Professor of Curriculum and Instruction and Educational Policy Studies at the University of Wisconsin–Madison. He has written extensively about the relationship between education and the structures of inequality in the larger society. Among his books are *Ideology and Curriculum* (1979), *Education and Power* (1982), *Ideology and Practice in Schooling* (1983), and *Teachers and Texts* (1986).

THOMAS E. BARONE received his doctorate from Stanford University in 1978. His publications reveal an interest in emancipatory educational theory for curriculum concerns. He has writen about and experimented with a variety of literary-style inquiry modes, including critical biography, forms of "new journalism," novelistic storytelling, as well as educational criticism. Barone is Associate Professor and Director of Secondary Education Programs at Northern Kentucky University.

HOWARD S. BECKER worked as a researcher at Community Studies, Inc. (Kansas City), 1955–1962, and at the Center for the Study of Human Problems, Stanford University, 1962–1965. He has been Professor of Sociology at Northwestern University since 1965 and became MacArthur Professor of Arts and Sciences there in 1982. In addition, he is Research Associate at the Center for Urban Affairs and Policy Research at Northwestern. His most recent major books are *Sociological Work: Method and Substance* (1970), *Art Worlds* (1986), and *Doing Things Together* (1986).

CHRISTOPHER M. CLARK is Professor of Education at Michigan State University, where he has taught educational psychology and done research on teaching since 1976. His graduate education at Stanford spanned the years 1970–1976, during which time he worked as a research assistant in the Stanford Program on Teaching Effectiveness. Prior to that he was a submarine officer in the United States Navy. Dr. Clark's research interests include teacher planning and decision making, the teaching of writing, and the relationship between research and the practice of teaching and teacher education.

ROBERT DONMOYER is Associate Professor at the Ohio State University. His areas of specialization include research utilization in policy making and practice, curriculum theory, instructional leadership, and qualitative research methods. Among his publications are "The Rescue from Relativism: Two Failed Attempts and an Alternative Strategy" in the December 1975 issue of the *Educational Researcher* and "The Principal as Prime Mover" in the summer 1983 issue of *Daedalus*.

MADELEINE R. GRUMET is Professor of Education and Dean of the School of Education of Brooklyn College, City University of New York. She is a curriculum theorist who brings phenomenological, psychoanalytic, literary, and feminist studies to research in education. Her book *Bitter Milk: Women and Teaching* (1989) is a study of the relation of our reproductive projects to epistemology, curriculum, and pedagogy.

EGON G. GUBA is Professor of Education at Indiana University, a position he has held since 1966. Following a twelve-year period as an administrator (Director of the Bureau of Educational Research and Service at Ohio State and Associate Dean for Academic Affairs, School of Education, Indiana University), he returned to teaching at Indiana only to find that his earlier commitment to positivism had been severely shaken. An invitation to be visiting scholar at the UCLA Center for the Study of Evaluation during the summer of 1977 provided the opportunity to clarify his mind and feelings with respect to paradigms. With Yvonna S. Lincoln, he has written a variety of papers and two books, *Effective Evaluation: Improving the Usefulness of Evaluation Through Responsive, Naturalistic Approaches* (1981) and *Naturalistic Inquiry* (1985). A third book, *Fourth Generation Evaluation*, is well along.

A. MICHAEL HUBERMAN is Professor of Education on the Faculty of Psychologie et des Sciences de l'Education, University of Geneva, Switzerland. He has been there since 1970, after having spent one to two years on research on adult cognition. Along the way, he has maintained that interest (*Adult Learning and Instruction from a Life Cycle Perspective*, 1971; *Cycle de Vie et Formation*, 1974) and expanded it to longitudinal studies of adulthood, notably in the teaching profession (*La Vie des Enseignants*,

1989). Huberman is conducting studies on research utilization and on "nonbehaviorist" versions of mastery learning.

PHILIP W. JACKSON is the David Lee Shillinglaw Distinguished Service Professor in the Departments of Education and Behavioral Science at the University of Chicago, where he is also Director of the Benton Center for Curriculum and Instruction. He has a Ph.D. from Columbia University and is a member of the National Academy of Education. His research interests focus on teaching. They include both empirical and conceptual studies. He is the author of *Life in Classrooms* (1968) and coauthor (with J. W. Getzels) of *Creativity and Intelligence* (1962). His most recent book is entitled *The Practice of Teaching* (1986).

YVONNA S. LINCOLN is Associate Professor of Education at Peabody College, Vanderbilt University. Prior to coming to Vanderbilt, she was on the faculties of Stephens College, Indiana University, and the University of Kansas. She is president of the American Evaluation Association. Besides numerous articles and conference presentations, she is the coauthor (with Egon G. Guba) of *Effective Evaluation: Improving the Usefulness of Evaluation Through Responsive, Naturalistic Approaches* (1981) and *Naturalistic Inquiry* (1985) and the editor of *Organization Theory and Inquiry: The Paradigm Revolution*.

MATTHEW B. MILES, a social psychologist, has been Senior Research Associate at the Center for Policy Research, New York, since 1970. Before that he was Professor of Psychology and Education at Teachers College, Columbia University. He has had a pervasive fascination with the field of planned change in education for more than thirty years. His long-term collaboration with A. Michael Huberman led to *Innovation Up Close*, twelve case studies of the implementation of NDN and Title IV-C innovations (1984); that experience underlies their discussant remarks. A comparative interest in school changes led to *Making School Improvement Work* (1985) and *Lasting School Improvement* (1987), compilations of knowledge about school change from fourteen countries.

D. C. PHILLIPS is Professor of Education and Philosophy at Stanford University. He is author or coauthor of *Theories, Values, and Education* (1971), *Holistic Thought in Social Science* (1976), *From Locke to Spock* (1976), *Perspectives on Learning* (1985), *Visions of Childhood* (1986), and *Philosophy, Science, and Social Inquiry Toward Reform of Program Evaluation* (1980), and he has authored numerous journal articles. He is on the review board of several journals and is North American editor for the international journal *Educational Philosophy and Theory*. He is coeditor of a new book series in Philosophy and Education for Reidel Publishing.

LESLIE G. ROMAN is an Assistant Professor in the Department of Curriculum and Instruction at Louisiana State University in Baton

Rouge, where she teaches graduate courses in critical ethnography, feminist theory, and sociology of the curriculum. She recently completed her doctorate in the sociology of education at the Department of Educational Policy Studies, the University of Wisconsin–Madison. She is the coeditor of *Becoming Feminine: The Politics of Popular Culture* (1989).

JANET WARD SCHOFIELD is Professor of Psychology at the University of Pittsburgh and a senior scientist at the Learning Research and Development Center. She has also served as a research psychologist at the National Institute of Education and the Office of Economic Opportunity and as a member of the psychology and sociology department at Spelman College. Dr. Schofield has published extensively on topics ranging from race relations to adolescent contraceptive behavior to research methodology. Her book *Black and White in School: Trust, Tension or Tolerance?* (1982/1989), which takes an ethnographic approach to the study of social relations in a newly desegregated middle school, received the Gordon Allport Intergroup Relations Prize from the Society for the Psychological Study of Social Issues.

LOUIS M. SMITH is Professor of Education at Washington University. He received his A.B. from Oberlin College (1953) and Ph.D. from the University of Minnesota in 1955. His major publications include *Educational Psychology* (with Bruce B. Hudgins, 1964), *The Complexities of an Urban Classroom* (with William Geoffrey, 1968), *Anatomy of Educational Innovation* (with Pat M. Koth, 1971), and the Kingston Revisited Trilogy (with several coauthors): *Educational Innovations: Then and Now* (1986), *The Fate of an Innovative School* (1987), and *Innovation and Change in Schooling: History, Politics and Agency* (1988).

JONAS F. SOLTIS is the William Heard Kilpatrick Professor of Philosophy and Education at Teachers College, Columbia University. In 1984 he accepted the editorship of the *Teachers College Record*, a quarterly journal of scholarship, opinion, analysis, and debate, which has continuously published since 1900 and is one of the most respected journals in the field of education. He has written numerous articles and books, including *An Introduction to the Analysis of Educational Concepts* (1985) and with Barry Chazan *Moral Education* (1973). After serving as president of the Philosophy of Education Society in 1976, he was chosen to be editor of the 80th Yearbook of the National Society for the Study of Education, *Philosophy and Education* (1981), which was the first NSSE volume since 1955 devoted to surveying the field of philosophy of education. He was elected president of the John Dewey Society for 1990–1991.

HARRY F. WOLCOTT is Professor of Education and Anthropology at the University of Oregon, a past president of the Council on Anthropology and Education, a former editor of the *Anthropology and Education*

Quarterly, a fellow of the Society for Applied Anthropology and the American Anthropological Association, and an active contributor to qualitative interests in the American Educational Research Association. His special interests within the broad field of anthropology and education include ethnographic research and cultural acquisition. His two well-known monographs that first appeared in the Case Studies in Education and Culture series edited by George and Louise Spindler, *A Kwakiutl Village and School* and *The Man in the Principal's Office: An Ethnography*, were recently republished by Waveland Press.

Index

Page numbers followed by *n* indicate footnotes and endnotes.

Accommodation, 190–191, 196–197
Accuracy, in research, 132–135
Administrative Science Quarterly, 4
Affect-laden knowledge, 189–190
African Beer Gardens of Bulawayo, The
(Wolcott), 135
Agar, M. H., 67*n*
Aggleton, P. J., 48–49
Allender, J. S., 315
Allport, Gordon W., 218
American Anthropological Association
(AAA), 252, 260
American Educational Research
Association (AERA), 3–6, 260, 264
American Educational Research Journal, 3
American Psychological Association
(APA), 252, 260, 264
American Sociological Association (ASA),
252
Amir, Y., 218
Andraea, Johann Valentin, 308
Andrews S. D., 4
Anonymity, 260, 262, 264–268, 271, 272,
279–280
Anthropology, 1, 4–6, 13, 138, 320
Anthropology and Education Quarterly, 5, 6, 138
Anyon, J., 320, 321
Apple, Michael W., 15–16, 38–73, 74, 77,
81–86, 88–90
Aronson, E., 218
Assimilation, 190–191, 196–197
Atkinson, P., 46–48, 51–52, 67*n*
Atwell, W., 102

Balance, in research, 133–134
Bandelier, A., 320

Barone, Thomas E., 12, 195, 301–303,
305–326, 339–349, 358–363, 365
Barrett, M., 55, 57, 58
Barthes, R., 313, 317
Bass, A. T., 324*n*
Becker, H. J., 214
Becker, Howard S., 122, 148, 150*n*, 173,
219, 233–242, 263, 267
Bensman, J., 122
Berg, B. L., 202
Berkeley, George, 21
Berlin, Isaiah, 189, 190
Bernard, H. R., 130, 150*n*
Bernard, J., 56
Bernstein, B., 42, 45
Bernstein, Richard, 116–117
Biases, 253
Bickel, W. E., 213
Biklen, S. K., 210, 219
Blumer, H., 180, 181, 188, 235
Bly, R., 107, 119*n*
Bogdan, R. C., 210, 219
Bolgar, H., 203
Boolean algebra, 207, 224
Bossert, S. T., 218
Bourdieu, P., 45
Bowen, E. S., 320
Bowles, S., 42
Brahe, Tycho, 26
Brewer, M. B., 88
Brinberg, D., 123, 126
Bronfenbrenner, U., 178
Brown, Roger, 124
Brown v. Board of Education, 218
Bruner, J., 188, 305, 306, 358
Buber, M., 179

Buchmann, M., 316
Bullough, E., 308

Campbell, Donald T., 7, 87, 88, 123, 201,
   205-206, 289, 318, 343, 347
Campbell, J., 176
Capote, Truman, 309
Carloye, J., 183
Case studies
   advantages of, 192-197
   aggregation of, 212-214, 222-224
   in elementary school qualitative
      research, 302, 327-338, 350-356
   generalizability and, 182, 183, 186-198,
      203, 205-206
   meta-analysis of, 206-207, 221-226
   multisite, 212-214, 222-223
   schema theory and, 192, 194
   See also Qualitative research
Case Studies in Science Education (Stake and
   Easley), 269-270
Case survey method, 207, 222-224, 227
Categorical imperative, 291-293
Cavell, Stanley, 165
CEMREL, Inc., 266-268
Cervantes, Miguel de, 320
Change, research on, 214-217, 249
Charters, Sandy, 124
Chekhov, Anton, 308
Chodorow, N., 117, 119n
Christian-Smith, L. C., 67n
Clandinin, D. J., 12, 344
Clark, Christopher M., 106, 301-303,
   327-338, 339, 350-356
Classical utopias, 308
Clifford, G. J., 348
Clifford, J., 66n
Cohn, M., 259
Coleridge, Samuel Taylor, 165
Collins, B. E., 88
Collins, T., 225, 226
Committed relativism, 264, 275, 287-288
Comparability, 208
Complexities of an Urban Classroom, The
   (Smith and Geoffrey), 12, 260-263,
   318
Complexity, and generalizability,
   177-179, 181-183
Computers, 214-217
Concrete utopias, 311

Conditions, site selection based on, 218
Confidentiality, 250-253, 278-280
Conklin, H., 175
Connelly, F. M., 12, 344
Consensual validation, 29-30, 75-77, 90,
   93
Consent, informed, 260, 264-268,
   272-273, 286
Consistency, in research, 134-135
Conspiracy, in literature, 313-314,
   318-323, 345-347
Constructivism, 89-90, 281-282
Contamination, 280
Contemporary Ethnography, 4
Context of discovery, 33-34, 77-78
Context of justification, 33-34, 77-78
Contract obligations, 253-254, 281
Control groups, 253
Cook, A., 308
Cook, S. W., 218
Cook, T. D., 87, 205, 343
Correspondence theory of truth, 24-25,
   97
Cowan, P., 190
Coward, Rosalind, 56, 57
Crandall, D. P., 212
Critical Hermeneutics (Thompson), 117, 118
Criticism, 30-31, 78-79, 249, 254-255,
   279, 282, 283
Cronbach, Lee J., 7, 123-124, 148,
   177-179, 204, 205, 208, 209, 215, 343
Culturalist tradition, 42, 45
Culture, generalizability and, 177-179

Dabbs, J. M., Jr., 4-5
Dean, J., 130
Deception, 251-252, 280, 292
Decision making
   career, 337
   in teaching process, 106
Defensiveness, case studies and, 196-197
Democratic liberalism, 274-275, 287
Dentan, R., 67n
Denzin, N. K., 202
Descartes, René, 21, 106, 119n
Description, 249, 251-252, 279-280, 283
Desegregation, 217-221, 225, 271-272
Dewey, John, 117, 179, 306-307, 359, 366
Dialectic, 90
Dialogue, 90, 271-273, 286

Diamond, J., 293
Dickens, Charles, 309, 321
Dictionary of Philosophy and Religion (Reese), 291–292
Differentiation, 190–191
Dilthey, W., 185
Discipline and Punish (Foucault), 167
Discovery, context of, 33–34, 77–78
Dobbert, M. L., 121, 123, 202, 214
Doing the Ethnography of Schooling (Spindler), 125
Donmoyer, Robert, 171–173, 175–200, 235, 238
Double-blind experiments, 219
Dray, W., 196
Dreiser, Theodore, 345, 360
Dunne, Faith, 5
Dwyer, D. C., 218, 264, 268–270

Easley, J., 269–270
Ecker, D., 324n
Educational Researcher, 4
Edwards, A. D., 47
Eggan, D., 186, 192, 193
Ego development, 103, 119
Einstein, Albert, 24, 177
Eisner, Elliot, 1–14, 19–20, 24–25, 29, 30, 32, 74, 92, 195, 248, 365–368
Elementary school studies, 302, 327–328, 350–356
Elliott, J., 258
Emerson, Ralph Waldo, 165
Empiricism, 21
Epistemology, 86, 90, 104–106, 168–169
   nonfoundationalist, 21–25, 76
   purity of, 342–344
   traditional, 21
Erickson, Fred, 6, 133, 136
Erosion of Childhood, The (Suransky), 195
Ethics, 243–299
   in Case Studies in Science Education project, 269–270
   in CEMREL experience, 266–268
   critical research and, 254–255
   descriptive research and, 251–252
   educational research and, 41–43, 49
   evaluative research and, 252–254
   in Federal Policy in Action project, 268–269
   interventionist research and, 254
   in Kensington School projects, 263–266, 270–272
   perspective and, 250–251
   principles of, 272–275, 286–288, 296–299
   professional codes of, 252, 260, 264
   in study of educational innovation, 263–266, 270–272
   teaching and, 255–256
   in urban classroom study, 260–263
Ethics of Teaching, The (Strike and Soltis), 247
Ethnographic research. See Qualitative research
Ethnography, 4–6, 12–13, 125, 214
   as evaluation, 204–205
   function of, 98
   meta-, 206, 224–227
   See also Feminist materialist ethnography; Naturalistic ethnography
Ethnography and Qualitative Design in Educational Research (Goetz and LeCompte), 125
Evaluation, 184–185, 249, 252–254, 279, 281, 283
   summative, 204–205
Evans-Rhodes, D., 215
Everhart, R., 66n
External validity, 123, 201–204, 206

Fairness, 252–253
Farrar, Kathy, 108–119, 158–160, 169
Faulkner, R. R., 4–5
Federal Policy in Action (Smith and Dwyer), 268–269
Feedback, in research, 129, 132–133, 155, 271–273, 332–337, 353–355
Feigenbaum, E. A., 215
Feinberg, S., 183–184
Feminism and Methodology (Harding, ed.), 55
Feminist materialist ethnography, 42–43, 52–64, 83–85, 88–90
   implications of forms of feminism for, 55–59
   implications of materialism for, 53–55
   social transformation and, 59–63
   theoretical and political adequacy of, 63–64
Fetterman, D. M., 204, 249, 282

Feyerabend, Paul, 21, 32
Field, W. C., 156
Fielding, Henry, 308
Filstead, W. J., 205
Finn, C., 318
Firestone, W. A., 204, 212, 213, 290
First impressions, 113–115, 129
Fittingness, 207
Flaubert, Gustave, 345, 360
Follesdal, D., 35
Ford, Joseph, 79
Formative evaluations, 204–205
Foucault, Michel, 167, 342, 343
Francis, W. D., 220
Freeman, L. C., 130
Freire, P., 104, 116, 119n, 179, 321,
    359n
Friedenberg, Edgar, 239
Frye, Northrop, 307
Fujimura, J. H., 235
Funded-project research, 253–254, 259,
    264–266, 273
Furlong, V. J., 47

Gadamer, H., 321
Gage, N. L., 156
Gagnon, J. H., 237
Galtung, J., 179
Geer, B., 234
Geertz, Clifford, 44, 116, 123, 126–127,
    139–140, 144, 147, 165, 202, 208,
    315, 319
Gellman, V., 259
Gender roles, 331–332
Generalizability, 10–11, 126, 171–242
    audience for, 235–236
    case survey method and, 222–223
    complexity challenge to, 177–179,
        181–183
    increasing interest in, by qualitative
        researchers, 204–206
    life experiences and, 172, 186–200
    literature on social science, 182–186
    meta-ethnography and, 224–226
    methodology and, 239–241
    paradigm challenge to, 179–182
    qualitative comparative method and,
        207, 224, 227
    in quantitative research, 171, 176–177,
        180–181, 183, 201–204, 233–235

reconceptualizing for qualitative
    research, 206–209
schema theory and, 190–192, 194–196
studying what could be, 217–221
studying what is, 209–214
studying what may be, 214–217
subject matter for, 236–239
traditional views of, 176–177, 180–181,
    183, 201–204
transferability versus, 185, 187–190
Geoffrey, William, 12, 260–263, 268,
    318
George, Ron, 271
Gerson, E. M., 235
Giallombardo, R., 240
Giddens, A., 48, 67n
Gilbert, G., 353
Gilligan, C., 275
Gintis, H., 42
Giorgi, A., 344
Giroux, H. A., 359n
Glaser, B., 51, 219, 344
Gleich, James, 79
Goetz, Judith P., 7n, 121, 123, 125–127,
    207–208, 210, 211, 219
Goffman, Erving, 165, 238
Good High School, The (Lightfoot), 12, 194
Goodwin, B., 311
Gould, S. J., 131
Gouldner, A., 362
Graduate Institute of Education (GIE),
    263–266
Gramsci, A., 70n
Grant, Linda, 7n
Green, A., 46, 197
Greene, Jennifer, 342n
Greene, Maxine, 313
Growing Up American (Peshkin), 205
Grumet, Madeleine R., 97–99, 101–120,
    154–165, 167–170
Guba, Egon G., 6, 7, 15–16, 74–91, 92–95,
    149–150n, 185–187, 204, 207, 208,
    211, 219, 238, 243, 279, 281, 282,
    288, 289–292, 301, 348, 365
Gustfield, J., 183

Habermas, J., 123
Haley, A., 309
Hamilton, D., 184
Hammersley, M., 46–48, 51–52, 67n

Handbook of Research on Teaching, 6, 201
Hanson, N. R., 21, 25-28, 36n, 76-77
Hansonism, 25-28, 76-77
Hansot, E., 308, 311
Harding, Sandra, 40, 43, 55, 58
Hare, R. D., 204, 206, 222, 225-227
Hare, R. M., 275, 287
Hargreaves, D. H., 48
Haydon, A. E., 272
Heald, K. A., 206-207, 222, 223, 227
Heath, S. B., 182
Heidegger, Martin, 316
Hemingway, Ernest, 308
Henriques, J., 106
Hermeneutics, 35, 38, 90, 105, 106, 117,
    123, 168-169
Heron, J., 286
Herriott, R. E., 204, 212, 213
Hersey, John, 309
Heshusius, L., 248, 282
Hester, S., 48
Himmelfarb, Gertrude, 165
Hintikka, M., 58
History, 6, 189
Holcomb, Harmon, 102
Hollands, R. G., 67n
Holloway, W., 106
Homans, George, 261
House, Ernest, 36n
Huberman, A. Michael, 123, 195, 212,
    219, 222, 223, 301-303, 339-357,
    358-363, 365
Huebner, D., 359n
Hughes, E. C., 234
Human Group, The (Homans), 261
Hume, David, 21
Husserl, Edmund, 343, 344

Ibsen, Henrik, 320
Identity, 103, 119
Illich, I., 314-316
Inferential statistics, 171
Informed consent, 260, 264-268,
    272-273, 286
Ingarden, R., 309
Instrumental knowledge, 314-318,
    320-321, 341-342, 358-359
Integration, 190-191
Intergroup relations, 217-221
Internal validity, 201, 203, 213

*International Journal of Qualitative Studies in
    Education*, 4
Intervention, 249, 254, 279, 281-283
Interviewing, in research, 127-128, 130,
    137-138
Iser, W., 310, 315

Jackson, Philip W., 7, 12, 99, 103-104,
    153-166, 167-170, 184, 210, 318
Jacob, E., 248, 282, 344
Jaggar, A., 51, 53, 54, 56-59, 83
James, H., 101
James, William, 35n, 161, 359
Jennings, Robert, 320
Johnson, Lyndon, 283
Johnson, Richard, 50, 61
Jones, A., 51, 53-54
Jones, E., 353
Jong, Erica, 308
Journal of Educational Psychology, The, 177
Journal of Thought, 4, 249
Justice, 252-253
Justification, context of, 33-34, 77-78

Kant, Immanuel, 181, 291-293, 297
Kaplan, A., 144, 260
Kassebaum, G. G., 240
Keat, R., 48
Keiser, R. L., 67n
Keith, P., 264, 265
Kennedy, M. M., 204, 209, 212
Kensington School Study, 263-266
    Revisited, 270-272
Kepler, Johannes, 26
Kerlinger, Fred, 29, 30, 34
Kermode, F., 311
Kerr, D. H., 359n
Killworth, P. D., 130
Kirk, J., 128, 202, 219
Kleibard, H., 180
Kleine, P. F., 264, 270
Klockers, C. E., 252
Knorr, K. D., 342n
Knowledge, 97-98
    affect-laden, 189-190
    instrumental, 314-318, 320-321,
        341-342, 358-359
    tacit, 188
Kohlberg, L., 275
Kramer, J., 324n

Krathwohl, D. R., 203
Kronenfeld, D., 130
Kuhn, Thomas S., 21, 31–33, 77, 90, 183
Kuhnism, 31–33, 77
Kurovsky, R., 320
Kwakiutl Village and School, A (Wolcott), 135

Lakatos, I., 21
Langer, S., 192, 307, 310–311, 318
Lather, P. A., 43, 56, 61, 62, 84, 182
LaTour, B., 135, 235
Lawler, R. W., 215
LeCompte, M. D., 121, 123, 125–127,
    207–208, 210, 211, 219
Lee, G. V., 218
Lewis, Oscar, 344
Lewis, Sinclair, 321
Life cycle of a phenomenon, 216–217
Life experiences
    in field work, 137–143, 157–158
    generalizability and, 172, 186–200
    in naturalistic ethnography, 137–149
    of teachers, 108–119, 159–160, 169–170
Life in Classrooms (Jackson), 12, 170, 210,
    318
Lightfoot, S. L., 12, 194, 195, 344
Lincoln, Yvonna S., 16, 86n, 89–90,
    185–187, 204, 207, 208, 211, 219,
    238, 243–245, 277–295, 296–299, 301
Listening, in research, 127–128
Literature, in qualitative research,
    167–170, 301–303, 305–326,
    358–363
    conspiratorial text in, 313–314,
        318–323, 345–347
    criticisms of use of, 339–349
    paradigmatic text in, 314–321
    romanticism and, 164–165
    using literary text in, 306–314
Locke, John, 21
Locke, L. F., 78
Lofland, J., 48, 50
Logical positivism, 281–282, 289–290
Lucas, W., 206

Macdonald, J. B., 359n
Malamud, Bernard, 308
Manicas, P. T., 343
Man in the Principal's Office, The (Wolcott),
    135, 155–156, 210, 225–226, 321

Mann, J., 192
Mannheim, K., 38
March, James, 320
Marcus, G. E., 66n
Marxist approach, 42, 55
Materialism. *See* Feminist materialist
    ethnography
Maughan, B., 218
McCarthy, C., 42
McCorduck, P., 215
McCorkle, James, 119n
McEwen, W. J., 123
McGrath, J. E., 123, 126
McLaren, Peter, 318–319, 321, 358
McPhee, John, 346
McRobbie, A., 45, 56
Meehl, P. E., 124
Mellor, R., 48
Melville, Herman, 361
Merleau-Ponty, M., 102, 103, 107, 154, 344
Meta-analysis, 79–80
    generalizability and, 206–207, 221–226
    of multisite studies, 212–214, 222–223
Meta-ethnography, 206, 224–227
Methodology, 4, 7–12, 86, 90, 344–345,
    349, 353, 360–362
    case survey method and, 222–223
    generalizability and, 239–241
    implications of feminism and, 55–59
    implications of materialism and, 53–55
    objectivity and, 78
Metz, M. H., 4
Michener, James A., 309
Microcomputers, 214–217
Miles, Matthew B., 123, 195, 212, 219,
    222, 223, 301–303, 339–357,
    358–363, 365
Miller, Arthur, 186
Miller, J. H., 309
Miller, M. L., 128, 202, 219
Mimesis, 102–106, 116–119
Mishler, E., 184
Mitchell, Julian, 301, 311–312, 341, 361
Modes of fiction, 315–318
More, Thomas, 308
Mortimore, P., 218
Multi-instrument approach, 130
Multisite qualitative studies, 203,
    212–214, 222–223
Myrdal, Gunnar, 15, 19, 30, 32, 35n, 92

Nachtigal, Paul, 5
Nagel, Ernest, 24, 26
National Commission for the Protection
     of Human Subjects of Biomedical and
     Behavioral Research, 254
National Institute of Education, 5, 271
National Science Foundation, 5
Naturalistic ethnography, 44-64, 82-86
     affinities with positivism, 48-52, 59-63,
          82-83, 87-88
     concept of validity and, 121-152
     described, 40
     ethics of, 41-43, 49
     feminist materialist perspective on,
          52-64, 83-85, 88-90
     politics of, 41-43
     reasons for appeal of, 44-48
Naturalistic generalizations, 184-187, 208
Naturalistic research. See Qualitative
     research
Neisser, V., 179
Nelson, R., 175
New Mimesis, A (Nuttal), 106-107
Newton, Isaac, 24
Newton-Smith, W., 32
Nietzsche, Friedrich, 165
Nisbett, R., 350
Nixon, Richard, 23
Noblit, George W., 140, 204, 206, 222,
     225-227, 317
Nonfoundationalist epistemology, 21-25,
     76
Norris, Frank, 345, 360
Notetaking, in research, 128-131
Nuttal, A. D., 106-107

Oakley, A., 43, 56
Objectivism, 40-41
Objectivity, 15-17, 19-37, 74-81, 86-88,
     92-95, 97
     in art versus science, 101-120
     context of discovery and, 33-34, 77-78
     context of justification and, 33-34,
          77-78
     group consensus and, 28-31, 75-77
     Hansonism and, 25-28, 76-77
     Kuhnism and, 31-33, 77
     methods of approaching, 126-135
     nonfoundationalist epistemology and,
          21-25, 76

truth and, 22-23, 75, 76
     ways to approach, 78-81
Object relations theory, 117-118
O'Connor, F. W., 252
Office of Education (OE), 264-266
Oliver, D. W., 274-275
Ontology, 86, 90
Orwell, George, 309
Osherow, N., 218
Ouston, J., 218
Outcomes, site selection based on, 218

Pagano, Jo Anne, 119n
Paggioli, Renato, 157-158
Paradigms, 31-33, 77
     challenge to generalizability and, 179-182
     in literary texts, 314-321
Parental Involvement in Federal
     Educational Programs, 212
Participant-observation, 130
Passeron, J., 45
Paternalism, 281-282
Patton, M. Q., 204, 210, 219
Peacock, J. L., 147
Pelham, B., 353
Pelto, Gretel H., 125
Pelto, Pertti J., 125
Pepper, S. C., 309
Percy, Walker, 322, 323
Perry, W. G., 264, 275
Peshkin, Alan, 1-14, 74, 121, 205,
     365-368
Peters, R. S., 359n
Pettigrew, T., 218
Phenomenology, 102
     relativist, 289-294
Phillips, Denis C., 15-16, 19-37, 74-81,
     83, 85-90, 92-95, 123, 178-179, 365
Philosophy, Science, and Social Inquiry
     (Phillips), 74
Piaget, Jean, 36n, 179, 181, 190, 191, 196
Pink, William, 140
Plato, 117, 119n, 308
Poetry, 107-108
Poetry and the Body (Vernon), 107-108
Pohland, P. A., 266
Polanyi, M., 185, 187, 315
Politics
     educational research and, 41-43, 49
     ethics and, 264-266, 281

Politics (*continued*)
  evaluative research and, 252–254
  feminism and, 57–59, 63–64
Popkewitz, T. S., 50
Popper, Karl, 21–23, 25, 30, 34, 77, 86,
  92, 94
Positivism, 90
  logical, 281–282, 289–290
  naturalistic ethnography and, 48–52,
    59–63, 82–83, 87–88
Postpositivism, 87–88, 90
Poulet, G., 307
Powdermaker, H., 188
Power
  methodology and, 38–44, 51–52, 55–59,
    60–63, 82
  social construction of reality, 196–197
Practical imperative, 292
Practice of Teaching, The (Jackson), 103–104
Predictive validity, 98
Primary data, in research, 129–130, 196
Principals, research on, 129, 133–135,
    155–157, 193–194, 210–211, 225–226,
    321
Prisons, 238, 240–241
Privacy, 251–252, 278–280
Prunty, J. J., 264, 270
Punk subculture, 45–48, 60, 62–64

Qualitative comparative method, 207,
    224, 227
Qualitative research
  characteristics of, 258–260
  conferences on, 6, 8–9
  criticism in, 249, 251–252, 279–280,
    283
  description in, 249
  in elementary schools, 302, 327–338,
    350–356
  ethnography and, 4–6, 12–13. *See also*
    Ethnography
  evaluation in, 184–187, 249, 252–254,
    279, 281, 283
  growth of courses on, 7
  history and, 6, 189
  intervention in, 249, 254, 279, 281–283
  literature and, 167–170, 301–303,
    305–326, 339–349, 358–363
  methodology of, 4, 7–12. *See also*
    Methodology

  publications on, 3–5
  purposes of, 249, 251–255
  quantitative research versus, 1–3, 7,
    233–235, 253
*Qualitative Research Methods for the Social
  Sciences* (Berg), 202
Qualitative Sociology, 4
Quantitative research
  generalizability in, 171, 176–177,
    180–181, 183, 201–204, 233–235
  qualitative research versus, 1–3, 7,
    233–235, 253

Rabinow, P., 67*n*
Ragin, C. C., 207, 222, 224, 227
Ratcliffe, John, 25, 31–32
Rationalism, 21
Reader response theory, 306
Reason, P., 287
Recordkeeping, in research, 128–131
Reese, W. L., 291–292
Reflexivity, 106–107
Reichardt, C. S., 205
Reichenbach, Hans, 33
Reinharz, Shula, 287, 293
Reisman, David, 234
Relativism, 289–294
  committed, 264, 275, 287–288
Reliability, 122–124, 126, 154, 202
Reliability and Validity in Qualitative Research
  (Kirk and Miller), 202
Replication, 203–204
Reynolds, D., 46
Reynolds, P. D., 252
Richardson-Koehler, V., 3
Ricoeur, P., 169*n*, 306, 309
Rist, R., 181, 184, 197, 320
Robbins, A. E., 212, 213
Roche, M., 168
Roiphe, A., 308
Roman, Leslie G., 15–16, 38–74, 77,
  81–86, 88–90
Romanticism, 164–165
Romney, A. K., 130
Rorty, Richard, 104, 105, 168–169, 316,
  317, 359
Rosaldo, Michelle Z., 43
Ross, L., 350
Rowan, B., 218
Rowan, J., 287

Ruby, J., 67-68n
Russell, H., 266
Rutter, M., 218
Ryle, Gilbert, 189, 208
Rynkiewich, M. A., 252

Sadler, D., 33
Sagar, H. A., 217-220
Sailer, L., 130
Sanders, C. R., 237
Sartre, Jean-Paul, 117
Schaps, E., 237
Schatzman, L., 46, 47, 50
Scheffler, Israel, 27-28, 30, 34
Schema theory, 190-192, 194-196
Schofield, Janet Ward, 171-173, 201-232
Schooling as a Ritual Performance (McLaren), 318-319
Schooling in Social Context (Noblit and Pink, eds.), 140
Schumacher, S., 266
Schutz, A., 46
Schwartz, R. D., 289
Science programs, 269-270, 330
Scott, S., 43, 56, 69n
Scriven, Michael, 28-30, 36n, 93
Sechrest, L., 289
Secord, P. F., 343
Secular humanism, 274-275, 287
Self-fulfilling prophecies, 181-182, 197
Shackle, G. L. S., 317
Shakespeare, William, 320
Sharp, Rachel, 46, 53, 54, 83, 197
Shaughnessy, J. J., 203
Shaver, J. P., 274-275
Shaw, George Bernard, 320
Sherman, R. R., 4, 249
Shulman, L. S., 248
Siegel, B., 321
Siegel, H., 32
Silverman, J., 104
Simon, W., 237
Site selection
    generalizability from one site to others, 220-221
    in studying what could be, 217-220
    typicality and, 210-212
Slavin, R. E., 218
Smith, A., 218
Smith, A. G., 212, 213

Smith, D., 56, 58
Smith, H. W., 202
Smith, J. K., 248, 278, 282
Smith, Louis M., 12, 243-245, 258-276, 277, 284-289, 291, 293, 297, 318
Smith, Mary Lee, 3-4, 282
Social interaction, 275
    in elementary education, 330
Socialization processes, 89, 331-332
Social Psychology (Brown), 124
Social realism, in literature, 308-314, 320
Social transformation, 59-63
Sociology, 1, 4, 48, 237, 252
Sociology of Education, 4
Sociology of Teaching, The (Waller), 233
Soltis, Jonas F., 243-245, 247-257, 277-283, 288, 291, 292, 294n, 296-299
Spender, D., 56
Spindler, George, 6, 125, 205, 214
Spindler, Louise, 6
Spradley, J. P., 252, 344
Stacey, J., 42, 43, 66n
Stake, Robert E., 7, 184-187, 192, 204, 207, 208, 211, 269-270
Standards for Evaluations of Educational Programs, Projects, and Materials, 252
Stanley, J., 201, 205, 318, 347
Star, S. L., 235
Steinbeck, John, 361
Stephan, W. J., 218
Stereotypes, 181-182, 195
Stoppard, Tom, 320
Strauss, A. L., 46, 47, 50, 51, 219, 234
Street Corner Society (Whyte), 235
Strike, Kenneth A., 247
Structuralism, 42, 44-45, 82
Study of Dissemination Efforts
    Supporting School Improvement, 212
Subjectivity, 15-17, 38-73, 81-86, 88-90, 97, 203
    in field work, 131-134
    naturalistic ethnography and, 41-64
    nature of, 38-39, 85
    power and method in, 38-44, 51-52, 55-59, 60-63, 82
    subject-object dualism and, 39-41
Summative evaluations, 204-205
Suransky, V., 195

Sykes, G., 240
Symbolic interactionism, 180

Tacit knowledge, 188
Taylor, K., 311
Teachers as Curriculum Planners (Connelly
and Clandinin), 12
Teachers Versus Technocrats (Wolcott), 131,
135–136
Teaching
decision making in, 106
ethics and, 255–256
learning from educational experiences
in, 331–332
life experiences of teachers and,
108–119, 159–160, 169–170
mimesis and, 102–106, 116–119
and qualitative research in elementary
school, 332–337
relationship to students in, 188
relations to the world and, 107–108,
117–118
transformation and, 103–105, 116–119
use of literary texts in, 301–302,
305–326
Teaching Public Issues in the High School
(Oliver and Shaver), 274–275
Tesch, R., 340, 344
Testing, 122–125, 148, 149, 154, 201
Therborn, G., 65
Thompson, John B., 117, 118
Thorndike, E. L., 177–182
Tikunoff, W. J., 6
Tolstoy, Leo, 79, 320
Tom, A. R., 359n
Total institutions, 238, 240–241
Toulmin, S., 316
Transferability, 185, 187–190, 207
Transformation, 59–63, 103–105,
116–119
Translatability, 208
Triangulation, 130
Trilling, Lionel, 341
Truth, 347–349
correspondence theory of, 24–25, 97
objectivity and, 22–23, 75, 76
in paradigmatic literary texts, 317–318
Truth tables, 224
Turner, T., 190
Twain, M., 309

Tyler, Stephen A., 149n
Typicality, 210–212, 218–221

Understanding, 98, 146–148
United Kingdom, 259
Updike, John, 302, 311–313, 321, 361
Urban decentralization, 222–223
Urry, J., 48
Urwin, C., 106
Utopias, 308, 311

Validity, 97–170, 202, 347–349
absurdity of, in qualitative research,
143–148
choice of subjects and focus, 160–170
consensual, 29–30, 75–77, 90, 93
defined, 97, 101, 124, 125
external, 123, 201–204, 206. See also
Generalizability
internal, 201, 203, 213
methods of achieving, 126–135
naturalistic ethnography and, 121–152
objectivity in art versus science and,
101–120
predictive, 98
types of, 122–126
unimportance of, 135–143
Vallence, E., 192
Value judgments, in research, 131–132
Van Maanen, John, 4–5, 143–144
Van Manen, M., 359n
Varieties of Qualitative Research (Van Maanen,
Dabbs, and Faulkner), 4–5
Vendler, Zeno, 146–147
Venn, C., 106
Verban, D., 215
Verification, 347–349
Vernon, John, 107–108
Vicarious experiences, 192–197
Vidich, A. J., 122

Wagner, A., 106
Wakoski, D., 107, 119n
Walker, D. F., 214, 324n
Walkerdine, V., 106
Waller, Willard, 233
Ward, B. A., 6
Ward, D. A., 240
Washington School study, 260–263
Webb, E. J., 289

Webb, R. B., 4, 249
Weber, G., 218
Weber, R. P., 123
Weiss, C. H., 183, 342n
Welty, Eudora, 320
Wexler, Philip, 4
Whyte, William Foote, 130, 210, 235
Williams, R. H., 320, 321, 324n
Williams, William Carlos, 165
Willis, P., 44, 45, 49–50, 66n, 68n
Willower, D. J., 320, 321, 324n
Winnicott, D., 116, 117
Wittgenstein, Ludwig Josef, 25, 165
Wolcott, Harry F., 97–99, 121–152,
    153–165, 194, 195, 204, 210, 214,
    225–226, 282, 321
Wolf, Robert L., 294n
Wolfe, Tom, 309, 340

Woods, P., 44
Woolf, Virginia, 101, 105, 154, 158–159,
    166
Woolgar, S., 135
Wordsworth, William, 165
Working hypotheses, 209, 238
    transferability and, 185, 187–190
Wouk, Herman, 320
Wright, E. O., 54
Writing, in research, 128–129, 132–135

Yates, D., 223
Yazdani, M., 215
Yin, R. K., 206–207, 222, 223, 227
Young, Philip, 149n

Zechmeister, E. B., 203
Zola, Emile, 345